What Others Are Saying About This Book

We've all experienced the excitement of learning at the hands of a truly gifted teacher. And most of us have experienced the bland, joyless drone of a poor one. Jerome Feldman and Doug McPhee have collaborated to create the definitive book on how to become that truly treasured, teacher—an excellent educator. Thoroughly researched and filled with inspirational quotes and stories, *The Science of Learning and the Art of Teaching* is written for our rapidly changing world. The authors, both talented educators in their own right, have woven together time-tested philosophy, cutting-edge research, and their own broad experience to form a useful guide for both young and seasoned teachers. They cover essentials for creating a solid learning environment, the impact of technology on education, inclusion strategies, and a vision of how the classroom is and will evolve in coming years. This gem is a must-read for all those who aspire to educational excellence.

—Mike Song
CEO & Author
Cohesive Knowledge Solutions, Inc.

The Science of Learning and the Art of Teaching is a commendable work that gets right to the heart of education. With its informative descriptions of best educational practices, including terms, methods and explanations, it will benefit all educators. It provides powerful insights and enables teachers to effectively match their delivery with their students, content, and situations. Reading this book I could hear the authors' voices speaking just to me—giving me rich data for reflection.

—Bobbi DePorter
President, Quantum Learning Network; Cofounder, SuperCamp
Author *Quantum Success,* Coauthor *Quantum Teaching*

In today's sprint-paced world, it is vital that nations, organizations, teams, and individuals learn better, think better, and teach better. "Better" does not only mean quicker—it means richer, deeper, broader, and with mind, heart, body and spirit engaged and growing. Jerome Feldman and Doug McPhee's *The Science of Learning and the Art of Teaching* helps everyone become such a learner, thinker, and teacher. It is a vital resource to all.

—Glenn Capelli
BA Dip Ed MACE CSP MENSA
Sir Winston Churchill Fellowship Awardee
Director True Learning Center

This is an excellent text to understand the learning process, which leads to better teaching. It will be especially important for beginning university professors as they usually enter the classroom without any formal teaching experience other than observing professors who taught them. Teaching is serious business that needs to be accomplished in an exceptional manner. *The Science of Learning and the Art of Teaching* by Jerome Feldman and Doug McPhee provides a detailed guideline to understand and become a better instructor. It will be required reading for all of my PhD students and new faculty that I mentor.

—Dr. Paul R. Krausman
Professor, Wildlife Conservation and Management
School of Natural Resources
University of Arizona

The Science of Learning and the Art of Teaching is a valuable both as an academic as well as a practical guide to teaching. I wish this text had been available when I started teaching.

I really appreciated the way the authors approach the aspect of a personal teaching philosophy. The manner in which the authors approach the preparation of lesson plans is a valuable insight into how one must approach the process of teaching. I really liked the way the authors cover not only learning styles but manage to blend the scientific theory of teaching into an artful roadmap to success in the classroom. This text is a wonderful resource for new as well as experienced teachers.

—John Poore, EdD
Professor
Keller Graduate School, DeVry University

Science and Art are not often associated with each other but often should be. Thankfully, *The Science of Learning and the Art of Teaching* makes an important contribution to teacher education by bridging together these critical aspects of the human education process. With thousands of teachers retiring and a teacher shortage due to arrive over the next decade, this enlightening book offers midlife career changers a way to become effective educators more quickly. The practical tips and helpful educational background will surely help those who want to become artful, effective instructors. Veteran teachers who want to infuse more powerful learning into their current practice will also find it practical and useful.

—Spence Rogers
President, Peak Learning Systems, Inc

The Science of Learning

& The Art of Teaching

Join us on the web at

careersuccess.delmar.com

The
Science
of
Learning

The
Art
of
Teaching

Jerome Feldman　　Doug McPhee

THOMSON

DELMAR LEARNING　Australia　Canada　Mexico　Singapore　Spain　United Kingdom　United States

The Science of Learning and The Art of Teaching
Jerome Feldman • Doug McPhee

Vice President, Career Education SBU:
Dawn Gerrain

Director of Learning Solutions:
John Fedor

Managing Editor:
Robert L. Serenka, Jr.

Acquisitions Editor:
Martine Edwards

Product Manager:
Jennifer Anderson

Editorial Assistant:
Falon Ferraro

Director of Production:
Wendy A. Troeger

Production Manager:
Mark Bernard

Content Project Manager:
Angela Iula

Director of Marketing:
Wendy E. Mapstone

Channel Manager:
Gerard McAvey

Marketing Coordinator:
Jonathan Sheehan

Library of Congress Cataloging-in-Publication Data

Feldman, Jerome A.
  The science of learning and the art of teaching / Jerome Feldman and Doug McPhee. -- 1st ed.
    p. cm.
    ISBN 1-4180-1616-0
  1. Learning. 2. Group work in education. 3. Teaching.
  I. McPhee, Doug. II. Title.
    LB1060.F456 2007
    370.15'23--dc22

                              2007020093

NOTICE TO THE READER

Contents

**UNIT 2
The Art of Teaching—
Translating Theory into
Skillful Practice / 125**

CHAPTER 4
Planning with the Mind in Mind—
Course and Lesson Planning / 137

CHAPTER 5
Preparations for Learning and Teaching / 153

CHAPTER 6
The Traditional Lecture: "The Good, the Bad,
and the Ugly" / 173

UNIT 3
**Learning without Limits: Proven
and Powerful Strategies for Learning
That Lasts / 303**

Acknowledgments

As I write this I am mindful of the Academy Awards ceremony and the desire of those who receive honors to recognize all the people who contributed to their success. The award winners often feel inclined to go on and on, trying to avoid leaving someone out. Likewise, there are many people who have influenced me and the writing of this book and its companion Field Guide to whom I am indebted. But rather than try to come up with a long list of names so as not to exclude anyone, I will keep this simple—my sincere thanks to all those whose contributions to education and the understanding of human learning have been both the inspiration and foundation for much of what these two books contain.

On a more personal note, I also want to express my gratitude to my family for their support over the past several years. Your help and encouragement made it possible for me to make it through a very difficult period in my life, even as I conceived and wrote these books. Without each and every one of you, this endeavor would not have been completed.

Finally, I want to acknowledge Doug, my co-author. I have come to realize you probably had no idea what you were getting into when you agreed to be part of this project. When I first conceived this book, I felt I could not do it alone and may very well have not even have pursued it if you had not said "Yes." Thank you.

—Jerome Feldman

Writing a book is a rewarding accomplishment, not to mention a lot of work. Although we write the words as authors, so many friends, colleagues, and students have influenced us that it would be difficult to name all of them. The challenge, of course, is naming those who have most influenced and supported the process of writing this book and its companion Field Guide while not leaving anyone off the list.

As a long-time educator and speaker I have been influenced by hundreds of educators and friends. My life experiences are broad, and offer me a perspective that is different from anyone else's. From my first teachers in elementary school to college professors to school administrators to the hundreds of speakers I have heard, I thank each of you. Know that you have provided some pearl of wisdom that I have lived in some fashion and that has influenced my thinking about learning and teaching. I especially thank Jerome Feldman for inviting me to work on this book—I've learned more as a result.

We started this project with the idea that we wanted to include illustrations that could be graphic representations of our writing. Christina Valenza started that process and, unfortunately, could not finish. Nancy Margulies stepped in and has added great value to the writing by offering her graphic interpretations of our words. We thank both Christina and Nancy.

The most important person in my life, my wife Cecelia, has offered tremendous support in so many areas of my life. The discussions we've had for over 20 years about education, teaching, and learning and, of course, life have each provided thoughtful reflection and heartfelt commitment to making a difference in learning and teaching. Those discussions and that reflection have been the greatest influence in my thinking about teaching. Cecelia is the most gifted teacher I have ever known and continues to challenge my thinking and support my growth and learning.

—Doug McPhee

The publisher and the authors wish to recognize the educators who reviewed this text, and to thank them for their time, expertise, and many thoughtful recommendations.

Michael Beaty
Campus President
Concorde Career Institute

Julie Conlon
Continuing Education, Buck Mickel Center
Greenville Technical College

Janet M. Cutshall
Professor, Sussex County Community College

Irene D. Gordon-Jasmine
Instructor, Nicholls State University

Paul Krausman
Professor, Wildlife Conservation and Management
University of Arizona

Jane Nowlin
Director, Platt College
Oklahoma City Central Campus

Ross W. Pearce
Facilitator, University of Farmers

Tara W. Ross
Keiser College

Susan R. Royce
Director Academic Services
Design Institute of San Diego

Mary Gormandy White
Mobile Technical Institute

ers of profes
this sor at a
book 4-year
likely univer
work in sity,
a vari balanc
ety of ing
subject your
fields teach
and ing
across load
a range with re
of dif search
ferent and
situatio writing
ns and and
set other
tings. profes
Per sional
haps obliga
you tions.
work in Maybe
a pri you are
vate a teach
career ing as,
and sistant
techni who
cal has just
school been
or a offered
public a new
adult assign
ment to
teach.
gram. Read
ers of
this
book
teach likely
need work in
teach a vari
ety of
ac subject
cour fields
and
across
educa a range
tion of dif
ferent
situatio
hands ns and
or au set
tings.
Per haps
you
work in
a pri
vate career
and
you techni
fish or cal
school
or a
public
part adult
time educa
full tion pro
time in gram,
structor where
in a you
2-year teach

INTRODUCTION:

Changing Notions for Changing Times—The Journey to Becoming a Masterful Educator

The future ain't what it used to be.

—Yogi Berra

The Times, They Are A-Changing

Readers of this book likely work in a variety of subject fields and across a range of different situations and settings. Perhaps you work in a private career and technical school or a public adult-education program, where you teach medical terminology or accounting or general education classes or a hands-on automotive repair course. Possibly you teach life sciences or English or engineering as a part-time or full-time instructor in a 2-year college, or as a full professor at a 4-year university, balancing your teaching load with research and writing and other professional obligations. Maybe you are a teaching assistant who has just been offered a new assignment to teach.

Or you are new to the teaching profession, seeking your first opportunity to do more with the expertise you have developed in your field over the years. As you contemplate your future in a classroom, you might feel you have little to guide you other than your own experiences as a student. If this experience was at all typical, you probably recall a few memorable teachers

who can serve as a model for what good teachers do. But more likely you possess a lot of vague memories of nondescript classes with sincere but (shall we be charitable?) not very dynamic or engaging instructors who (and here is a scary thought) did not really seem to know more about teaching than you do. When it really comes down to it, what you mostly have to start with are notions about teaching that match the ways of learning that suited you as a student—and your determination to provide a better experience for your students than you had as a learner.

It is also possible that you are an experienced instructor, with a number of years of teaching behind you. If you were to think back for a few moments, you would probably acknowledge that things were a little rough for you when you started your career. But you now feel pretty confident, having developed a reliable repertoire of teaching routines and practices with which you are comfortable. There is a good chance that you have learned to do more than just lecture at length and that you regularly mix in discussion sessions and a few other activities that seem to keep students engaged. Yet, at the same time, you may also be aware that there is more that you can do and, as good as these methods have been, there is still room for improvement.

Certainly, there are many other ways we could characterize the professional lives and personal circumstances of teachers such as you. However, it would be difficult to do so, given the enormous variations across all possible settings and situations. Simply put, the world of postsecondary education is a big place. It is a world populated by almost 3 million educators teaching thousands of different courses to over 15 million students from countries across the globe in approximately 6,400 public and private institutions. Some of these schools are quite small, with only a single career curriculum, such as cosmetology or medical assistance, while others offer courses of study beginning with general education classes and continuing all the way to the postdoctoral level. Yet, despite the diversity found across the landscape of postsecondary education, one generalization can be made—education at this level is an increasingly complex enterprise, and we educators are and will continue to be expected to succeed at what we do in the face of new and emerging challenges that require levels of knowledge and skill significantly greater than those who worked in the past.

> *Nothing in education is so astonishing as the amount of ignorance it accumulates in the form of facts.*
>
> —Henry Adams

Why Is This So?

Why are the times changing? For one, the students we find in our classroom are not like those from previous generations, who were, by and large, kids from middle- and upper-class backgrounds fresh out of high school. Statistics reveal that our learners are and will continue to be increasingly diverse in age and ability and in social, economic, language, and cultural backgrounds. They are also older, mostly female, increasingly foreign-born and often part-time, with enormous demands on their time and energy as they try to balance work and families with their studies.

Moreover, things have dramatically changed in the world of work, because of powerful economic, social, and technological forces. Almost every report on the need for educational reform of the past 20 years has repeated the same findings and conclusions—we have largely failed to and, therefore, must learn how to better educate and train these diverse students to succeed in increasingly demanding career fields with highly complex and technical knowledge bases. The message coming not only from the ivory towers of academia but also from the shop floors of our factories is the same—it is no longer good enough for students merely to possess knowledge; they must also be able think deeply about and with that knowledge so that they can reason, solve problems, work collaboratively, and communicate effectively in the often ill-defined and ambiguous settings of the "real world."

If all this was not enough of a challenge, the very foundations of many of the disciplines we teach are also shifting beneath our feet. Along with technological innovations and the need for increased worker productivity in a highly competitive global economy, beyond basic core introductory classes, the knowledge base in many disciplines is changing rapidly. Whether computer programming or the environmental sciences, medicine or engineering, automotive mechanics or graphic arts, most knowledge domains are not the same today as they were even a decade ago. Consequently, most efforts to cover course content in a typical term, whether through traditional face-to-face instruction or through computer-mediated distance learning, leave students with knowledge that is often, at best, "a mile wide and an inch deep" and woefully inadequate in today's demanding workplace.

Lastly, economic trends and political forces are beginning to have an impact on public expectations of postsecondary education that may require a significant shift in school policies—and classroom practices.

Postsecondary education is big business in the United States. As mentioned, it consists of more than 6,400 institutions that serve over 15 million students. Total public and private expenditures for this education are well over a $100 billion a year, with tuition rising significantly faster than family incomes and inflation. Given these increasing costs, there is concern about the continuing affordability of postsecondary education. Members of Congress are hearing from parents and students who are increasingly worried about the costs of a postsecondary education. These officials are concerned that at a time when the federal government alone makes available far in excess of $50 billion a year in student financial assistance, parents and students are afraid they will not be able to pay for college. Moreover, there is the issue of whether students and the government are getting sufficient "bang for their buck," with the federal government beginning to ask questions

A man should first direct himself in the way he should go. Only then should he instruct others.

—Buddha

about the quality of this education in order to determine whether the instruction received justifies the high price paid.

At present, it is primarily privately operated national and regional accreditation associations that evaluate school programs and set professional standards. However, the evaluation procedures and standards established by these accrediting agencies are not always consumer-friendly and easily available to the public. As a result, critics contend that these measures fail to give students a meaningful way to gauge the quality of a school. Recent congressional hearings have called for legislation to create greater transparency in these assessment systems, so they can provide more quantifiable and easily understood measures of program quality to consumers. Similar to trends toward greater accountability in K–12 education, these efforts include proposals for easily understood, well-defined benchmarks and rigorous measures of teacher effectiveness and student learning, Yet the only qualification for most teaching in postsecondary education is some degree of subject-matter expertise. Therefore, it is highly likely that schools will be expected to provide faculty more formal and rigorous professional-development programs to give them the training that can improve their teaching methods.

> *Things do not Change; we Change.*
>
> —Thoreau

The Emperor Has No Clothes

The bottom line is this: Traditionally content has been king in the classroom. But today the mantra of educational experts and policy makers is "covering content is no longer enough." In many ways the "emperor has no clothes"—or at least is not appropriately attired for today's world of formal education. To succeed academically and professionally, our students need more than instructors who are subject-matter experts who can competently and proficiently "cover the content."

Subject-matter expertise is only the first step in the enterprise of education. Instructors also need to know how to move students, who come to us as novices, toward greater and greater degrees of expertise. This can come only from a grasp of what they are taught that goes beyond an ability to dutifully reproduce information for tests. As their instructors, we need to thoughtfully present what we know not merely as information and isolated facts but as a carefully constructed and coherent body of knowledge organized around core concepts and principles. We need to be able to clearly identify and represent these essential ideas in a variety of ways that give this knowledge personal meaning and the power to change how our students behave and think. And we need to help our students develop intellectual and personal skills that they can carry with them when they leave our often highly structured and relatively static classroom environments and enter into the dynamic, unstructured, and complex situations of today's workplace and living.

So, What's New?

Given the ongoing dialogue in educational circles about the pressing need to meet the above challenges, one would assume that what goes on in postsecondary and career-school classrooms has substantially changed in recent years. Unfortunately, this is not the case. It is true that the *face* of career and postsecondary education has changed, as new ways to "deliver" instruction through advances in computing and communication technologies have been widely implemented. But in many cases what has not changed is what teachers regularly do in their classrooms every day. What most instructors do today is often not significantly different from what was done decades ago. Yet doing the same old things in different guises will not suffice in our increasingly complex and rapidly changing world.

It is not the face of education that we must change, but its heart. The centuries-old paradigm of instruction as a system of "delivering information" must be modified, if not replaced altogether, to better fit the dynamics of shifting social, economic, and technological trends. And it must also conform to a growing body of knowledge about what good learning and teaching are all about that is emerging from research in educational psychology, cognitive studies, and more recently, neuroscience research.

The Purpose and Design of This Book

So, how can the heart of the teaching enterprise change? No single book can completely answer this question. But it is possible to suggest an answer, which is the goal of this text (and the companion Field Guide, which we strongly recommend you get).

The answer we offer unfolds in three parts: (1) a conceptual framework for understanding the rationale for your personal teaching style and what we know about human learning, (2) specific and practical teaching strategies and techniques that best reflect this understanding, and (3) suggestions for effective professional and organizational development efforts that can serve as the foundation for ongoing meaningful and sustainable program- and institution-wide improvements in teaching and learning.

The content of the text aligns with these three dimensions. Unit 1 sets the foundation for professional growth by looking at the personal rationale for what we do in our classrooms, the dominant learning theories that shape how most of us teach, plus important research findings about how the brain works and other thinking about human learning, such as emerging ideas about the nature of intelligence, that can inform our practice. Units 2, 3, and 4 include a good deal of the "nuts and bolts" of many basic as well as innovative classroom practices, from initial course design to final assessment. (The companion Field

Definition of insanity—doing the same things in the same way and expecting different results.

—Albert Einstein

The real voyage of discovery consists not in seeking new landscapes, but in having new eyes.

—Marcel Proust

Guide goes even further into many of these ideas, with additional guidelines and detailed ideas for implementing them.) Unit 5 provides a plan for creating professional development programs and institutional processes that foster innovations that yield not only better classroom learning and teaching, but also greater student satisfaction and retention and overall organizational effectiveness.

How to Best Use This Book: Our Recommendations

Make a Mess of It

This is not an expensive college text to be kept in pristine condition so that it can be sold back at the end of the term. There is no end of term here—professional growth is lifelong. Think of this book not as an expense but as an investment in this professional growth. So dog-ear it until its edges are as soft as tissue. Underline, highlight, and comment in it with wild abandon. Cover the naked margins with sticky notes. We believe this book (as well as the companion Field Guide) is something that you will want to refer to again and again as your experience as a teacher changes you.

Note this icon throughout the text. It will guide you in locating material on related topics, found in other units and chapters of the text.

Do Not Just Read This Book

Reading, as we usually read, just touches on surface of knowledge. Meaningful learning requires that we do more than just read; we must also reflect. If real estate is all about location, location, location, then learning that lasts is all about reflection, reflection, reflection. It is often said, "we learn from experience," but it is not necessarily so. Consider how often we are inclined to make the same mistakes again and again, despite our experience. We learn not from experience alone, but from *reflecting* on our experience and extracting the deepest meaning possible from it. One of the premises of this book is that real learning is about deep understanding; reflection is needed if you want this kind of understanding. So take time to pause, process, and personalize the information.

Start with a Clean Slate

Whether you are an experienced educator or someone who has just made the decision to become a teacher, try to approach this text with a "beginner's mind." Teachers who attend weekend conferences and participate in professional development workshops often express little concern for theory; what they want is something they can "use Monday morning," techniques and tools for better teaching that can easily become part of their daily repertoire. We certainly have no argument with this. This text and its companion Field Guide are designed to provide you with many research-based, proven, and practical methods and tools. However, as we discuss in Unit 1, improving your teaching is not just a matter of knowing "what works" or how to use specific methods or techniques. It is also a matter of possessing a clear rationale for what you do—of understanding concepts and theories to help you know "why" things work, "when" they work, for "which" specific purposes and contexts, and for "whom"—the particular students they work best for. Sometimes tedious, you must be willing and able to wrestle with each of these questions and enter the place where they converge. Then you will have entered the bright crucible of change, where the science of learning meets the art of teaching, where the known and the unknown mix in an alchemical process of transformative teaching and learning. A beginner's mind is the key that opens the door to this place.

Adopt a Metaphor for the Journey

> Learning becomes more miraculous and ever present when the human heart is engaged.
>
> —Dr. Laurence Martel

There are many ways to conceptualize the process of learning to improve one's teaching practice. We would like to offer one, at least for a start. Consider this process to be a journey in which one is traveling to another country rich with its own history, traditions, and values, possessing unique landscapes and terrain.

If you are new to the teaching enterprise, consider this your first visit. You may have some familiarity with this land, possibly having read of its people and seen pictures or perused a map. Yet you have never set foot onto its soil and breathed its air and reveled in its sights with your own eyes. Therefore, much will be quite "foreign" and will take time to assimilate and adjust to.

If you are an experienced teacher, consider this a return visit. You have been here before, developed your opinions about this land, and found some favorite places that you return to again and again. But, as this is a vast land, there are many new places to explore and new things to learn. So you have decided to venture out from the familiar places to discover what the unknown country has to offer. You, too, will need to adjust as you give up your "old favorites" for some new terrain.

Be Willing to Travel Far from Home

We trust you want to go deeper and beyond what we can only touch upon in this book to learn more—much more—about the very important and often highly complex topics we discuss. To encourage you to do so, we have tried to make it as easy as possible and have taken a different approach to reference materials and sources than most professional development texts for educators. Most, if not all, of these

Are there not . . . two points in the adventure of the diver: One—when a beggar, he prepares to plunge? Two—when a prince, he rises with his pearl? I plunge!

—Robert Browning

books tend to be quite academic in tone and format. Although we have based everything we say here on the findings and/or experience of many qualified and thoughtful theorists, researchers, and educators, we have deliberately avoided slowing you down as you read and reflect with the baggage of lots of footnotes and long lists of references. We have distilled the thinking and research from hundreds of valuable and reliable sources into an accessible format that not only gets you started on your journey, but makes it easy for you to travel far and wide with ease. Therefore, in lieu of the typical footnotes and bibliographic text and Internet references, we provide at the end of each chapter a simple "just-in-time" research guide called "Springboards for Further Learning" for deeper exploration and study. We also offer a recommended reading list in the appendix that represents some of the sources of inspiration and the knowledge base for much of this book and our own teaching practices over the years.

The rationale for this is quite simple. Just about every topic and idea you might want to know more about can be easily, immediately, and freely found on the Internet with a good search engine. Thus, we provide at the end of each chapter, Springboards, a brief list of key terms and key names that can lead you directly to live links for additional study and insight into the topics discussed in each chapter. Of course, you can still buy books and subscribe to professional journals if you like. But with the guide we give you, you can "travel far" into the universe of teaching and learning at no cost, without delay, and without having to leave the comfort of your home or office whenever you feel so inclined.

Get the Companion Field Guide

This text, close to 400 pages, may seem to be a pretty hefty tome. However, the topics we explore here are rich, deep, and varied, and we have barely scratched the surface of many important ideas and teaching practices. To get full value from your reading, reflection, and study, we believe you will need and want more. For this reason, we have written the companion Field Guide. It is loaded with valuable supplemental and complementary materials. Throughout this text, you will find an icon that makes it easy to cross-reference all the additional information, activities, and exercises found there.

Refer to Field Guide

Who We Are—Our Experiences and Beliefs That Define Our Philosophy of Teaching and Learning

We thought a brief personal introduction would be helpful in giving you an understanding of where we are each coming from and our personal perspectives on teaching and learning that are the grounds for much of this text and the companion Field Guide.

Jerome Feldman

I have been teaching adults for over 25 years. My first assignment began 2 hours after my first interview. No, not because I was *so* good—obviously I had never taught a class before—but because the hiring administrator was *so* desperate to get someone to cover a class whose instructor had just resigned. After "winging" it for the first 2 years, I came to the realization that there was a lot more to teaching than knowing my discipline and a reliance on teaching routines that simply reflected how as a student I had always been comfortable learning. So I enrolled in a master's program to gain a deeper and more fluid understanding of my discipline, as well as to develop my teaching ability through a formal study of different theories and methods.

This further education was good enough for about another 10 years. In the early 1990s, I came across some recent findings about the human brain and its incredible capacities. The first was that learning and the development of personal intelligence is a result of and reflected in the nature and amount of connections that different brain cells (neurons) make with each other. The second finding was that each brain has about 100 billion individual nerve cells (give or take a few billion), with each of these cells able to connect to up to 10,000 different neurons. As one researcher (who either was very smart or had a lot of time on his hands) calculated, *the number of possible combinations of these connections is greater than the number of atoms found in the entire universe.* Knowing the universe to be a pretty big place, I knew that was a lot of atoms—and a lot of connections—and a lot of potential "smarts." I realized that the way I had been teaching—even with my advanced training—was not good enough to tap into and draw out this enormous individual potential, which I came to accept as the true meaning of education when understood in its Latin derivative (*educaré*) as "a drawing out" of what is already there.

Simply put, my perspective on teaching and life as an educator has never been the same since this "pedagogical epiphany" about a dozen years ago. Since then I have read and reflected upon hundreds of books and articles, attended and taught dozens of conference presentations, and written articles for local institutions. These experiences have shaped and continue to shape my understanding about the nature of teaching and learning, and now have led to this book, an ambitious but still humbling effort to make clear to others what teaching—maybe not the oldest but, in my opinion, the noblest profession—is all about in its highest expression.

Doug McPhee

Much like Jerome, I was hired virtually on the spot. The fact is, in college I did not decide until the middle of my junior year that I would be a teacher. I loved college and the variety of things I could learn. I was

Live as if you will die tomorrow. Learn as if you will live forever.

—Gandhi

joyfully taking classes with no plan in mind and came to a point at which I was asked what my major was. I did not have one. I was encouraged by friends and the Dean of the Education Department to pursue an elementary teaching credential. I did so and was hired before I finished my student teaching. I taught kindergarten through sixth grade for 20 years while continuing to learn the art of teaching.

I began early in my career doing workshops for other teachers and presenting at conferences. As the years went by, I learned more and more about teaching more effectively. In the early 1980s I discovered a method, accelerated learning, that was a breath of fresh air for me and that aligned with my beliefs about learning and teaching. It was from that discovery that I left the school district and became a full-time consultant to schools, community colleges, and four-year institutions on improving instruction. In addition, I worked as a coach and administrator for eight summers in SuperCamp, a program for people 13 to 21 years of age that taught the skills of learning and also touched the emotional side of these young people, turning many of them around from failures to successes. (SuperCamp has transformed into Quantum Learning Network (QLN), based in Oceanside, California.) Teaching adults at three universities has further influenced my beliefs about learning. I have also worked with a number of corporations to design and deliver training in more effective and powerful ways. Over several years, I worked with The Ken Blanchard Companies, designing a course and delivering their content to corporate clients. However, more importantly, my growing understanding of research on the brain and learning has shifted how I design instruction.

One of the greatest values of continually seeking new ways of doing our work is finding something and trying it in the "real world" of teaching. I continue to do this as a way of improving my practice, adding new colors to my palette for the "art of teaching."

A pitfall for many teachers and instructors is that we get complacent. We find a technique or a certain practice that works and we overuse it rather than building a broader repertoire. Of high value to me is learning new ways of doing old things. This is sometimes disconcerting to the educational system and causes some angst, yet if the results are positive, it is a good thing.

My basic beliefs about teaching and learning have not changed much in many years. With that said, I must emphasize that I struggled for several years to understand how I would contribute to this noble profession. As a son of two teachers who were also missionaries, I had to find my way by reflecting on my practice, reading extensively, and trying new ways of instruction that I concluded might make for more powerful learning for my students. I can design instruction with all the best practices of many years to provide creative and important connections for students and the content I may be teaching. Still, it is

Learn not only to find what you like, learn to like what you find.

—Anthony J. D'Angelo

from more than 30 years of instructing that I have come to realize that I will never know all I need to reach every student. That is what this book is about, offering you our expertise knowing that you will have to draw your own conclusions to really continue on a journey of learning for yourself.

A Brief Statement of Our Mutually Shared Teaching Philosophy

Learning

- Learning is natural, and everyone can learn when provided with the proper conditions for learning.
- Personal connection to content enhances interest and motivation, and leads to more powerful learning.
- The more active we are in the learning process by being engaged in thinking about and processing our learning experiences, the more we will be able to understand and retain and apply to settings outside the classroom.
- Metacognition, as an awareness of how one learns, is an important element of effective learning that good learners possess and that can be taught.
- An awareness of research on the brain and learning, as well as our personal teaching philosophy and style, provide important information for teachers to consider in their planning and presentation.

Teaching

- A learning environment that fosters curiosity and a positive attitude about learning and lots of student engagement balanced with purposeful content acquisition offers an effective setting for learning.
- Using multiple models and methods offers students the most productive possibilities for successful learning.
- Instruction should be designed around essential content elements, highlight students' prior knowledge, and provide students with clear expectations regarding what they will need to know and be able to do.
- Control and authority in a classroom needs to be flexible, balancing teacher and student roles according to each desired learning goal and specific task.

Live with the questions now. Perhaps you will gradually, without even noticing it, live along some distant day into the answer.

—Rilke

Unit 1
An Exploration of the Science of Learning— The Philosophical and Conceptual Foundations for Our Teaching Style and Practices

In making choices about what to teach and how to assess it, clarity about the character of learning . . . must be an essential bedrock for what we do.

—Ted Marchese,
The New Conversation about Learning

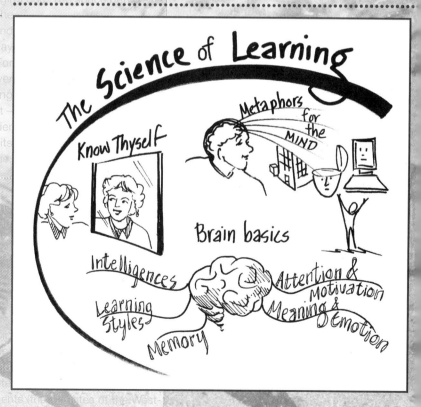

First Things First

There is a universal question that all teachers ask at different points in their careers. It is a question that the new teacher will certainly ask many times before she walks into her first classroom. But it is also a question even the best and *most* experienced among us continue to ask throughout our careers—*How can I best teach my subject?* It is an important question. Yet it is not necessarily the *most* important one.

There are more fundamental questions that lie at the heart of the issue of what makes for quality and effective instruction. However, contrary to what one might first suspect, these are not questions about teaching. Rather, they are questions about the nature of learning, for the true measure of the value and effectiveness of our teaching can only be truly determined by gauging not what we do or how we feel about it but by what our students actually learn. Simply put, we need to begin to go beyond asking ourselves what makes for good teaching and begin to deeply reflect on what makes for good learning.

This unit offers a conceptual foundation for understanding what we mean by *learning,* and how it occurs based on various theoretical approaches. We include some important theories proposed by different educational psychologists and cognitive scientists, with a historical perspective on the ideas that have dominated thinking about what constitutes learning and good teaching practices. In addition to these models, or paradigms, we provide an overview of specific research findings and leading thinking into how the brain and mind work and the implications for classroom practice. Together, these theories and research constitute what we consider to be the foundation of a science of learning. However, before we explore what this research and thinking can tell us about the nature of human learning, it is important to be clear about what we actually mean by a "science" of learning.

Theories of Human Learning: Hard Science or Fascinating Speculations?

For many, the term *science* may suggest that we have arrived at a well-defined and possibly conclusive understanding about how people learn, akin, for example, to what we know about sending a rocket to the moon—which involves well-understood principles from astrophysics to metallurgy and the chemistry of fuel propulsion. For others, especially those involved as researchers in what is considered the hard sciences, such as physics or biology or chemistry, the idea of a "science" of learning may evoke a more skeptical response, given the enormously complex and largely unobservable workings of the human mind. These individuals may consider the claims of such a science to be more speculation than fact, the effort to develop formulas for good teaching not much more fruitful than efforts of alchemists of old who sought to change lead into gold; maybe alchemists knew a little about chemistry, but certainly not enough to realize the limitations of their knowledge and the futility of their efforts.

Yet, like many things, this subject is not an "either/or" matter. The reality lies somewhere in between.

One way to understand the state of thinking and research in learning and teaching is to consider the field of physics. Physics is clearly a legitimate science, comprised of a body of knowledge that includes indisputable facts, conclusively proven theories, and irrevocable laws. However, physics is still an evolving discipline that, along with the proven facts and accepted laws, also includes a host of unexplained observations, tentative suppositions, and emerging theories. For example, we know what it takes to harness nuclear power, even as we continue to strive to grasp the ultimate nature of matter. Indeed, core principles, such as Heisenberg's Uncertainty Principle, suggest that we may never be able to develop indisputable explanations of certain phenomena given that the very character of what we wish to explain is changed by the very act of our observation of it. At the same time, Chaos Theory proposes that despite the otherwise seemingly random nature and therefore unpredictability, of many events, there is an underlying order present that we cannot observe and understand at the level of our ordinary experience. We could go on with other illustrations of ideas in modern physics that are counterintuitive and even defy the logic of everyday perception and thought, and yet, at the same time, are the foundation for major breakthroughs in our understanding of the nature of the material world.

In many ways, the current status of what educational professionals refer to as "the science of learning" is not much different. On one hand, the learning sciences—educational, social, and cognitive psychology, along with the neurosciences, and even the newest, evolutionary psychology, using the same research tools as other scientific endeavors—have produced a body of data and comprehensive theories that go a long way in explaining how people acquire, retain, and recall knowledge. These findings are not only an important part of efforts by educators to improve the quality of our schools, but also a part of popular culture. In recent years, magazines such as *Time* and *Newsweek* have had major stories on the brain and learning. Given the fast pace and significance of these findings, some even claim that just as the last decades of the 20th century brought a revolution in information technology, the next several decades may very well represent the "age of the brain," with our emerging understanding of how the human mind works transforming not only educational practices, but the quality of our everyday lives.

Yet there are still many who remain somewhat circumspect and cautious about research findings in the learning sciences.

It is argued that much thinking in this area is often at best educated guesses, embryonic models, or unproven theories able to describe in only limited ways the highly complex processes involved in learning, cognition, and teaching. These critics contend that there are still too many unanswered questions, and it is premature to attempt to use these findings to formulate new instructional principles that can reliably be applied in our classrooms to improve teaching and learning. For example, in *In Search of . . . Brain-Based Education,* John Bruer, a noted researcher in cognitive studies, states that we need to proceed slowly when it comes to looking for or making claims about the direct classroom applications of neuroscience research into right–left brain differences or theories about multiple intelligences, even as well-known and intuitively appealing as these ideas might be. We agree that we have to move slowly and take into account the most recent research.

"Excuse Me, but Is Your Paradigm Really Shifting?"

There is another useful analogy between physics and the emerging science of learning that can characterize the contrasting views of the current state of affairs in the latter that can help us develop a balanced and proper perspective. This has to do with the nature of paradigms and the way scientific thinking changes over time.

In the 1970s, Thomas Kuhn wrote a landmark book, *The Structure of Scientific Revolutions.* In it, he proposed a theory to explain changes in science and how fundamental conceptual frameworks, or paradigms (which he is credited with popularizing), do not slowly evolve but radically shift in a revolutionary matter, completely breaking with that which came before; in this shift, new thinking does not build on old ideas, but displaces them. For example, in physics, quantum concepts that developed in the first part of the 20th century did not arise from the older Newtonian model that dominated scientific reasoning for several centuries, but completely superseded these Newtonian notions.

Some apply this theory of scientific revolutions to the shift that has occurred in our theories of human learning and what constitutes best educational practices over the past several decades. According to this view, what is transpiring is not just a progression in our thinking about the nature of learning, but the development of a revolutionary new understanding of how the human mind works and what comprises good teaching in the "information age."

However, there are others who argue, in looking back on the history of thinking about the best educational policies and practices, there is no such radical departure from earlier perspectives on learning and teaching, What these critics observe is a see-saw struggle between

16

competing views that, while reflecting fundamentally different outlooks, do not represent indisputably better or necessarily incompatible outlooks on the nature of learning and effective instruction. For example, E.D. Hirsch, the author of the 1987 bestseller *Cultural Literacy* and a long-time critic of many popular educational reform efforts, sees very little real improvement and certainly no "paradigm shift" transpiring in our schools today. What he does believe, as he writes about in *The Schools We Need: And Why We Don't Have Them,* is that at present there are too many misconceptions and overgeneralizations of research and overly zealous teachers and policy makers uncritically accepting what is the latest reform, theory or practice "du jour."

So, What's Next?

As the title of this unit suggests and as stated earlier, we believe that our understanding of the nature of learning and what constitutes good teaching is evolving. Like other scientific disciplines, the science of learning is moving forward but with fits and starts, as different and even contradictory ideas emerge and then compete for attention and agreement in the educational community.

At the same time, though, we may be far off from articulating what some may consider a science of learning that offers a coherent and unitary description of how people think, remember, and learn. There has emerged over recent decades a significant body of knowledge and ideas that can intelligently inform educational practice. And we have been able to develop over recent years some stable and reliable understandings of what contributes to effective learning and teaching that, while not necessarily fitting neatly together into a single theory, still offer powerful insights that can guide and improve our practice. These understandings and insights are explored in Chapters 2 and 3 of this unit. In Chapter 2, An Exploration of the Evolving Science of Learning, we examine the shifts in the two dominant theories about learning of the last 100 years and their relevance for classroom practice. In Chapter 3, Learning with the Brain and Mind in Mind, we go into detail about more recent thinking and research into specific areas of interest, such as memory, attention, motivation, and intelligence.

We preface this discussion with Chapter 1, Exploring Our Personal Teaching Philosophy: Teacher, Know Thyself. We do so because it is our experience and the conclusion of researchers into the nature of learning itself that before any one of us can fully appreciate, accept, and possibly even understand any new ideas (in this case the body of knowledge and various paradigms in the learning sciences) we must also consider our personal "paradigm" or perspectives and prior knowledge on the subject of our study (in this case teaching and learning) that predispose us to certain ways of approaching this study and our teaching practices. For this reason, before we present these ideas and research, we take a little time to help you to reflect on your beliefs and practice so that you may formulate and solidify a cogent personal education philosophy that can accommodate ideas from the science of learning. If you write your thoughts you will be able to reflect on them and edit, adopt, or adapt them to best match what you want to be in the classroom.

CHAPTER 1

Exploring Our Personal Teaching Philosophy: Teacher, Know Thyself

It isn't what people think that is important, but the reason they think what they think.

—Eugene Ionesco

Do You Know:

- Your capacity for improving your teaching is a function of not only what you know but also what you believe and value about teaching and learning?

- These beliefs and values comprise our teaching philosophy or perspective and are largely based on unconsciously held assumptions?

- Across a broad range of subjects and teaching contexts, there are a only small number of different teaching perspectives, with each teacher adhering to one or at most two dominant perspectives?

- How your beliefs about and orientation to teaching and learning align with the approach of other educators?

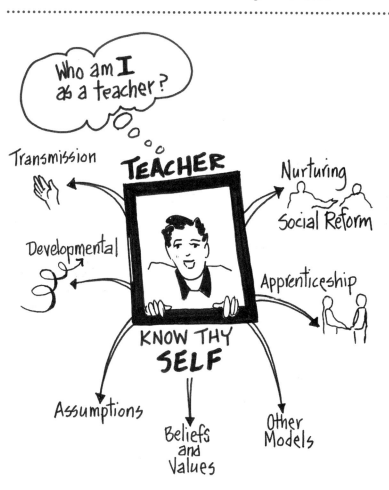

19

Introduction

As stated earlier, fast-changing economic, technological, and social forces are redefining the goals of education and reshaping the task of teaching in postsecondary and career-technical schools. These changes have raised the bar on what students must know and be able to do to succeed and, therefore, increased the demands on us, as educators.

Covering the content is no longer enough, especially since the very knowledge base from which we teach is quickly expanding. We need to not only cover the content, but also to uncover student learning. We need to make sure this content is taught in flexible ways that can be transferred to new settings by making students capable of thinking critically, solving problems, and communicating effectively. Faced with such challenges, one would assume that what goes on in our formal institutions of learning and our classrooms has changed in recent decades to meet these challenges. Yet in many cases this is not true.

To be able to effectively respond to these challenges and improve our teaching practices we need to go beyond the common questions that look at the surface and observable elements of the teaching/learning transaction—what we are to teach and how to best go about it. We also need to understand how people learn. Yet, as suggested in the introduction to this unit, our quest to understand the character of learning needs to begin with questions that first take us to a deeper and more personal level of inquiry that can reveal our basic assumptions and beliefs about what it means to learn and how best to teach.

> We teach
> who we are.
>
> —Parker Palmer

Understanding Your Personal Teaching Philosophy

Parker Palmer, in his book *The Courage to Teach,* explores the notions of our teaching persona and personal teaching philosophy by raising four questions that he believes underlie the ongoing dialogue about what comprises good teaching and learning. The first two are the typical questions asked in teacher training and professional development programs. These are the questions of the "what" and "how" of teaching—the content to be taught, our subject matter, and the best methods and techniques needed to teach this material. However, Palmer proposes we learn to ask two further questions. These are questions of the "why" and "who" of teaching, which reside at a significantly deeper level, as they concern how we personally define the purposes of our teaching and our roles as educators.

The what and how questions are fundamental and must be asked; indeed this book and its companion Field Guide focus on these two questions as the core elements of our understanding the science of learning and our means to a progressive mastery of the art of teaching. As Palmer states, he has "no quarrel" with these questions and neither do we except, as Palmer continues, "when they are posed as the only questions worth asking."

The logic here is simple. To improve what we do in our classrooms, we need to change the way we think. To change the way we think, we need to understand why we think as we do, especially any biases we may have in our approach to teaching in certain and possibly rigid and limited ways. Such understanding requires that we possess insight into the origin and make-up of our fundamental and overarching perspective or philosophy on teaching and learning. Only then can any of us become sufficiently receptive to learning new and more effective and flexible ways of thinking about the nature of learning and teaching. Without surfacing and examining these largely unconscious ideas, our efforts to meaningfully change our teaching practices will most likely prove to be extremely frustrating and difficult.

So, What Do We Mean by a "Teaching Philosophy"?

> *To change your reality you have to change your inner thoughts.*
>
> —David Bohm

At first thought, the idea of a teaching philosophy may sound highly academic and abstract, something more suitable for an "ivory tower" discussion in a graduate-school seminar or for conversation among gray-haired professors over lunch at the faculty club at an ivy-league university. A teaching philosophy is, however, quite the opposite. It is deeply personal and directly relevant to each of us as classroom teachers, having its greatest influence when it remains removed from our immediate concern and unexamined.

A good working definition of a personal teaching philosophy is *it is a set of beliefs, values, intentions, and attitudes about learning, teaching, the nature of knowledge, and the role of students and teachers in the classroom.* Every teacher possesses a teaching philosophy simply because all of us invariably hold such beliefs, values, and attitudes that are the root of our teaching persona.

Everything we are and do as teachers flows from this philosophical wellspring of our teaching. It is a personal teaching paradigm, the mental model of how we see the world of teaching and creates our "teaching persona" and preferred teaching style. It determines our perceptions of ourselves as teachers. It defines our expectations of our students, and the amount of control we wield or are willing to yield to them. It frames our view of what it means to know and learn something, the topics we highlight as the core concepts of our courses, and the content we believe needs only be touched upon or can even be ignored. It influences the kinds of questions we ask or do not ask and how we ask them, the way we measure learning and deal with the mistakes our students make and how we judge the results of what we do.

As the ethical foundation for their work, medical doctors take the Hippocratic oath, which includes the dictum to "do no harm."

Educators have no similar statement of professional ethics as a guide for proper professional practice. If we were to choose one, perhaps ancient Greek philosophical imperative to "know thyself" might serve well.

The Origin of Your Personal Teaching Philosophy

Basically, there are three sources for our beliefs, values, and attitudes about teaching and learning. These are our culture, our personal experience, and our formal study and training as teachers.

The first are the beliefs that are part of tradition and operate within our system of formal education and even as elements of popular culture. These might go back all the way to Aristotle, who said, "What we have to learn to do, we learn by doing," or to Galileo, who said, "You cannot teach a man anything; you can only help him find it within himself." Looking at more contemporary sources for our beliefs, we may have the idea that a person's capacity for learning is a matter of intelligence as measured by IQ and is fixed for life. Or, drawing from more recent influences, we may have come to the conclusion that "males are better at math than females," that "everyone has different learning styles," or that "knowledge is power." It is possible to go on.

Another, and the most common and influential source of what we believe about learning and teaching, is our own personal educational experience as students. Although some of this learning may have been what is known as incidental learning, the kind that happens outside the classroom (learning how to ride a bike, understanding the game of football, etc.), it is likely that our experience in formal educational settings has had the greatest influence. This experience consists of what we saw teachers doing, as well as what we felt comfortable with as learners. Beyond our early education in elementary school, this most likely meant sitting and listening to lectures while taking notes, reading textbooks and doing homework outside of class, and memorizing and reproducing what we studied on tests. It may include the personal beliefs that "learning is hard work" or "learning for its own sake is exciting," or that "it is not okay to make mistakes."

Lastly, the roots of our teaching philosophy may come from formal training and study in education. This could include inquiry into learning theories, such as behaviorism, cognitive science, and constructivism, or teaching methods, such as direct instruction or problem-based learning. (These are explored in the following and subsequent chapters.) It may also involve an awareness of more esoteric subjects, such as the historical and philosophical roots of modern education, and the differences between knowledge, understanding, and wisdom as articulated by the ancient Greeks and modern philosophers. Although these distinctions may seem on the surface to have no immediate relevance to improving one's craft of teaching, the ideas are the very

> *Before we choose our tools and techniques we must choose our dreams and values.*
>
> —Anonymous

> We will not
> cease from
> exploration
> and the end
> of all our
> exploring will
> be to arrive
> where we started
> and know the
> place for the
> first time.
>
> —T.S. Eliot

foundations of the dominant approaches to teaching that all educators take. Just as importantly, they have a powerful influence on how we envision the purposes of our professional development and go about our efforts to improve our practice. For example, for the early Greeks *knowledge* meant basic comprehending, *understanding* meant knowing something well enough to be able to do it, and *wisdom* meant the capacity to act wisely. Applying these concepts to teaching, most teachers can be said to possess *knowledge* as a comprehension of the subject they teach and possibly a grasp of effective teaching practices, with *understanding* as expressed in their ability to successfully practice their field. But how many of us can lay claim to *wisdom*? How many of us possess both a depth of understanding of our discipline as well as a grasp of the science and art of good teaching to the degree that allows us to consistently make the right choices and do the right things in our classrooms to promote our students' learning?

Reflecting on Your Personal Teaching Philosophy

Think about your views on teaching and learning. This can include your beliefs and attitudes about teacher and student roles, the nature and goals of learning, and the kinds of activities that promote learning.

Why you *really* need to do this.

If this exercise seems to be an abstraction or just a distraction with little perceived value, consider the following:

- Many of the best teachers take the time to do develop a teaching philosophy. (Just type in "teaching philosophy" on Google and you will find many examples.)
- Consider it a matter of "enlightened self-interest." It is becoming increasingly common for students to expect their faculty to be able to state their philosophy of teaching.
- If this is a remote concern, then consider such as statement as an excellent way of articulating what you do as a teacher as preparation for a possible job interview.
- Finally, and as a more immediate application, a few brief sentences about your approach to teaching stated in a course syllabus will be an invaluable aid to your students' success in your class. There will be fewer unpleasant surprises for all, since it will serve as an explicit expression of the expectations all teachers have but rarely make clear beyond a brief course description. Furthermore, as a personal statement of who you are, it is a great way to begin to make a more personal connection to your students—something that most students say they highly value and see as a quality of the best teachers.

Take a few moments to write down what beliefs and ideas come immediately to mind, using the questions listed below as needed for prompts.

Questions to Guide This Introspective Exercise

***Unit 2
Introduction***

- How do you decide what is important to teach and what your students should know?

- How do you determine that students have learned what they need to know? (Objective tests, demonstrations of and the ability to use knowledge?)

- How do you use feedback from student performance in the classroom?

- Do you consider that things other than content knowledge, such as the development of intellectual skills, are also important? If so, what are these other areas of learning you include and how much importance do you place on them?

- How would you describe an effective learning environment and what you consider the best conditions for learning to be?

- Besides lectures, what other teaching activities do you use in your classroom and how and when do you decide to use them?

- What kinds of questions do you ask, and how often and when do you ask them?

- How much freedom do you give to students to explore and discover for themselves what they need to learn?

- How would you characterize your relationship with your students? Formal and authoritative? Casual and facilitative?

- What are your preferred learning styles (reading, listening to presentations, discussions, etc.), and how are these expressed in your teaching style and techniques?

Refer to Field Guide

Certainly, there are many more questions that can be asked. If you are interested and willing to do so, we would suggest that you consider your answers to these questions as the first step to writing a formal statement of your teaching philosophy. You'll find an exercise to complete in the Field Guide. There you will find a complete guide to constructing a statement of your teaching philosophy, with a host of related resources.

Putting Your Perspective into Perspective—Different Orientations to Teaching and Learning

Many teachers are curious about and find it helpful to know how their personal teaching philosophy aligns with that of other professionals. Fortunately, there are a number of researchers who have characterized the predominant teaching approaches postsecondary teachers take to instruction, which can help you get a perspective on your views of learning and teaching.

Most noteworthy is Dan Pratt, who has spent over two decades researching and describing different philosophical orientations to teaching. His work corresponds to that of other researchers. Pratt characterizes these orientations as teaching perspectives, which he defines as an educator's fundamental intentions and beliefs about what constitutes and influences learning and gives direction to teaching. Through surveys of teachers from around the world, he has investigated the conceptual roots of different views on what it means to be an effective teacher. He has discovered that across a broad spectrum of disciplines, contexts, and people, educators differ in four basic dimensions, which he calls BIASes. Applying an awareness of his findings on dominant orientations and where you locate yourself among them can be quite useful in clarifying the rationale for the decisions you make each time you walk into a classroom and, therefore, how you can begin to improve your practice.

If a man does not keep pace with his companions, perhaps it is because he hears a different drummer.

—Thoreau

So, What're Your BIASes?

As defined by Pratt, these BIASes are as follows:

B = Beliefs about learners, learning, our subject matter, and the roles and responsibilities of teachers and students.

I = Intentions about what we expect students to learn; that is, what we are trying to achieve.

A = Actions that we take in the classroom as our teaching methods and techniques to help students learn.

S = Strategies, or the ways our beliefs, intentions, and actions come together in an overall strategy and process of decision making.

These 4 BIASes are expressed in different patterns that Pratt has categorized into five perspectives on teaching:

1. transmission,
2. apprenticeship,
3. developmental,
4. nurturing, and
5. social reform.

According to Pratt's research, about 90 percent of all teachers will identify with one or at most two perspectives. He also has concluded that no single perspective is the basis for what might be considered "good teaching." Each approach has the potential to lead to effective teaching, with no single way consistently better than another. Pratt, therefore, advises educators to be cautious about adopting one dominant view of

When I first came across Daniel Pratt's research into teaching perspectives, I had a bit of an epiphany. I realized that while I had evolved a pretty varied approach to my teaching over years of practice, these diverse teaching practices were rooted in a fairly consistent perspective on the nature of teaching and learning—just as Pratt discovered in his research. The perspective that comprised the core of my values and beliefs was a fairly even balance between what he has described as the developmental and nurturing approaches. What became apparent was that no matter what particular techniques and methods I used, which included elements of all five of his perspectives and seemed rather eclectic on the surface, I almost invariably wove them together into a consistent personal system. This framework was much like a web of interrelated beliefs, attitudes, and behaviors that was held together by a core belief that people learn best when they are encouraged to learn for themselves and that they are supported in this through the creation of challenging but self-empowering learning environments and practices.

Pratt's work also reinforced a natural inclination to share my personal teaching philosophy. When I first started doing so early in my career I did it as a way of connecting with my students, since I had long felt that students would benefit from a heads-up on my teaching style. But I also came to realize that just telling them the "what" of my practice was only part of what they needed to know and could benefit from. I discovered that when students understood the "why" of how I evolved my beliefs and attitudes, they were much less resistant to my learner-centered approach, which often placed much more responsibility for their learning on their own shoulders—something that most were not used to and were initially uncomfortable with because of their educational experiences. Possessed with an understanding of the rationale for this approach and the personal journey I traveled to arrive at it, they became more willing partners in the learning experience.

learning and teaching. What he believes is most important is the authenticity of one's approach, meaning to be an effective teacher above all requires that you be yourself. This is an important conclusion that Parker Palmer has also drawn in his book, *The Courage to Teach,* referred to earlier, and which we have found also to be true from our combined 50 years of experience as educators.

Pratt points out that it is important not to confuse these teaching perspectives with a particular teaching method or set of techniques. A perspective operates on a deeper and more personal level than our behaviors as instructors. Despite the personal and diverse preferences for certain ways of teaching among instructors, Pratt has found that

Chapter 2

> *Not perfection as a final goal, but the ever-enduring process of perfecting, maturing, refining is the aim of living.*
>
> —John Dewey

there is a great deal of commonality among each perspective, with the same teaching actions, such as lecturing, discussions, problem-based learning, and others, present across perspectives. Perspectives are differentiated not by teaching techniques, but how a specific technique is used and for what purpose based on each educator's fundamental values and beliefs. As you consider the following five perspectives, do not be concerned about finding a "perfect fit"; rather, look for the one or two with which you mostly identity. Also, before proceeding, we strongly encourage you to assess your own fundamental orientation. You can do this quite easily by taking a free instrument developed by Pratt, *The Teaching Perspectives Inventory,* found on the Web at teachingpersectives.com. (*Note:* Along with each perspective, we briefly reference specific theories and research in education and the learning sciences that align with the different philosophical perspectives. Bear with us. Some of these labels may seem rather obtuse at this moment, but they are explained in the next chapter.)

Transmission Perspective

The Philosophy. The transmission model is the most prevalent of the five approaches among secondary and postsecondary teachers, and it is the easiest to explain. Though not by definition rooted in any specific theory of learning and teaching, it finds support in behaviorist psychology and direct instruction. In this view, "content is king," and the aim of instruction is to convey the subject matter accurately and efficiently. As characterized by Pratt, the learner is a container to be filled, with learning seen as a process of accumulation of knowledge over time. Knowledge is seen to exist outside the learning and is found in what the teacher has to say or in texts. Success of instruction, then, is believed to be based primarily on a teacher's subject-matter expertise and ability to structure this content.

The Practice. Teachers who adopt this orientation generally spend a good deal of time in preparation, beginning with the basics of the subject and then systematically proceeding through a set of tasks that lead to the learner's mastery of the content. Pratt's research shows that the transmission method, when done well, follows common guidelines on traditional methods of teaching: establishing clear objectives, presenting well-organized and well-paced lectures that make efficient use of class time, answering questions to clarify misunderstandings, pointing out errors, offering reviews and summaries, helping students find relevant resources, and assessing learning through largely objective means that determine mastery of the content.

The Challenge. Pratt indicates that the transmission model is the one most often cited as an example of problematic teaching, and instructors who adopt this orientation share a number of common difficulties.

Foremost, with a focus on content rather than on learners and the learning process, those operating within a transmission approach may fail to appreciate the difficulties students may have with the subject matter and frequently find it hard to recognize the need for and come up with examples and ways of connecting content to where the students are. Also, these teachers frequently dominate the classroom with their own talking, and when students ask questions or offer some comment, they respond by talking more rather than engaging the students themselves in the learning process. This does not mean a transmission perspective cannot be done well. Those most successful with this approach have an excellent grasp of their subject, a clear passion for it, and the ability to deliver it with an enthusiasm that engages students and engenders within them a respect for it.

Developmental Perspective

The Philosophy. In this view, the learner is seen primarily as an information processor, somewhat like a computer. As explained in the next chapter, the theoretical foundation for this approach is a cognitive-information processing model of learning and training. The belief here is that people are predisposed or "preprogrammed" to learn in certain ways as a result of preexisting mental models and their previous experience, which filter and determine the ways in which they are inclined to interpret and understand the subject. Thus, learners do not so much receive or acquire knowledge as they *construct* it on the foundation of what they already know. An educator who operates from this orientation believes that good teaching starts with this knowledge base and that real learning involves students being able to make sense of what they need to learn by relating it to what they already know. The desired outcome looks similar to that of the transmission model—the learner's improved subject matter knowledge and thinking ability. However, in contrast to the transmission model, in which the teacher dominates instruction and learners are expected to somewhat passively recall and reproduce the knowledge of the instructor or texts, here students are called on to be active participants in their learning and to integrate new material into their thinking in complex ways that go beyond surface, factual reproduction to a deeper, conceptual understanding.

The Practice. Teachers who operate within this orientation believe they need to begin instruction by connecting the learners' old ideas and ways of thinking to the new knowledge and thinking abilities they wish their students to develop. This includes directly surfacing (triggering) their students' prior knowledge, as well as any possible misconceptions they may have about the subject matter that can interfere with understanding new material. The frequent use of questions and

> Man's mind stretched to a new idea never goes back to its original dimensions.
>
> —Oliver Wendell Holmes

other techniques for eliciting feedback are important elements in this process. Unlike questions that might be used by a teacher who adopts a transmission perspective, here the questions are designed to do more than promote recall; rather, they are intended to reveal how and why students think the way they do, expose possible learning difficulties, and challenge students to become more engaged in the material. Examples, illustrations, case studies, and problems are commonly used for connecting old and new ideas, grounding unfamiliar concepts, and moving learners from simple to more complex ways of reasoning.

The Challenge. Approaching instruction from this perspective is not as easy as using a transmission orientation. Developmental teachers need to not only be knowledgeable and efficient, but also must be able to constantly adapt their knowledge to learners' ways of understanding. Also, it is difficult to ask questions that elicit more than factual responses or surface understanding to reveal where in the learning process students are and help them acquire critical-thinking capacities. Moreover, it takes patience and a real appreciation of the sometimes slow process of deep learning to allow students the time and space they need to discover ideas; with the common pressure to cover content, it is much easier to tell them what they need to know rather than let them reason through the material themselves. Finally, when teachers try to teach from this perspective they need to develop ways to elaborate on the material and design assessments that reflect the learning outcome they seek, which is the students' increased ability to reflect on, analyze, evaluate, and apply rather than merely recall and reproduce what they learn.

> *Education is not preparation for life; education is life itself.*
>
> —John Dewey

Apprenticeship Perspective

The Philosophy. As the name suggests, this orientation is one familiar to those working in skills-based programs or those involving internships, though it is becoming increasingly common in more traditional classroom instructional settings. The theoretical foundation for this perspective is somewhat mixed, including notions from cognitive–social constructivism and situated learning. The dominant metaphor is learner as novice and the goal of instruction is to help the learner develop a new identity by becoming a proficient participant in a particular field as a member of a professional community. This happens when the learner successfully makes the transition from a naive outsider to an expert in a "community of practice" or profession able to perform in a skilled manner. In this view, a learner needs not only to possess an objective body of knowledge and be able to reason in ways appropriate to a particular vocation, but also to internalize the core values and beliefs held by those who are experienced in their field. Within this perspective, teachers see themselves as "masters," who not only teach didactically and demonstrate through their own example and behavior the desired outcomes they seek but also convey what it looks like and means to be a member of a community of professionals.

The Practice. Operating from this perspective, a teacher generally will try to create a learning environment that involves authentic tasks that replicate as much as possible real situations in which students will be called on to demonstrate or apply their knowledge. The instructor attempts to model as much as possible the values, knowledge, thinking skills, and behaviors of a skilled participant in a particular field. A process known as scaffolding is the primary teaching tool. Scaffolding breaks down complex tasks into basic components and leads the learner into increasingly more difficult and core elements of a desired performance.

In a manner akin to the approach of a developmental instructor, in this model the teacher will also seek to identify students' point of entry or their level of competence in relation to a new skill and the degree to which they can perform on their own and how much assistance they need. Ideally, this point will shift continually as students progressively learn to think and behave in ways consistent with those of experienced members of their profession; consequently, the role of the instructor will also change. At the beginning of instruction, the teacher will demonstrate as the students observe. Then through the process of scaffolding, the learners will begin to practice what has been modeled for them. As students assume greater responsibility for their performance and become more and more independent, the teacher provides less and less guidance, until the students are able to enter the "community of practice" that comprises their profession.

> *Smart people don't learn . . . because they have too much invested in proving what they know and avoiding being seen as not knowing.*
>
> —Chris Argyris

The Challenge. Within this approach, there are several difficulties instructors commonly have to deal with. One is to accurately assess a student's point of entry and to properly balance between a student's ability and the degree of scaffolding needed to help the student progress. Another is to find authentic learning tasks that mirror the kind of real-life situations the student will encounter outside the classroom. An adequate degree of authenticity and matching problems and cases with each student's level of competence takes time and careful consideration; a significant degree of individual attention is necessary to achieve this. Finally, scaffolding is not just a matter of demonstrating a particular performance task but being able to break it down into its constituent parts and being able to explain them. An expert will, by definition, be knowledgeable and proficient in their field. Yet knowing what you know and being able to explain what you know are quite different matters. It is quite common for experts to be unable to clearly articulate actions that have become habits and find the words needed to tell others how to do what they can do so well themselves without much conscious thought.

Nurturing Perspective

The Philosophy. Here the metaphor for learning and teaching is, according to Pratt, the "vulnerable self," and is common among those who teach in adult education programs. This orientation has its theoretical roots in theories of andragogy and humanistic psychology. Nurturing teachers maintain that the learner and learning need to be approached both intellectually and emotionally, with special attention given to each student's self-concept, affective needs, and freedom to be self-directed. A primary goal of learning is a learner with greater self-confidence and increased self-direction. The dominant underlying belief is that a student's prior educational experience has often been a negative one and led to a poor self-concept as a learner. It is also assumed that students need to be able to assume a good deal of responsibility for their own learning if they are to succeed. This perspective holds that learners are more likely to succeed when they are working toward the fulfillment of self-determined goals within a supportive, positive learning environment. Such an environment balances the learner's necessary independence with a caring teacher–student relationship and learning tasks that provide an appropriate level of challenge. When these proper conditions are not present in the classroom, it is assumed that learning will be obstructed and possibly fail.

> What sculpture is to a block of marble, education is to an human soul.
>
> —Joseph Addison

The Practice. Teachers who take this approach maintain a focus on the learning environment and actively seek to balance academic achievement with strategies that build their students' self-concept and self-confidence and capacity to learn. Common strategies include getting-to-know activities, collaborative learning exercises, and attending to students' emotional states and needs. In many ways counseling becomes as important as teaching, and providing encouragement is an integral role for the teacher. Assessment often includes measures of an individual's progress in addition to a student's mastery of subject matter. Some see this approach as failing to provide the rigor students need to succeed academically and not adequately emphasizing the importance of standards that all students must meet; however, a nurturing perspective does not preclude setting high goals for learners. Nurturing teachers, rather than just leaving students to fend for themselves when faced with significant learning challenges, seek to ensure that demands are reasonable and work hard to help their students prepare for tests.

The Challenge. As Pratt points out, the very label *nurturing* perspective has some negative connotations and, although many teachers might not apply this specific label to themselves (remember, this is Pratt's name for it), the nurturing orientation is not an uncommon one, and those who identify with it are frequently criticized for their approach. Critics believe that nurturers often lower their standards in order to help people succeed, which is often perceived to be in conflict with institutional expectations for student achievement. Though there may be some truth to this, those who correctly practice this approach do not see high standards and personal encouragement as incompatible; on the contrary, they see demonstrating competence and achievement as the very means to building self-confidence. Still, it can be quite difficult for some to effectively balance academic requirements with emotional needs. Thus, it is easy for nurturing instructors to be tempted to compromise academic standards in efforts to help their students feel good about themselves as learners and even out of a personal need to be liked by their students.

Some people would rather die than think.

—Bertrand Russell

Social Reform Perspective

The Philosophy. The final perspective that Pratt identified in his research is that of social reform. In many ways this perspective has its roots in the same humanistic psychology of the nurturing approach, but also finds a rationale in what is known as a social constructivist framework. (Remember, this and other possibly unfamiliar terms are explained in the next chapter.) Within this perspective, the focus shifts from the learner as an individual to someone shaped by and operating within the context of the larger society. Therefore, the learner, the learning process, and teaching can be understood only in terms of the social, cultural, and historical setting within which they occur. Teachers who work from this perspective are distinguished by a strongly held set of personal ideals that motivates their teaching. The goal of learning is not only to change a student's personal thinking but to shift larger cultural, political, and social values and beliefs. Pratt has found that this is the most difficult perspective to characterize, since it encompasses no particular or uniform set of characteristics and strategies. He has discovered that it is present among those working in such diverse fields as community development and AIDS awareness to automotive mechanics and medical education. As Pratt puts it, the one constant is that the teacher who adopted this approach was either a "leader or a rebel."

The Practice. With no unique teaching method that characterizes the classroom practices of a social reformer, elements of effective teaching from the other perspectives are found here. Good social reform educators organize and deliver content clearly, help their learners connect new knowledge with their prior experiences, develop greater and greater levels of expertise in their field together with a personal sense of self-efficacy and confidence. What distinguishes this approach are the ideals that drive instructors, their success at expressing these ideals, and their ability to get learners to adopt them as their own by questioning personal beliefs and values about their field of study and life in general.

We need to be the authors of our own life.

—Peter Senge

The Challenge. Social reformers are quite rare, and although they are found teaching in many contexts, clearly they will do best when working in a program that explicitly states as its primary goal greater personal, social, and political awareness coupled with collective change rather than education or training for the purpose of individual career or academic advancement. As advocates of changes, social reformers are most successful when they are able to effectively balance their strongly held personal ideals with a respect for their students and colleagues and a tolerance for ideas that do not reflect their personal values.

CHAPTER WRAP-UP

Whether you are an experienced instructor or new, full-time or part-time, articulating your individual teaching philosophy provides the foundation for clarifying goals and guiding your behavior in the classroom each day by describing your identity as a teacher. It also is a necessary step in learning how to effectively improve your teaching practice.

We have suggested that it would be helpful to make your teaching beliefs and values explicit by possibly taking an inventory of your teaching goals and beliefs and writing a formal statement of your teaching perspective. However, you can also go about exploring your identity as a teacher more informally and begin with the simple question, "Why am I teaching?" as a foundation for the "what" and "how" of your teaching. Rather than trying to come to a definitive response, simply allow the answer to evolve over time through day-to-day reflections. Once you are clear about the "why," the "what" and "how," which we explore in the remainder of this text, will more easily make sense and fall into place and hopefully lead to a natural unfolding of the knowledge of what makes for effective teaching, and the wisdom of what it means to be a great teacher.

Have patience with everything unresolved in your heart and to try to love the questions themselves. . . . the point is to live everything. Live the questions now. Perhaps then, someday far, you will gradually, without even noticing it, live your way into the answer.

—Rainer Maria Rilke

Summary of Five Teaching Perspectives

Transmission*   *Effective teaching requires a substantial commitment to the content or subject matter.* Good teachers have mastery of the subject matter or content. It is a teacher's primary responsibility to represent the content accurately and efficiently for learners. It is the learner's responsibility to learn that content in its authorized or legitimate forms. Good teachers take learners systematically through sets of tasks that lead to content mastery. Such teachers provide clear objectives, adjust the pace of lecturing, make efficient use of class time, clarify misunderstandings, answer questions, provide timely feedback, correct errors, provide reviews, summarize what has been presented, direct students to appropriate resources, set high standards for achievement, and develop objective means of assessing learning. Good teachers are enthusiastic about their content and convey that enthusiasm to their students, and for many learners, they are memorable presenters of their content.

Apprenticeship   *Effective teaching is a process of acculturating students into a set of social norms and ways of working.* Good teachers are highly skilled at what they teach. Whether in classrooms or at work sites, they are recognized for their expertise. Teachers must reveal the inner workings of skilled performance and must now translate it into accessible language and an ordered set of tasks. Learning tasks usually proceed from simple to complex, allowing for different points of observation and entry depending on the learner's capability. Good teachers know what their learners can do on their own and what they can do with guidance and direction, namely, engaging learners' within their "zone of development." As learners mature and become more competent, the teacher's role changes, and over time, teachers offer less direction and give more responsibility as they progress from dependent learners to independent workers.

Developmental   *Effective teaching must be planned and conducted "from the learner's point of view."* Good teachers must understand how their learners think and reason about

(continues)

the content. The primary goal is to help learners develop increasingly complex and sophisticated cognitive structures for comprehending the content. The key to changing those structures lies in a combination of two skills: (a) effective questioning that challenges learners to move from relatively simple to more complex forms of thinking, and (b) "bridging knowledge," which provides examples that are meaningful to the learner. Questions, problems, cases, and examples form the bridges that teachers use to transport learners from simpler ways of thinking and reasoning to new, more complex and sophisticated forms of reasoning and problem solving. Good teachers work hard to adapt their knowledge to each learner's level of understanding and ways of thinking.

Nurturing

Effective teaching assumes that long-term, hard, persistent effort to achieve comes from the heart, as well as the head. People are motivated and productive learners when they are working on issues or problems without fear of failure. Learners are nurtured by knowing that: (a) they can succeed at learning if they give it a good try; (b) their achievement is a product of their own effort and ability, rather than the benevolence of a teacher; and (c) their efforts to learn will be supported by their teacher and their peers. The more pressure to achieve, and the more difficult the material, the more important it is that there be such support for learning. Good teachers promote a climate of caring and trust, helping people set challenging but achievable goals, and providing encouragement and support, along with clear expectations and reasonable goals for all learners. They do not sacrifice self-efficacy or self-esteem for achievement. Therefore, the assessment of learning considers individual growth or progress as well as absolute achievement.

Social Reform

Effective teaching seeks to change society in substantive ways. From this point of view, the object of teaching is the collective rather than the individual. Good teachers awaken students to the values and ideologies that are embedded in texts and common practices within their discipline. Good teachers challenge the status quo and encourage students to consider how learners are

(continues)

positioned and constructed in particular discourses and practices. To do so, common practices are analyzed and deconstructed for the ways in which they reproduce and maintain conditions deemed unacceptable. Class discussion is focused less on how knowledge has been created, and more on by whom and for what purposes knowledge has been created. Texts are interrogated for what is said and what is not said; what is included and what is excluded; who is represented and who is omitted from the dominant discourses within a field of study or practice. Students are encouraged to take a critical stance to give them power to take social action to improve their own lives; critical deconstruction, though central to this view, is not an end in itself.

*Used with permission of Daniel D. Pratt and John B. Collins.

SPRINGBOARDS FOR FURTHER LEARNING

Key Names
Tony Grasha
Parker Palmer
Daniel Pratt

Key Terms
inventory (of teaching goals)
personal teaching philosophy
teaching goals
teaching goals inventory

teaching perspectives
teaching perspectives survey
teaching styles

CHAPTER 2

An Exploration of the Evolving Science of Learning: Metaphors for the Mind

For all the talk of learning amongst educational policymakers and practitioners, there is a surprising lack of attention to what it entails. . . . It is almost as if it is something is unproblematic and that can be taken for granted. Get the instructional regime right, the message seems to be, and learning . . . will follow. This lack of attention to the nature of learning inevitably leads to an impoverishment of education.

—M.K. Smith

Do You Know:

- How learning occurs, and what factors influence learning?
- What the prominent theories of learning are?
- How these theories relate to contemporary educational and training practices?
- What types of learning are best explained by each of these different theories?
- What the strengths and limitations of these theories are?
- How your own teaching perspective aligns with these different theories of learning?
- How you can use these theories to improve your own teaching practices?

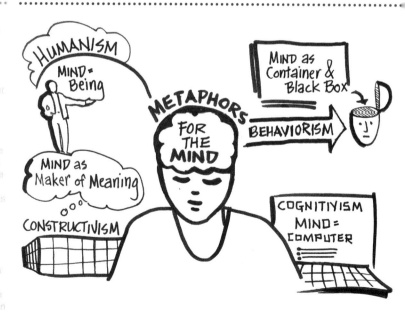

37

Introduction

Over the past century, many instructional approaches have been studied and implemented across a wide variety of educational and training settings. These established perspectives, as well as many newer ones, are often the subject of skepticism and ridicule or passionate advocacy as proponents and critics of a particular approach position themselves. Teachers are caught in the crossfire of the debate, with the implications for their classroom practice often unclear and even confusing.

You can sort through this debate by grounding what you do in your classrooms in an explicit statement of your philosophy of teaching and learning. In this chapter, we continue our journey across the landscape of postsecondary education by exploring the dominant theories of learning that shape this landscape to help you develop a sound and reliable rationale for your teaching philosophy.

Some theories focus on ways to describe and control observable behaviors and events. Others attempt to build descriptive frameworks to explain and influence workings of the mind we cannot directly study, such as the nature of attention, the way memories are formed and recalled, or how we come to process, understand, and give meaning to knowledge. Still others look to the social environment as a determiner of our ways of knowing and learning.

Unfortunately, the boundaries between these theories are not always clear and, as often is the case in many scientific investigations, each theory is not a distinct set of constructs. The same concepts and theorists may be associated with more than one theory. Furthermore, each theory is not always singular, but is often a meld of related yet independent principles and models; in some areas, competing theories may even overlap. Moreover, each is subject to and has undergone various modifications over time. As a result, teachers who desire to ground their teaching practices in proven principles are faced with multiple conceptualizations of learning that can be complementary, as well as conflicting, and whose applications to instruction are not always apparent. When considered in terms of different learning settings, tasks, and goals, each offers legitimate views on the character of learning, and it is probably safe to say that no single theory can adequately account for all aspects of learning.

The challenge is to sort through all these ideas to understand the relationships among them and then derive sound educational principles that can be applied to the design of effective curricula, instruction, assessments, and learning environments. In what follows, we do the "heavy lifting" of this work for you. After reviewing the most influential theories of learning put forth over the past century, we have distilled them into four basic groups: behaviorism, cognitivism, constructivism, and humanism. Each set of constructs is characterized in terms of its own prevailing metaphor for the human mind and views on learning. We then briefly describe the educational

The greatest obstacle to discovery is not ignorance—it is the illusion of knowledge.

—Daniel Bornstein

A Valuable Preview of What's Ahead

To help you getting a better grasp of the four learning theories and how they influence classroom practices, we suggest you take a quick look at the table included in the Chapter Wrap-up. The table presents a description of the learning theories as a continuum of concepts and practices, with behaviorism and cognitivism as somewhat related theories at one end and constructivism and humanism at the other.

As further help, consider the following: Imagine you are thinking of enrolling in a foreign language program to learn Spanish in preparation for a trip to Mexico. You have a choice between two teachers in the program. To decide which class you want to take, you are invited to observe each one for a day. Both classes are in their third week of instruction.

In the first class you observe the following: The instructor begins by doing a quick drill in which all students in chorus repeat the Spanish alphabet as pronunciation practice. Next, she goes over a vocabulary and phrase list that explains some of the new words introduced in a reading from a textbook, which each student has. She goes over the rules for the correct pronunciation of each of these, with the students repeating them after her. Students then read the passage silently and afterward take turns reading the dialogue in pairs. After that, they answer questions in Spanish regarding the passage and go over the answers, doing an exercise to practice the conjugation of verbs used in the past tense in the dialogue. Finally, the teacher assigns as homework some of the new phrases she wants the students to memorize and use in their own sentences. She also gives an additional exercise that has drills for practicing verbs in the past tense. She tells the students that she is going to quiz them on the new words the next day by asking them to write their definitions. She uses English to conduct most of the class. This includes her directions for activities, her explanations, and answers to student questions. Your overall impression is that the class was somewhat formal but conducted in an efficient manner.

The next day you visit the second classroom. The differences between this and the other class strike you immediately. Though it is only the third week of the course, the teacher is using only Spanish. The students have no books out. The instructor, who points to objects in the class and names them, with the students repeating each word after him, conducts the lesson. Each item is labeled in Spanish. He then uses a number of different objects in simple actions, for example, writing with a marker on a whiteboard, describing in Spanish what he is doing. Rather than translating what he has said, he keeps repeating the statement and asks the students to repeat it with him several times. He asks the students in Spanish to

(continues)

write down the statement to the best of their ability. He invites a few volunteers to come put on the board what they have written. Afterward, the teacher writes the statement on the board, spelling and pronouncing each word. There is a great deal of laughter, for it is obvious that most of the students had a lot of mistakes. It is only at this point that he takes a moment to explain in English a rule of Spanish pronunciation that most of the students seemed to have trouble with. This same process is repeated with a few other objects and actions. At the end of the class, he gives them in English the assignment to prepare to mime a simple activity for the class next day that the class as a group will have to describe in Spanish. He tells them about an upcoming field trip to a local Spanish market. But rather than explaining this in English, he does so by holding up a picture of a market and then acting out with Spanish comments (walking, going in to the market, and making a purchase, etc.) what they will be doing. Your overall impression is that though he used Spanish almost entirely during the class the students seemed to get a lot out of it and had a good time doing so.

Two classes. Same course. Same learning goals. Yet entirely different methods. The first class reflects a hybrid behaviorist/cognitivist approach, the second a hybrid constructivist/humanist approach. Keep each scenario in mind as you read this chapter. They can embed otherwise abstract ideas in a concrete example that, we are confident, will add a some "meat" to the "bones" of these different theoretical approaches to learning and teaching.

implications of each theory, including its corresponding teaching perspective and associated teaching methods, and conclude the chapter with a critical evaluation that highlights their relative strengths and limitations.

Behaviorism: The Mind as a Container and "Black Box"

The first theory explored is the oldest, with roots going back to the early part of the past century. As a theory of learning and teaching, it had its greatest impact in the first half of the past century but still influences a broad spectrum of educational and training practices today.

The Metaphor

Behaviorists conceive the mind as an empty, opaque container, or "black box." In this conceptualization, the mind is unavailable to direct study and holds only that which is placed there from outside sources, completely subject to these external influences. From this perspective, human learning can be explained only in terms of observable behaviors (therefore the moniker) and the environmental conditions that influence them. Any attempt to describe hidden mental operations, such as attention, perception, thinking, memory, and understanding, is considered to be philosophical speculation rather than solid science.

Foundations and Key Principles

Mention behaviorism and, for many people, experiments with salivating dogs and rats in mazes may come to mind, with the names of Pavlov (does that ring a bell?) and B.F. Skinner having become part of our popular culture. There are also less recognized individuals who made significant contributions to educational psychology and practice. Each of these theorists' ideas represent different developments that advanced behavioral learning theory with successive elaborations of its core tenets and its educational applications.

The fundamental tenet of behaviorist theory is that all human activity—everything from our emotions and reasoning to all behaviors—can be described and predicted in terms of the associations between external stimulations and the responses to these stimuli. Behaviorists assert that the same principles of association can be applied to both animal and human behavior without having to make assumptions about what goes on inside the mind. In some cases these associations are reflexive and automatic, such as salivating when hungry or jumping at a loud noise. This is known as classical conditioning. Other associations are deliberately learned and can be taught and modified. This is known as operant conditioning.

All of the dominant forms of behaviorism postulate three things:

1. that there is a predictable and reliable link between a stimulus and the response it produces.

2. by studying and manipulating the environmental conditions that influence behavior, it is possible to predict and shape with a high degree of certainty what someone will do in a specific situation.

3. learned behavior can be strengthened or weakened by introducing various kinds of reinforcement.

These three principles, as elementary as they may seem, became the foundation for most traditional teaching of the past century.

Implications for Teaching—Key Concepts

Knowledge

Behaviorists construe knowledge not as something that resides in the mind and guides our actions but rather as an ability to do things. In this view, knowledge is a repertoire of actions or the rules of action that can

Learning theories do not give us solutions, but they do direct our attention to those variables that are crucial in finding solutions.

—S.B. Merriam and R.S. Caffarella

be demonstrated or performed. For example, to know what a fork is means to have the capacity to use a fork for its intended purpose, even though at any particular moment a person may not demonstrate that ability.

Learning

From a behaviorist perspective, learning is defined as a change of behavior due to experience and the creation of habits. Proper conditioning produces and shapes desired patterns of behavior by associating the preferred responses with particular stimuli and by strengthening or weakening this connection through the introduction or withholding of positive or negative reinforcements. Complex behaviors are to be learned by breaking them down into their component elements and then presenting them in a step-by-step manner.

Motivation

The motivation to learn, as learning itself, is believed to be entirely external to the student, driven by the positive and/or negative reinforcements in a learner's environment. Behaviorist methods typically rely heavily on the use of positive reinforcements. Pleasant experiences— praise, recognition, good test scores—provide the positive feedback that will reward and strengthen the connections between specific stimuli and appropriate responses. It is up to the instructor to provide the correct reinforcements at the appropriate time in order to strengthen learned behaviors.

> *Great ideas originate in the muscles.*
>
> —Thomas A. Edison

Implications for Teaching—Key Classroom Influences

By the 1950s behaviorism was the orthodoxy in psychology and education, with schools dominated by approaches to instructional design and practice that favored a behaviorist model.

Teaching Perspective—Transmission

Behavioral psychology aligns with the transmission perspective of teaching (introduced in Chapter 1). The teacher serves as a subject-matter authority who controls the amount, manner, and sequence of the delivery of information. Teaching is largely the transfer of information from teacher to learner as the transmission of an appropriate repertoire of behavioral responses to specific stimuli. These responses, as desired learning outcomes, can be strengthened through effective reinforcements. In this model, lecturing is often the dominant instructional practice, though it is only one possible way of delivering course content.

Course and Instructional Design

Although behaviorist instructional design and teaching practices vary depending on the setting, they do share common principles and provide the framework for a number of enduring teaching and training models.

Treatment of Course Content and Subject Matter. Behaviorist methods are most effective in teaching topics for which there is a single correct response, easily memorized materials, and/or discrete content such as facts, formulas, definitions, and vocabulary. This approach is also useful when teaching manual skills and other performance activities with simple sequences of steps.

Courses incorporating behaviorist design principles emphasize the identification and presentation of content as discrete sets of facts and elementary ideas rather than broad concepts or complex and abstract ideas or thinking skills. Large topics and complex skills are identified and broken down into small learning units that are the basic components and approximations of the final learning outcomes. This content is then arranged into logical and easily manageable segments, which are sequenced for difficulty or complexity for easier acquisition.

Characteristic Teaching and Learning Activities. The most significant influences of behaviorism on instructional design derive from three principles that specify three basic instructional stages:

1. a statement of learning objectives in terms of a measurable behavior at the outset of instruction or training.

2. the specification of the conditions under which the desired behavior should be demonstrated.

3. the evaluation of the acceptable performance of this behavior.

These objectives inform learners of what will be taught and how their learning will be measured. They all reflect the belief that through careful specification of learning goals and the careful control of all learning activities at predetermined, externally controlled times, learners will be able to demonstrate what has been learned as a result of instruction. These three principles have been a powerful influence on many educational and training instructional design practices since the 1950s.

Course material is presented solely by the instructor or through other appropriate instructional media, such as books and computer technology. This material is then reinforced for memorization and recall via a number of teaching methods. However, most behaviorist guides practices tend to be so-called skill-and-drill exercises. These provide the repetition of content and the practice of skills that, together with positive reinforcements, build and strengthen student response patterns. Other techniques may include sequenced question (stimulus) and answer (response) frameworks, with questions of gradually increasing

> *A great teacher makes hard things easy.*
>
> —Ralph Waldo Emerson

difficulty, as well as guided practices and regular reviews of material. Behaviorist assessment focuses on the reproduction of information or the demonstration of skills using easily measurable markers of learning, such as objective written exams and observations of performance of tasks. To maximize learning, individual learners may be pretested and then directed to skip certain sections of material based on these assessments. Below are examples of the most prominent teaching and training methods that incorporate these behaviorist concepts.

Implications for Teaching—Key Instructional Strategies and Practices

> *Learning without thinking is labor lost; thinking without learning is dangerous.*
>
> —Chinese Proverb

Behaviorist theories are the basis of a number of common and enduring instructional design models. If you are new to teaching or training or have no formal background in these areas, you may not be familiar with these approaches. However, they are all prominent models that have influenced employment and workplace training programs, online and computer-based training, and several well-known academic teaching approaches. (*Note:* These models have their roots in behaviorist design concepts. All are built around the three core design principles discussed above. However, they do not necessarily reflect only "pure" behaviorist principles. They all have been modified and elaborated upon using ideas and findings from cognitive research, which are explained in the next section.)

Employment/Work-Based Skills Training

The two most prominent employment-related and workplace training designs are Robert Gagne's Conditions of Learning and the Dick and Carey Model.

Robert Gagne's Conditions of Learning. Robert Gagne's instructional design model has influenced many other approaches to instructional design. His basic framework incorporates core behaviorist ideas concerning the identification of learning objectives, the creation of the ideal conditions for supporting learning, and determining the sequence of instructional events. Gagne's instructional design model consists of nine

Gagne's Nine Instructional Events

1.	2.	3.	4.	5.	6.	7.	8.	9.
Gain Attention	Inform Learners of Objective (s)	Stimulate Recall of Prior Knowledge	Present Information	Provide Guidance	Elicit Performance	Provide Feedback	Assess Performance	Enhance Retention and Recall

learning events, which focus on the three learning stages:

1. preparation for learning (gaining attention, informing learners of the lesson objective, stimulating recall of prior learning),

2. knowledge acquisition and performance (presenting the stimulus, providing learning guidance, eliciting performance, and offering feedback), and

3. evaluation, application, and enrichment.

He also classified learning goals into five categories that represent the variety of performance outcomes and the different conditions favorable to each domain of learning. These goals are verbal information, intellectual skills, cognitive strategies, attitudes, and motor skills. The importance behind this classification is that each learning level requires different types of instruction. For example, cognitive development is facilitated by opportunities to solve problems, while the learning of attitudes calls for learners' exposure to a proper role model or effective persuasion.

The Dick and Carey Model. The Dick and Carey Model, named after its two developers, incorporates much of Gagne's approach. It is also a step-by-step approach to learning and training that provides a highly efficient method. The process begins with the identification of performance goals and an analysis of learners and contexts as the basis for written performance objectives. It then progresses to the development and precise selection of instructional strategies and materials, and concludes with the design and conduct of formative and summative evaluation of instruction and any needed revisions of instruction.

Computer-Based and Online Learning Programs

Most computer-assisted instructional programs are built on a behaviorist teaching framework. They commonly sequence the presentation of subject matter in graded steps, from simple to complex, which the students work through independently at their own speed. After each step, the learner's comprehension is assessed and often followed by immediate feedback and possibly information for further study. This design matrix was used quite commonly in the 1960s and 1970s in a system known as programmed instruction. At that time, books and devices known as teaching machines were used as the media for instruction, which allowed only linear instruction. With advances in information technology, computer-based instruction today permits more "branched" instruction that can teach more complex bodies of information and higher-order skills than could the early technology.

Academic Subject Applications

Behavioral design tenets have also been successfully incorporated into the teaching of traditional academic courses. Prominent among such approaches are two closely related and widely researched

> *Try not to have a good time. . . . This is supposed to be educational.*
>
> —Charles M. Shultz

Chapter 4

> *Simple things should be simple. Complex things should be possible.*
>
> —Alan Kay

(and sometimes confused) models of learning, Mastery Teaching and Learning, and Direct Instruction. Both methods address learner differences and emphasize the importance of pacing and sequencing instruction to meet the varying learning capacities of individual students, a common and popular theme among educators today.

Mastery Teaching. As in all behaviorist-inspired teaching approaches, mastery teaching begins with the establishment of clearly defined learning objectives that organize knowledge into relatively small learning units, each with its own objectives and assessment. The goal of instruction is the mastery of each objective through proper instruction, which includes the following: teaching, modeling, practice, formative evaluation, reteaching, and reinforcement, and summative evaluation. Units are preceded by brief diagnostic tests to provide supplementary instruction to help students overcome problems. Time to learn is adjusted to fit each student's aptitude, with no student allowed to proceed to new instruction until basic materials are mastered.

Direct Instruction. Direct instruction, developed during the 1960s, after a number of years of decline, has been reintroduced in many schools as a way of addressing declining rates of academic achievement, particularly among high-risk students. It, too, is a highly structured and carefully scripted program, one that is often able to quickly move students to mastery of basic academic skills. Although the early mastery of basic skills is a key element, the program also addresses students' general comprehension and analytic skills.

Cognitivism: The Mind as Computer

Even as behaviorism was reaching its zenith in the 1950s and 1960s, thinking about human learning began to change. New lines of inquiry, investigative methods, and research protocols were developed. Researchers in a number of disciplines began to look beyond external behaviors to describe and explain how people learn by getting inside the behaviorist "black box" to understand the invisible workings of human thought. These efforts gave birth to cognitive science. Some have been bold enough to call it a new "science of the mind," which we, as a theory of learning, refer to as cognitivism.

The Metaphor

Cognitivists use the metaphor of the human mind as an information-processing device or computer. Like a computer, how the mind operates is described in terms of programs or rules that govern the ways it receives, processes, stores, retrieves, and acts on information. Cognitive researchers have developed theories and models to explain human thinking by examining diverse mental phenomena, such as the kinds of mistakes people make in reasoning, the ways we form and apply concepts, and our speed of thinking and performance in solving problems. Over the years, cognitive theories have evolved and been supplemented by various lines of thought and study. These range from fields of psychology and the neurosciences to logic and even robotics. Much mainstream cognitive research and findings, however, frequently deemphasize or exclude outright some topics addressed by these related subdisciplines. These include questions of human development and emotion, and the social and cultural factors that bear on the nature of the human mind and learning, and the computational metaphor persists as the dominant image of the mind at work. (Our third learning theory, constructivism, discussed in the next section, addresses some of these vital topics.)

Foundations and Key Principles

Cognitivists do not entirely reject behaviorist principles. They recognize the role of environmental influences in the shaping of learning and also study changes in behavior to understand learning. Yet they do not try to explain all learning in terms of these changes, but only as visible indicators of what is going on in a learner's mind. A number of different sub-theories together describe human thinking and learning from a cognitivist perspective. Among these are schema, stage, and cognitive load theory.

Schema Theory

Schemata are dynamic, evolving cognitive representations that function as "mental maps" or knowledge networks used by the mind to focus attention, organize memory, interpret experience, and govern behavior. According to this theory, our understanding and recall of what we experience largely depends on how the content of this experience interacts with and modifies these preexisting mental models. Differences among people's understanding, learning, and problem-solving abilities can be explained in terms of differences in their mental schema. (Think of the difference between what chess masters and novice players understand. Masters have a large body of organized information about chess that enables them to quickly glance at a chess game in progress and understand each player's strategy and remember the position of each piece. Those without a well-developed schema for chess would have no clue, even with an extended observation of the game.)

Stage Theory

Stage theory examines how we process information and experience in terms of three steps:

1. the input of sensory data.
2. the processing of this data in short-term memory.

Ten geographers who think the world is flat will tend to reinforce each other's errors. . . . Only a sailor can set them straight.

—John Ralston Saul

3. if important, the transfer of this information to and consolidation in long-term memory.

According to this theory, sensory information transferred to short-term memory can be retained for only about 20 seconds, unless rehearsed or grouped into meaningful parts. Information goes into long-term memory when it is deliberately committed to memory through rehearsal and overlearning or if it possesses strong emotional content.

Cognitive Load Theory

This theory states that the amount of information a person can handle and learn is determined in many ways by the rules and limits of memory. A key concept is chunking, based on the finding that information organized into "chunks," or units, is more easily manipulated and transferred into longer-term memory. About seven bits or pieces of information are considered the maximum amount that can be held in short-term memory. (The use of seven digits for phone numbers is a commonplace example of this capacity.)

Other Key Concepts

The following key cognitivist principles represent singular findings rather than theories that have significance for teaching and learning:

- Meaningful Effects—Meaningful information is easier to learn and remember.
- Serial Position Effect—Items at the beginning or end of a list are easier to learn.
- Distributed Practice Effect—Practice that is done at intervals rather than all at one time is more effective.
- Interference Effects—Prior learning, especially misconceptions, can interfere with new learning.
- Advance Organization Effect—Previewing information by organizing subject matter to reveal the relationships of ideas enhances learning.
- Dual Encoding Effect—Memory consists of two separate but interrelated systems for processing information, one verbal and the other visual.

Implications for Teaching—Key Concepts

Knowledge

Cognitive science, as with behaviorism, characterizes knowledge as external to and independent of the learner. Knowledge is treated as an "object" that can be manipulated by an instructor and transferred to

> *It is not enough to have a good mind. The main thing is to use it well.*
>
> —Descartes

and deposited in the mind of the learner. However, whereas behaviorists describe knowledge only in terms of observable demonstrations or performances, cognitive scientists also view knowledge in terms of the unobservable representations of the world transmitted to the mind and held there in dynamic mental networks. (This notion of knowledge as "objects" stored in the mind—perhaps a bit abstract and even obtuse—is an important one, for it distinguishes much thinking in cognitive science from our third theory of learning, constructivism.)

Learning

Schema theory stands not only at the center of the cognitivist view of the mind but of its explanation of the processes of learning. Schemata provide simplified explanations of complex phenomena that can be modified by new information and experiences. This modification of our mental representations and subsequent changes in our thinking is what cognitivists generally define as learning. The processes involved in learning, as with all operations of the mind, are described in terms of sets of conditions and rules. Sets of mental rules govern and explain how new information is related to and integrated into old ideas to yield learning. If new ideas are not successfully accommodated because a learner cannot connect them to existing schemata, or there is an information overload, learning is impeded or may not happen at all. In addition, there are rules describing how the amount and organization of information to be processed influences learning. Information that is clearly and meaningfully organized and sufficiently elaborated on is more easily grasped, applied, and transferred to new settings. Attention to the limits of memory is given special consideration in cognitivist learning designs.

Motivation

The primary motivators in learning are seen as intrinsic, with learners themselves the most important source of the drives for their learning. Cognitivists acknowledge that external forces can and do influence the motivation to learn; however, they claim that the motivational forces that arise from learners themselves are more powerful and should be emphasized in the classroom.

Implications for Teaching—Key Classroom Influences

Though cognitivist learning theories have not led to the development of comprehensive and systematic teaching models (as behaviorist theories have), the influence of cognitive science on instruction is significant. These theories have resulted both in the modification of earlier behaviorist instructional approaches, as well as giving rise to uniquely cognitive teaching practices.

Little things affect little minds.

—Benjamin Disraeli

Teaching Perspective—Transmission/Developmental

The teaching approach that best correlates with cognitive theory is a hybrid of Pratt's transmission and developmental perspectives. From a cognitivist's perspective, the primary goal of instruction is to effectively communicate or transfer information for efficient processing. However, in contrast to a purely behaviorist approach, here instruction is not seen as something mostly done to students but also an activity that seeks to incorporate prior knowledge, personal motivations, and ways of thinking. A cognitivist-themed design is also developmental in that it attempts to help learners develop their thinking capacities and ability to demonstrate what they know in ways that go beyond the simply reproduction of knowledge.

Course and Instructional Design

There are a variety of instructional approaches that reflect the findings of cognitive investigations into how the mind works.

Happiness is nothing more than good health and a bad memory.

—Albert Schweitzer

Treatment of Course Content and Subject Matter. In a cognitivist-inspired approach, course content and classroom activities are planned and presented in a manner consistent with the rules and processes that govern how the mind works. Ideally, this accounts for students' prior understanding plus their information-processing and memory limitations, so they can better attend to, comprehend, store, and recall new information. Some topics may progress from the simple to the complex to facilitate learning, as in a behaviorist design, but they do so in order to mirror the way the mind naturally processes information—for example, to reduce the load on memory—and not to just simplify content. Course lessons also seek to highlight conceptual frameworks and sometimes complex relationships between ideas rather than always break content down into small and sometimes isolated bits of information.

Characteristic Teaching and Learning Activities. With a focus on knowledge transmission, cognitive-based instruction is largely teacher-directed. The instructor is chiefly responsible for managing the pace and character of the information "input and output process" and for creating the teaching materials and classroom environment needed to facilitate students' acquisition, retention, and recall of knowledge. There are a fair number of strategies that can be used for these purposes. These address the rules and conditions that govern how the mind works best, as already mentioned. Cognitive teaching practices, however, have not been integrated into popular and comprehensive systems of instruction (as with behaviorist-inspired approaches) and remain more as a collection of strategies and techniques than as unified models. Below we discuss some of the most prominent practices.

Refer to Field Guide

One of the most important trips a person can make is that involved in meeting the other person halfway.

—Unknown

Implications for Teachings—Key Instructional Strategies and Practices

Each of the following strategies and practices may be implemented in a variety of ways, either in isolation or combination. (Elaborations of some of these ideas, along with additional ones, can be found in the companion text.)

Activation of Prior Knowledge

Opening instruction with activities to spark existing knowledge is among the most commonly used cognitivist teaching tools. The activities are geared to help learners see the relevance of new information and link what they already know to what they are to learn. This can be achieved in a variety of ways, such as by simply asking questions, by providing or eliciting student summaries of previously learned material, or by preview "quizzes" that assess prior knowledge.

Organization and Sequencing of Information

Materials are organized to help students remember more by deliberately presenting information in manageable chunks. With short-term memory limited to seven or so bits of information, chunking increases the capacity to remember by increasing the size of each separate item to be recalled. (For example, a string of eight numbers, such as 68473219, is easier to remember when the numbers are grouped in pairs, 68-47-32-19, requiring storing only four bits of info instead of eight.) This technique can be used for the recall of many different kinds of discrete data or facts, such as lists of terms or formulas. In addition, attention is given to the order in which information is presented (e.g., serial position effect) and the timing of study (distributed practice effect) to promote better recall.

Dynamic and Multiple Representations of Knowledge

Included here are diverse ways of presenting information to engage many levels of thinking and types of processing. Their shared purpose is to enhance comprehension and recall, as well as to make explicit the relationships among ideas within a body of information. Here are several key methods:

- *Advanced organization of subject matter:* This is one of the most often recommended methods of cognitivist-inspired instruction. As a thinking tool, advanced organizers give students the opportunity to both link new information to their prior knowledge and also to understand the organization of this new information by highlighting the structure of content. They connect wholes to parts so students can see the "big picture." They can be either text-based or graphic representations of information, such as diagrams, tables, grids, outlines, graphs, and conceptual maps.

Refer to Field Guide
Unit 2

- *Use of visual learning and thinking tools:* Verbal learning is greatly enhanced when supported by visual illustrations of material. (You know the old proverb: "a picture is worth a thousand words.") A cognitivist classroom will include, in ways appropriate to course content, visual representations of information to promote deeper processing and better recall. These may include some of the same graphic tools used as advance organizers, which also can serve other purposes when used at different points during instruction, For example, a variety of visual thinking tools, such as Venn diagrams or comparison grids and other kinds of charts, can be used to explain difficult and complex concepts, to promote interaction among students for better understanding and recall, or for review and for consolidation of learning.

- *Use of computer modeling and simulations:* A cognitive view of the mind naturally leads to the use of computers as an extension of the human mental modeling system. Mental models can be closely aligned with computer-based programs, such as simulation tools and computer-generated graphics. (Although research into the use of software tools as modeling systems has become quite advanced, curriculum designers are only beginning to address the role of modeling activities as teaching tools.)

It is tempting to want to sort, categorize, and place everything that we need to do together with our students' learning experiences into nice, neat "conceptual boxes." Long-established and emerging learning theories can lead us to believe that this is possible and desirable. However, just as our personal experiences reveal that few things in life are black or white but are frequently many shades of gray, as each of us matures professionally we also discover that teaching and learning are equally nuanced.

I am by nature inclined to embrace a blended cognitive/constructivist/humanistic approach to my teaching. Still, I appreciate and see value in some of the highly objective constructs of behaviorism and an ability to manage instruction through traditional teacher-centered designs. Clearly, there are numerous occasions on which a focus on content and the transmission of information are central to student learning. Moreover, the constraints of departmentally predetermined curricula and course syllabi often seem to leave little room for flexibility in the use of my contact time with my students. Still, as a result of my study of the science of learning and through the confidence that comes from experience, I am often able to adopt and adapt a variety of approaches and methods to create powerful learning experiences for my students. On the surface and

 to the casual observer, these practices may seem to be an eclectic "grab bag" of tools and techniques. However, they are actually quite systematic. Because they are rooted in theory and research and my own teaching philosophy, I believe my practice on most occasions meets both the program demands of covering content, as well as the critical need to address the sometimes complex and nuanced processes of my students' learning.

Constructivism: The Mind as Maker of Meaning

In recent years constructivism has become the center of contemporary theories of learning. In many ways, it dominates conversations about educational policy and reform today. Constructivism has roots in cognitive science, incorporating a number of its key findings and principles. However, it also draws from a broad range of thinking regarding human development and learning and stands in many ways as a distinct view of how people learn.

The Metaphor

The constructivist depiction of the mind shifts the metaphor from the mind as a well-programmed and efficient computer to a view of the mind as a "builder" or "maker of meaning." Essentially, constructivists assert that knowledge is what we make of it, and that without minds there would be no knowledge. In this metaphor, the mind does not merely accumulate information as a container, or process and store information like a computer. The mind builds what it knows in an organic and subjective fashion to create meaning from experience through the interpretation of this experience.

Foundations and Key Principles

The main ideas underpinning constructivist thought are not new; they span centuries of philosophical thought. Some see its origins with Socrates, who claimed that the basic conditions for learning are in the mind of the individual and that inquiry, as a dialogue between teacher and student driven by questions, was the best tool of instruction. The purpose of Socratic dialogue was not the conveyance and reproduction of information but the development of a deeply personal grasp of knowledge—the theme at the core of constructivist-based learning. More recent precedents are found in the philosophy of progressive education from the early decades of the past century. Among other things, this view held that education was not about being told things but about learning through experience.

You don't just learn knowledge; you have to create it. Get in the driver's seat, don't just be a passenger. You have to contribute to it or you don't understand it.

—Dr. W. Edwards Deming

Various constructivist theories have risen from these and other philosophical traditions. Like cognitivism, constructivism is considered a metatheory of learning that brings together several related but distinct conceptualizations of the nature of knowledge and learning. Although there is debate about the viability and validity of the different brands of constructivism, two complementary strands—cognitive constructivism and social constructivism—have emerged as the dominant theories. Cognitive constructivism emphasizes the personal, individual character of learning, while social constructivism emphasizes the social–cultural nature of learning. The two share the assumption that people cannot be given or transferred information that they then can immediately understand and use. These theories assert that although information can be imposed, understanding cannot, and must come from within. Because of the many interwoven elements of these theories, their roots are explained in some detail below to clarify some of their similarities and differences.

Cognitive Constructivism

> Knowledge is not a transferable Commodity and Communication not a Conveyance.
>
> —E. von Glasersfeld

The cognitive constructivist outlook draws many of its insights from elements of the cognitive science model of the mind. However, it departs from a computational metaphor with an emphasis on the developmental aspects of human thinking abilities and the ways knowledge becomes personally meaningful. There have been a number of modern thinkers who have had a major influence on the cognitive strand of contemporary constructivist theory and its central concepts and principles. Prominent among them are Jean Piaget and Jerome Bruner.

Conceptual Development. Piaget was the first to theorize that conceptual change and intellectual growth result from interactions between our existing cognitive structures, or schemata, and our new experiences. However, he is best known for his description of the stages of cognitive development in children. His core ideas of childhood cognitive reorganization have been echoed in descriptions of the thinking changes presented in adult learning. Through this process people continually generate theories about the external world, which are then accepted or rejected depending on whether they are seen to be working or not in practice.

Assimilation and Accommodation. Piaget also postulated that thinking is changed, enlarged, and made more sophisticated through two complementary processes, assimilation and accommodation. Assimilation is a relatively passive process by which a person fits a new concept into an already existing one. For example, a child who is familiar with dogs as small, furry animals with a tail might see a cat for the first and think it is also a dog because it shares the same characteristics. Accommodation is a more advanced process. It is an active reorganization of knowledge. In the above illustration, for instance, accommodation might occur if the child were explained the differences between dogs and cats and began to restructure thinking around this new information.

Knowledge Construction. Jerome Bruner first introduced the notion of learning as knowledge building or construction. He developed his views through the systematic study of how people form concepts and categorize their thinking about their experiences. His theory expresses the core theme that learning is an active process in which learners build new ideas based on their past and current knowledge and which enables them to go beyond given information to develop deeper and more personal understanding.

Concept Formation and Concept Attainment. Bruner described the ways people develop their mental representations of the world as a dual-stage process of concept formation and concept attainment. Concept formation is the initial understanding that all things and phenomena have distinguishing characteristics that allow them to be sorted and categorized. Concept attainment is the next development, in which we determine what these specific attributes are and how they are used to identify similarities and differences among things that allow us to group them. (Unlike Piaget, Bruner's work led him to make specific recommendations for educational practice. He proposed a discovery-based model of learning, in which students are encouraged to discover facts and relationships for themselves and continually build on what they know. He also introduced the idea of a spiral curriculum to reintroduce the same topics at higher levels and to reinforce learning.)

Social Constructivism

As the label suggests, social constructivism moves beyond strictly personal and individual influences on learning and examines its social origins and character. Incorporated into this perspective are theories of social cognition and situated learning, which emphasize how people learn through observation and as a result of the context in which learning happens. Here, too, several theorists have contributed to the emergence of contemporary social constructivist theory. The most significant is Leo Vygotsky, with additional influence seen in the work of Albert Bandura, who contributed ideas to both cognitive and social constructivist thought.

Social Interaction. Social interaction, according to Vygotsky, plays a fundamental role in the development of cognition. The full potential for this development is determined not just by what an individual can do on his or her own but by what someone can do with help from another, more capable person.

Zone of Proximal Development. A core foundation for social constructivist thinking is Vygotsky's concept of the zone of proximal development

> *On those who overanalyze his music: "When you tear the wings off a butterfly, it is no longer a butterfly."*
>
> —Claude Debussy

(ZPD; "proximal" simply means "next"). Vygotsky observed that when children were tested on tasks on their own, they rarely did as well as when they were working in collaboration with an adult. ZPD refers to the gap or difference between what children can learn unassisted and what they can learn when aided by an adult or a more capable peer. Initially used to describe the intellectual growth of children, it has been incorporated in modern social-based theories of adult learning as well.

Scaffolding. Scaffolding, a term also coined by Vygotsky, is guided support for learning that enables a learner to perform and achieve more difficult tasks than they can do alone. It does not necessarily involve someone directly teaching another how to perform a task. It can be any open-ended series of interactions through which a more capable person enables others to refine their own thinking or their performance to make them more effective. The everyday ideas that align closely with this model are that of "stretching" learners and teaching through mentoring and apprenticeships, both of which can be applied to learners of all ages.

Modeling, Metacognitive Awareness, and Motivation. Bandura also offered a theory of social learning. Initially it emphasized imitation or vicarious experience as a form of learning. However, he also noted that modeling alone was not sufficient to explain learning and development, and he later turned to a focus on the role of cognitive processes, such as memory, language, and evaluation in the integration and mental representation of experience. This perspective further evolved to include the role of metacognitive skills, such as self-regulation, self-perceptions, self-reflective thought, and the power of belief as critical components of the learning process. Moreover, the theory emphasized that although individuals may pay attention to, learn, and even practice certain actions, their motivations affect whether they will perform a behavior on a regular basis.

Implications for Teaching—Key Concepts

Knowledge

More so than in any other learning paradigm, the nature of knowledge is critical to constructivist thinking and teaching. Many actually consider constructivism to be as much a theory of knowledge, or epistemology, as a theory of learning. In both behaviorist and cognitive theory, knowledge is something transferable from one mind to another. On the other hand, constructivism assumes that knowledge is not some "thing" that exists outside the mind to be passed whole and intact from one person to another. Each learner through experience, active reflection, and personal interpretation can only gain knowledge individually, not by passive absorption or mental manipulation according to fixed rules. Constructivism does not deny that knowledge has objective qualities external to the mind that people can agree on. Rather, it

> *If education is always to be conceived along the same antiquated lines of a mere transmission of knowledge, there is little to be hoped from it in the bettering of man's future.*
>
> —Maria Montessori

reworks this idea with an emphasis on people's specific and unique understanding and use of knowledge. Where cognitive and social constructivism diverge is in their view of this meaning-making process. Cognitive construction sees it as highly individualistic, whereas social constructivism proposes that knowledge is created through social interactions and the collective meanings they generate.

Learning

Schema theory is central to both cognitive and constructivist views of learning; however, for constructivists, learning is not knowledge *acquisition* but knowledge *construction*. It involves more than adjusting schemata to match the ideas of an authority (such as an instructor) or to mirror "true" representations of external reality. Understanding emerges when external information is made personally meaningful and through social interactions that permit the sharing of multiple perspectives. Also, in the constructivist view, what a learner knows at any one moment is accepted as an incomplete and inaccurate representation of the world. Errors that occur in learning are seen in a positive light and as natural; they are even valued as a means of gaining insight into how students are developing and organizing their thinking. Deep and enduring learning proceeds when misconceptions or missing conceptions are identified and examined and corrected through exploration and reflection with the assistance of an instructor.

Motivation

Natural motivation is intrinsic (as in a cognitivist framework), though cognitive and social constructivist views differ on its sources. In cognitive constructive theory, learners are driven by the innate need to make sense of experience and find internal, mental balance. (The presentation of new information is seen to create a cognitive imbalance that motivates a learner to return to equilibrium, by either assimilating or accommodating the novel material.) In social constructive theory, social encounters are believed to significantly influence and improve a learner's motivation. (Social relationships and classrooms are ideally organized into "learning communities" that provide support and assistance to underpin motivation.)

Implications for Teaching—Key Classroom Influences

Constructivist ideas have yet to provide a foundation for a comprehensive instructional model. Yet they do provide a collection of principles with important implications and applications for teaching and learning.

Teaching Perspective—Developmental/Apprenticeship

A hybrid developmental/apprenticeship perspective best captures a constructivist orientation to teaching. A constructivist-inspired instructor seeks a fundamental and qualitative change in the thinking

> *Learning is a social process that occurs through interpersonal interaction within a cooperative context.*
>
> —D. Johnson and R. Johnson

of learners. The highest learning goal is students' reaching a deep and personally meaningful understanding achieved through their own efforts. The social orientation of constructivist-based teaching is seen in the apprenticeship concept of the teacher–learner relationship. Here the goal is to develop not only new information and skills, but also the ways of thinking and the values possessed by experienced members of a specific field of study. This means a learner, as a novice, progressively acquires a professional sense of identity and a place as a participant in a community of practitioners.

Course and Instructional Design

One way to capture the essential character of constructivist teaching is to think of instruction as the orchestration of student learning experiences rather than the management and control of the content and context of learning. In this sense, constructivist teaching is dynamic, holistic, and adaptive rather than linear, fixed, and prescriptive. Although appropriate for any level of instruction, constructivism is especially well suited for teaching complex concepts and advanced knowledge, procedures, and skills, and where learning processes and/or outcomes are open-ended, such as with problems that have no single answer or way to arrive at a solution.

Treatment of Subject Matter. Constructivist-guided teaching emphasizes the processes of learning rather than the content of instruction. Instruction is not so much driven by the subject matter or what instructors do to present information but by what students do to arrive at their understanding of the material. Therefore, content is not completely "packaged" (i.e., prespecified, sequenced, and organized for ease of assimilation). This approach is not dismissive of subject matter; however, it is often minimalist. Rather than try to disseminate the maximum amount of information in the shortest amount of time, as in most other teaching, the goal is to produce the most learning with the least amount of teacher control and delivery of content.

Characteristic Teaching and Learning Activities. There are common themes that permit the design and use of constructivist teaching–learning environments and teaching practices. Constructivist-inspired teachers can weave these practices together to suit the purposes and particular contexts of different teaching situations and learners, although there are a number of constructivist design models.

Focus on the "Big Picture." Constructivist teaching emphasizes a "big picture" approach to course content in its emphasis on students' deep understanding rather than memorization of information. Topics are set into the context of the larger framework of a discipline, and organized around its big concepts and central questions. Teaching topics are

> Memorization is what we resort to when what we are learning makes no sense.
>
> —Anonymous

ideally driven by broad themes to create better connections to students' experience and interests, and may even be interdisciplinary.

Communication-Rich Environments. Classroom communication is at the heart of and has many roles in constructivist learning. Dialogue and interactions among the instructor and students, and among students themselves, are used to:

1. clarify and deepen thinking by requiring that learners to express their ideas.

2. allow students to learn from the questions and responses of others.

3. build a sense of community and collaboration by breaking down the power relations between teacher and students and barriers between students.

4. create knowledge that is more than the sum total of the ideas of the individual students.

Learners as Explorers and Learners as Teachers. Students are seen as active discoverers rather than receptacles of knowledge so that information is not merely digested at a superficial level. Learning tasks and outcomes are often open-ended, to give students plenty of space to explore and discover ideas for themselves. This, however, does not assume that meaningful learning necessarily just happens, but recognizes that it often needs to be facilitated by teachers. This facilitation may involve the way subject matter is introduced, when and how learning activities are integrated into instruction, the manner in which questions are asked and answered, and what kind of boundaries are established within the learning environment. Constructivist practices also present teaching and learning as processes that either students or teachers can perform. The design of material to be learned is ideally structured to promote and encourage student interaction and collaboration to make the classroom a community of learners. The physical environment to support this may include clustered desks or tables and work spaces for peer instruction, collaboration, and small-group instruction.

Authentic Learning and Assessment Tasks. Constructivist-style teaching and learning is concerned with students developing their ability to successfully handle problems so they can meet the challenges they will encounter outside the highly managed and controlled environment typical of most instruction. Commonly, classroom instruction presents a well-defined problem with only one answer or solution, or a task that has just one or only a few ways of performing it. However, in the "real world" students will constantly face ill-defined problems that have no unique solution or situations that can be handled in a variety of different ways depending on the circumstances. Constructivist teaching practices, therefore, try to prepare students for these

Learning is not so much an additive process, with new learning simply piling up on top of existing knowledge, as it is in active, dynamic process in which the connections are constantly changing and the structures reformatted.

—K. Patricia Cross

challenges by presenting authentic learning activities that reflect these complexities and ambiguities. Students are given opportunities to apply what they have learned in authentic contexts or, if it is not feasible, to practice on real tasks or through case studies and/or simulations that mirror real-life settings that engage higher-order thinking abilities.

Context-Sensitive Instruction. Constructivist-based instruction is also highly sensitive to both the personal and the social contexts of instruction. The social context of learning is captured in the notion of situated cognition, which states that what is learned is inseparable from the situation in which learning takes place or will need to be transferred to. It highlights the importance of creating an environment for learning that links knowing and doing. The personal context includes the learners' goals, the perceived value of instruction, and the learners' individual learning styles. To address these learner differences, constructivist classrooms provide multiple presentations and representations of material and seek to make explicit student misconceptions so they can be actively engaged to reveal how they may interact and possibly interfere with new learning. (This contrasts with a cognitivist approach, in which only knowledge that is a prerequisite for new learning or needed to organize the subject matter is reviewed prior to instruction.)

Promotion of Metacognitive Awareness. Metacognition is our awareness of what we know and our ability to understand and control our own thinking processes. Highly skilled and efficient learners have a well-developed metacognitive awareness. An instructor can promote students' learning skills by helping them to understand the role of metacognition in learning. These skills generally fall into three categories:

1. metamemory—an understanding of how memory works and strategies to use for improving memory.

2. metacomprehension—the ability to monitor how well one understands something, to recognize what one does not understand, and to know how to remedy the misunderstanding.

3. self-regulation—the capacity to adapt one's learning process by adequately choosing, using, and evaluating the first two strategies without assistance.

Ongoing Feedback and Assessment. Evaluation of student learning progress is frequent and ongoing. Assessment is not seen just as a way to assign grades but to provide feedback to students and teachers alike. Errors are not seen as mistakes but as indicators of where learning problems may exist. This feedback is then used as a source of information so students and instructors alike can modify what they are doing as instruction proceeds to improve learning outcomes.

> There is no difference between living and learning. . . . Teaching is communication and like all communication is elusive and difficult.
>
> —John Holt

Unit 3

Implications for Teaching—Key Instructional Strategies and Practices

Examples of constructivist learning are found in a number of teaching approaches. Each in itself does not fully encompass all the dimensions of constructivist theories. Still, together they offer valuable guidelines for generating the quality and kind of learning constructivist designs seek to achieve. Among these are cognitive apprenticeships, inquiry or discovery learning, and cooperative learning.

Cognitive Apprenticeship

Cognitive apprenticeship is not a uniquely constructivist approach to instruction. Indeed, it is often associated with developments in cognitivism, and is used for the teaching of basic skills and knowledge in competency-based fields of study with very specific learning outcomes, such as those found in most vocational and career education and corporate training environments. For these purposes cognitive apprenticeship it is not as open-ended as other constructivist methods. It is largely bound by prescribed learning goals tied to a prespecified body of knowledge, and there is less emphasis on personal exploration and interpretation. Moreover, tasks are often simplified and separated into basic components or steps to ease their comprehension.

> *Teaching is the achievement of shared meaning.*
> —D.B. Gowin

At the same time, cognitive apprenticeship within the framework of constructivism is distinct in a number of important ways. Its orientation to instruction rests almost entirely on the teacher–student relationship as one of expert and novice in close collaboration to develop students' abilities beyond the point possible without this interaction. In this regard, it uses scaffolding throughout instruction to help students extend their current skills and knowledge. In this model, the instructor (or possibly a more competent peer) acts like a coach by entering into a personal dialogue with learners and modeling the knowledge level and skills to be attained. The instructor as coach tries to understand learners' personal grasp of the material to be learned, and to help them progressively refine their understanding and skill level. Like scaffolding around a building under construction, the support is removed in stages so learners are able to perform or demonstrate their knowledge with greater and greater independence.

Inquiry-Based Learning

In inquiry-based learning, the content of a course acts as a means to an end, rather than an end in itself, with curriculum materials and teaching activities allowing and requiring student exploration of topics in a process of self-discovery. A premise underlying this strategy is that the knowledge base for most disciplines is constantly expanding and changing, with no one ever able to learn everything. However, it is believed that all can develop the learning skills and attitudes necessary to continue the acquisition and examination of knowledge throughout their lives. Another premise is that knowledge discovered for oneself is more meaningful and more readily put to work in settings outside the original instructional setting. Inquiry in this method is more than simply asking a lot of questions. Its proper application consists of several factors, which include a structured context or framework for questions (often a problem to be solved), a specific focus for questions, and many different levels of questions. (There are several variations of inquiry-based learning, including the discovery learning concept of Bruner, problem-based learning, case-based learning, and anchored instruction, a specific and promising technology-based learning approach developed at Vanderbilt University.)

Cooperative Learning

Cooperative or group learning captures the character of much of what goes on in most constructivist-based classrooms. An assortment of learning activities come under the label, and it can be used for both short-term and long-term learning goals and for both in-class and out-of-class learning. This kind of learning is more than just a matter of students working together to accomplish certain tasks, When properly designed and implemented, it is a highly structured approach to group learning facilitated by clear guidelines that create roles for each learner, well-defined boundaries, and specific learning goals that keep the group learning on track and on task. There are other less-structured versions that one can use as well.

> *Socrates was not a Content provider.*
>
> —David Noble

Thematic Instruction

Thematic instruction is considered more an approach to the design of curricula rather than a specific instructional practice. It involves the organization of a curriculum or course around macro "themes" that integrate basic disciplines, such as science or even history, around broad subjects. It also places instruction into contexts that connect what is being taught in the classroom to other real-world and other relevant subjects. It may involve team teaching, with instructors from different subject areas working together to teach the same students over the course of a term or an even longer period of instruction.

Specific Constructivist Design Models

A number of frameworks have been suggested for the creation of constructivist learning environments.

The Five E's. A convenient constructivist framework has been defined by the Biological Science Curriculum Study (BSCS). In this model, the process is explained by using five E's—Engage, Explore, Explain, Elaborate, and Evaluate.

- *Engage:* This provides the opportunity to find out what students already know or what they think they know about the topic and concepts to be developed, as well as to stimulate interest and involvement.

- *Explore:* This segment provides an opportunity for students to get directly involved with the learning materials and share a common set of experiences to compare what they think about what they are observing and experiencing.

- *Explain:* This portion provide opportunities for students to make sense of their inquiry and exploration. They begin to "label" their experience or conceptualize the main ideas of the module. This stage also involves the introduction of any formal language, scientific terms, and other information the students may need to accurately describe and explain what they are learning.

- *Elaborate:* Elaboration allows students to apply or extend their formal understanding of concepts in new situations and relate their previous experiences to new ones.

- *Evaluate:* Evaluation of students' conceptual understanding and ability to use skills is an ongoing process that begins with the engagement stage and continues throughout each stage of the model. It serves to both provide feedback to monitor student understanding and as a way of assessing student performance for grades.

The Learning Cycle. This is a three-step design that can be used as a general framework for many kinds of constructivist activities. This cycle may repeat many times throughout a lesson or unit.

- *Discovery:* the teacher encourages students to generate questions and hypotheses from working with various materials.

- *Concept introduction:* Here the teacher focuses the students' questions and helps them create hypotheses and design experiments.

- *Concept application:* Students work on new problems that reconsider the concepts studied in the first two steps.

Humanism: The Mind as Being and Becoming

The Metaphor

Humanism is both a philosophy and a psychology concerned with human freedom, dignity, potential, and self-fulfillment. As a theory of learning, it is the most difficult to explain in terms of a metaphor that

---

Teachers may think they are stuffing minds, but all they are ever affecting is the memory. Nothing can ever be forced into anyone's mind except by brainwashing, which is the very opposite of genuine teaching.

—Mortimer Adler

---

concisely captures its concept of the human mind and how we learn. It is as concerned with the mind as it is with everything that defines us as humans—our thoughts and emotions, our needs and motivations, our values and morality. Within this perspective, the human mind is not considered an object to be manipulated and influenced, or to be studied and described, or even as an instrument with which to build knowledge. Rather, it characterizes the mind as the seat of identity and in terms of the dynamics of personal transformation and growth. From a humanistic perspective, then, the mind might be viewed as both "a state of being and a process of becoming," with the capacity for and goal of self-actualization. Still, this perspective does include assumptions about teaching and learning, ideas that have profoundly influenced education for many decades, especially the nature of teacher and student roles and relationships and the importance of creating positive learning environments.

Foundations and Key Principles

Humanists give primacy to the study of human needs and interests with the assumption that human beings behave out of a personal sense of purpose and values. They also believe that we cannot dissect people or their behaviors or thought processes into parts. Each person must be understood as a unique and whole being that grows and develops over a lifespan. The study of motivation and the achievement of psychological health and fulfillment are of special interest. In light of these assumptions, the chief goals of humanistic-based education are to promote positive self-direction and independence and to help people develop and maintain the desire and creativity needed to foster lifelong learning. Humanistic learning theory has roots in and is drawn largely from two areas of study—humanistic psychology and andragogy, a philosophy of adult learning.

Humanistic Psychology

Although there are a number of humanistic psychological theories, two ideas have had the most direct influence on educational policies and practices—facilitative learning and self-actualization.

Facilitative Learning. The psychologist Carl Rogers developed facilitative learning. The thrust of the idea is that people are engaged in a lifelong process of "becoming" or self-realization, though the way in which individuals are socialized often blocks this process. Rogers believed that it is important for people to experience positive relationships based on unconditional positive regard, empathetic understanding, honesty, and integrity in order to best fulfill their potential. Such relationships help people develop the capacity to take responsibility for the direction of their lives and the choices they make. This notion of self-direction lies

> The mind is not a vessel to be filled, but a fire to be kindled.
>
> —Plutarch

at the heart of the theory of facilitated learning, which claims that knowledge cannot be simply transmitted or transferred to another. The only knowledge that can significantly influence behavior is self-discovered and personally appropriated and assimilated through direct experience.

Self-Actualization. The theory of self-actualization is a conceptualization of human motivation developed by Abraham Maslow. It explains human needs in an ascending hierarchy: physical survival, personal safety, love and belonging, esteem, and self-actualization. The first four levels are described as "deficiency" needs. A person must be able to meet these lower needs prior to working toward the needs at the next level. As with Rogers, Maslow designated self-fulfillment or *self-actualization,* as he termed it, as the highest level of human growth, and where one's potential has been most fully realized. Maslow proposed that self-actualizers possess a number of qualities that distinguish them from others:

1. a strong and independent but flexible self concept that can tolerate ambiguity and uncertainty.

2. an ability to accept themselves and others.

3. a freedom to act in accord with their own values without being bound to the common beliefs and practices of the culture they are part of.

4. a highly ethical concern for others.

The theory of self-actualization, as a general theory of human motivation, offers no direct suggestions for educational practice. However, it does point to the primary drives and goals of human learning, with self-actualization as its highest achievement. The theory has influenced and been incorporated into various approaches to adult education, including andragogy.

Andragogy

Andragogy is the most direct and explicit expression of a humanistic theory of adult learning, and has been the center of most discussions of adult education over the past four decades. However, the theme of this discussion has not necessarily been singular. For some, andragogy is a prescriptive set of guidelines for teaching adults, for others a philosophical position regarding the psychology of adult development and learning. Still others see it as an ideology regarding individual freedom, the relationship between individual and society, and the aims of adult education.

The most prominent voice in this discussion has been that of Malcolm Knowles, whose work has had a significant impact on thinking about adult learners. He used the term *andragogy* as a unique conceptualization of adult learning, curricula, and teaching methods to distinguish

Teaching that impacts is not head to head, but heart to heart.

—Howard G. Hendricks

adult education from the education of children, or pedagogy. (The practice of *pedagogy,* often used as a synonym for *teaching,* in its literal meaning refers to the education of children.) Knowles introduced five distinct principles of adult learning (explained below) that address the unique needs, motivations, and experiences of adults and proposed a framework for the planning, implementation, and assessment of instruction.

Implications for Teaching—Key Concepts

Knowledge

Humanism posits no particular theory of knowledge and what it means to know something, as the other theories do. Rather than focus on subject-matter knowledge, humanistic educators are largely concerned with self-knowledge. This kind of knowledge is not something that can be received from the environment or put in the mind of the learner by others, but it is an understanding developed and drawn from within. It also deemphasizes objective knowledge with the argument that today and in the future we are facing an exponential growth in information and technological advances that make acquiring knowledge less valuable than possessing the capacity to continually learn, adapt, and grow.

Learning

Humanistic concepts of learning echo many of the ideas of constructivism. The individual, and not the external environment, largely determines learning. Meaningful learning comes through reflection on personal experience and a process of interpreting, integrating, and transforming one's experiential world. An instructor helps learners take advantage of the opportunity and tools needed to investigate their own experiences, supplements past experiences with new opportunities, and helps learners extract lessons from their insights and experience.

Motivation

Concern for learner motivation lies at the heart of humanistic education. The desire to learn must come from within, created by the need for personal growth and fulfillment, and cannot be controlled from outside the learner. It is assumed that students will be naturally driven to learn when given the freedom and support to do so. Learner motivation relates directly to the question of students' interests and available time, energy, freedom, and ability to plan and control their own learning activities. (This is in contrast to the beliefs of constructivists, who see discovery, or the making sense of experience, as the primary drive in human learning.)

Implications for Teaching—Key Classroom Influences

Humanistic approaches to education are best characterized in terms of general orientations and intentions rather than a prescriptive guidelines and practices.

> *Teaching, is not just a job. It is a human service, and it must be thought of as a mission.*
>
> —Dr. Ralph Tyler

Teaching Perspective—The Nurturer/Social Reformer

The unmistakable orientation is the instructor as nurturer, as described in Pratt's teaching perspectives framework. In this outlook the learners' self-concept and self-development are placed at center stage. Attention to feelings and self-determination, as reflected in learner autonomy, along with mutual respect and understanding among teachers, learners, and others, are as important as intellectual development. To a lesser degree, the social reform perspective may be found here. It is evident in the assumption that individuals find meaning by combining personal growth and satisfaction with a commitment to social change and the welfare of others by improving education and emphasizing equity, consensus, and collaboration through democratic participation in the learning process.

Course and Instructional Design

Humanistic education is seen as a lifelong process designed to produce individuals able to live humane, meaningful, and self-directed lives. The hallmark of humanistic education is the blending of emotions, intellect, and behavior in a framework of values derived from the humanities, including freedom, responsibility, equality, and moral action.

Treatment of Subject Matter. As with constructivist education, learning processes are highlighted over products or content of learning. Learning how to learn is more important than acquiring a lot of information. Content is not an end, but rather a means of promoting the goal of self-actualization. In its most emphatic form, humanistic education sees anything that can be taught to another person as relatively inconsequential, with the most significant learning being that which leads to insights and understanding of others and oneself.

Characteristic Teaching and Learning Activities. Humanistic education suggests a number of principles that shape its approach to teaching and learning:

- *Allow learners to assume control of their learning:* Humanist learning activities are student-centered. This means learners are treated as individuals who bring a unique set of experiences and needs to the instructional situation. Learning is best when self-directed, with a strong emphasis on learners and instructors negotiating objectives, methods, and assessment criteria. Whenever possible, students are given a choice in the selection of tasks and activities and in setting realistic goals.

- *Foster a classroom culture supportive of learning:* Individual development does not take place in isolation and is best fostered in a cooperative, supportive, and noncompetitive environment. The classroom should be psychologically and emotionally, as well as physically, nonthreatening, within an overall culture that encourages

> *Our goal is not so much the imparting of knowledge as the unveiling and developing of spiritual energy.*
>
> —Maria Montessori

cooperation, risk-taking, and growth. Students are expected to participate in group work in order to develop social and affective skills. The instructor is seen as a role model for the attitudes, beliefs, and habits that need to be fostered. This is the one area where humanistic educators have had the most significant impact on current educational practice.

- *Promote intrinsic motivation:* Learning is highly personal. Humanistic educators believe it is essential to get learners' buy-in and commitment in achieving learning or training goals. The most valuable learning occurs when what is learned is perceived to be important or meaningful to the learner, and when learning is self-directed. This is achieved not only by demonstrating the value of the learning or training. It is also by cultivating the participants' sense of confidence in their ability to achieve their goals, since the way one feels about a program also influences the commitment to it. A person who feels secure, respected, esteemed, and empowered is likely to make a strong effort, and if threatened, anxious, hostile, or demeaned, is more likely to resist.

Implications for Teaching—Key Instructional Practices and Strategies

Already introduced above, there two prominent humanistic-inspired approaches to education. Knowles's Andragogy is the most dominant and widely discussed. Of lesser influence is Roger's Facilitative Learning.

Andragogy

Andragogy systematically incorporates into instruction five principles that reflect the assumptions and values just explained:

1. Adults seek independence and are capable of directing their own learning, and teachers need to be able to facilitate learners' self-directedness.

2. Adults possess a depth of personal experience that is an important resource for learning and needs to be taken into consideration.

3. Adults are geared to learn things that relate directly to their life roles and to help them achieve personal goals and solve problems.

4. Adults need to know the purpose for which they are learning something and desire knowledge that has immediate application in their lives

5. Adult learning is generally driven by internal factors, such as self-esteem and well-defined personal goals.

Based on these ideas, Knowles proposed a framework for the planning, implementation, and assessment of instruction. This framework

If you want to build a ship, don't drum up people together to collect wood and don't assign them tasks and work, but rather teach them to long for the sea.

—Antoine de Saint-Exupéry

covers considerations for

1. the creation of classroom environments conducive to adult learning.
2. the selection and organization of course content and methods of presentation.
3. the choice of instructional technologies.
4. forms of evaluation suitable for adults.

These include creating a classroom climate that promotes mutual respect and trust, emphasizes cooperative learning, and makes learning nonthreatening. Instructors using this approach also involve students in mutual planning of content and method, in determining their own learning needs and challenges, identifying the resources and strategies they need to achieve their learning goals, and evaluating their own learning, principally through the use of qualitative methods.

Facilitative Learning

As with andragogy, facilitated learning encourages students to have a high degree of involvement in all aspects of their own learning. The technique is used most frequently in university education, especially seminar courses, and in business learning and training environments, in which the goal is not just the gaining of knowledge but the promotion of more effective communication and working styles and positive workplace relationships. It is also a central piece in open education, a movement that promotes learner independence and control over the goals and processes of their education.

The teacher's role, as the name suggests, is that of facilitator and organizer, who provides resources and support to learners. In turn, the participants learn with and from each other as they identify and implement solutions to challenges, problems, or other developmental issues. They might also set their own objectives and be responsible for learning assessment.

Teachers who are more highly facilitative share a number of characteristics:

1. They attend to and respond to student feeling.
2. They use student ideas in ongoing instructional interactions.
3. They enter into discussions with students (dialogue).
4. They praise students.
5. They tailor contents to the individual student's frame of reference (explanations created to fit the immediate needs of the learners).
6. They are more spontaneous and expressive.

> My heart is singing for joy this morning. A miracle has happened! The light of understanding has shone upon my little pupil's mind, and behold, all things are changed.
>
> —Anne Sullivan, teacher of Helen Keller

Some may consider much of this "fluff." However, research has consistently shown that the quality of teacher–student relationships is a critical factor in the quality of student learning experiences and outcomes. Students have higher attendance levels for classes of facilitative teachers, and they demonstrate more self-confidence and higher levels of academic achievement.

Critical Evaluation of Learning Theories

As the conceptual foundation for classroom contemporary instructional practices, behaviorism, cognitivism, constructivism, and humanism each possess their strengths and limitations. Given the brief scope of the descriptions provided in this chapter, we can only be similarly brief in a critical evaluation of these theories. Ultimately, as a classroom instructor, you must decide how you wish to align yourself with these approaches. To do so, we encourage you to go deeper into these topics with your own research. (See Springboards for Further Learning at the end of this chapter.)

Critique of Behaviorism

As the oldest theory, behaviorism has the longest history of application to education, and is also subject to a long list of concerns.

Theoretical Perspective

The full range of human learning cannot be adequately explained in terms of simple stimulus-response relationships, external reinforcements, and other behavioral principles. Also, many behaviors are learned without reinforcement, such as most social behaviors that are part of normal human development.

Teaching Implications

Dissecting topics and ideas into simpler elements by breaking down course material into isolated units to narrowly focus learning objectives and then sequencing this material for increasing levels of difficulty is not suitable for all subjects and learning tasks. Behaviorist learning environments can be highly contrived and mechanistic, and thus fail to engage more natural ways of learning that incorporate the elements of real-life situations or settings similar to those in which what is taught will need to be applied.

The behaviorist view that the goals of schools are to modify human behavior and transmit information conflicts with more contemporary and liberal ideas that education should liberate learners to become independent thinkers. Behaviorism is often out of step with the current shifts in teacher–student classroom roles in education. These place less emphasis on teacher control and more on the need for student-centered activities that foster student responsibility for learning.

Educate: from the Latin, meaning, "leading out or leading forth."

—Webster's Dictionary

Behavioral-based applications can produce inflexible, rote learning that is only the reproduction of information or habitual performance of a skill or procedure rather than deep learning. Routines and memorization become a substitute for higher-order thinking skills and learning strategies needed for a more flexible understanding of material that can be transferred to new situations, such as more advanced courses of study or the workplace.

Behaviorist-based measurement is too narrow in its scope. Limiting the working knowledge of a subject to a finite number of tasks or facts, and then assessing only that which can easily be measured in objective terms can give the illusion that something has been learned. In reality, it may only tell us that when provided with a prompt, learners responded in a programmed way in the setting of the classroom, not that they actually possess competence.

The Bottom Line

The behavioral model of learning and teaching can be faulted for failing to capture the full range of human experience involved in learning. In addition, its assumptions that learning is always reflected in overt behavior and that instruction should be designed to control behavior to produce change do not accord with the personal teaching philosophy of many teachers. As a consequence, the behaviorist paradigm is currently on the wane in psychology and education, and some scholars even question whether it can make any contribution to informed scholarship and contemporary educational practices.

This is unfortunate. Some have gone so far as to condemn many forms of poor teaching, such as a long-winded lecture delivered to uninvolved students, as behaviorist, even when they have no relation to behaviorist theory. Behaviorist learning theory has provided the basis for many innovations in teaching over the past century and continues to bring attention to important dimensions of effective instruction. Core behaviorist principles, such as reinforcement and repetition, immediate feedback, and the importance of the organization and sequencing of content, are still recognized as valuable elements of instructional design and have applications for a range of learning goals, from skills-based learning to subject matter that calls for the retention of a large amount of factual information. Core behaviorist teaching practices also have merit. Many instructors today rely on the simple and intuitive elegance of behavioral design and teaching practices in their classrooms. They provide clear-cut and easily workable strategies for course design, the implementation of instructional practices and the use of assessment tools appropriate for many kinds of learning and continue to be used with success in vocational–technical, career, corporate, and military training programs, as well as traditional academic classroom settings.

Behaviorists may have overstated their ability to describe human learning, and its principles and practices are perhaps a bit mechanistic.

> *Pedagogy is what our species does best. We are teachers, and we want to teach while sitting around the campfire rather than being continually present during our offspring's trial-and-error experiences.*
>
> —Michael S. Gazzaniga

And though behaviorist tenets have been largely supplanted by new ideas, its ideas that educators must give attention to behavior and know how to influence it effectively are still at the center of many teaching and learning activities today.

Critique of Cognitivism

Cognitivism is based on more contemporary research than behaviorism and draws ideas from thinking in a variety of independent fields of study. However, as the foundation for educational practices, is not without limitations and concerns.

Theoretical Perspective

The claim that human minds work by developing mental representations and in accordance with computational rules is still largely conjecture, and might be fundamentally mistaken. Many see the mind not as a computing device but as a dynamic, adaptive, and highly complex system that cannot be understood by reducing it to elementary components or accurately explained entirely in terms of logic and computational rules. There are those who also challenge the conclusions of mainstream cognitive studies and their application to education because they largely neglect the role of emotion, physical environments, and social influences in human thinking.

Teaching Implications

As with behavioral psychology, the emphasis on defining limited, predetermined expectations and goals for instruction and acquiring skills and procedural knowledge can limit the potential for learning deeper conceptual knowledge and higher-order thinking skills. Some cognitivist instructional designs may fail to consider the intangible, yet important role of informal learning that occurs in and is facilitated by unstructured learning environments, which some believe are a more natural reflection of how the mind works.

In trying to formulate rules that describe how the mind works, cognitivist practices can lack the flexibility needed to address individual differences in the processing of information and learning. Teachers, accepting cognitive research without reflection, may be inclined to apply cognitivist strategies without trying to accommodate the different learning needs and preferences of students. It can be a challenge to systematically and correctly implement cognitivist strategies, especially for novice instructors. Unlike the behaviorist-inspired instructional models that offer comprehensive and prescriptive guidelines for instruction, the classroom applications of cognitive research are not always as clear and evident. They are primarily distinct techniques rather than well-organized models.

The harder the conflict, the more glorious the triumph. What we obtain too cheap, we esteem too lightly; it is dearness only that gives everything its value.

—Thomas Paine

The Bottom Line

When compared to the explanations of behavioral psychology, cognitive theories tend toward the more abstract, and seem tentative in many areas of study. The ability to make a scientifically valid picture of the inner workings of the mind to explain learning processes is an enormous challenge, and in many ways is still beyond the reach of current cognitive theories. Moreover, cognitive science, with its many subtheories or partial theories, lacks the unity and clarity that can make its concepts and findings readily accessible to educators concerned about their direct applications to classroom practice.

Still, this computational view is limited, but not necessarily false. Though it has not yet risen to the challenge of explaining all we may need to know to understand human thinking and learning, it offers many important insights that teachers can rely on. We know with confidence that effective instruction needs to take into account learners' prior knowledge and the structure and organization of knowledge to be learned and be appropriate for all skill levels and experiences. We also know much about the systems and processes of attention and memory. These findings and other research have yielded valuable guidelines and strategies for practice that, when integrated into teaching, can result in improved learning outcomes. With continuing advances in research protocols and new technologies, we can anticipate more fascinating and important insights into human learning that can help instructors develop more effective and efficient tools for teaching.

Critique of Constructivism

Constructivism has an intuitive appeal to many teachers. Yet as a theoretical foundation for teaching practices it is still evolving, and raises complex issues that pose many questions.

Theoretical Perspective

Constructivism had been criticized for being more a philosophy of knowledge than a theory of learning and the mind. It is less amenable to research and experimentation than either behaviorism or cognitivism, and some critics consider it more of a folk theory than a scientific one that can provide effective and comprehensive guidelines for teaching.

Teaching Implications

The suggestion that the only knowledge worth acquiring is that which students discover for themselves, although intuitively appealing, may be counterproductive. Some teachers may be led to believe that sophisticated knowledge and skills can be attained only through individual effort, without the systematic and deliberate intervention in their students' learning processes.

An education isn't how much you have committed to memory, or even how much you know. It's being able to differentiate between what you do know and what you don't.

—Anatole France

Constructivists rarely prescribe or predetermine instructional activities and sequences. Rather, they highlight the design of facilitative learning environments. Many, if not most, teachers may find it challenging to figure out what to do in their classrooms on a day-to-day basis when operating only from a constructivist perspective.

Too much focus on learning processes and higher-order thinking skills may fail to provide students the knowledge base they need to succeed academically and professionally. To construct knowledge, learners need a "tool kit" of thinking skills and "the nuts and bolts" of facts, concepts, and other concrete information to build knowledge with.

Some learners have a preference for instruction that moves from specific details to more general ideas and do not always benefit from the broad conceptual approach of constructivist teaching. In addition, a good deal of procedural training is often more effective when independent parts are taught and practiced first, before presenting them in their full complexity.

The constructivist assumption that instruction should be grounded in concrete situations or in authentic learning tasks may not always be valid. Many concepts transfer from one context to another when taught directly without regard to the context of learning. Also, successful transfer can in some cases depend more on the amount of practice rather than on the original learning context.

There is the question of how teachers ensure that valid and sufficient learning has taken place when each individual is responsible for developing knowledge and course subject matter is open to individual interpretations and experiences in the learning process. In many cases, this is a question that has no definitive answer, which instructors, especially novices, may find unsettling.

In encouraging the expression of individual differences, teachers may often find it extremely difficult to effectively and efficiently respond to a multitude of student interests because of a lack of resources in the classroom or the school. Similarly, providing learners with a measure of control over their learning, while a worthy ideal, may not accord with reality. Many learners simply do not want or resist this responsibility.

Adequate time is needed for teachers and students to learn and practice the many roles suggested by a constructivist perspective. Also, a good amount of time is required for the open-ended kind of activities favored and for responding to the individual constructions of students. It can be a challenge to properly manage time and provide boundaries to produce desired learning outcomes within the limits of a particular class or even an entire course.

Creating learning environments that are authentic representations of real-life situations and giving learners the opportunity to replicate what people do in them can also be challenging. Aside from internships or workplace learning settings, a single instructor within an existing school or other environment that may not have the resources to foster

Teaching Consists of equal parts perspiration, inspiration, and resignation.

—Susan Ohanian

this kind of learning must create authentic learning tasks within the constraints of a single classroom.

The Bottom Line

In current educational discourse, there is much talk about constructivism, and many consider it to be the dominant model of the past several decades. In some circles, it has even become a reform slogan used to separate "modern" and "advanced" practices of learning and instruction from old-fashioned and "obsolete" practices. However, the constructivist vision of learning is not without its critics. They contend that this movement has not fulfilled its idealistic promise of more "meaningful" learning and has failed to provide a practical model for implementation because of its highly subjective and open-ended notions of knowledge and learning.

Moving from theory to practice always presents challenges, be it in education or in any other endeavor. And when there are multiple brands of theory, as with constructivism, the task becomes that much more demanding. However, despite its weaknesses, constructivism does not lack an effective design process or framework for good teaching. Constructivist learning environments, while highly flexible, are not unsupported, chaotic, and confusing, as many contend or fear. Numerous researchers, educators, and authors are actively engaged in using constructivist principles every day in their classroom to create powerful learning experiences. These teaching designs balance the process of knowledge acquisition with knowledge construction to produce deep understanding and develop independent critical thinking and problem-solving abilities. Interestingly enough, technology is increasingly being touted as an optimal medium for the application of constructivist principles to learning. There are growing numbers of constructivist-based computer-mediated instructional methods that use software tools that allow for branched, networked formats that mirror the complex character of human reasoning that constructivism sees as the heart of learning. So despite its possible flaws, constructivism continues to and will likely influence discussions about how to best improve teaching and learning for years to come.

> *Teaching, without learning, is just talking.*
>
> —Unknown

Critique of Humanism

Though humanism reflects the personal values of many educators, as a theory of learning it has a number of potential limitations when applied in many instructional settings.

Theoretical Perspective

The humanistic view of the adult learner represents a largely Western view of human nature and may not address students' non-Western cultural and social backgrounds that can influence the goals and processes of their learning. Today's learners are increasingly diverse in terms of abilities, values, culture, language, race, gender, and age. Humanistic values rooted in uniquely Western concepts of individualism and self-determination may not reflect students' beliefs, values, attitudes, and goals. Also, it is assumed that students can be given the responsibility for their learning. Critics, including experienced teachers, contend that this is somewhat fanciful thinking and is much easier said than done.

Classroom Implications

Learner self-direction is difficult to attain, at least within the limits of a term of instruction. It develops by a continuing process and requires foundational qualities and skills, such as self-confidence and self-awareness, and the ability to set goals and monitor one's own progress. Environments that nurture, sustain, and develop an individual's full potential, while valued, are not easy to create. Moreover, not all learners appreciate or benefit from attention to affect, and a neutral environment may be better suited for some students. Moreover, those with a humanistic teaching perspective may fail to properly balance students' affects with the need for knowledge acquisition.

Many factors support student motivation. Not all of them arise from the intrinsic drive to learn and grow. Also, not all teachers will agree on exactly what contributes to students' finding personal meaning and relevance in what they do in any particular course on any particular day, and trying to address each student's personal motivators can be difficult.

The emphasis on possessing learn-to-learn skills is important to student success and helping students become independent, lifelong learners; although this is a worthy goal, it can be difficult to plan and implement. Many instructors find it impractical, if not impossible, to achieve this, given the curricula and time constraints they must contend with for most courses.

Many aspects of humanistic education cannot be assessed according to the standards of mainstream educational practice and seem to be unsuitable in today's reform-minded world of education. Self-evaluation may be a meaningful form of assessment, but there is also the need to develop a student's ability to meet external expectations set by others and satisfy their criteria for success.

The Bottom Line

Like the other learning paradigms we have explored, the humanistic model does not remain unproblematic. It shares some of the perceived limitations of constructivist orientations to teaching and is believed to be inappropriate by some and even to some extent misguided. Several decades of critical analysis suggest that humanism in general and andragogy in particular (as the most widely recognized humanistic-oriented approach to adult learning) does not adequately serve as a

> Many instructional arrangements seem "Contrived," but there is nothing wrong with that. It is the teacher's function to Contrive Conditions under which students learn. It has always been the task of formal education to set up behavior which would prove useful or enjoyable later in a student's life.
>
> —B.F. Skinner

One striking fact is that the complex world of education— unlike defense, health care, or industrial production— does not rest on a strong research base. In no other field are personal experience and ideology so frequently relied on to make policy choices, and in no other field is the research base so inadequate and little used.

—From *Improving Student Learning,* National Research Council

comprehensive theory or even offer a reliable set of methods that can be universally applied. Although offering a guide to practice, many believe that humanism is best considered as a body of philosophical assertions that offers a narrow and culturally relativistic perspective of adult learning and adult learners.

On the other hand, more so than any other model or view of education, humanism identifies and seeks to educate the much-needed development of self-directed, lifelong learning skills for achieving academic and personal success. These are the personal capacities individuals require to succeed in the information age, where many of today's jobs and workforce skills call for the capacity to learn and adapt to the frequently changing demands of a highly competitive and technologically advanced economy. Furthermore, the humanistic tenet that the cognitive and affective domains of learners cannot be separated and that students learn best in emotionally supportive, nonthreatening environments is not only appealing, but is an area in which significant contributions have been made to our knowledge base about what supports effective learning. So although humanistic educational principles may not be a planned part of the classroom practices of many teachers, its values drive discussions about both the goals of education and training and the best ways we can create instructional environments to achieve those goals.

CHAPTER WRAP-UP

The complexity of human learning is reflected in our complexity as biological, cognitive, and social beings. Theories exist, each focusing on different aspects of our make-up as humans. As explained, behaviorists emphasize our observable behavior, cognitive psychologists and constructivists our mental processes, and humanistic psychology our personal and interpersonal development. Each of these approaches suggests particular instructional strategies. However, they do not determine these strategies fully, and a great deal of educational and learning research and theory is steeped in controversy and debate. The debate by its very nature polarizes these approaches with the question, "Which is best?" This polarization is unfortunate, for the issue is more complex. The critical question is not, "Which is the best theory?" but "Which theory is most effective in teaching and learning a specific body of knowledge in any particular circumstance?" And, of course, the answers will vary. There are many categories of learning tasks and thinking, all of which have a place in education and training, with some teaching methods are better suited than others for each kind. Each theoretical perspective offers benefits according to the content and context of each instructional setting.

Though these theories have been presented as distinct conceptualizations, they also overlap in many areas. We propose that they can be positioned on a continuum, where they fall into two camps, the behaviorist/cognitivist and constructivist/humanist.

Although each end of the spectrum represents a different outlook on the nature of knowledge, learning, and the best designs and methods for instruction, these perspectives are not necessarily incompatible. To make the best choice you need to understand the strengths and weaknesses of each learning theory. Your choices can be made only in light of your personal intentions, preferences, and expectations, the purposes of instruction, the specific subject matter and instructional conditions, together with the characteristics and learning goals of your students.

In considering any teaching approach, what matters are not just the principles underlying a particular practice or method, but also the appropriate match between techniques and goals and the context of learning, together with the actual results one gets. Bad teaching and poor learning can happen with any teaching method, no matter what the stripe, when the underlying principles of that method are not properly applied. The consistency, artistry, and skill with which these principles and practices are used are critical to their success.

Both behaviorism and cognitivism are useful in contexts in which the objectives to be attained are unambiguous, in which their attainment can be judged according to commonly agreed upon criteria of successful performance, and in which a clear imbalance exists between your and your learners' areas of expertise. Examples might be the acquisition of information needed in an introductory course, such as basic bookkeeping procedures, or novices learning to become proficient doing things in highly prescribed ways, such as giving injections, or using problem-solving tactics when defined facts and rules apply, as might be necessary when learning to operate a sophisticated machine. Although no learning is without elements of reflection or emotive dimensions, these examples are all located primarily in the domain of task-oriented, instrumental learning that fits most easily with a behaviorist/cognitivist hybrid approach.

On the other hand, a constructivist/humanistic orientation might be more appropriate for challenging learners familiar with course content and ready for self-directed learning and practicing the skills needed to face ill-defined learning problems that mirror the unpredictable nature of everyday living and working commonly experienced. There are few examples of situations today outside the classroom for which objectives are unambiguous and success can be commonly agreed upon by the all those involved. In the information age, rules change daily. To face such unpredictability and variation, we need approaches to instruction such as those offered by a constructivist/humanist orientation.

> *Never become so much of an expert that you stop gaining expertise. View life as a continuous learning experience.*
>
> —Denis Waitley

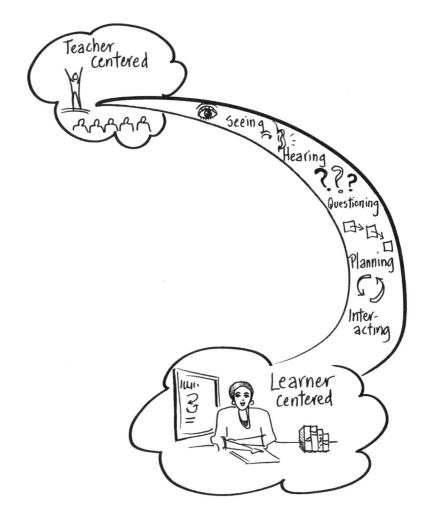

Life is like playing the violin solo in public and learning the instrument as one goes on.

—Samuel Butler

The bottom line is this—the goal of improving teaching and enhancing learning is achievable if you do not limit yourself to any one approach. This is not because we have not yet discovered the one correct learning theory. It is simply because we learn in many different and complex ways that cannot be described by any single theory. Given the dynamic relationship between all of the dimensions of the teaching–learning transaction, you need to be willing to consider a combination of different learning theories and the practices they suggest. However, such a flexible strategy should not just be an eclectic grab bag of ideas that mixes and matches techniques and strategies as one chooses. Your strategy needs to be well crafted.

You can begin by learning to recognize and apply standard rules, facts, and operations in a prescribed and somewhat formulaic manner. But you also need to learn to be creative and adaptive. Just as your students develop knowledge and skill through experience, progressing from rote learning to skilled practice, you too need to be willing to grow along your own knowledge/skills continuum. You need to learn how to extrapolate from general rules and procedures and become proficient in developing and testing new understandings and actions when familiar categories and ways of thinking fail in the face of unfamiliar situations and challenges. If you learn how to do this you will have progressed from: *knowing what,* to *knowing how,* to creatively *knowing-in-action.* And you will then have progressed from novice teacher to masterful educator, being able to adapt to changing, fluid teaching environments in which optimal conditions do not always exist but the best kind of learning often occurs.

SPRINGBOARDS FOR FURTHER LEARNING

Behaviorism

Key Names

Benjamin Bloom
Robert Cagne
Dick and Carey
Madeline Hunter

Robert Mager
B.F. Skinner
Edward Thorndike

Key Terms

direct instruction
feedback
instructional design
mastery learning
operant conditioning

performance and behavioral
   objectives
programmed instruction
reinforcement
task analysis

Cognitive Science

Key Names

David Aushbel
Jerome Bruner

John Bruer
George Miller

Key Terms

advanced organizers
cognitive flexibility
information processing
memory

mental models
schema
visual tools for learning

Constructivism

Key Names

Albert Bandura
Jerome Bruner
Roger Bybee
John Dewey
Jacqueline Grennon Brooks

D. Merrill
Seymour Paper
Jean Piaget
Lev Vygotsky

Key Terms

authentic learning
cognitive apprenticeship
cooperative learning
inquiry-based learning
problem-based learning

reciprocal teaching
situated cognition
situated learning
thematic instruction

Humanism

Key Names

Malcolm Knowles
Abraham Maslow

Carl Rogers

Key Terms

andragogy
facilitative learning

self-actualization
self-directed learning

CHAPTER 3

Learning with the Brain and Mind in Mind: A Brief Exploration of Thinking and Research in the Neurosciences, Cognition, and Educational Psychology

Teachers try to change the brain every day. The more they know about how it learns, the more successful they can be.

—David Sousa, Ed.D.

Do You Know:

There's been more research on the brain in recent years than in all of history preceding them?

Meaning and memory are all about relationships?

Four key research findings that will help you increase learning?

It is not possible to always keep your students' attention, no matter what you do?

How you can influence the motivation to learn?

There are numerous types of intelligence?

Teaching students about intelligence increases it?

Introduction

For millennia humankind has gazed upward into the heavens to wonder at the stars and the vastness of the space that contains the seen and unseen universe, a universe that we know today contains thousands upon thousands of galaxies, each with billions upon billions of stars stretching across a space many light-years from one still unknown end to the other.

In recent years, we have begun to gaze in another direction, inwardly into an equally mysterious space, the invisible universe of our own minds. Some consider the mind seeking to understand itself is not unlike trying to lift yourself by your own bootstraps. Yet, with the aid of brain-scanning technologies developed in the past decade or so, researchers are able to peer into the previously inaccessible, enormously complex workings of the human brain. This inner space is its own cosmos, containing more than 100 billion individual neural cells, each able to connect with 10,000 other cells, generating a number of different possible combinations whose number exceeds the total of all the atoms in the entire known universe. These almost infinite possibilities of design create countless individual human minds each with its own unique pattern of organization shaped by nature and personal experience, producing drives, thoughts, feelings, and behaviors that create identities as different as each snowflake that has ever fallen and will ever fall for all time to come.

As you contemplate the complexity of the human mind, you can begin to appreciate the equally complex challenge you face each time you walk into your classroom. You stand before not just one of these marvelous creations, but perhaps several dozen or even hundreds. Despite the enormous efforts being made to improve teaching, students still seem to learn slowly and with difficulty, sometimes even resisting the effort. Still, the work of one person seeking to teach another can and does succeed every day. Theories and research on how the brain works and how we learn can give you more confidence to make your teaching more efficient and effective.

The 1990s, declared "The Decade of the Brain" by George H.W. Bush, saw an acceleration in federal and private funding leading to research and findings regarding the brain and cognition with parallels to the tremendous growth in information technology of earlier decades. In part, these discoveries have emerged out of the learning theories discussed in Chapter 2. But they also include theories and findings that are coming out of their associated disciplines, including the neurosciences, biology, chemistry, sociology, anthropology, and even the new field of evolutionary psychology. The power and significance of these insights exceed all prior discoveries, and have laid a solid foundation for advances that continue to accelerate as multiple colleges and universities investigate the brain and the mind–brain connection in many areas of interest.

The research base on learning and teaching has not been consolidated in a way that gives a clear, consistent message in formats that are useful for practice.

—*How People Learn*
The National Research Council, Committee on Developments in the Science of Learning

Although there are controversial issues and much more we need to understand, educators today have access to an enormous body of scientific thought and hard research about the mind/brain that can inform and powerfully improve our practice. The purpose of this chapter is to highlight a few specific areas of research and thinking that have important implications for learning, teaching, and training. These include:

1. explorations of the basic structure and operations of the brain.

2. the roles of meaning, emotion, memory, attention, and motivation in learning.

3. learner differences.

4. the nature of intelligence.

Brain/Mind Basics

Neuroscience both confirms and contradicts common beliefs about learning and memory.

—Valerie Strauss

This is not a lesson in brain structures, chemistry, or biology, as valuable as that might be. It is not our intent to overload you with information that will not contribute directly to your chosen craft. (There is, however, a glossary of terms at the end of this chapter that will offer you some further insights into organs and structures in the brain.) This is a simple overview of some of the things we have learned about the brain and how it processes information that may be useful in your teaching journey. Indeed, it will be valuable as our knowledge grows to keep abreast of new findings in brain research.

From Brain Scan to Lesson Plan

Not all the conclusions arrived at by researchers have direct teaching applications. Some of these findings result from "hard-core" scientific investigations in the neurobiology and information-processing research of cognitive science, involving the use of highly advanced brain-scanning technologies and controlled experiments. Other findings, however, are still somewhat tentative and even speculative, the result of scholarly considerations of how people learn and behave. These have descriptive power, but remain unproven according to the accepted scientific research standards. Moreover, even when the research is solid, much of it is done at the cellular, biochemical, and genetic level—investigative domains far removed from what "whole" people do. Consequently, not all findings when carried into the classroom can be assumed to have more weight than beliefs until proven by further study, their connections to teaching only implied, not proven. Unfortunately, well-intentioned educators have extended research beyond their scientific backing and have drawn conclusions about certain teaching methods and techniques not supported by research. Moreover, there have been a host of popular books written and probably countless workshops given that make claims that "brain research proves X, Y, or Z" when the research can, at best, suggest possible strategies for consideration and guidelines for good teaching. To help you sort through all this, when possible we will point out when this research points to direct teaching applications and when one must be cautious in drawing the connections between research and classroom practice.

A Brief Research Primer

Brain research is done from the "bottom up" and the "top down." With the development of sophisticated instruments and procedures, such as magnetic resonance imaging (MRI), functional magnetic resonance imaging (fMRI), computed tomography (CT). and positron-emission tomography (PET), the bottom-up approach has become a major research area during the past 15 to 25 years. Those who study from the bottom up are generally neuroscientists who focus on small units, individual cells, or small systems of cells within complete systems. This offers them opportunities to determine physical reactions and chemical interactions in the brain. This perspective argues that understanding the basic units of a system is essential to understanding the whole system. However, these subunits are not necessarily connected to the whys and wherefores of more complex cognitive, emotional, or psychological functions.

The top-down approach is broader, and includes the study of more readily observable and higher-order cognitive functions and/or behaviors, such as learning, movement, and language. Cognitive psychologists, linguists, physical anthropologists, and philosophers are some of those who study from the top down. They study the functions that take place on these higher levels—the final expression of the deeper physiological processes studied by the neurosciences—though the top-down investigations have increased our capacity to better understand the physiology of the brain as well.

Among the most prominent findings that have emerged from brain research have come from Marian Diamond at the University of California at Berkeley and her husband, Art Scheibel, M.D., at UCLA. Dr. Diamond is credited, with her colleagues, with conclusive research that the environment can affect the brain. Called *cortical plasticity*, it is the idea that the structure of the brain could change in an experience-dependent way. Dr. Scheibel has studied the development of the brain in utero and determined that cells migrate and multiply to form the human form as we know it. His detailed research on brain development laid the foundation for much of the research on chemistry and cell development in the brain being done today.

> *You Can't go from neuroscience to the classroom, because we don't know enough neuroscience.*
>
> —Kurt W. Fischer

During the early period of brain research, educators tried to draw conclusions on what the findings meant to teaching. Unfortunately, there were conclusions that were inaccurate and yet accepted as accurate. Now we know more, yet it is still not well known how brain processing affects learning. Even with the most sophisticated methods of imaging there are questions. There are some conclusions that can be drawn, but you must continue to have an open mind and keep current. In the next two sections you will read specifics about the brain and meaning, emotion, and memory. A third section provides a short overview of some findings that have important implications for more effective learning. This information will help you in designing your course activities. You will also find a section in the workbook suggesting activities for you to consider.

Making Meaning—It's All About Making Connections

Creating meaning or what has meaning to the learner is at the heart of effective teaching and quality learning. When there is meaning, things make more sense. What we experience has personal relevance and forms lasting memories. We find meaning when connections are made. There are three kinds of connections that contribute to the creation of meaning:

1. cognitive connections.
2. personal connections.
3. emotional connections. (In many ways, these are not separate processes; indeed, they are quite related. But for our purposes here we have made these distinctions to aid this explanation.)

Cognitive Connections

Imagine being given a puzzle with a thousand pieces. The pieces are taken from their original box and tossed on the floor, and now it is your job to put them together. Your first question may be, "Where do I begin?" Your second will probably be, "Can I see the cover of the box to see the picture of the completed puzzle?" This is a logical question that reflects how the mind naturally wants to make sense of what it does not understand—by looking for patterns that connect small bits of information to make larger concepts. Meaning in terms of information-processing research is a matter of the matching of new stimuli with information stored in memory, prior knowledge, or pattern recognition. Seeing patterns or relationships among bits of information and isolated ideas allows us to "connect the dots," so to speak. And making these

Human beings are disposed to make sense out of new information, events and experiences.

—Bill Cerbin

connections to weave together fragments into wholes is how we make sense of what we experience in our everyday lives.

Personal Connections

Beliefs, interests, and values also contribute to creating meaning. Greater and deeper meaning is generated when personal connections are made to what we experience. Unless there is a personal interest and personal relevance is found in an activity, the mind/brain will generally lack the motivation to pursue or persist at new experiences. Think about it from your own learning experiences. When you were taking a course or a lesson on a topic that was of great interest to you, you probably paid more attention. Perhaps you enjoyed history more than English literature. History may have had more meaning because of your travel experiences. Or perhaps you loved math because you were good with numbers or had an inspiring teacher. Then again, physics may have held your attention better than biology because of the difference in lab classes.

Emotional Connections

In addition to our values or beliefs, and interests, we also place more meaning on some things because of the emotional power of the experience. What we are emotionally connected to will have more meaning for us. From tragedy to blessing, our emotions help us experience more meaning and remember more. Did your parents divorce, or did you lose someone close to you? Did you have an accident of some sort, or a relationship that went badly? What about a recognition award, or baby being born? If you think about these experiences, they all had a powerful and meaningful impact on you. Even if you try to forget, they are still there because of the emotional state you experienced at the time. The most important thing to know is that meaning is critically linked to emotion.

There are two ways to consider emotion: emotional attachment to or rapport with the instructor and emotional attachment to the material. Again, your own experience may prove the point. Did your most effective teacher tell stories, or use illustrations to keep your attention? Was the teacher you best remember tied to you through a strong relationship? If you liked a teacher, you did more to please him or her. You felt more comfortable asking questions and getting help. You spent more time on that subject than others, and you learned more. Even in informal teaching settings, rapport, which is based on emotion, makes a difference in what students learn.

This emotional connection also applies to subject matter. You are a subject-matter expert for a reason; you liked most of the topics in subjects of your greatest interest. As you learned more, you became more deeply connected to the material and probably passionate about it.

No man can be a good teacher unless he has feelings of warm affection toward his pupils and a genuine desire to impart to them what he himself believes to be of value.

—Bertrand Russell

This is natural, and you cannot forget it when you are teaching others. What held true for you holds true for your students.

Four Critical Findings on Learning

Research done by David Perkins and Lauren Resnick at Harvard University and Gaea Leinhardt at the University of Pittsburgh's Learning Research and Development Center concluded that there are four enlightening keys to learning that are very different from what educators usually think about learning. These findings in the early 1990s affirmed beliefs held by many without the brain/mind research backing that has since emerged. (As you may recall, these ideas were discussed in Chapter 2. The research is solid, and it turned time-honored beliefs on their heads; unfortunately, it has not made much difference in the way teachers teach. Personal beliefs are sometimes too strong to be influenced by research.)

Prior Knowledge

The easiest finding to understand is that learning that is connected to prior knowledge shapes new learning. In simple terms, if you know something about the brain, it will influence how you interpret the information presented here. We question new material based on our prior knowledge. Any misconceptions are included in the filters that you use to process new knowledge. The most effective way to acknowledge this is to build on prior knowledge and get conceptions out in the open by using discussions about student understandings and beliefs about the topic. This will help you discover misconceptions so that you can address them. This research has not been widely accepted and practiced because of the very misconceptions and beliefs about learning held by many educators.

Social Interaction

The research notes that social interaction is a big part of learning. In other words, the interaction during discussions helps in the learning process. The cooperative/collaborative learning movement has proven to be very successful for just this reason. Students talking among themselves about a topic are not acting out, but rather are processing information socially. The challenge for instructors is not knowing exactly where a discussion may go. When instructors allow for robust discussion, things change. The teacher is no longer the only one in the classroom responsible for all the knowledge. This concept promotes not only deeper thinking but mutual respect.

Learning Is Situated

The next finding, according to Lauren Resnick, is the most radical of all. The idea is that learning is very much tied to particular situations. We used to believe that learning in one situation is easily transferred to

> *Learning from programmed information always hides reality behind a screen.*
>
> —Ivan Illich

another. (For example, it might be assumed that skateboarding is easily transferred to snowboarding.) There is some transfer, but much less than we used to think. Because we create knowledge as we go, we adapt it to each current situation. It is like a new start each time we are faced with using new knowledge. This finding justifies the apprentice-to-journeyman programs in the trades. It also supports internship programs and experiential learning initiatives.

Use Multiple Strategies

Unit 3

The fourth of these findings is that teachers should be using numerous strategies to embed learning more deeply. Perkins suggests that "fancy thinking" should be taught explicitly. Comparing and contrasting, synthesizing, and evaluating offer learners tools that can be applied in many instances. We use plain thinking all the time, and by purposely teaching fancy-thinking skills, we will better prepare students to face new situations and use their knowledge successfully.

Classroom Implications and Applications

Refer to Field Guide

As classroom practitioners it is crucial to know and use the most current information in designing and delivering instruction. The most important implication, then, is to be continually aware of the latest in research on the brain. Here are some valuable suggestions to get you started. You'll find more specific applications for the following ideas in the Field Guide.

- Remember your passion about the subject, and do not hide it.
- Build a strong relationship with your students. Listen to them carefully. Keep your appointments. Greet the students at the classroom door and any other place you might see them.
- Know your students' interests and activities (try a first day of class survey). Find common threads if you can. This will allow you to design lessons relevant to their lives.
- Make materials as vivid and engaging as possible from the students' perspective.
- Create strong emotionally charged stories that connect students to the content.
- Plan your lessons to include multiple real-world situations (especially the students' world).
- Use multiple strategies to present and help students process and apply new knowledge.
- Build on prior knowledge, and correct incorrect beliefs and assumptions.

- Offer continuous opportunities for student learning and interaction through discussions, blogs, and any other means available to you.
- Create as many situations in which the new knowledge can be applied and practiced.

Thanks for the Memories—How Memory Works

There are hundreds of memory courses offered through public seminars, community colleges, books, tapes and CDs, and consultants to companies and organizations. All these have one thing in common: people forget things that are important to them, or to someone else. Though the same things that help us make sense of and find meaning in our experiences do apply to how memories are made, there are other factors that are involved in memory processes that we know today.

The study of memory is long-standing and deep. It is probably the most studied of brain functions because of its importance in disease (i.e., Alzheimer's and dementia) and education. There are thousands of researchers in neuroscience and cognitive psychology who have studied and continue to study how we remember and how the brain processes information. We still do not have a complete understanding of how it all works, and the findings that follow could change with ongoing research.

Three Memory Systems

There are three systems involved in memory: sensory, short-term (sometimes called working memory), and long-term. Each serves an important purpose in the memory-forming process. When we experience something, our senses are the first receptors. We see, hear, touch, taste, or smell something and form a sensory memory of it. Sensory memory is not always conscious. For example, have you ever been in a near accident? If so, you probably ignored the details and just reacted. Your unconscious was operating to help you avoid a dire situation. You may not have remembered the incident because it all happened so fast. Sensory memory can take up to a second, but usually takes a much shorter time—a millisecond or less—to form. Sensory memory can help us form an impression that can move to short-term memory, but this is true only if the input is not ignored. We have many experiences that are superficial or inconsequential and that we ignore. When ignored, the information is instantaneously discarded so you have no perception or memory of it.

Any sensory impression, if not ignored, is transferred electrochemically in the brain. Now it is in short-term memory, where it will remain for about a minute unless it is processed in some fashion to move it to long-term memory. (Remember "chunking," from Chapter 2?) The short-term memory can hold seven items plus or minus two. The seven items might be numbers, words, or a phone number, for instance.)

Long-term memory is the next stage in memory formation. Have you ever called information, dialed the number, and found it busy, only to call information to get the number again? This is because you have not transferred the information from short-term to long-term memory.

There are several keys to move information from short-term to long-term memory. Rehearsal and repetition are the most important ones, unless the short-term memory is strongly emotionally based. (Strong emotionally charged memories seem to occur without the conscious practice of saying, "I need to remember this!") Think of your own experiences. Perhaps at some time you "crammed" for an exam. You may have found that you did okay on the exam, but soon after (maybe less than 24 hours) you forgot the content you studied. In fact you may have blanked out on information that you knew you had studied. You did not spend enough time rehearsing the information or spread out your study (distribution effect) to sustain it for long-term memory. Your strategy was to "learn" just at a surface level enough to help you pass an exam, which is not a very effective way to learn.

We can also consciously move short-term memory to long-term memory by attaching the short-term/sensory information to something we are already familiar with or our prior knowledge. The pathways for familiar information are easily maneuvered, and by attaching a new chunk of information to something already known, the brain more easily creates a new neural pathway so the information is easier to retrieve. This is true because of the association with a stored memory.

Three Types of Memory

In addition to the three memory systems just described, the workings of memory may also be understood in terms of three different types of memory: episodic, declarative, and procedural. Each of these is believed to be governed by its own mechanisms and brain circuits. One important distinction is how easily they are formed. Think of memory in terms of capturing experiences like a camera might take a picture. Episodic memory is thought of as involving a one-time mechanism. You need only one exposure to an episode to remember it. Declarative memory and procedural memories, on the other hand, require multiple exposures to the contents of memory, with these contents updated and strengthened with each exposure.

Episodic Memory

This is memory of personally experienced events. It is memory of specific moments in time. It is considered a form of declarative memory, since it can be consciously recalled and discussed. However, it is memory

> The lasting measure of good teaching is what the individual student learns and carries away.
>
> —Barbara Harrell Carson

that is tied to the time and place of the experience, whereas factual declarative memory is not. You can think of episodic memories as the stories we tell about the events in our lives. These kinds of memories are easily formed and can endure for a long time with no conscious effort to store and strengthen them. Episodic memories are strengthened when associated with strong positive feelings (your first kiss, or the time you learned you were to have your first child) or moderately negative ones (the day you had a car accident).

Declarative Memory

> *How can you do new math with an old math mind?*
>
> —Charlie Brown,
> *Peanuts*

Declarative memory (sometimes called semantic memory) is the kind of memory used to store facts. It is "what" memory. It is called "declarative" because it is memory we can consciously talk about or declare. It deals with the kind of learning and memory most associated with schooling—for example, textbook knowledge, concepts, and other academic subject matter. It exists independently of any particular time or place. For example, you can remember George Washington's birthday though you have no recollection when you first learned this fact. This kind of memory is easily formed but also easily forgotten. Declarative memory is strengthened by rehearsal, the use of memory techniques (mnemonics), spaced repetition, and frequent retrieval.

Procedural Memory

These are "how-to" memories, involving learned skills and procedures. They are stored without regard to the time or place they were created (though it is possible to remember the time they were acquired). They are hard to form, yet very lasting. Procedural memories are solidified with repeated practice. Just think of learning to ride a bike. Although you may remember little about the actual events associated with the development of this ability, you can still get on a bike and ride even decades after having last been on one.

Brain Matters: How the Brain Processes Memory

Memory is processed mainly in two small organs in the brain, the amygdala and the hippocampus, after being routed by the thalamus. We have experiences every minute of every day and must decide whether the experience is worth remembering. As already stated, this process takes place in microseconds or nanoseconds. The relationship between emotion and memory is complex and not entirely understood, but generally, it seems that emotion increases the likelihood that an event will be vividly remembered later. The amygdala is thought to be the seat of emotions, sorting out fear and pleasure and also sending messages to other parts of the brain that

(continues)

trouble is imminent. The thinking process about how to respond is set in motion by signals from the amygdala. The amygdala is located in the limbic area of the brain, while the hippocampus is closer to the temporal lobe, just below your temples.

The hippocampus helps us form long-term memory although it is more involved in acquisition rather than storage or retrieval. It helps combine new memories with previous experiences. The formation of new episodic memories requires the hippocampus. Without the involvement of the hippocampus, for example, one is able to form new procedural memories (such as riding a bike) but cannot remember the events during which they happened. At this time we know that the hippocampus is directly related to memory formation and helps form the unconscious recognition pathways around complex experiences. We know that Alzheimer's disease damages the hippocampus before other areas of the brain.

Classroom Implications and Applications

From using repetition and mnemonic memory systems to creating vivid stories and experiences, there are many techniques that can be used to form and more easily recall memories. Along with meaning and emotion, discussed earlier, they all work to the degree that you practice them and have the intention to remember. Below are a few suggestions. These ideas are not about how you can form stronger memories for your students, except in a very general sense. (We encourage you to look into the many resources that, as noted, deal with many specific techniques for improving memory.)

- Provide ample opportunities for repetition and rehearsal in class. Continuously review previous material and, just as importantly, distribute this review and study at intervals.

- Again, make your class materials and presentations as vivid and personally meaningful as possible.

- Match your learning activities to your learning goals. If you want students to learn a skill, do not just have them memorize facts and other information. Embed the learning in performance activities.

- Share with your students how memory is formed to encourage them to review past material and preview new material.

Most importantly, keep in mind that good teaching is not just about the efficient transfer of information. It is also about creating experiences. There are many clever ways to have students rehearse and repeat the content. This brings together the different systems involved in episodic,

Unit 2

declarative, and procedural memory so that they reinforce each other. Partner sharing, choral response, minute papers (responses written in a minute), mind mapping (a graphic organizer), writing a song/rap, acting out, and creating skits are just a few of the ways you can have students become engaged with and practice your required content.

Your Attention, Please!

Many students believe that they can learn while doing several other things at the same time, like talking to a friend, listening to music, and thinking about what they are going to do after class. You do not have to be a teacher to agree. Anyone with a teenage son or daughter who claims to be reading while watching TV will attest to the same. We also may fall subject to this belief because of our own experiences, such as cruising down the freeway at high speed caught up in our own thoughts and completely oblivious to everything around us. When we realize we have not been paying any attention to our driving, all we can do is wonder how we managed to avoid a terrible accident.

However, contrary to these common observations, the brain is unable to focus on more than one stimulus at a time. What information-processing research tells us is that what may appear as simultaneous focus or multitasking is in fact a rapid alternation of focus. The more routine something is, the less it demands our attention and the more easily we can shift our attention to something else.

Stages of Attention

Pre-Attention

Attention is not a singular activity, but a complex process involving a number of steps. To begin, a sensory signal must trigger a neurological response. This action is called "pre-attention," and involves the formation of a sensory memory. For example, in the case of vision, light will strike the eye and create a sensory imprint that will last only milliseconds. (There is some evidence that with auditory signals these will last somewhat longer.)

Perception

Because the brain cannot consciously attend to the huge amount of incoming sensory information we are bombarded with at any given moment, the brain filters out most of this data by selecting what to discard and what to further process or turn into a percept or perception. Only when some kind of significance (meaning) is assigned to raw sensory information does it become perception. In other words, what the senses respond to and what we actually see or hear, etc., are not the same. For example, presented with a nondescript image, the

> We teach what we like to learn, and the reason many people go into teaching is vicariously to re-experience the primary joy experienced the first time they learned something they loved.
>
> —Stephen Brookfield

natural impulse for the human mind is to try and figure out what it is. As explained earlier, it does so by attempting to organize it into something familiar or at least something similar to what is already known. We activate certain mental representations held in memory (prior knowledge) and "map" this crude data to them. This matching process is called pattern recognition, and it helps us to begin to make sense of our experience through the formation of our initial perceptions.

Immediate Attention

So how does perception result in attention? The brain is constantly monitoring the environment. Attention is highly selective, and most perceptions are quickly dropped. (They are not transferred from sensory to working or short-term memory.) But through evolution and a primal survival instinct, we are programmed to automatically distinguish between and give immediate attention to signals based on certain attributes:

- *Intensity:* The brighter, louder, more powerful, etc. sensory signals are, the more likely it is that they will get attention.
- *Novelty:* One bit of sensory experience is different from other sensory impressions.
- *Motion:* That which moves will attract attention.

Sustained Attention

There is no such thing as "not paying attention." We are always paying attention to something, even if this attention is constantly shifting. The operations leading to initial attention are automatic mechanisms. Clearly, though, we do not want our students sensing what is going on in our classroom in an unconscious manner; we want them to give sustained attention to what is important.

Meaning is one element that determines whether something is relevant and worthy of our students' deliberate focus. Information with meaning moves from the sensory background to the foreground of the their minds. A person may, for a moment, attend to something that is novel or intense, but generally will not attempt to process it further if the perception does not have some kind of meaning. If something fails to make sense for a certain length of time, then the matter will be dropped and attention given to something else. Emotion is an even more powerful force that can drive attention. As explained earlier, the brain is hardwired to respond to anything that has strong emotional content. Our most primal urge is to react immediately to what represents a threat. Also, that which has a positive emotional value will draw and keep our attention.

Most models [of learning] assume that the purpose of learning is to incorporate new information or skills into the learner's existing knowledge structure and to make that knowledge accessible. . . . Learning begins with the need for some motivation, an intention to learn. The learner must then concentrate attention on the important aspects of what is to be learned and differentiate them from noise in the environment.

—Marilla Svinicki, Anastasia Hagen, and Debra Meyer

Cycles of Attention

Getting attention and keeping attention are two very different things. In order to keep attention it is important to understand the differences. When you take the following information into account you will be better able to keep attention for longer periods of time.

Time Cycles

The ability of a person to sustain her attention on one thing varies according to age and physical condition. Young children have trouble staying focused for more than a few minutes. Adults, on the other hand, can maintain attention for longer periods, 15 to 20 minutes for the average person (less when tired, dehydrated, or not properly nourished). This is a much shorter span than what teachers often expect of their students. (An interesting aspect is that children and adults can focus for longer periods of time when they have special interests, like video games or sports practice.)

Focus Cycles

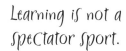

Learning is not a spectator sport.

—D. Blocher

Humans have many temporal cycles—hormonal, cellular, biochemical, and electrical, among many others. Our attention also operates in these cycles, naturally drifting from an external to an internal focus, at a frequency and length of time according to our personal psychology and thinking styles. It is believed that these changes play an important part in the ways we need to process, store, and retrieve information.

State Changes

Refer to Field Guide

Shifts in attention and our ability to sustain it are influenced by our general biological makeup, and our physiology at any particular moment. Think about working at a computer and sitting up straighter to become more engaged. This can be a matter of our fatigue levels, what we have eaten or drunk recently, and our level of activity. For example, dehydration, low blood sugar, or raising blood sugar too quickly (think soda or candy on an empty stomach) can quickly lead to fatigue. Unlike other factors genetically programmed, these are all under our personal control and thus open to influence. Purposely activating state changes during class can increase attention and hence learning. State changes are as simple as adjusting your position in a chair to doing a "gallery walk" of posters around the room created to represent content. Simply having everyone snap their fingers after completing an activity will not only offer a state change but will mark completion. (The brain likes to know when things are finished.)

A Final Note: Role of the Unconscious

From the viewpoint of mainstream cognitive research, attending to what we want to learn is necessary for learning to happen. However, there is ample evidence that we are not only bombarded by many signals that remain outside our awareness, but also that such information or messages received below the level of conscious awareness, or subliminally, can actually interfere with or enhance conscious learning activities. The more emotionally laden these signals are, the greater their impact. (Remember the section on meaning and emotion?) Although this whole topic is somewhat controversial and open to debate, it points to the importance of the overall tone and content of the learning environments created in our classrooms. This includes the way we speak, behave, and even dress, which can influence how our students feel about us, the subject matter, and their overall experience in the classroom. It also includes what our students say and do in class.

Classroom Implications and Applications

Many things compete for our students' attention from the moment they enter our classrooms. It may be thoughts of their commute, the work awaiting them at their job, the growling of their stomachs, an attractive classmate across the room, or the noise of cars passing outside. We could easily go on. Clearly, we have no control over many of the things we likely consider distractions. However, we do have the ability to influence our students' attention by using our understanding of what governs it.

- Vary what you do to create novelty and accommodate naturally occurring cycles of attention and the need for reflection.
- Vary the tone and volume of your voice and your position in the room.
- Vary what your students do to keep them alert and engaged by inducing state changes. Shift their physiology by getting them to move, so they are not just sitting in one mind (and probably butt) numbing position too long.
- Inform your students of proper nutrition and hydration, and encourage them to drink water regularly and eat a light but balanced meal before class. These two things alone can make a huge difference in your students' attention levels. Provide water and food breaks if you can.
- Investigate and use classical music as a backdrop to your content input sessions.

Education, n. One of the few things a fellow is willing to pay for and not get.

—Leonard L. Levinson

Unit 2

- Provide an environment that is accepting, and maintain high academic standards.
- Have students change seats during longer classes. Assigned seating is not conducive to student focus or attention.

Motivation

I never teach my pupils; I only attempt to provide the conditions in which they can learn.

—Albert Einstein

Rarely will one hear a parent or a teacher of young children complain that they are unmotivated. Yet the question "Why are so many of my students unmotivated?" is an almost universal lament of educators. Who has not witnessed their students sitting not only at the fringes of the classroom near the walls or exits, but also at the "edge" of the course itself, reluctant to become engaged and seek out the heart of the subject matter and give their all to learning? The quest to increase learner motivation is considered to be the "holy grail" of teaching—a compelling and sometimes seemingly futile endeavor. Even when students are in direct pursuit of important career goals, teaching or training them can be like pulling teeth—both a struggle and a real pain. Why is this so?

In fact, all students are motivated. However, they may not be very motivated about your class or subject. They may be much more motivated to stay in bed or spend more time with friends rather than with books. A frightening truth is that you can't motivate others. But you can create the environment or arrange the conditions in which they will be motivated. (A primary aim of this book is to support you with numerous tools for creating a class setting that motivates your students to be engaged and to learn more and faster.)

As children we were all naturally curious adventurers with a seemingly insatiable appetite for learning. We impulsively searched our environment to make sense of it, first crawling and then rambling awkwardly but with determination, pushing and pulling everything in sight to find out what it does. But then as we get older, commonly this spirit of exploration diminishes. Learning often becomes associated with drudgery instead of delight. A large number of students will drop classes or leave school altogether.

There are many reasons why this is so, and explanations abound in the literature of educational psychology. Most of these have to do with developmental issues (younger learners are much more willing to take risks than older ones, since they see effort as having a generally positive result) and socialization experiences in school (where we begin forming beliefs about school-related successes and failures that have important implications for how we approach and cope with learning situations). You cannot explore all these explanations and actually do not need to in order to understand your learners' motivations.

Chapter 17

What you do need to understand is that their motivation never totally disappears; all our students have interests outside our classes, things they enjoy and want to do, whether it be playing guitar, finding a date, or figuring out how to deal with a problem at work. What has become diminished is their *motivation to learn*. This involves the reasons, value, and benefits of academic or training tasks to learners that underlie their involvement or noninvolvement in these activities. The correct question then we ask ourselves as teachers is not "Why are our students unmotivated?" but "Why do they lack the motivation to participate with more interest, effort, and even enthusiasm?"

Understanding the Motivation to Learn

As an instructor you do not need to understand everything there is about human motivation to increase your students' engagement in the learning process. But you do need to understand a little about the character of their commitment to participate in this process, that is, their *motivation to learn*.

Students may be equally motivated to perform a task, though the sources of their motivation may differ. Behavioral theories tend to focus on extrinsic motivation (i.e., rewards) or biological drives (hunger, sleep), while cognitive, constructivist, and humanistic theories deal with intrinsic motivation (i.e., psychological needs and personal goals). Linked to classroom learning, extrinsic motivation means getting good grades, passing courses, or other outside incentives, like recognition by others. (You will likely agree that stickers and candy or taking away privileges, like recess, will not work for your students like they do with young children.) On the other hand, intrinsically motivated students actively engage themselves in learning out of curiosity, interest, or enjoyment. They may wish to achieve their own intellectual and personal goals, and hence are more likely to be excited by challenging activities.

Although any kind of motivation is obviously preferable to none, there is compelling evidence that students who are more intrinsically than extrinsically motivated do better. In fact, some research demonstrates that using extrinsic motivators to engage students in learning can lower achievement and negatively affect student motivation. Students who are motivated to complete a task only to avoid consequences or to earn a certain grade rarely exert more than the minimum effort necessary to meet their goal. And when students are focused on comparing themselves with their classmates, rather than on mastering skills at their own rate, they are more easily discouraged, and their intrinsic motivation to learn may actually decrease. Although external rewards may sustain productivity, they can also decrease interest in a learning task, diminishing the likelihood that the task will be continued outside the context of the classroom.

The teacher if he is indeed wise does not teach bid you to enter the house of wisdom but leads you to the threshold of your own mind.

—Kahlil Gibran

Students who are intrinsically motivated, on average, come out ahead in a number of areas. These students are better adjusted to school and achieve more. They also experience greater confidence about their ability to learn new material and are inclined to use learning strategies that demand more effort and enable them to learn more deeply. Overall, students with intrinsic motivation are more likely to engage in and persist at challenging tasks. They are also likely to be life-long learners, who continue to educate themselves outside the formal school setting. Although every educational activity cannot, and perhaps should not, be intrinsically motivating, these findings suggest that capitalizing on existing intrinsic motivation brings important benefits.

At the same time, it should be noted here that some researchers object to describing student motivation as either intrinsic or extrinsic. They argue that many complex and interrelated factors influence students' motivation to succeed in school and that most successful people are motivated by both internal and external factors. Most experienced teachers would probably agree. It is, therefore, suggested that you build on *both* types of motivation when working to engage students more fully. Some students seem naturally enthusiastic about learning; these kind of learners still need or expect their instructors to inspire, challenge, and stimulate them. Therefore, all students will benefit from your efforts to support the interest that brought them to the course in the first place, regardless of the kind and level of motivation they possess. Their learning will be transformed, for better or worse, by what happens in your classroom. You certainly cannot control everything, but you can influence a lot. Your passion and excitement about what you do will have an amazing affect on your students.

> *The task of the excellent teacher is to stimulate "apparently ordinary" people to unusual effort. The tough problem is not in identifying winners: it is in making winners out of ordinary people.*
>
> —K. Patricia Cross

Classroom Implications and Applications

Seminars on how to improve learner motivation are popular among educators and trainers. Many instructors come looking for a "silver bullet." Unfortunately, there is no single magical formula for motivating student learning. Students' histories accompany them into each new classroom setting, and many things affect a given student's motivation to work and to learn. These include factors outside our control, such as their interest in the subject matter, perception of its usefulness, general desire to achieve, self-confidence, and self-esteem, as well as patience and persistence.

Though you cannot directly motivate your students, there is much you can do to influence them and to foster greater engagement and commitment to learn. Your role is to create the conditions for each and every student to find motivation within themselves and, just as importantly, to avoid doing things that can demotivate your students. This is not as complicated as it may first seem. Research has shown that good everyday teaching practices can do more to counter student apathy than special efforts to attack motivation directly.

So, what can you do to create the environment and circumstances for students to experience more motivation? Research done at UCLA offers some basic findings to consider:

- Too much tension or concern can demotivate students. ("This test will determine if you pass or fail this course.")
- A moderately pleasant or unpleasant feeling tone increases motivation while excessive amounts of either positive or negative affect interfere with productivity.
- The more interest generated the greater the learning.
- Success and the right degree of difficulty support stronger motivation.
- When students get specific feedback on their performance, motivation increases.
- If the activity is rewarding, intrinsic motivation increases.

Thus, the right amount of tension, feeling, tone, interest, success, meaningfulness, and knowledge of results will help you create an environment that will increase intrinsic motivation and, in the end, achievement.

Here is a list of more specific ideas for enhancing learner motivation. You will find these to be consistent and will reflect what most students identify as the qualities of good teachers and their favorite classes. For an elaboration of these ideas and others see Units 2 and 3.

- Offer a well-organized course that provides a clear sense of direction.
- Set clear expectations and performance standards. Students should know exactly what is expected of them.
- Use appropriate, concrete, and understandable examples, analogies, and visual tools when presenting core concepts.
- Be enthusiastic about what you teach, and demonstrate a genuine interest in students and what they learn. When students feel you care about them and what they have to say, they will care about what *you* do and have to say.
- Be sensitive to students' attitudes and beliefs about learning, and be aware of your own beliefs about teaching and learning. High expectations lead to higher performance. If you expect your students to be motivated, hardworking, and interested in the course, they are more likely to be so.
- Vary teaching and learning activities to keep students curious and engaged. Variety reawakens students' involvement in the course and their motivation. Break routines by incorporating multiple strategies.

I have never in my life learned anything from any man who agreed with me.

—Dudley Field Malone

Refer to Field Guide

In even the most mature person, understanding is a mixture of insight and misconception, knowledge and ignorance, skill and awkwardness.

—Grant Wiggins

- Give frequent, early, specific feedback that provides knowledge of results and supports students' beliefs that they can do well. Offer students feedback on how to improve. (Watch your "buts" versus "ands," and use of "don't forget" versus "remember to." The first carry a negative connotation, while the alternatives empower students.)

- Avoid public criticisms of students' performances and the kind of competition that pits students against each other.

- Put students into cooperative working groups. Students are more attentive, learn better, produce more work, and are more favorable to teaching methods when they work cooperatively rather than compete as individuals.

- Ensure opportunities for students' success by assigning tasks that are challenging and achievable. Encourage students to focus on their continued improvement and learning, and not on individual test results.

- Help students find personal meaning and value in the material; capitalize on students' existing needs and satisfy their own motives for enrolling in the course.

- Create an open and positive atmosphere. If students experience the classroom as a caring, supportive place where there is a sense of belonging and everyone is valued and respected, they will tend to participate more fully in the process of learning.

- Help students experience a sense of autonomy and respect. Elicit student feedback and input into the learning process so they feel they have some sense of control and freedom.

Use respectful messages that positively reinforce your power as an instructor. For example, instead of saying, "I require," "you must," or "you should," stress "I think you will find . . . ," or "I will be interested in your reaction." Ask students directly what they find more or less motivating in their classes. This can be a written survey about your class. Or try a simple and more indirect approach: request that students recall and describe two other classes, one that they found motivating and one that they did not.

If you prefer to try a more systematic approach, one author, John Keller, presents a straightforward instructional design model (ARCS) for motivation that is based on a number of other theories and pulls these separate elements into a prescriptive framework. His model suggests a design strategy that encompasses four components of motivation:

- Arousing *Attention*
- Creating *Relevance*
- Building *Confidence*
- Producing *Satisfaction*

Helping Discouraged Students
These ideas will support you in helping those students who are unmotivated.
- Recognize that strategies that are ultimately self-defeating, such as a lack of effort, cheating, and procrastination, are often an attempt to protect a student's sense of self-worth.
- Portray effort as investment rather than a risk and skill development as an incremental and task-specific process that takes time for everyone who is learning new things.
- Try the process of attribution retraining, which involves modeling and practice exercises. The goals are to help discouraged students to
  1. focus on the tasks rather than on becoming distracted by fear of failure;
  2. respond to frustration by reviewing steps to find mistakes or figuring out new ways of handling a problem rather than giving up; and
  3. attribute their failures to insufficient effort, lack of information, or reliance on ineffective strategies rather than to lack of ability.

Learning Styles

Every one of us perceives and processes experiences in different predisposed ways. Our personal preferences for how we perceive, respond to, remember, and think about information, along with how we make decisions and solve problems can be described as our learning style. There is great diversity in learning styles in any single class; hence, knowing more about patterns of learning styles will provide you with helpful information in designing instruction and adjusting class environment.

Dimensions of Learning Style Preferences

Learning style theory and research begin with the fundamental insight that people, because of age, personal and sociocultural experience, individual psychology, and brain physiology, rely on perceptual, cognitive, and affective filters or lenses to orient their experience and understanding of the world. Learning style models are almost as diverse as are learners. A systematic classification developed by the educational psychologist Lynn Curry can help make sense out of our current understanding of human learning differences. This categorization looks at learning styles in terms of different and somewhat overlapping layers, like layers of an onion. (*Note:* References are made to specific learning style models, each of which is briefly explained in the section that follows.)

*Opposites
are not
Contradictory
but
Complementary.*

—Niels Bohr

Instructional and Environmental Preferences

These are the outermost layers of the onion, the most observable traits, which include sensory preferences for receiving and expressing what we learn. These traits are highlighted in the popular and generic visual/auditory/kinesthetic–tactile (V/A/K) learning style description, as well the Dunn and Dunn Learning Styles Inventory, which overlaps to a significant degree with other "layers."

Social Interaction Preferences

This level considers ways in which students in specific social contexts adopt certain strategies—for example, how strategies used by students vary by gender and maturity, and how they are responsive to the teaching context in which students finds themselves. Here we find the Grasha and Reichman Student Learning Interest Scales.

Information-Processing Preferences

To think is to differ.

—Clarence Darrow

These describe the middle layer in the onion and the processes by which information is obtained, sorted, stored, and used. Included here are ideas about the right brain/left brain, such as Hermann's Brain Dominance model; Kolb's approach to experiential learning, which has become a much used model; and to some measure, Soloman and Felder's Learning Styles Preferences. Others we might include here Howard Gardner's Theory of Multiple Intelligences, though it also serves as an emerging theory of intelligence and is discussed later in this chapter.

Personality Preferences

Here we are at the innermost layer of the onion, the level at which our deepest personality traits shape the orientations we take toward the world. These personality factors rate individuals along tendencies in their attitudes toward engaging the world, which includes not only how they respond to experience but also choose to express themselves. Myers and Briggs's (a typological approach to personality) well-known inventory is found at this level.

Learning Style Models

Simple models and techniques work better. There are numerous models to consider, and if one can call up information quickly and use it to enhance the learning immediately, then it is more worthwhile. You have a hundred things to think about every minute you are with your students. You should be able to act quickly and make connections with the students in as effective a manner as possible. With detailed styles surveys and indicators that take up pages and pages or even books, there is too much to remember or think about. Below are short descriptions of several models that we have found valuable. As you study them, though distinct in some ways, you should easily be able to detect their correspondences as suggested by the "onion" categorization.

V/A/K

This is the most common and simple characterization of learning styles that addresses the methods people prefer for receiving information and how they express what they have learned. Its history lies in neurolinguistic programming. There are three main modalities for learning: visual, auditory, and kinesthetic/tactile. You'll recognize that these modalities are actually senses, so there are really five. Taste and smell are not used to a high degree in learning settings, though they might prove useful when we have more research on their influences on learning. You probably already have an appreciation of how these modalities are involved in learning. Just think of your own educational experiences and learning preferences. Imagine you are being taught for the first time how to change a tire. Some of you probably do well having the process described to you (auditory). Others, however, may prefer sitting alone with a written explanation and reading it. Still others might need to see things to get them and prefer visuals and other graphic representations, or might just need to watch someone else do it first. Again, some of you might just want to roll up your sleeves and do it yourself with a bit of coaching. This is a bit of a simplification. For with just about everyone, each of these methods interacts and supports one another to different degrees. Still, most people rely on one or two more than others. So when you are thinking about students and designing learning plans, it will be helpful to know about and take into account their modality strengths.

Human beings start out as butterflies and end up in cocoons.

—Anonymous

Kolb's Learning Style Inventory

Kolb classifies students as having a preference for concrete experience, abstract conceptualization, active experimentation, or reflective observation. He maps out four quadrants that indicate how people take in and then internalize information and shows how they can serve as stages of holistic learning.

The four quadrants' descriptors are:

1. Concrete Experience (CE), which has to do with feeling.

2. Reflective Observation (RO), which has to do with watching.

3. Abstract Conceptualization (AC), which has to do with thinking.

4. Active Experimentation (AE), which has to do with doing.

He goes further, to combine quadrants on a model described as Diverging (CE/RO), Assimilating (AC/RO), Converging (AC/AE), and Accommodating (CE/AE).

Intelligence is knowing what to do when you don't know what to do.

—Art Costa

This conceptual model is a simple one, but one that can run very deep. It is the kind of model that works well.

4-Mat

Bernice McCarthy developed the 4-Mat model. It consists of the following four components:

Type 1: Innovative Learners are primarily interested in personal meaning. They need to have reasons for learning—ideally, reasons that connect new information with personal experience and establish that information's usefulness in daily life.

Type 2: Analytic Learners are primarily interested in acquiring facts in order to deepen their understanding of concepts and processes. They are capable of learning effectively from lectures, and they enjoy independent research, analysis of data, and hearing what "the experts" have to say.

Type 3: Common Sense Learners are primarily interested in how things work; they want to "get in and try it." Concrete, experiential learning activities work best for them—using manipulatives, hands-on tasks, kinesthetic experience, etc.

Type 4: Dynamic Learners are primarily interested in self-directed discovery. They rely heavily on their own intuition, and seek to teach both themselves and others. Any type of independent study is effective for these learners. They also enjoy simulations, role-play, and games.

Traditionally, instructional techniques commonly used in public schools best address the needs of the Type 2 Analytic Learner, with heavy emphasis on linear sequential processing of information.

Dunn and Dunn

Dunn and Dunn identify five dimensions that mark various preferences:

- *Environmental:* regarding sound, light, temperature, and class design
- *Emotional:* addressing motivation, persistence, responsibility, and structure
- *Sociological:* for private, pair, peer, team, adult, or varied learning relations
- *Physical:* related to perception, intake, time, and mobility
- *Psychological:* based on analytic mode and brain-hemisphere dominance

Myers–Briggs

The popular Myers–Briggs Type Indicator categorizes people as extraverts/introverts, sensing/intuitive, thinking/feeling, and judging/perceiving. This model anchors our preferences in our very makeup according to their preferences on scales derived from Carl Jung's theory of psychological types. It is used in many settings, both educational and corporate.

Index of Learning Styles

The Index of Learning Styles is an online instrument used to assess preferences on four dimensions (active/reflective, sensing/intuitive, visual/verbal, and sequential/global) of a learning style model formulated by Richard M. Felder and Linda K. Silverman. Richard M. Felder and Barbara A. Soloman of North Carolina State University developed the instrument.

Hermann Brain Dominance

The Herrmann Four Quadrant Whole Brain Model is the only instrument that quantifies a person's preference for thinking in four different modes based on the task-specialized functioning of the physical brain.

Classroom Implications and Applications

The insights provided by the various learning style models explained here suggest a number of perspectives for designing learning opportunities that respond effectively to the diversity of learning characteristics exhibited by today's students. No one model may suit your purposes, your teaching styles, or the needs of your learners. Even where you find some congruence and agreement, you still need to figure out how to use these sometimes complex models in your classrooms. You may feel that this is too much of a task given the demands on your time and the need to cover subject matter. But addressing learner differences is important for students' success. Here are some basic considerations and strategies you can use to better address them.

A Simple Place to Being–Awareness of Teacher/Learner Mismatch

Too often our focus as educators is on teaching content and not the processes of learning. Despite our best intentions, we wear blinders that prevent us from noticing the variations in how our students learn. We either do not think about how they learn or, more commonly, assume that others learn like we do. Consequently, we may see variations in learning patterns as deficiencies rather than as natural differences. However, your students will possibly struggle to be successful when limited to activities that are not compatible with what they bring into the learning situation. One learning style is neither preferable nor inferior to another; it is simply different, with different characteristic strengths and weaknesses. A goal of instruction, then, should be to equip students with the skills associated with every learning style category, regardless

> We don't have to make human beings smart. They are born smart. All we have to do is stop doing things that make them stupid.
>
> —John Holt

of the students' personal preferences, since they will need all of those skills to function effectively as learners as well as professionals.

Some Practical Strategies

Though there are some educators who do not think much about learner differences, it is likely that you are among those who do appreciate student differences and are concerned about how they can impact learning. Use a survey to determine learning styles. Your students will benefit, especially if they understand the results. You will be better equipped to design activities that engage your students.

Among those that offer the clearest set of guidelines are Kolb's Experiential Learning Cycles and V/A/K. We encourage you to study these further, for they provide effective frameworks that with practice can make significant improvements in learning outcomes.

Variety—The Spice of Teaching and Learning

> *Many Children struggle in schools . . . because the way they are being taught is incompatible with the way they learn.*
>
> —Peter Senge

If you are feeling pressed for time, and are not ready to use any particular model, we encourage you to entertain one simple idea: *introduce variety into what you do.* As all these models tell us, it is likely that among the students sitting in your classroom, there are or will be those comfortable with theories and abstractions; others who feel much more at home with facts and observable phenomena; some who prefer active learning, and others who lean toward introspection; and some who prefer visual presentation of information, and others who prefer verbal explanations. Obviously, there are many approaches that you could use in designing learning environments that respond more effectively to the needs of students. We suggest starting slowly and systematically, by introducing multiple ways of presenting information and activities to engage diverse students according to their learning styles. By doing so you will create rich learning environments and achieve greater congruence between teaching styles and learning styles that better meet the needs of those who sit in your classroom.

A Final Note: Gender Differences

There have been numerous studies on gender differences in learning. A good number of them indicate that there are differences between how women and how men learn. As an example, boys tend to volunteer to answer questions more often than girls. However, it seems that the actual differences are not as much about gender as about confidence, interest, and social factors.

You do not need to be up on all this research to make a difference in how your students learn. The most important thing is to be aware of your own beliefs about gender differences. Perceptions about individual capabilities influence how you respond to and treat women and men. If you believe or perceive that men are better at math and science, for instance, then you will expect more of men and conversely expect less of women. If you expect women to be more capable in the humanities, they will perform better than men do. These expectations affect performance, be it at a higher level or lower one.

The social belief that there are differences in capabilities allows this perception to continue. In reality, when provided the same opportunities and expectations, men and women can perform well in both the sciences and humanities. Your job then is to hold high expectations for every student entering your class.

Intelligence

Study and speculation about the nature of human intelligence goes back many centuries. The earliest modern approach goes back to Franz Gall, who invented phrenology in the early 1800s. Phrenology is the study of an individual's bumps on the skull, which supposedly reveal character traits and mental abilities. At its height, there were dozens of phrenological societies in the United States and in Great Britain, where it was seriously proposed that members of Parliament be chosen by the shape of their skulls. Some phrenologists even molded children's heads to accentuate good qualities and minimize bad ones. We clearly have come a long way since the days of Franz Gall, and modern psychology has formalized the study of intelligence over the past 100 years. How to define and measure intelligence, however, is still a matter of debate, and ideas continue to change. In this regard, the issue is not unlike other areas of psychological and educational research and theory we have presented, including the preceding discussion about learning style differences.

At the same time, this issue is much more contentious than just about any other area of research. In examining differences between people, theories about intelligence not only seek to describe and measure these differences but also make highly sensitive judgments about them to decide who is smart and who is not. Our notions about intelligence can powerfully influence our self-concepts and beliefs about the abilities and potential of others. Therefore, it is important for you to keep an open mind on this matter. Such a perspective can help you move beyond preferred viewpoints based on older, yet debatable, notions that have melded with possible personal biases and permit you to consider alternative perspectives, particularly those supported by the most recent research and thinking.

Classical Views of Intelligence

In the history of modern thinking about intelligence, there have been many ideas about what intelligence is and how to measure it.

> Most learning disabilities are actually teaching disabilities on the part of the school.
>
> —Retired Teacher

The most influential and commonly understood approach throughout most of the past century is the notion of IQ (intelligence quotient) tests. First developed by the French psychologist Alfred Binet, this measure took a pragmatic approach, choosing a series of 30 short tasks related to everyday problems of life. It was later modified for use in this country by Lewis Thurman of Stanford University and became the Stanford–Binet test. In this revision, IQ first appeared as a score to quantify intellectual functioning so people could be compared. To arrive at an IQ score, Thurman used a formula expressing the relation between an individual's mental and chronological ages. By convention, overall intelligence test scores are usually converted to a scale with 100 as the average and which places approximately 95 percent of the population between 70 and 130.

Individuals rarely perform equally well on all the different aptitudes, or subfactors, such as memory, verbal comprehension, and number facility, included in the traditional IQ test. One person may do better on verbal than on spatial items, for example, while another may show the opposite pattern. Some theorists, therefore, developed alternative approaches, which emphasized the importance of a general factor that can be extracted from a diversity of tasks given as indicators of intellectual ability. One common view today is something like a hierarchy of factors with the general factor at the apex. But there is no full agreement on what this general factor actually means. It has been described as a mere statistical pattern, a kind of nebulous mental energy, a generalized abstract reasoning ability, or an index of how fast a person's brain works.

There have been many disputes over both the concept of IQ and other measures of intelligence that focus on subsets of mental abilities, and there are a number of alternative approaches that propose a general capacity of intelligence. There are also some theorists who are critical of the entire testing approach. These critics do not dispute the fact that tests can predict certain forms of achievement—especially school achievement. They argue, however, that to base a concept of intelligence on test scores alone is to ignore many important aspects of mental ability. Some of those aspects are emphasized in other approaches, which are reviewed below.

I believe babies are born as innovative personalities. . . . But our social processes work to stamp out exploration and questioning.

—Jay Forrester

Emerging Views of Intelligence

Over time, theorists have sought to break intelligence down into subfactors that remain components of one overarching mental capacity. They also propose distinctly different kinds of intelligences, each with its own attributes and psychological reality. We briefly discuss four notable contemporary efforts: Gardner's Theory of Multiple Intelligences, Sternberg's Successful Intelligence, Perkins's Reflective Intelligence, and Resnick's Effort-Based Intelligence.

Gardner's Theory of Multiple Intelligences

Howard Gardner of Harvard University is the most well known theorist to argue that intelligence is not a single attribute but comes in different expressions. The most widely cited version of Gardner's concept of multiple intelligences is that there are seven different types of intelligence, although he has adjusted this number and suggested several more intelligences. His primary seven intelligences are:

1. Verbal (language and reasoning)
2. Mathematical (facility with numbers and formal logic)
3. Musical (not only for musicians, but also for the mechanic who can diagnose sounds)
4. Spatial (ability to navigate in unfamiliar territory, like a new city)
5. Bodily/kinesthetic (movement such as dance and manual skills)
6. Interpersonal (social skills)
7. Intrapersonal (self-understanding) functioning

The additional intelligences proposed by Gardner are

- Naturalistic (think of zoologists and skilled survivalists)
- Existential (the concern with ultimate philosophical issues)
- Spiritual (recognition of and sensitivity to spiritual outlooks and values)

Gardner argues that these different intelligences are independent of one another. The first three are somewhat similar to components of intelligence identified by earlier approaches, whereas the others are more novel. He believes these develop differently in different people because of heredity, environment, and training and that all need to be considered to provide a truly global assessment of intelligence.

Others have also proposed multiple forms of intelligence. What is different about Gardner's work is that he does not attempt to support his approach purely through statistical analyses of intelligence test data. He argues that tests address only linguistic and logical plus some aspects of spatial intelligence and that other forms have been entirely ignored. He asserts that conceptions of intelligence should be informed by work with both children and adults and should specifically include studies of gifted individuals (Mozart could write music before he could even read, suggesting distinct brain systems), people who have suffered brain damage (which may sometimes impair one intellectual skill while other skills remain at least partially intact), and individuals from diverse cultures. He proposes including distinct developmental patterns among basic competencies (spoken language fully develops effortlessly in normal people, while few progress to an understanding of higher mathematics even with formal schooling).

> "I cured the patient but he died" is as logical as saying "I taught the pupil, but she did not learn."
>
> —Christopher Bowring-Carr and John Burnham West

In navigating our lives, it is our fears and envies, our rages and depressions, our worries and anxieties that steer us day to day. Even the most academically brilliant among us are vulnerable to being undone by unruly emotions. . . . We need to place as much importance on teaching . . . the essential skills of Emotional Intelligence as we do on more traditional measures like IQ and GPA.

—Daniel Goleman

Gardner's arguments have attracted considerable interest. His thinking seeks to explain a broad range of individual differences in mental performance, along with the kind of "smarts" that help people live more productive and fulfilling lives. It also has an intuitive appeal that has been embraced by many teachers, given their everyday observations of learners. Finally, Gardner's theory suggests that cultural and racial differences are the result of some abilities being highlighted and valued over others, providing an "anti-theory" to unitary theories of intelligence, which have been used by some to justify the intellectual superiority of some racial groups.

Still, this theory is not without its critics. There are those who wonder at the changing number and abstract character of some of these intelligences and question whether these aptitudes can really be characterized as "intelligences" or whether they are just abilities, and what the differences really might be. In addition, many do not accept Gardner's modular notion that different intelligences emanate from different parts of the brain and are independent of each other. (Although neuroscience may prove that indeed different sections of the brain account for different types of processing.) Moreover, though the rationale for this theory is based on several independent indicators, the validity of performance tests in these new domains has yet to be conclusively demonstrated according to some of the standards used to support other theories.

Sternberg's Successful Intelligence

Robert Sternberg, noted Yale psychologist and former president of the American Psychological Association, also believes that theories of a single mental ability fail to account for the complexity of the human mind. Like Gardner, he proposes multiple dimensions to intelligence, though he associates them with different expressions of personal competency rather than distinct brain functions, as Gardner suggests.

His three-part theory identifies:

1. Analytical intelligence
2. Creative intelligence
3. Practical intelligence

Only analytical intelligence is measured to a significant extent by mainstream tests. Sternberg is concerned with what can predict success in the real world and helping individuals develop components of intelligence needed to perform well, rather than trying to identify individual differences among people. He suggests a need for personal balance between analytic intelligence and creative intelligence and especially practical intelligence, which he believes best translates to real-life success.

Analytic abilities include metacognitive skills and effective knowledge acquisition. Analytic problems tend to be clearly defined, with all the information needed to solve them coming from life experiences. They call for a single right answer that can be reached by only one method and are removed from ordinary experience with little or no intrinsic interest (the kind of learning that behaviorist/cognitivist instruction favors). Practical and creative capacities involve insight, synthesis, and the ability to deal with novel situations as well as to adapt to everyday problems. The challenges calling for these kinds of intelligences tend to be poorly defined and require information seeking and the application of existing knowledge, have several acceptable solutions, are embedded in personal experiences, and call for personal motivation and involvement. (These are the kind of problems addressed effectively by constructivist/humanistic teaching designs.)

Sternberg believes that intelligence is culturally sensitive, and a person considered intelligent in one culture may be seen as unintelligent in another. He suggests that his theory can explain why people defined as intelligent by standard tests often fail in their everyday lives. He sees this as being due to factors that can include a lack of motivation, impulse control, and perseverance; a fear of failure; procrastination; an inability to delay gratification; and too little or too much self-confidence. See Emotional Intelligence below.

Chapter 8

Perkins's Reflective Intelligence

David Perkins of the Harvard Graduate School of Education also proposes that there are three kinds of intelligence:

1. *Neural intelligence:* linked to the fixed efficiency of one's neurological system and what is measured by IQ tests.

2. *Experiential intelligence:* one's accumulated knowledge and experience in different areas.

3. *Reflective intelligence:* one's broad-based strategies for attacking problems, for learning, and for approaching intellectually challenging tasks. This includes general metacognitive abilities plus attitudes that support persistence, imagination, self-monitoring, and self-management.

Perkins contends that the three of these forms of intellect work together. He gives most of his attention to reflective intelligence, because he thinks that it contributes most directly to intelligent behavior that leads to personal success in the world. He refers to it as "fancy thinking," versus "plain thinking." In this regard, he parallels Sternberg's interest in what can help people gain control over and improve their lives.

Research shows that all three expressions of intelligence can change. Today there is general agreement that brain systems that determine neural intelligence have a "use it or lose it" characteristic. They are strengthened by stimulation and can be maintained, and indeed increased, by use. Experiential intelligence grows through years of accumulating knowledge in both informal and formal learning environments. Such knowledge and experience can lead to a high level of expertise in one or more fields, and can be increased by experience in "rich" learning environments. However, it is reflective intelligence that is the most amenable to change and the best target for educational intervention. The neural component of intelligence does not change very much with instruction or practice, although there are nutritional and maturational effects. Experiential intelligence in a particular area takes years to build. However, reflective intelligence, which acts like a control system that helps to make effective use of neural intelligence and experiential intelligence, can be increased through practice. A person can learn mental management strategies and develop what Perkins calls the proper "mindware" (metacognitive skills) in rather short periods of time, months not years, to make more effective use of neural intelligence and experiential intelligence.

In this model, mere practice is not reflective process. There is reason to believe that practice alone is not enough and that it can actually reinforce old and incorrect thinking habits rather than change or improve them. In contrast, activities in which people think about their thinking can lead to the development of new mind habits: patterning, repatterning, and depatterning. *Patterning* means organizing thought, and *repatterning* is adopting new cognitive strategies, while *depatterning* is opening one to new possibilities. Together, these three processes help people adapt mindware to their own needs or even invent their own mindware, needed to develop better thinking. In this regard, better thinking means not just more efficient, faster thinking, which practice alone would yield, but fundamentally reorganized thinking, which, according to Perkins, requires direct attention to mindware. Perkins does have ideas about how to nurture these thinking skills.

Educators ask, "How do I develop mindware in students?" Perkins proposes that what is needed and what research shows is called for, is the integration of the teaching of thinking in a deep and far-reaching way with specific subject matter instruction. Each discipline has its distinctive ways of explaining and validating ideas. For example, mathematics highlights formal deductive proof, the sciences emphasize empirical evidence from experiments, and history depends on evidence from primary sources. Therefore, teaching intelligent behavior calls for teaching the habits of mind that represent the kind of thinking strategies appropriate for a particular field of study. Such strategies need to be embedded in these courses along with the facts and knowledge of each discipline.

Socrates's, injunction "Know thyself" speaks to this keystone of Emotional Intelligence: awareness of one's own feelings as they occur.

Daniel Goleman

Chapter 15

Resnick's Effort-Based Intelligence

Lauren Resnick and her colleagues at the University of Pittsburgh's Learning Research and Development Center are also challenging the enduring and widely accepted idea that intellectual ability is fixed by nature. They have been studying what happens to students who are immersed in demanding, long-term intellectual environments. What they have discovered parallels Perkins's notions that important dimensions of intelligence are mutable and teachable. Resnick calls this kind of intelligence "intelligence-in-practice," or effort-based intelligence.

In this conceptualization, intelligence is the habit of persistently doing the following:

- Understanding things and varying strategies until a workable solution is found

- Knowing what one does and does not know

- Seeking information and organizing that information so it makes sense and can be remembered

- Practicing habits of mind (much like Perkins's reflective intelligence)

With the support of studies in educational and cognitive psychology, Resnick points out that what people believe about the nature of talent and intelligence—about what accounts for success and failure—is closely related to the amount and kind of effort they put forth in situations of learning or problem-solving. If people believe that intellectual ability is fixed, then effort has little role in success; they develop a "you either have it or you don't" attitude. This attitude becomes a barrier to trying and learning new things. However, if people believe that talent and intellect grow and can be developed incrementally, they tend to invest energy to learn something new or to increase their understanding and mastery. But it is not just brute effort that distinguishes these learners from people who think of intelligence as a fixed commodity. When these thinkers encounter difficulties, they are likely to apply metacognitive skills (Perkins's reflective intelligence), seek opportunities to sharpen their skills and knowledge, and see the difficulty and any occasional setbacks as part of a learning challenge rather than as evidence that they lack intelligence. These characteristics can move such learners on a continuously upward trajectory of increased talent, intelligent behavior, and success.

> *In order for the brain to Comprehend the heart must first listen.*
>
> —David Perkins

Emotional Intelligence

Emotion has long held a central place in the field of psychology and therapy, but its place in the study of intelligence and educational and personal success is relatively new. There are several prominent approaches to the concept of emotional intelligence (EI). The one that

An ordinary degree of understanding is routinely missing in many, if not most students. It is reasonable to expect a college student to be able to apply in a new context . . . that which she just demonstrated mastery [of] in her class. If when the circumstances of testing are slightly altered, the sought-after competence can no longer be documented, then understanding—in any reasonable sense of the term—has simply not been achieved.

—The Unschooled Mind

has introduced this idea to the popular culture and most educators has been Daniel Goleman.

As used by Goleman, the term *emotional intelligence* encompasses five characteristics and abilities:

- *Self-awareness:* understanding and discriminating between emotions and recognizing them as they occur
- *Mood management:* emotionally responding in appropriate ways to a particular situation.
- *Self-motivation:* "gathering up" feelings and being able to move toward a goal, despite possible negative emotions or self-doubt or inertia
- *Empathy:* recognizing and respecting feelings in others
- *Managing relationships:* being able to effectively handle interpersonal interactions, conflict resolution, and negotiations

Research on the brain and learning suggests that emotional health and intelligence are fundamental to effective learning and are a critical element for a student's success in school. According to Goleman, key traits of EI are confidence, curiosity, intentionality, self-control, relatedness, a capacity to communicate, and an ability to cooperate.

The idea of emotional intelligence has inspired research and curriculum development. Researchers have concluded that people who manage their own feelings well and deal effectively with others are more likely to live contentedly. Plus, happy people are more apt to retain information and do so more effectively than dissatisfied people. Emotional intelligence has proven to be a better predictor of academic and future success than traditional methods such as grade point average, IQ, and standardized test scores. Hence, there has been much interest in emotional intelligence on the part of corporations, universities, and schools nationwide.

Despite this broad interest, how to teach and train EI or whether there is much room in classroom schedules for EI is unknown. In early years, children need guidance and instruction. However, older students and adults are expected to bring emotional skills to their situations. As a society we have not offered a realistic understanding of EI through our schools, and yet EI is critical to our well-being. When you include an understanding of EI in your classes you will offer students another level of skill to master.

Classroom Implications and Applications

Though the issue of intelligence is a complex and controversial one, understanding your own views and then helping students understand theirs as well are important places to begin.

Teach *About* Intelligence

The debate over intelligence can be confusing. There are a number of essential questions, such as:

- "What makes people smart?"
- "What does it mean to be smart?"
- "How am I smart?"
- "Is intelligence fixed?"

Not one of these questions has an easy or agreed-upon answer. Both teachers and their students can easily become trapped in personal or incorrect beliefs about the nature of ability and aptitude. These beliefs make it hard to evoke effective academic effort from students and for them to want to even try. Although many allow that hard work can compensate for lower doses of innate intelligence, most also assume that aptitude largely determines what people can learn in school. There is some truth to this, but not the entire truth, as confirmed by converging research from educational psychology and cognitive science. The conclusion to be drawn is that there may be fixed aptitudes or hardwired genetics, but intelligence under a broader consideration is not absolute. People can learn how to make the *right* kind of effort and can develop metacognitive and other abilities or habits of mind that lead to better academic performance and overall life success.

The bottom line, then, is this—as educators we need to accept these possibilities ourselves, and then convey them to our students. Students may be discouraged by prior experiences and a sense of limitation—imposed by themselves and by others. These experiences hold them to low expectations and an unwillingness to break barriers erected by their acceptance of the judgment that inborn aptitude matters most and that they have not inherited enough of that capacity. By embracing the belief that intelligence can be developed, we can help our students liberate themselves from the stranglehold of beliefs that block both their academic and personal success.

Teach for Intelligence

In addition to shifting their beliefs, we can also begin to teach students the tools and attitudes they can use to improve how they learn. This includes encouraging persistent effort, and creating opportunities for students to prove to themselves they can do better. You may not see this as your job or may not think you have the time to do so. Yet few can argue that it is not a worthy and important endeavor, one that can make a significant difference in student motivation to learn and learning outcomes.

And it is not as hard as it may seem. Not only is intelligence not absolute; neither are people's beliefs about it. We know that students who, over an extended period of time, are treated *as if* they are intelligent, actually become so. If they are taught demanding content and are expected to explain and find connections (as well as memorize and repeat), they learn more and learn more quickly. They think of themselves as successful learners. They are able to bounce back in the face of short-term failures.

People respond to the situations in which they find themselves. This means that it is possible to help students develop learning-oriented goals and an incremental view of intelligence and thus set them on the upward spiral by which they can become smarter and deliver high-level academic achievement for everyone. We should not be afraid of academic rigor and challenging learning tasks. It is this rigor we need to put in place to give students—who are properly prepared—an opportunity to stretch and strengthen their mind "muscles." When we combine high expectations, rigorous content, and learner-centered instruction, we provide the means for every student to succeed.

CHAPTER WRAP-UP

There is currently a great deal of debate over much research and thinking regarding how the mind works and how people learn. By grounding this debate, as well as your personal views and teaching practices, in a deeper understanding of and appreciation for the enormous diversity and amount of ideas available, you can begin to improve the quality of your teaching.

You can also do much to improve the quality of your students' learning. Do not consider what is discussed here as some secret to be kept from your learners—begin to familiarize your students as you familiarize yourself with this knowledge. The more they know, the more they will enable their metacognitive abilities and be able to deal with the complexities and common frustrations associated with learning well. If they understand, just as you do, that many factors influence their ability to learn and that intelligence is not fixed, they may have greater patience and persistence as they strive to educate themselves. Our experience is that when students have an understanding of intelligence and learning styles and how they learn, they become more interested and engaged in the classes we teach. They seek out learning activities that match their needs and learn to manipulate their environment to include elements that enhance their own learning. Learning-to-learn skills are just as important as any specific subject matter.

Over time, research in the neurosciences, cognition, educational psychology, and other areas will certainly reveal more about how to select among different teaching methods and tools that can enhance our teaching style and help our students expand their own repertoire of learning styles. What is needed is a more purposeful and continuous dialogue between those who work in the classroom and those who work in the laboratory. Hopefully, as we move forward, what has been announced in the past in a piecemeal fashion in both professional journals and the popular press will become increasingly integrated. This will make it easier for educators (and their students) to become informed of and stay current with research in all areas of study with implications for teaching and training. With a better and more rigorous interface between learning discoveries and the practical world of education, there is no reason to think this won't happen. More and more educators at every level are striving to determine the most effective and efficient fashion in which to craft their instruction to better meet students needs.

Brain Matters: An Incomplete Glossary of Brain Terms

Knowing the following brain basics will not necessarily improve your teaching. However, if you wish to begin making better connections to neuroscience and how it may affect teaching, it would be valuable to recognize some of the organs and structures in the brain. What follows is not an extensive list. The 30 terms listed are what we consider to be the basics. In many of the definitions some information about how the term may relate to learning is included.

Amygdala: This almond-shaped complex, located in the limbic section of the brain, is a critical processor for the senses, mediating threat and fear. It plays a role in emotionally laden memories, an important key to long-term memory.

Axons: Long fibers that extend from neurons that carry output to other neurons. There is one axon for each neuron, and it can subdivide to connect with many dendrites. They are usually about a centimeter long and can be up to a meter long.

Brain stem: Links the lower brain to the middle brain and cerebral hemispheres. It is located at the top of the spinal cord and manages all the automatic/autonomic functions such as breathing, gland secretion, and heartbeat.

Broca's area: Located in the left frontal area of the cerebrum, this converts thoughts into sounds or words, and sends this message to the motor area. Impulses come from Wernicke's area (see below).

Cerebellum: Located next to the brain stem, it is cauliflower-shaped and in the past has been linked to balance, posture, coordination, and muscle movements. Current research also links it to cognition, novelty, and emotions. It is one home of procedural learning, reflexive learning, and conditioned responses.

Cerebral cortex: The outermost layer of the cerebrum. It is wrinkled, six layers deep, about 1/4 inch thick, and packed with neurons. *Cortex* is the Latin word for "bark" or "rind." A thinking part of the brain.

Cerebrum: The largest part of the brain, composed of the left and right hemispheres. It is composed of four lobes, temporal, occipital, parietal, and frontal.

Cingulate gyrus: Located in the midbrain, this mediates communication between the cortex and other midbrain structures. May help link emotions to thoughts.

Corpus callosum: This four-inch bundle of hundreds of millions of nerve cells connects the left and right hemispheres of the brain.

Dendrites: The strandlike fibers emanating from the neuron (see below). Much like spiderwebs, they are the receptor sites for axons (see above). Each cell has multiple dendrites. The more dendrites are developed around a topic (literally the more connections) the more likely it will be transported to long-term memory.

Frontal lobes: One of four main areas of the upper brain area, the cerebrum. Controls voluntary movement, verbal expression, problem solving, willpower, and planning.

Glial: One of two major types of brain cells. Glials, also known as interneurons, outnumber neurons 10 to 1. Glial carry nutrients, speed repair and may form their own communication network.

Hemispheres: The left and right cerebral sections connected by bundles of nerve fibers. Each hemisphere processes things differently, and early assumptions about hemisphericity are outdated. In general, the left hemisphere processes things more in parts and sequentially. The right hemisphere processes more holistically and less sequentially. Both sides of the brain are activated in learning.

Hippocampus: Located deep in the temporal lobe, this crescent-shaped organ is strongly involved in learning and memory. It mediates semantic (also called factual, taxon, linguistic, and explicit) and episodic (also known as spatial, event, and contextual) memory.

Hormone: A substance formed in some organs of the body and carried by a bodily fluid to another organ or tissue to serve a specific purpose. The pituitary gland controls the manufacture and release of hormones. The hypothalamus regulates the pituitary and the production of the hormone adrenaline (also known as epinephrine), which is released from the adrenal gland and travels to the liver, where it releases glucose for rapid energy. Abrupt increases in adrenaline levels caused by anger or fear can constrict the heart vessels, requiring the heart to pump with higher pressure. This is one reason to ensure that you have a pleasant classroom environment.

Hypothalamus: Located under the thalamus in the bottom center of the brain. The hypothalamus regulates certain metabolic processes and other autonomic activities. It links the nervous system to the endocrine system.

Limbic system: A group of connected structures in the midbrain area. It includes the hypothalamus, amygdala, thalamus, fornix, hippocampus, and cingulate gyrus. Term is now discounted with current brain research about emotions and the brain. Still useful from a metaphoric sense.

Medulla oblongata: Channels information between the cerebral hemispheres and the spinal cord. It controls respiration, circulation, wakefulness, breathing, and heart rate.

Myelin: A fatty white shield that coats and insulates axons. Myelin can help make neurons more efficient and facilitate electrical impulses to travel up to 12 times faster (up to 200 mph). This is like insulation on a wire; the more layers the faster the electrical impulses. Habits may be a result of myelinated axons.

Neuron: One of two types of brain cells. Made up of the cell body, an axon, and many, many dendrites. We have between 100 billion and 300 billion of these. Dendrites bring stimulation to a neuron. Neurons communicate to other neurons by firing a nerve impulse along an axon. Neurons process information from the senses electrochemically.

Neurotransmitters: The brain's more than 50 biochemical messengers. They act to stimulate neighboring neurons or to inhibit activation of the electrical impulse from the cell body down the axon. These are the chemicals of learning. *Acetylcholine,* partially involved in long-term memory formation, present in higher levels during rest and sleep (justifies reflection time). *Dopamine,* common in regulating emotional responses (moods or feelings). Plays a role in movement. *Endorphin,* a natural opiate similar to morphine, produced in the pituitary gland. Protects against excessive pain. *Glutamate,* amino acid found in every cell in the body, used as a "fast excitatory." *Noradrenaline,* primarily involved in our arousal; fight, flight, metabolic rate, blood pressure, emotions, and mood. *Serotonin,* controls switches that affect various emotional states. Most responsible for inducing relaxation, states of consciousness, mood (depression, euphoria, anxiety), and regulating sleep.

Occipital lobe: Located in the rear of the cerebrum in the upper brain. It processes our vision, an obviously important part of learning.

Parietal lobe: The top of the cerebrum. It deals with reception of sensory information from the body's opposite side. It plays a part in reading, writing, language, and calculation. Also holds some working memory.

Peptides: A class of hormones made of chains of amino acids. These proteins also serve as information messengers for states, moods, and thinking. They travel throughout the body. *Oxytocin* is a peptide sometimes known as the "commitment molecule." It is released during sex, pregnancy, childbirth, and lactation, and influences "unlearning" (how one unlearns something) and pair bonding (i.e., between mother and child).

Pons: A critical relay station for sensory information located at the top of the brain stem.

Prefrontal cortex: A region of the front part of the cortex. It holds data in working memory and coordinates the activities of the sensory regions in the service of higher reasoning.

Synapse: The junction communication point where neurons interact. When an axon of one neuron releases neurotransmitters to stimulate the dendrites of another cell, where the reaction occurs is a synapse. The adult human has trillions of synapses. This is where neurochemical learning takes place.

Temporal lobe: Located on the side of the cerebrum, near our ears, this an area believed to be responsible for learning, hearing, senses, listening, language, and memory storage.

Thalamus: Located in the limbic system, or middle of the brain, this is the key sensory relay station. It is also intimately involved in self-reward.

Wernicke's area: An area at the upper back edge of the temporal lobe that converts thoughts to language.

SPRINGBOARDS FOR FURTHER LEARNING

Neurobiology of the Brain and Educational
Psychology for Educators

Key Names

Marion Diamond	David Perkins
Howard Gardner	Lauren Resnick
Eric Jensen	Robert Sylwester
Gaea Leinhardt	Patricia Wolf

Key Terms

downshifting	meaning
emotion	memory
hemispheric dominance	triune brain

Student Attention and Motivation

Key Names

Jere Brophy   Mark Lepper
Abraham Maslow

Key Terms

attention   intrinsic motivation
extrinsic motivation   perception

Student Learning Styles

Key Names

R. Dunn and K. Dunn   David Kolb
Richard Felder   Bernice McCarthy
A. Gregoric   Myers-Briggs
N. Hermann

Key Terms

learner differences   learning styles inventory
learning styles

Emerging Concepts Intelligence

Key Names

Art Costa   David Perkins
Marian Diamond   Laura Resnick
Howard Gardner   Art Scheibel
Daniel Goleman   Robert Sternberg

Key Terms

effort-based intelligence   multiple intelligences
emotional intelligence   practical intelligence
habits of mind

Unit 2
The Art of Teaching— Translating Theory into Skillful Practice

> *Science may tell us what learning is, and what influences it, but to apply this knowledge effectively is nothing if not an art.*
>
> —James Zull

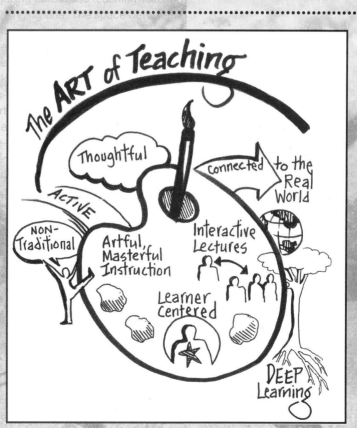

125

In Unit 1 we provided an overview of a wide array of theories, research findings, philosophical considerations, and scholarly thought that represent important landmarks and guideposts in the teaching/learning landscape of contemporary education. This is a large territory, and our tour of differing perspectives was relatively brief. However, this survey serves as a solid foundation for you who are first developing your teaching practice, as well as providing a coherent framework for more experienced teachers ready to reconsider and improve what you already do in your classrooms. Still, understanding your personal teaching philosophy along with learning research and theory and their implications for instruction is only the first step in enhancing your practice. The "science of learning" can only tell you *what* to do and *why* and, to some degree, the *how* and *when* of teaching. There are no scientific formulae or rules that can tell you the best ways to weave these elements together in the moment-to-moment and ever-changing dynamics of any particular course or class session. This skillful practice calls for your understanding of the "art of teaching."

Teaching—How Much Science and How Much Art?

If you were to ask the question "Is teaching primarily a science or is it essentially an art?" the answer would be, "Well, it all depends." This may seem a flippant response or a feeble attempt to avoid answering a difficult question. But it really isn't. The answer *does* depend on a number of factors, most especially where you stand as a teacher.

New instructors will look frequently to the science of learning and teaching—its theories, prescriptions, and procedures—to help them navigate the unknown terrain between themselves and their learners.

On the other hand, experienced instructors believe that no matter how much theory and research we now know and regardless of what advances may come in the future, ultimately teaching is and will always be an art. When gazing across the teaching/learning landscape, these educators see it as ever-changing. The space between a teacher and learners is like the shifting sands at the ocean shore, shaped by unpredictable forces of wind and wave—we may walk the same beach every day but we will never walk the same path twice. For these experienced instructors, teaching will forever be as much art as it is science, if not more so, calling for the qualities that are the hallmarks of any art—creativity, innovation, and imagination.

Consider music. No doubt it is an art. It is a craft that in its highest form demands and draws on the unique, creative expression of each person who participates in it, whether an instrumentalist, vocalist, or composer. We can all likely agree that although some people may possess natural ability, such inborn talent cannot alone yield a skilled performance. The mastery of this discipline also requires the study of the theories and principles that underlie it and, of course, a great deal of practice. For the novice, the path to mastery begins with a little of the art and a lot of the science and the routine of regular drills. Only when an individual becomes knowledgeable about basic theory and proficient in the fundamental techniques, does he or she find the freedom to give creative and personal expression to what is ultimately an infinite number of combinations of only a few basic elements (the 12 notes of the Western musical scale, for instance).

If a doctor, lawyer, or dentist had 40 people in his office at one time, all of whom had different needs, and some of whom didn't want to be there and were causing trouble, and the doctor, lawyer, or dentist, without assistance, had to treat them all with professional excellence for nine months, then he might have some conception of the classroom teacher's job.

—Donald D. Quinn

The craft of teaching is much the same. Each time you walk into a class, your work calls for the creative and somewhat unpredictable composition of the many distinct components that comprise the teaching/ learning transaction—content, context, people and processes—all orchestrated into some kind of unified and satisfactory whole. This challenge remains no matter what are the particular circumstances or settings of the courses you teach or how much experience you have under your belt. You could faithfully apply behavioral conditioning techniques or religiously follow the steps of mastery learning, relentlessly use computers and information technology and develop all kinds of theories to explain how people think and learn, but then what? Nothing can be ensured to work in the same way with the same results every time. Every class will always be a mix of many minds (including your own) in many moods with many manners of expression interacting in ways that can change not just from day to day but also from moment to moment.

And even if we could eventually come to a perfect and complete knowledge of human biology and psychology, and even if such knowledge could help you predict and control every aspect of human behavior and learning in any particular setting, would you really want to reduce teaching and learning to a rigid routine and drab formula that left no space for freedom of expression and nothing to your imagination and creativity or that of your students? Students are not automatons, and neither are you. Even in the most routine situations, all of us are continually driven to seek new experiences and self-fulfilling methods of personal expression.

The bottom line is this: Teaching is both **a science** and an art—and always will be. You will always be faced with unique individuals and circumstances in every course and classroom experience. Good teaching will always rely on research-based theory and principles that go hand in hand with your personal judgments and decisions that are based on factors that dynamically and unpredictably unfold during a term and even the duration of a single class meeting. As you navigate that mysterious terrain that lies between you and your learners, theories and prescriptive methods can act only as signposts to guide your judgments. Ultimately, these judgments will still call for the exercise of imagination and innovation and a good measure of intuition and, at times, even inspiration.

Becoming a More Artful Educator— The Question of Style

Associated with the notion of teaching as an art is the question of style. Just as students have distinct learning styles, teachers in the practice of their craft have unique teaching styles. And just as with learning styles, there is no clear agreement on the common elements that comprise an individual teaching style.

A good teacher is better than a spectacular teacher. Otherwise the teacher outshines the teaching.

—William Glasser

Anthony Grasha was an educator and scholar who wrote extensively about teaching and learning styles. He characterized these styles in terms of general classroom behaviors, the qualities of popular instructors, the roles teachers play (facilitator, counselor, etc.), models of teaching (teacher-centered or learner-centered), and even the use of formal psychological personality theories to describe teacher dispositions. Among these different perspectives, Grasha concluded, there are key similarities that reflect common qualities of good teachers from across all fields of study and professions. These largely include the personal qualities and behavioral preferences that are often the indicators others—such as students, peers, and administrators—use to judge an instructor's effectiveness. How these characteristics come together comprises one's teaching style.

Before you continue reading, take a moment to reflect on your own education. You have had scores of teachers in your lifetime. You probably remember only a few, those who were the best and those

Reflection

Before you continue reading, take a moment to reflect on your own education. You have had scores of teachers in your lifetime. You probably remember only a few, those who were the best and those who were the worst. Who were these teachers you had? What characteristics separated the bad or mediocre from the outstanding, memorable ones? This is a simple exercise, but a very valuable one. If you desire to become a better teacher, these are very important questions. See the companion Field Guide for a worksheet with a list of questions for your consideration.

Refer to Field Guide

Doing It with "Style"—The Qualities of the Best Teachers

So what are the characteristics of an effective teaching style? Descriptions of good teachers have been written in books and can be readily found on various Web sites, including those of a large number of colleges. Some of these are based on overviews of educational research, while others are original work derived from student surveys conducted at these schools themselves. There is a great deal of consistency across these findings, and a number of themes have emerged. Most of these studies make the same point—what students consider to be the qualities of good teacher have little to do with training or with prescriptive methods and have a lot to do with *you*—the person and presence you bring into your classroom each day. What some have spent years discovering, studying, and writing about, you and your students already know—the best teachers:

1. are knowledgeable about their subject matter,
2. can present what they know in an organized and engaging manner and, most importantly,
3. care about their discipline and their students.

In what may as well be starkly smug satisfaction, an amazing 94% (of college instructors) rate themselves as above average teachers. . . .

—K. Patricia Cross

129

Good Teachers Are Subject-Matter Authorities and Are Prepared to Teach

- **Knowledgeable:** They know their subjects well. They possess basic factual knowledge as well as grasp the overarching concepts, principles, and other key ideas that lie at the core of their discipline and which give structure to and help students make sense of the material.

- **Prepared:** They come to class organized and ready to teach. This demonstrates not only their subject-matter authority but also their dedication and commitment to teaching.

Good Teachers Possess Effective Communication and Teaching Skills

- **Enthusiastic:** They are excited about the subject they teach and present the material in an engaging manner. They challenge students at an appropriate level to keep learning interesting.

- **Clear:** They establish for their students the relevance of the content to current issues and weave together ideas to create meaningful patterns that reveal the relationships of ideas. They also effectively communicate these connections and help students make their own.

- **Focused on Learning:** They provide frequent and specific feedback. Assessment is used not just to grade students (formative) but to help them learn, communicate to them their progress, and evaluate the effectiveness of instruction (summative).

- **Humorous:** They have a sense of humor. This humor is both purposeful and respectful of students.

- **Humble:** They can be self-effacing at times. They laugh at themselves, demonstrating that there are times to be serious and other times not to. They are willing to admit mistakes.

- **Innovative and Creative:** They use a variety of ways to present and represent information that include different learning preferences.

Entertain great hopes.

—Robert Frost

Good Teachers Are Attentive to Teacher–Student Relationships

- **Fair:** They treat students equally, and their expectations and standards are firm and clear. They are also sensitive to individual differences and capabilities.

- **Caring and Personal:** They establish rapport with students and create a sense of community in the classroom. They are friendly, approachable, and accessible.

- **Respectful:** They honor and appreciate individual differences, which are seen as a source of divergent ideas rather than as problems or sources of potential conflict. They accept the mistakes students make as a natural part of the learning process.

- **Have High Expectations:** They possess a positive attitude and convey their confidence in their students' ability to learn even as they challenge their long-standing ideas and values.

> Interestingly, in numerous workshops with educators at all levels that I have conducted, informal surveys show that the most important aspects of effective teachers have little to do with subject-matter expertise. Responding to the following prompt—"What was the most important characteristic of your memorable/favorite teacher(s)"—hundreds of instructors and administrators have responded with answers other than brilliance in the subject being taught.
>
> Responses have been 30:1 about personal characteristics such as: cared about me, respected me, they were enthusiastic about the subject, held me to a high standard, and had a sense of humor. The responses about expertise were secondary: loved their subject, knew a lot about what was being taught, and could answer even the most difficult questions about the topic.
>
> With this in mind, as you think about your practice make sure to consider your personal characteristics and your subject knowledge. Your approach and persona will have as much impact as your knowledge and methods.

From Science to Art—From a Teacher-Centered to a Learner-Centered Approach

Bringing together the "soft" skills of the creative practice of one's craft with the "hard" science of learning will come more easily to some than to others. This is true whether you are new to teaching and trying to develop a basic repertoire of methods and techniques or are someone who has many years of experience under your belt and now wishes to modify and add to your teaching tool kit. In general, your professional development will be easier if new concepts and practices closely align

131

with your present teaching philosophy and natural teaching style. Where this natural fit is absent, you may experience some confusion and difficulty as you first move into unknown territory. Making the shift from where you are now to a new way of thinking and doing things may be easier when looked at in terms of transitioning from a teacher-centered to a learner-centered approach. Discussions about how to transition from teacher-centered to learner-centered teaching environments and practices are at the heart of many efforts to improve instruction and learning outcomes. Unfortunately, the meaning of the concept of learner-centered teaching is frequently assumed but not always understood.

The mediocre teacher tells. The good teacher explains. The superior teacher demonstrates. The great teacher inspires.

—William Arthur Ward

What exactly does *learner-centered* mean? Traditional classrooms largely influenced by behaviorist, and to a lesser degree cognitivist, ideas have primarily viewed students as vessels to be filled with knowledge. Because this has been so predominant in the personal educational experiences of most teachers, you may have difficulty understanding how to become more learner-centered. However, it can be really fairly easy to grasp this perspective.

Remember the teachers you had who talked the entire time you were in class? Compare those to the ones who engaged you in the information through activities, discussions, and exercises. Consider the instructor who assigned reading and writing and rarely discussed how that would benefit you in better understanding the subject. Compare that to the teachers who told a story, used a metaphor or analogy, or offered an illustration that made the topic come alive in your world. Those teachers made you want to read and learn more. Some did so without a lot of planning or designing, they had a gift. Others, on the other hand, carefully crafted their courses and lessons to fully engage students in the learning process. Yet, whatever the source of their skill, each kind of teacher made learning a powerful and memorable experience.

To make this a bit more concrete, think about training someone to use a new software program. You can start by explaining things, presenting steps and know-how apart from the "doing." Students are given additional resources after instruction to study and practice with the topic or procedures. This is a traditional teacher-centered orientation. It focuses on the content of learning. This approach has its place for "downloading" information. And, obviously, in learning some procedures, such as how to use a piece of machinery, the teacher/content-centered approach is valuable because of safety issues. But in these situations, when a procedure is only talked about or demonstrated, it is not learned effectively.

On the other hand, you can first set up a learning environment so that participants see a demonstration, get a brief explanation as needed, but then start to practice skills as soon as possible, perhaps regrouping to continue with participant demonstrations. No attempt is made to explain everything up front, to have students memorize a lot of facts, and/or to minimize mistakes. Rather, learners are given a chance to "jump in," to make personal discoveries, and to figure things out by themselves as much as possible. You coach as needed, but emphasize exploration and direct experience over explanation and demonstration. This is a more learner-centered approach. It focuses on the context and processes of learning, as well as on the content. This learner-centered perspective seeks to provide and promote the most productive, enriching, and supportive environment for learning that is possible.

There are two dimensions to the concept of learner-centered teaching—the learning outcomes as the expected content or skill mastery *plus* the learning processes and contexts involved in reaching these outcomes. When designing courses and activities, you need to consider both. Thus, the artful educator is not only a subject-matter authority. The artful educator is also skilled at designing and planning for powerful learning to occur.

From the Science to the Art: A Framework for Guiding Your Practice

Becoming more skillful and creative in the practice of your craft will come more easily to some than to others. As noted, change and growth will be easier when new concepts and practices align with your present teaching philosophy and natural teaching style. Whatever your personal situation, we believe a brief introduction to the matrix upon which Unit 2 is based would be helpful. This matrix incorporates elements of both a traditional teacher-centered approach as well as a more learner-centered one.

Planning with the mind in mind: What is the subject matter to be taught and what are the learning goals to be set?

The Preparation for Learning and Teaching: What are the methods and means to prepare the learner and the learning environment for powerful learning?

(continues)

133

Presentation of Content: What are the most appropriate and best ways to help students acquire knowledge?

Personalizing Knowledge: What are the most appropriate and best ways to help students take a deep approach to learning to making this knowledge "their own"?

Performance Standards: What are the most appropriate assessment measures that indicate what students have learned?

Unit 2: A Matrix for Course and Lesson Design

Unit 2 consists of seven chapters that correspond to the primary components of any orientation to the design and implementation of instruction. This design framework answers five fundamental questions.

Preparation and Planning

Ch. 2.1 Content	What Shall I Teach?
Ch. 2.2 Context	How Can I Create the Best Learning Environment?

Presentation

Ch. 2.3 and 2.4	How Shall I Present the Content to Be Learned?

Personalization

Ch. 2.5	How Can Students Deepen and Personalize Their Understanding of the Content?

Appraisal

Ch. 2.6 and Ch. 2.7	How Can I Determine What Each Student Has Learned and the Value and Effectiveness of My Instruction?
	How Do I Decide Grading Policies and Effectiveness?

Chapter 4: Planning with the Mind in Mind— Course and Lesson Planning

What is the subject matter to be taught, and what are the learning goals to be set?

You'll consider the content you are expected to teach and add your own expertise. We also include tips about preparing a syllabus, course descriptions, and lesson design and planning. These practical tools lay the groundwork for you to prepare.

Chapter 5: Preparations for Learning and Teaching

What are the characteristics of the instructional setting and students, and what are the methods and means to prepare the learner and the learning environment for powerful learning?

Too often at all levels of education the assumption is that once the content is covered the students have learned. We do not subscribe to this assumption. We believe that the instructor is responsible for providing the environment that facilitates learning the content. Another way of describing that is that learning is uncovered around the content to grow knowledge. There are two aspects that effective teachers manage: the physical environment and the emotional environment.

Chapters 6 and 7: Presentation of Content

What are the most appropriate and best ways to help students acquire knowledge?

The process of presenting content is described in Chapters 6 and 7. Here you will discover strategies that you may be familiar with and some that you will want to use in your practice. In Chapter 6, we offer descriptions of the traditional lecture and how to make them quality presentations. In Chapter 7, we go beyond the tried-and-true formulas of customary lectures to show you how to create a more powerful learning experiences. If your goal is to become an artful practitioner, this chapter will provide some foundational tools to include on your palette.

Chapter 8: Personalizing Knowledge: Taking a Deep Approach to Teaching and Learning

What are the most appropriate and best ways to help students take a deep approach to learning, to making this knowledge "their own"?

Knowledge that is personalized is more than information memorized but also information that is deeply understood and enduring. It is a knowledge that often comes only from engagement with content on a thoughtful level. This is commonly referred to as critical thinking, but we also refer to it as habits of mind. Habits of mind are the thinking skills and aptitudes we need in business and at home to be more productive and smarter in everyday things. By teaching for deep, personal understanding, you will not only help your students learn more, you will also be encouraging habits of mind that offer your students a gift that will be appreciated for a lifetime.

Chapters 9 and 10: Performance Standards

What are the most appropriate assessment measures that indicate what students have learned? How do I determine grading policies and gauge effectiveness?

What would education be if we did not include assessment? Chapter 9 offers reasons for testing and valuable traditional and non-traditional methods of testing for understanding and mastery. You will find descriptions of assessments that you can use to indicate when learning is happening during a course of study. Included are specific examples and suggestions for designing tests and exams. Alternative assessments are described and examples given. Finally, we make some suggestions about grades and grading standards and policies.

This is likely a unit you will dog-ear and mark up. Use those sticky notes to quickly find sections you want to refer back to. Mark on the tab or the page what you want to remember and use in the future.

CHAPTER 4

Planning with the Mind in Mind—Course and Lesson Planning

To teach is to learn twice.

—Joseph Joubert

Do You Know:

- Planning can take two times the time spent in class?
- A well-designed content plan is only part of instructional success?
- What it means to begin with "the end in mind"?
- Important things you should do the first day of class and continue to do for every class?

Planning for Learning—Content Orientation and Process Orientation to Teaching

Maybe you have worked in your particular field for years and you really know your subject. But that does not mean it will be easy to teach it. This is especially true if you want to provide your students with experiences they will remember and with expertise in and excitement about the subject you are teaching. Plan for learning is an art.

Two approaches emerge when teachers plan their instruction—a content orientation (most often) and a process orientation. Content is about

137

the expected knowledge to be gained. Process is how we structure and guide learning so that the learner not only gains new and useful knowledge but also does so in the most effective and memorable manner possible. Both are useful and, in fact, essential. However, if one uses only one or the other, then students will not learn as effectively.

The content approach is fairly simple in determining the specifics that are listed to gain mastery. This is often included in the course syllabus (see below) and is often found in the table of contents of the textbook you probably are using. When content orientation is your primary approach to planning, once the main topics have been identified, you then write a specific objective or set of objectives for each one and determine the level of proficiency in order to pass the course. For content experts, as most instructors are, "content rules." But you have to be careful. It is easy to become so content-driven that you leave the students behind. In designing a course of study, content is the driving force and the logical place to begin. Still, you have to keep the learners in mind.

This is where attention to process comes in. You also have to have content that has meaning and makes sense. Your classroom activities and processes should be based on the principles that reflect what we know about the science of learning. These processes shape the content into forms that are suited to how people learn best. They guide you to teach with the "mind in mind." It is when you combine content outcomes (product) with strong process outcomes that powerful learning occurs. This unit offers specifics on building a course and including all the elements of powerful learning that will take place with your content.

> *The art of teaching is the art of assisting discovery.*
>
> —Mark Van Doren

Refer to Field Guide

A Helpful Framework

A simple-to-use framework for course and lesson planning includes five basic elements. (See the Field Guide for elaborations on several matrices that can be used in course and lesson planning.) This framework involves a process that is recursive and not necessarily linear. This means you will often likely have to go back and forth between the different elements as you plan your course and lessons. You may start with content, for example. However, you may find that you cannot fully specify your teaching and learning goals until you have carefully considered the context of instruction—that is, the level at which your students stand when they come to you. You may also not be clear about some of the desired learning outcomes until you have sat down and thought about, even written, your tests and other assessments.

- *Content:* What is the subject matter to be taught?
- *Goals:* What do you want learners to know and to be able to do with the content?
- *Context:* What is the instructional setting and composition of students?

- *Processes:* What teaching practices and learning activities serve the learning goals?
- *Assessment:* What will be the indicators and measures of the achievement of expected outcomes?

Course and Lesson-Plan Guide

Content: Subject Matter	What are the most important topics that you will need to cover?
	At what level? An introductory course? An advanced level?
Learning Goals and Purposes	Acquire basic facts? Master complex concepts? Skill performance at rudimentary level? An advanced level?
Context: Setting and Students	What is the instructional setting? Large lecture hall? Small classroom? Lab? Online course?
	What are the characteristics of students? Full or part-time? Young? Older? Learning aptitudes? Motivation and interests?
Learning Processes	What kinds of teaching and learning activities will best serve your teaching goals? Lectures? Discussions? Interactive student activities? Lab and performance exercises?
Assessment and Feedback	What kinds of feedback and assessments techniques will you use to support and measure the desired learning outcomes? Will you use only formal measures to assign grades and/or also informal feedback as indicators of students' progress and learning needs?

Out of intense Complexities intense simplicities emerge.

—Winston Churchill

Your Content—Selection and Organization of Subject Matter

The department or programs in which you work will often predetermine content through the curriculum used. You may also be given a broad course outline. You will likely also have a textbook to guide you in the selection and organization of the course content. All these resources will make your job easier. And of course, your experience in the field will contribute to how you use these resources to get you started.

It can be tempting to rely on these materials entirely in putting together your course syllabus (see below) and your specific lesson plans. If you are a new instructor, this is understandable and reasonable. However, we strongly recommend that you attempt to go further with your own elaboration and enhancements and tailor the content for your own purposes and the needs of your students. You can and should add value by adding to the core content, adapting it to what you know happens in the real world and to the interests of your students. (This has to do with the instructional context as explained further below.)

For example, you probably know or will discover that broad course outlines and textbooks do not always make the most sense in the real world. They offer information and organization through the sequence in which this information is presented. But they can pose challenges for mastery and application of learning. Thus, once you have reviewed the text or outline you may have, you will want to compare the content offered and the objectives for the course that you personally find important. Then it is time for you to use your creativity and knowledge to arrange your course in a fashion that makes the most sense to you and will best engage your students in the learning process.

Your Learning Goals—Start with the End in Mind

Your course goals and standards set the bar for achievement and drive accountability. These are about what students should be able to do, understand, care about and know as a result of your teaching. The best way to figure this out is to begin with "the end in mind."

If you do not know what you expect students to learn by the end of a course it is like going on a trip with no destination, much less a map. One way to begin with the end in mind is to write your final exam first and then work backward. To write the final exam you need to consider the most important content specifics that you want to have covered and have your students master. You have to know what you expect to take place for your students to succeed on the final exam. What new connections will they be capable of making after they have completed your course? How you ultimately measure what they learn is also important to consider as you design your course. (Because everyone is familiar with written tests, that is a good place to start. We will provide alternative assessment possibilities later in Chapter 9.)

After you have written the exam you can determine how you wish the course to proceed over the weeks of instruction. It is a good idea to outline the major points to include in the sessions that will take place.

High aChievement always takes plaCe in the framework of high expeCtation.

—Jack and Garry Kinder

Chapter 9

Consider what might be the most challenging content for learners to understand and apply to their worlds—you will need to spend more time designing those content areas. Once that is done you should prioritize the list to begin determining the best sequence for instruction and the processes you need to proceed through to reach this final outcome.

(At this point you can list the resources necessary for students to reach closure on each topic and any activities for personalization and elaboration you want to include that will enhance their learning.)

Finally, you will want to decide how students will be assessed throughout the course at certain milestone points. This way you can make sure you include all the most valuable content in the course design. You will also want to craft those milestone quizzes, exams, and/or authentic assessments before you complete the course design.

Chapter 8

The Learning Context—Your Learners and the Learning Environment

> *If you fail to plan, you plan to fail.*
>
> —Old Saying

One of the most important things to remember, as indicated by a great deal of research and scholarship into learning is that content has to be "situated" for the learner. In other words, when planning for delivering crucial content you have to determine where in the students' lives they have a common reference point for your content. A common experience that relates to them and to your content will situate the content so that they not only remember it, but they also can relate it to their situation. When crafting your course and delivery, if you always keep the learner in mind you will be successful.

The context or setting is determined not only by the nature and needs of your learners, but also by the character of the learning environment. This includes the physical and affective or emotional factors that can and often influence learning. Because of the importance of this often-neglected part of teaching, we cover and elaborate on this topic in Chapter 5.

The Teaching/Learning Process: From Course Design to Learning Designs

Process is the means by which you facilitate students reaching mastery. Process is the how. Process design includes your methods of presentation and delivery of content. But it is much more. A focus on presentation is a teacher-centered approach only. You will, as we have emphasized, want to incorporate learner-centered processes. These are activities, exercises, experiences, debates, skits, projects,

Chapters 6 and 8

and so forth that you include in the plan to support the learning of content. Process is where you use the creative juices to design activities that ensure involvement and learning. Often the process is more important that the actual content. This is especially true if you use your work experience to plan activities that are based in the real world.

Assessment

Chapters 9 and 10

Assessment is often the most neglected or underappreciated component of course design. It often comes as the final stage in course design for most instructors or sometimes even as an afterthought. However, the point we have just made offers a logical and valuable place to begin your course and lesson designs. Moreover, assessment has many forms and purposes that are not understood by many teachers but have a critical role in all dimensions of teaching and learning. Given the importance of this topic, it is explained in great detail in the chapters on assessment.

> *In action be primitive; in foresight, a strategist.*
>
> —René Char

Course Design and the Syllabus

Every institution requires a course description and syllabus. This is simply a concise description and an outline of your course. Often it comes straight from a text you have been assigned. Usually the syllabus is distributed at the first meeting of a class, with discussion centering on the course requirements. We suggest that you take it beyond the requirement and the table of contents and "design" a course. Course design is much like design in any other field such as designing a house. In house design, you take into account how each room will be used and the specific design elements that will best suit the purpose. Designers have resources that offer them options that might be considered in the design process. They always keep in mind who will occupy the house, and if they are custom designing, they listen carefully to the owners. They use their expert knowledge to design homes that meet the needs of their clients. The same is true in course design. The trick is to know all your options. What methods will you use to deliver the content? How much time will be spent on activities and projects? What experiential plans will you include? In what ways will student competence be measured? Will you use a final exam or some other method of assessment to determine competence? Is there a place for "authentic" assessment? What particular content "chunks" are the most critical, and how many times should you have students review and work with these particular "chunks"?

Refer to Field Guide

Man arrives
as a novice
at each age
of his life.

—Sebastien
Chamfort

Syllabus Basics

There are many versions of syllabi, and there are some basic elements that are included. Below we have included the basics with short descriptions. Obviously, some of the items are self-explanatory and, hence, are only listed. You will find a template for this model in the Field Guide and on the CD. Your institution may require other elements, and we suggest a couple that may not be required and are nice to include for clarity.

Course Title: This is the official catalog title. You can add a tagline if you wish, but it is not necessary to do so.

Course Description: This is the catalog description. This section may include more detail than offered in the limited version listed in a catalog.

Meeting Days and Times

Course Instructor's Name, Office Location, Office Hours, Phone (Cell Phone too?), and E-Mail Address

Texts and Supplemental Readings: This section includes the required resources as well as suggested reading material and other resources (i.e., articles, research studies, audio programs, videos, DVDs). You can also include in this section Web sites that will support students in reaching the outcomes of the course.

Course Purpose: Explain why this course is being included as part of a course of study, who might be in the class, and why they might be taking the class. Some of this may be clear because of the subject you are teaching.

Course Methods: Here is where you will entice the students with a variety of methods that will be used during the course. You can offer a short description of each one and explain to students how it will benefit their learning. Note that there will be various methods used and that to be successful in the class they will be asked to participate at their highest level.

Program/Departmental Goals: List the goals and expectations from the department or division of study and how this course meets those goals.

Course Objectives (or Outcomes): Note your specific outcomes for this course.

Course Requirements: This will include all the required papers and projects. Be as detailed as possible so that students know what your exact expectations are.

Prerequisites: Let students know that if they do not have certain prerequisites this is not the right course for them.

Assessment/Grading: Describe all the ways you will assess progress and determine a final grade. Include any cooperative activities that will be used to determine success in the course.

When I teach college courses I start the first class by noting that as of that time everyone has an "A." We then go through the syllabus and at each point of discussion I ask what they might have to do to keep their "A." This works extremely well and lays out all the expectations for my class. And isn't it true, they do all have an "A" when they first walk into your class?

Course Outline: List everything in order of its expected place in the course. You should also note that sometimes this changes depending on discussion and guest speakers.

Course Timeline: This should match the section on Course Outline.

Attendance Policy: This should indicate both your expectations and how attendance may or may not be part of your grading policies.

Academic Honor Code: This is where you include the code of conduct at your institution. If there is not one from the institution, you should still include your expectations about cheating and plagiarism.

In course design, the object is to make sure you are creating a flow to the content that will best suit the course objectives and student learning. Each session has elements that should enhance the content. Over many years of experience we have discovered that it is best to follow a basic rule: Design with the end in mind. What is your expected result by the end of the course? If you determine what the students should know and be able to do at the end of the course you will be ahead of a majority of instructors.

> We're drowning in information and starving for knowledge.
>
> —Rutherford D. Rogers

Lesson Design and Learning Plans

Lesson design, as the smaller sections of your course design, provide you a guide for individual class sessions. Lesson plans include the details of what will be included in a lesson. Seems obvious, and it is. There are many different forms and templates. If you do a search on Google for "lesson plans" you find hundreds of thousands of resources. However, it is obvious that there are certain components of lesson planning that cross all disciplines and, for that matter, all levels of education. The basic sections found in all templates include: topic, lesson objective/outcome, materials/resources, information/content, activities, practice, assessment, closure, and after-class assignments.

Below we outline examples from the two basic orientations to teaching and learning that represent the continuum of approaches to teaching and learning we discussed in Chapter 2—the behaviorist/ cognitivist and constructivist/humanist. These also correspond to

Emphasis on discovery in learning has precisely the effect on the learner of leading him to be a constructionist, to organize what he is encountering in a manner not only designed to discover regularity and relatedness, but also to avoid the kind of information drift that fails to keep account of the uses to which information might have to be put.

—Jerome Bruner

the teacher-centered and learner-centered continuum described in the introduction to this unit. At the same time, we suggest that you adapt these and/or you find or design a form that works for you. Whatever your template is, it should include the basics and your personal purposes that reflect the particulars of your course and subject matter. It should be used as a thought process, not as a form to fill in. It is through design that you will provide the most powerful learning for your students.

Teaching for Mastery: A Behaviorist/Cognitivist Model

As stated above, there are many templates, and we like the following model from Madeline Hunter and Doug Russell at the UCLA Lab School. There are seven things to consider. This is not a checklist; it is not about absence or presence of any of the elements. Rather, it is about looking carefully at each element and consciously deciding to include it and deciding how it might be best used in the design for the results you desire. Like an architect designing a home, you consider the possibilities using your expertise and use what will best support reaching your end goal. You have to determine the objective for your lesson before you can design it. Below we describe the seven elements in detail.

Anticipatory Set. This is the "hook" or how you get the learner's attention, just like bait on a fishhook. This can take many forms and may not be necessary at all in cases in which the content is already of high value or inherently "grabs" attention. The idea here is to focus attention on the lesson. Determine how you create a framework for the ideas and information that will be delivered. Sometimes referred to as a "scaffold" or an advanced organizer. Just as a scaffold for a building helps to frame it and allows the workers to work safely on completing the building. a learning scaffold holds the lesson together and helps the learners frame what the content is and how it fits for them.

Sometimes an activity at the beginning of a session that gets students moving or acts as an icebreaker will help set the stage for the session's intended outcome. The anticipatory set may also extend the understanding and/or application of abstract ideas by using an analogy or metaphor to introduce a topic. An anticipatory set may also happen at the end of one lesson as a "hook" for the next lesson.

Input, or Presentation. This is how you provide the information. You can choose to lecture, which is appropriate for a certain portion of any course. Be careful not to overuse lecture or direct instruction. Students will not respond positively to lectures all the time and will not retain the information as readily unless you mix up your presentations. You might use a video or DVD to make a point. Your plan may also include a "jigsaw" activity, in which you assign sections of a textbook to small groups to deliver to the rest of the class.

Another method of presenting material is designing an experience for students, perhaps through a metaphor that will result in their understanding the content.

Two colleagues and I designed a course on basic statistics that used a grocery store as a metaphor. Everything from the selection of groceries to the checkout stand and the distance to the store was used to illustrate statistical tools. The metaphor was very successful because everyone is familiar with grocery shopping. The statistical terms were easily learned when embedded in a familiar metaphor.

Modeling. Once the material is presented, the application of the content should be modeled in ways the learners will use it in the real world. What is expected of them in applying their new knowledge? The application of the content is critical to learners complete understanding. Problem solving using the content will ensure that the learner is capable of using it. As the instructor, you model various ways of using the material. Perhaps you are teaching a specific skill in patient care or documentation. You have to model the use of that skill, material, or process so that the learners can situate it in the real world.

Checking for Understanding. It is easy for us to say we understand while not really understanding. Everyone wants to appear competent and confident. There are many times when we are not. Checking for understanding is a critical step in the learning process. It will help you determine whether the learner really "got it." Practice is the key, skill practice. (We prefer using the term *skill practice* versus *role play,* as it has a stronger impact because it is real, not bogus or phony.) In skill practice, you have designed a scenario for students to apply what has been taught in an environment that is nonthreatening. A lab setting is very useful. If students are successful, great; if not, you should reteach in another way that will ensure their understanding. (*Note:* This does not mean in a louder voice.)

Guided Practice. Students have an opportunity to practice the new learning on their own through an exercise or activity directly under your supervision in class. It happens in a safe environment. This is the lab setting that works so effectively in the sciences, and it should be used more in other courses, such as the one you are teaching. When it is done well, praise the learner and move on to the next person or group. If they are struggling, offer a prompt and return later to observe their success.

Closure. Just as the anticipatory set begins a lesson, closure closes the lesson. It is when you as the instructor "tie a bow around the

> *The true art of memory is the art of attention.*
>
> —Samuel Johnson

package" and bring everything together. The truth is you do not have to do it yourself. This is a great opportunity to have students debrief the lesson and share their conclusions with you and the rest of the class. This helps them organize their learning, offers a coherent picture, consolidates the learning so students have a context for applying it in the future, and provides you with feedback as to their level of understanding. By having them offer their conclusions the closure is stronger and more valuable than if you do it. If you have done a good job designing the lesson or session the value will be evident to every student.

Independent Practice. Often referred to as "homework," independent practice provides reinforcement for the learning. This may take the form of homework, or group work in class, applying several concepts in a larger context. Independent practice offers learners different contexts in which to use the learning, thus moving it to long-term memory. Applying the material to relevant situations and contexts ensures that they will be able to use it in the real world. Independent practice is only used with content that has already been discussed and experienced in class. It is practice on topics the student already knows about and has experience with in a controlled and safe setting.

The Five E's and Discovery Learning: Two Constructivist/Humanist Models

The two models briefly outlined here reflect many of the principles of constructivist and humanistic approaches to learning and teaching. They incorporate elements that encourage self-direction and exploration and the discovery of personal meaning and understanding. Unlike the previous model, the teacher plays less of a role in controlling the learning process. Here, the teacher serves to facilitate and orchestrate. Instructional activities are more open-ended and are set in a communication-rich, highly interactive learning environment.

The Five E's. This model is easy to understand and implement. It was developed by Rodger Bybee and the Biological Science Curriculum Study. The model is based on the assumption that adults, as well as children, acquire knowledge by constructing it for themselves and building on what they already know. It follows a logical progression and offers the same kind of structure as the Lesson Design Model from UCLA described above.

- *Engagement:* This starts the lesson, activates prior knowledge with the content and stimulates thinking. Using something novel, opening a demonstration by reading from a pertinent source, or analyzing a graphic organizer are options to consider.

> *The art of progress is to preserve order amid change and to preserve change amid order.*
>
> —Alfred N. Whitehead

- *Exploration:* When students explore, they think, plan, investigate, and organize. They solve problems, construct models, and do experiments by reading authentic resources and collecting information.

- *Explanation:* Students analyze their exploration. They work to clarify their understanding and modify by reflecting on their work. They support their work with evidence and discuss the reading they have completed.

- *Extension:* Students use this as an opportunity to expand and solidify their understanding of the concepts and apply them to the real world.

- *Evaluation:* Teachers may use a scoring tool to evaluate or may work with students to create a rubric to assess their work.

Discovery Learning. Discovery learning is one of the most natural ways we learn. It starts when we are very young, with our first experiences. We discover our world and learn how to live in it. The older one is, the more discovery learning has been done. It can be a valuable a tool for the classroom. You will need to determine a specific task and be willing to allow students to work out the problem. Discovery takes longer than other designs because of the nature of discovery itself. Thus, you will have to allow for mistakes and provide materials for more than one attempt to discover results. Stepping back may be difficult, but it is necessary. You can offer encouragement with failure and success. Finally, you should plan a method to record procedures, discoveries, and results.

Below is a short description of a discovery learning situation. This set of questions should be considered in preparing such an experience. They are arranged in a rough chronological order, but discovery-based planning is particularly recursive, meaning early steps may be returned to and repeated at various stages of the process. (Because discovery learning is related to inquiry-based learning, you'll find a more detailed description of this method in Chapter 13.)

Chapter 13

- What stimulating ideas, objects, problems, etc. might students wish to explore?

- What are the probable outcomes that will come out of the exploration of such "stimuli"?

- How is such an exploration doable? What will I, as a teacher, have to gather and organize?

- What is the likely time frame for such an exploration?

- How will I help my students form constructs as they carry out their exploration?

- To what degree will I allow this exploration to be student-directed? In what instances might I need to step in?

- What groupings of students might I use, and how will these groupings share their conclusions?

- How will we bring this exploration to closure?

- How can we link the learning arising from this exploration to other explorations and to the curriculum in general?

The First Day of Class—A Pivotal Moment

The first meeting of a class sets the standard and tempo for all future meetings. Make it personal and interesting. Tell the students about your history in the field and something personal that will relate to them that you are a real person. Explain that this may be the most interesting and exciting class they have ever experienced. (Don't scoff; it could be, if you make it so.) Remember all you have read in this book and you will create memorable and powerful learning experiences.

Harry Wong, a gifted educator in the San Francisco area, wrote *The First Days of School: How to Be an Effective Teacher.* He describes many activities and processes that the most effective teachers use. Even though his audience is high-school teachers, his ideas are valuable for any educator wishing to become more skilled at teaching. It is a books worth including in your library. Wong's ideas are not new or even unique; what he has done is include many things in one book. You will find that some of that information is in this book because it makes sense and it is the right thing to do.

There are basics about the first class that you will want to consider to set the tone and expectations for future sessions. The basics also apply to every class in the future. Everyone has a degree of nervousness when beginning something new. Even if you have taught the same course before, no two classes are the same. Students are curious, if not also nervous. Your most important job during that first class is to ensure that students feel comfortable and know the course expectations. Here are seven things to include during that first session.

- *Greet students at the door as they arrive:* Yes, you read it here. This may seem hokey, but it can assure students that you are real and are interested in their success in your course. You are totally prepared for the first class; doing any last-minute things will not distract you, they are already done. Taking time to greet each student as they come in the room will give them confidence that you are a real person, you are friendly, and the class will be built around student–teacher relationships. How do you greet them? Exactly what you do does not matter as much as that you are at the door doing something to put them and yourself at ease. Introduce yourself, shake hands, hand out an icebreaker activity, and encourage them to participate.

- *Use an icebreaker:* Think of how you can engage students in an activity that will have them thinking and getting to know others in the class. There are many to choose from, and you will find a section in the Field Guide on several that we like to use. This is also a great opportunity to participate with the students; do the activity too. If you can adapt the icebreaker to have something to do with the course content you are teaching, then that gives it more value.

- *Debrief:* The value of using any activity is greatly increased when you plan time to debrief. Simply put, ask students what happened, what the expected outcome was, and how they felt about the experience. Icebreakers are meant to create relationships in a group. Plan them that way. You can use icebreakers on a regular basis to build a group so everyone has fun and learns more because they continually feel valued and safe.

- *Ask questions and listen:* Remember when you started a class and the instructor did all the talking, maybe not only the first class, but every class? The most effective instructors ask more than they tell. During that first class you might ask: How will the class benefit students? Why did they decide to enroll? What do they expect to walk away knowing that they did not know before? What do they want to be able to do as a result of the class? You may have other questions too. You can ask them to write some answers before discussing with a partner or small group.

- *Review the syllabus:* If you handed out the syllabus at the door, the students have had a chance to look it over. Take some time to review the course as you have written it up for them. Ask them what things mean, or if they know about any of the topics in the syllabus. Ask if this is what they expected.

- *Set standards and expectations:* This is a great opportunity to really enroll them in your course. In some of my college-level courses, I started this by telling the students that they all started with an "A" or Pass. Then I proceeded to share how they could maintain that status. I set the expectations. Then I started a discussion with them so they could help determine what would be reasonable for accomplishing mastery. This was always interesting because they were used to being told what had to be done. It took longer to get them going because of their limited experience of setting their own standards. We also talked about what kinds of assessment would be helpful in knowing that they knew.

- *Stick around:* When you make yourself available, especially after the first class, you open up opportunities for students to ask questions and seek clarification in a one-on-one fashion. You also offer them time to get to know you and to build a mutual learning relationship.

These are not difficult ideas to implement, and if you have the intention of offering your students a more learner-centered environment, each will build a strong model for all your future classes. By setting this tone, you set a standard for student involvement. By giving students choices, you increase the potential for their learning. Choices in that first session include participating in the icebreaker, asking questions, and setting their own group standards for success.

CHAPTER WRAP-UP

Lesson design and planning is a critical element to your success and should become a natural part of your instructional prowess. You might think after reading this chapter, "These things are easy to describe and hard to implement." But that is not really the case. There is logic to everything here, and planning is the key to your success. It really is not that hard to do, but it does take a great deal of time to plan courses and each individual lesson. But it is time well spent. If you have spent the time looking at the materials, knowing the outcomes you expect, and planning the delivery, you will find that once you get into class the job becomes much easier. Once you know your students, you can tailor your design to better meet their needs. You have choices of how to approach each class and every interaction. The key is to remember that if you spend twice as much time planning as the allotted class time you will be prepared for any eventuality. As an instructor, you should be doing the work before class so that students can do the work during class.

We have offered a couple of planning models. There are many others, and most teachers design their own model or method to prepare courses and lessons. You will discover your best planning method after several courses and a number of lessons. Our idea here is to give you a good start and things to think about, as you become a masterful instructor.

If you do an Internet search, you will find loads of tools for planning lessons. You will find sample lessons probably in your subject area. The resources available to you are infinite, and could be overwhelming. As you grow into your new career, use templates and models that work for you. Some you will adopt with no changes, and others you will adapt to better meet your specific needs. The point here is you do not have to reinvent any template or model for planning.

Also, keep in mind that the first class is so important to your success and the learning of your students that you cannot spend enough time planning for it. The list we have included is just something for you to think about. You will come up with your personal "rituals," your introductory remarks, and activities that will leverage your strengths in the classroom. Again, we emphasize the concept of making students feel welcomed not only the first day of class but also every class session they attend. These ideas work every day.

SPRINGBOARDS FOR FURTHER LEARNING

Key Names

Jerome Bruner   Doug Russell
Rodger Bybee   Harry Wong
Madeline Hunter

Key Terms

constructivism   lesson design
course design   lesson plans
discovery learning   practice
goals   standards
inquiry   syllabus

CHAPTER 5
Preparations for Learning and Teaching

If I had eight hours to chop down a tree,
I would spend 6 hours sharpening an axe.

—Abraham Lincoln

Do You Know:

- That the learning environment is more than a classroom?
- The two key elements of a powerful learning environment?
- That "everything speaks"?
- How music can be a powerful learning enhancer?
- Why classroom routines and rituals are important?
- How you can ensure that each student is ready to learn?
- The most crucial interaction that you should plan for in every class session?

Introduction

Have you ever met someone for the first time and felt that you had known each other forever? All your thoughts surfaced in their words. You did not want the conversation to end, and you knew there would be another time you would make contact because it was such a strong connection. You found so many connections to your values

153

and passion. The conversation was rich and intriguing. Instant rapport was truly evident.

Perhaps you can think of a time when you went to a class and were surprised to find a room that was filled with exciting and interesting materials, realia, pictures, and posters. "Overwhelming" may have been your first reaction, and yet your curiosity was piqued. Each of these things helped to make you want to know what was going to happen. You were immediately engaged and enrolled in the learning process without a word spoken.

Can you create an environment that is so rich and enroll students in such a personal fashion? Yes, you can! In this chapter you will learn about the most important and practical considerations and strategies for creating a powerful learning environment. It describes our view of the learner-centered classroom. We offer guidance on the elements you should consider as you set up your room, to create the most productive, enriching, and supportive learning environment possible. You will also learn how to ensure that the students entering your classes are ready to learn and that you yourself are ready to teach.

The Learning Environment

The learning environment is both the physical setting and emotional climate in which learning takes place. The phrase "everything speaks" is used by Quantum Learning Network (QLN), a program for creating accelerated learning settings. The term is used on a regular basis to help both teachers and noninstructional staff understand the influence of even the smallest thing on the learning environment. "Everything speaks" is a reminder that every interaction, every person, every activity, every part of the physical environment, and every time interval makes a difference for learning. Just as Bobbi DePorter, founder of QLN, has said for many years, the phrase, "everything speaks" is the essence of this section.

> *Teachers who cannot keep students involved and excited for several hours in the classroom should not be there.*
>
> —John Roueche

The Choices You Have and the Choices You Can Make

An attractive physical setting and positive learning culture at all levels contribute to student success in schools. Included here are the school location and facilities, its mission and values, and the faculty and administrative interactions.

Perhaps you are thinking there are elements of the setting or culture of your school that do not contribute to a positive learning environment. You may also believe you do not have many options when it comes to creating such an environment. Maybe your campus is nothing more than an office building in a busy urban setting. Or maybe there are administrative or staff or program issues, which are so often part of any organizational system. Yes, it may be more difficult to change the environment of a school in an urban office building than one in a found in a country setting, and problems in a school can be a distraction for both you and your students. Still, you can begin to create a positive space even if the surroundings are less than supportive.

In just about any postsecondary school, once you close the classroom door, it is your world. You make the choices that make a difference. This can be good and bad. It is good because you have an enormous amount of freedom and flexibility when it comes to doing what you feel is best. At the same time, you live with not only your successes but also your failures. If you close the door and never discuss what goes on with other educators, you are doing yourself and your students a disservice. The value of reflection and discussion is too great to deny yourself and others.

Our advice (and that of many educational scholars) is to enroll your colleagues in the process of building a learning community in your school. If your ideas are good and are working, you should share them. And if a situation or a process that did not work as planned puzzles you, thinking about it gets you only so far. Describe it to other instructors and ask for their observations. Working in teams, you and your colleagues can get valuable insights, as well as promote a positive learning culture that will influence not only your classes but also your entire institution.

> *Create an environment with frequent change. . . . Exposure to new information, experiences, and material has an engaging effect on the brain.*
>
> —Anonymous

The Physical Environment

The classroom you are assigned is the space you have to work in. "What you see is what you get," and your choices are limited. You probably cannot make it the perfect environment, and will likely need to leave it as you found it because other instructors share the space. But because you share the space does not mean that you cannot personalize it each time you are there. All you need are the intention, the time, and the materials.

The Peripheral Environment

One thing you can probably easily do is place a few things on a bulletin board or perhaps a poster or the like on the walls. One of the tenets of accelerated learning is the use of peripherals, items placed on walls around a classroom that support the learning and the learning environment. Being exposed to these peripherals reinforces the expected learning in a subconscious fashion.

Unit 3

You can get your students involved in the process too, which can be very valuable in the entire enrollment process for a course. Here is one practice. During the first class session ask each student to write a quote on an 11-by-17-inch (ledger size) sheet of paper. Provide colored markers and the paper. The quotes are to be positive and could be made up or from someone else. It's great if they remember who said it, but it really does not matter. Thoughts may come up about things students heard at home when growing up. This is okay. The most important part is that the quotes must reflect something upbeat. The quotes offer insights into each personality in the room. Put them up for several sessions, along with larger posters of exercises and lists from activities. It is different enough from other classes that students can better be engaged in future classes.

Using the Space

The traditional classroom most of us grew up in had rows of desks. The teacher had a desk at the front or sometimes to the side. Traditional rows and a teacher desk at the front is a very authoritative model. The teacher was clearly in charge, and all the information in the class came from the teacher. That is not to say that the traditional setting is bad or good. This configuration works for the lecture or direct instruction setting. Too often, though, it is never changed or adjusted to more learner-centered designs. The important thing to remember is that you may have and should use the flexibility of the space and furniture. You should plan your room arrangement so it matches your teaching goals and activities. When you have alignment like this you bring the expected learning more effectively and easily.

Regardless of how the room looks when you arrive, it does not dictate how you can use the space to the benefit of your course. Whether you have a room with desks or tables, unless they are fixed, you can rearrange furniture easily. For example, your first class session might be set as a circle. This is a good setup because everyone can see each other. Sharing the syllabus and expectations in a circle creates an atmosphere of collaboration right from the start. Students will also feel more secure about asking questions. You can learn names faster this way too, by doing introductions while everyone can see each other. A circle arrangement is also good for review sessions.

Small clusters of three to seven desks are another option. This allows students to work in small groups for discussions or to complete assignments and projects. If there are tables and chairs, you may just need to move the tables aside. Groups of three to seven (odd numbers) work well.

The best part is you do not have to do all the work. If you want to mix up your instruction and still leave the classroom a certain way for

The environment is everything that isn't me.

—Albert Einstein

the next instructor, guide your students in rearranging the room. The first session you will have to do it all and plan your time so you can finish before students start arriving. But after that, you can enlist their help. One way to do this is to put instructions on the board to show how the room needs to be set at the beginning of each class session. Often the instructions can be just a word or phrase. ("small groups today" or "lecture"). In a matter of minutes, all the work is done for you. At the end of the class session students return the furniture to its original state. This practice is also a great one to help them to "own" the space they work in. Because you offer something novel, some of your students are often willing to show up early to help.

As an adjunct instructor at three universities, I faced the same challenges you face. Assigned rooms, old/odd furniture that never seemed to be the "right" furniture, poor lighting, and no supplies, to name but a few. I decided I could control the space to a certain degree. I could not select the room I was assigned, and it was never ideal, whatever *ideal* means. I brought my own chart holder and chart paper and colored markers to record our discussions, questions, and conclusions. Each class session, we placed posters or charts from previous sessions on the walls with masking tape. The posters were mind maps, lists, illustrations, and group work that students had completed as group or individual projects. We put them up at the beginning of each class, and rolled them up at the end. Students were more than willing to help put them up each session. This simple practice allowed the students to "own" the space we shared, and it helped them remember all the content we had previously discussed and experienced. I used music during every class to bring students together and to enhance the learning and interaction. Music is an important element in creating a friendly and productive classroom.

I did most of my instruction with adults who had full-time jobs and were in class to learn more about teaching or to work toward a teaching credential. A number of the classes I taught were after regular working hours so many students came straight from work. I do not know about you, but I need a little "down time" after work and some sustenance. For many of those classes, we determined a schedule for bringing snacks and drinks. I brought water to every class, and for the first class I provided the snacks. Anything from popcorn and chips to fruit and sub sandwiches was okay. This provided the nourishment needed for 2 or 4 hours of class. This plan acknowledged that to be strong learners we need food and drink, especially after a full day at work.

(continues)

I truly believe that the students in my classes were happy to be there and made great strides in their learning because of their involvement in creating an environment that was powerful. The novelty of music, food, and water was so different from their other classes they learned more and had more fun doing it. I loved it too.

Lighting

The lighting in the typical classroom is fluorescent. The "buzz" in this type of lighting sometimes is more invasive than any other distraction. If you cannot control the fixed lighting, you can use a small incandescent lamp to create a "softer," more inviting learning space. This is especially effective in a small classroom, and this minor change can do much to change the mood. Natural lighting, of course, creates the best mind state for learning. If you have a daytime class, consider turning off some of the overhead lighting. If you are assigned a classroom with no windows, request a change if others are available.

Some classrooms, such as auditoriums and lecture halls, are designed with stage lighting. Rooms with a soffit loaded with lighting offer a better atmosphere than direct fluorescent lighting. This can be very useful if you have access to the control panel. You can adjust lighting so it matches your lecture or activity. Usually the lighting is targeted to the front of the room, but it can be aimed in different directions. You can probably also dim some of the lights.

> Music is the language of the spirit. It opens the secret of life, bringing peace, abolishing strife.
>
> —Kahlil Gibran

A Few Other Important Considerations

Nutrition and Water

Have you ever been famished, with no time to eat? People come to class at the last minute and sometimes have not had much to eat or drink before arriving at your doorstep. This is not good for the potential learning. We do not think or learn very effectively if we are hungry or thirsty. Although you should not be expected to provide food and drink each class, if you do so for the first class it is a sign of your commitment to effective learning. Bottled water is fairly inexpensive by the case. You can purchase snacks in bulk, or bring popcorn. One of the discussions during that first class period could be asking whether students want to set up a rotation to bring food and water so everyone will be in a better place for learning. It usually goes well as long as you keep it simple. You also need to talk about cleaning up when they leave.

Water is fundamental. Water keeps the body hydrated and provides needed sustenance. If you offer water only, that is fine. Discourage soda because it is not healthy, and if it is spilled it is messy to clean up.

Healthy snacks or salty snacks are better than sweet snacks. Sugar will give an immediate burst of energy, but the effects wear off soon after, and we feel ourselves in a slump. Packaged snacks are easiest, and fruit is good too. Sometimes students volunteer to bring in vegetable platters and even pizza. All of these are great and help set your class apart from others, creating positive feelings and stronger affiliation.

Consider that there may be a policy that will not allow you to have food in a classroom. If you do not know of such a policy, or if there is not one, you still have to make sure that you leave the room better than when you arrived. (Go by the belief that forgiveness is often easier than permission.) By doing so you will not get complaints from other instructors or custodial staff. Napkins and paper towels are essential, in case there are spills or crumbs. When you recognize that water and nourishment are essential pieces to the learning puzzle, you will become a more successful instructor. If you are committed to your subject and your students and have passion about being a masterful teacher, you will do whatever it takes to be successful. Taking care of basic needs becomes part of that.

Breaks

Breaks in the action are good for two reasons. First, they give students time to process information in a less formal way. Second, taking care of personal needs leads to better attention. You should include a break of about 10 minutes every hour or hour and a half. Also, it might be useful to note that students can take their own breaks without penalty. (If you need to go, you need to go.)

When you do offer a break, be sure to say how long it will be and what time students should be back and ready to start again. Too often instructors say, "Let's take 10 minutes." More likely than not, the 10 minutes turns into 20, and time is lost. That is one of the main reasons that breaks are not planned, because there is no strategy to get students back. Be specific with your return time and they will be ready to start again.

Music

You know that music can affect you. Think of the time you last heard a radio blaring, or perhaps elevator music. How about that favorite song from high school or college that you still can remember word for word? Then there is the special song from your first love. Finally, how many times have you had a tune in your head for no particular reason and you cannot seem to change the tune or stop it from repeating over and over? Music allows us to be in touch with emotions and thoughts. The memories flood as we think of the events and people associated with these songs.

We are influenced by music every day. So why not use it to the best benefit in schools? Too many students find schools an unfriendly

Music excites the inherent brain patterns and enhances their use in complex reasoning tasks.

—UC Irvine Research Team

Musical training is a more potent instrument than any other, because rhythm and harmony find their way into the inward places of the soul, on which they mightily fasten, imparting grace, and making the soul of him who is rightly educated graceful, or of him who is ill-educated ungraceful.

—Plato

Accelerated Learning
Chapter 12

place, even when they choose to be there. Classrooms should be welcoming places. Just think of the lobby of a nice hotel. Would you rather stay in the Ritz-Carlton or Hotel Six? Classrooms should be as welcoming as hotel lobbies are, with soft music playing. Music can be an invitation to learning. The bonus is that you will like the atmosphere as well. You will find yourself energized and more relaxed. You will plan better and be better prepared to change plans in the flow of the moment.

Benefits of Music. Music, though rarely appreciated as a learning adjunct, can help create the kind of environment that engages learners and increases learning possibilities. There are good reasons to include music in your classroom including:

- To energize
- To align groups
- To induce relaxation
- To manage classroom activities
- To stimulate thoughts of prior experiences
- To develop rapport
- To set the theme of the tone of the class or course
- To teach, creating connections between right and left brain
- To lend a sense of fun to the class
- To appreciate musical variety
- To inspire learners to make their best efforts

Music has so much value to human learning and performance that it has been researched deeply. Research by Gordon Shaw and others at the University of California at Irvine determined that after listening to classical music for 10 minutes before taking an IQ test, scores were better for those who listened versus those who did not. Though the brain-boosting effect was temporary, it does point to the simple power of music.

Georgi Lozanov, a psychiatrist and educator interested in how to facilitate learning, discovered the role of rhythm in enhancing brain activity and learning and used music extensively in his Suggestopedic method. He developed passive and active concert readings of new material—specifically, learning a second language—using a background of music that increased manyfold learners' ability to retain new vocabulary and other language skills. (Think about the ABC song. You can probably sing the entire song, even though you may not have thought of it for years. Having students use tunes they know to make new songs using your content is a great way to encourage thinking and also to embed learning into long-term memory.)

Music Works

From Plato to Einstein to the present day, many creative and productive scientists and others have used music as an outlet. Einstein would play his violin when he could not seem to solve a problem. After playing for a time, he would return to his work and find solutions. Music has been used for generations to relieve stress and relax us. Research done at Loma Linda University School of Medicine in conjunction with the Mind-Body Wellness Center, Yamaha Corporation, and Applied Biosystems found that music actually reduces stress at a genomic level. The implications are significant. In the not-too-distant future, it is possible that we will be able to control stress at a DNA level, based on individualized solutions. In the meantime, we have affirmation that playing musical instruments and listening to music will better prepare learners for learning.

If I were not a physicist, I would probably be a musician. I often think in music. I live my daydreams in music. I see my life in terms of music.

—Albert Einstein

Getting Started. It is fairly easy to introduce music into your classroom. When planning your lessons, include a prompt for music in your plan, so you remember to use it and use it at the right time (see below). Just bringing a small boom box with you to each class will help you get into the mindset to start using music. You do not need to invest in a high-end sound system. A portable, inexpensive boom box will work well. (If you pay a little more for one with a remote control, you may find it useful.) If you do not already have a good selection, start collecting music CDs that you like (because you are more likely to play them), preferably instrumentals, such as contemporary light jazz, classical, and new-age compositions. (Music with lyrics can be distracting for students if they are the wrong ones or if they are played at the wrong time.) Find stores that have used CDs, or look online.

Keep in mind the importance of being sensitive to your students when you use music. You should tell them that you will be using music and explain its purpose in the learning process. It might sound something like this: "I use music in my classes because I know that it helps with learning. In fact, the research is pretty clear that your learning will be even greater if music is part of the process in class and out of class. I use music to smooth our discussions, move us from the door to our seats, as a backdrop for activities and to move us out of the room when it's time to go. I will also use it when I ask you to write a minute paper or reflect on something we've discussed. Music offers great value to us." (Also, by offering students an explanation for your use of music and other techniques you use, you help them to better understand the way people learn. Learning to learn is an untapped arena—many students have never been told about how people learn.)

> *I never learned*
> *anything while*
> *I was talking.*
>
> —Larry King

Refer to Field Guide

How to Use Music. When and how you use music are the keys to its successful use in your classroom. Consider the following:

Transitions: This is an easy time to remember to use music. As students enter or leave your room, use upbeat instrumentals or vocals to create excitement, promote feelings of success, and build interest. (Use music that energizes you and it will likely energize your students.) You can also use very short music interludes as you shift from one activity to another, such as when you change a topic during a lecture or when you stop a presentation to have students move into groups for a discussion or group assignment. The music will not only keep up the energy during the transition but, as an added bonus, will give you a few moment to collect your thoughts as you prepare for what comes next. Turn the volume up as students move about and stop the music at its highest volume at the end of the transition so everyone can hear that the music has stopped. You have their attention now, and can make an announcement or go forward with your plans.

Background: Another logical time to play instrumentals is when you have students in discussion groups or involved in other activities, such as when processing a lecture or writing. You do not want the music to be too loud because it can be distracting, and yet you want it to be loud enough to give a sense of security that no one will hear another group's discussion. You may find that music will prompt deeper discussions, as well as adding a stimulating influence. The appropriate volume is a fine balance that you will learn to make with practice. During this time you can circulate and listen to the groups and determine how you will debrief the activity. (See the Field Guide for more on debriefing activities.)

Classroom Management: You can also use music to manage individual or group activities. Rather than using music just as background, you can also use it to time an activity, by telling students to stop when the music ends. Again, it is useful to use the volume controls. You can gradually raise the volume of the music to get their attention as you approach the end of an activity and then lower it slowly and completely fade it out. This makes it a soft closing for the activity, which allows the completion of thoughts and reflection.

"Concert" Readings: After you become accustomed to using music during transitions and activities, you may want to try using it as background to content presentation, such as part of a lecture or demonstration. This method is considered an active or passive "concert reading." The students just listen to your voice with classical music in the background as you read your material. You can do this successfully if you find just the right piece of music and practice timing it to the content

Chapter 12

and length of the material. It is not necessary to spend hours, but it will be effective only if you practice until you are comfortable. (This may seem a bit exotic, but it has been demonstrated to be very effective in reinforcing learning and recall. You can learn more about active and passive concert reading in Chapter 12.)

The Emotional Environment

The physical environment is fairly easy to manage if you set out with the intention to do so. For setting the right emotional environment you will likely have to have even greater intention. The truth is that some people have an easier time building emotional safety and rapport than others. What is important is for you to know the key ingredients of a setting that offers support, comfort, and the best inducement to learning. Each of the following sections provides short yet important elements to consider.

Create a Sense of Ownership

Ownership means students have a sense of belonging to something they have helped create. In planning your first class, think about how you can ask students to do things in the room that will give them a sense of being a part of it. It has already been suggested that you have them hang posters on the walls or move furniture to help create a space they "own." Here we suggest that you go further and lead a discussion about what the ideal classroom would be like and then ask how you can make it so together. Take a few minutes by yourself to brainstorm what that classroom would be like for you to get the discussion going. (Part of the discussion should be how to transform it each class session so that it may be easily returned to its original state.)

Provide Relaxed Interaction

Relaxed interaction starts at the door. Whether you are totally prepared or not, you should intend to and be ready to greet students at the door as they arrive for class. This small gesture can provide amazing results. Students feel they are important and known by you and, as a result, they will be more likely to participate in class. They feel after that short personal interaction at the door that they have rapport with you, and they do. You have personalized their experience by greeting and interacting on a personal level, even if it was only for seconds. There are numerous other things you can do to create relaxed interaction, including really listening to students, responding to things you can change to ensure they understand content, providing time during each

> Low self-esteem is like driving through life with your hand-break on.
>
> —Maxwell Maltz

class for open questions and discussions, and spending time after class with the purpose of being available. All of these create a more relaxed environment.

Watch Your Language

Use Affirming Language

The words we choose influence others in ways we sometimes do not think about. The use of "and" versus "but" is a good example. When the word *but* is used, it often does not just set up a contrast to what has been said before but can actually negate it. Consider this example, "I like your paper, *but* did you think about giving more examples?" This is a common way teachers comment on students' work, a style that weakens the positive or diminishes the strengths and highlights the problem or weakness. Wouldn't it be more effective to say, "I like your paper *and* did you think about giving more examples?" Another emotional effect that changes with the words we use is evident in the difference between "challenge" and "problem." They cannot always be substituted for each other, and yet often they can, with just a little forethought and consideration. Also, how many times do you hear or receive notices reminding you "Don't *forget to* . . ."? How about substituting that with "*Remember* to . . ."? The latter image is clear and strongly positive. Positive talk does influence our thinking and learning. Make those self-fulfilling prophecies positive and you and your students will be much happier.

Avoid Put-Downs

Many of us engage in what is sometimes called "playful teasing." This is a natural thing to do and can be a healthy way to create more relaxed interactions. The challenge comes when we cross that invisible line between playful teasing and put-down. You may not do so on purpose, but put-downs can happen without your intending them to. Most critical is the acknowledgment that we have mistakenly stepped over the line. Too often our response to hurt feelings is one of denial, "Come on, I was just kidding!" The truth is, if the recipient of our teasing is hurt by the words or a misperceived intent, we need to own our mistake. It is awareness of these kinds of incidents that will help build and nurture emotional safety in a classroom or anywhere else. Instructors have to model taking care of a mistake in order for students to know how to apologize and make it right. So the bottom line is, apologize and move on.

Pay Attention to Your Body Language

There are various studies that describe how we process information, and the overwhelming conclusion is that actions speak louder than

> I will speak ill of no man, and speak of all the good I know of everybody.
>
> —Benjamin Franklin

Chapter 6

words. We portray with our face and body more than by speaking alone. This is one reason why face-to-face meetings and real live classes will never be completely replaced by virtual learning. When you are conscious of how your physical responses match your verbal responses you will be more congruent. You can probably remember times when you have seen someone say one thing aloud and not portray the matching physical response. You have to model behaviors that match your words; otherwise you lose credibility. There are entire books on this topic, and what is meant here is to simply pique your interest to discover more.

Excellence is the result of caring more than others think is wise, risking more than others think is safe, dreaming more than others think is practical, and expecting more than others think is possible.

—Anonymous

Build Self-Confidence

There are five factors that affect self-confidence—security, selfhood, affiliation, competence, and mission or purpose. These are not entirely independent and may be self-evident, but you should know a little about how they enhance student confidence.

Security

Security has to do with feeling safe both physically and emotionally. If you work in an urban area, providing a setting that is physically safe may be difficult. But security also has to do with individual feelings of safety or comfort. Providing an environment that is emotionally safe and has strong rapport between students and with the instructor as we have already talked about will suffice.

Selfhood

This is the feeling that one matters. Your greeting students at the door can help provide this to each student. You also contribute to a students' worth by offering specific feedback on their contribution to each class. This is more than just general praise, such as telling a student that he or she has done "a nice job" or saying "that was a good comment." (Remember the old saying about "damning someone with faint praise.") Tell students in very specific terms what makes their contributions good. This will show that you really mean what you say. (See more on acknowledgments in the next section.)

Affiliation

The third factor is knowing that one belongs to a group, like your class. We affiliate with groups that provide personal value and align with our beliefs. Some affinity groups are natural, like family, school, or church for some. When students have affinity, they feel a sense of well-being. (Interestingly, corporate giant Home Depot encourages employees to become involved in volunteer organizations, believing that they make better employees by doing so.) You can create this sense of belonging in many ways. One is way is to bring students' personal interests into the classroom (which also affirms their self-worth). Another way, which should be part of your every class session if possible, is to create a lot of opportunities for positive student interactions.

Competence

If you know you are good at a task and others also acknowledge it, you have both competence and confidence in your ability. When you have competence, you have a sense of achievement. You contribute to this for your students by challenging them to do well and then acknowledging their competence when they succeed at a specific task. This could be with an exam or assignment, the subject itself, class relationships and conduct, or something as simple as asking pertinent questions. (One way we know we are good at something is because people ask us to do it with them or for them.)

Mission

Finally, when you have a mission, your life has a purpose. We get that purpose from how we are driven, our parents, or other mentors or models. Your mission at this point in your life may be to become the best instructor you can be. People's missions and purposes change over their lifetimes. The point is that you should have something from which you seek fulfillment.

When you know the factors affecting self-confidence, you can be purposeful about how you interact with your students. Who knows, you may be the model who gives students the purpose they may be seeking in their life.

A Note on Acknowledgments

The influence of teacher acknowledgments is often underappreciated in postsecondary learning. Many instructors think this is a topic suited for elementary education, and not the teaching of adults. However, adults are really not much different when it comes to their need for recognition. (Don't you value praise and approval?) So, give the importance of acknowledging student participation and work its due. This means honoring what students do in your course as often as you can. This begins with, of course, recognizing what students have added in a current class session. But it also involves more. For example, note how much you are anticipating the contributions they will make next session. Or, while students are departing, take a few minutes to tell several of them specifically how they contributed to and made the class more meaningful for themselves and others. You can select students who need the feedback to get them more involved. You could also tell students about how someone else contributed to the class

Comedy is simply a funny way of being serious.

—Peter Ustinov

and made a difference. And again, do this in a very specific fashion. Some specifics you might address could include, "You asked an essential question that led to a very important discussion today. Thanks." Or "The point you made about [insert topic] was right on. That kind of contribution is welcome anytime." Or "Your presentation today was both well prepared and helped me better understand your commitment to the class." These and other very specific feedback statements will encourage more involvement.

Be Aware of Your Presentation Styles

Chapter 3

Students relate to teachers based on many factors. One of those is the way teachers match student learning style. It is a challenge to match every style of every student. You do not have to conduct a formal learning styles survey to get a sense of your students' preferences. Just by paying attention to wording of responses and observing behaviors in class you can get a good idea of the styles you should address. You can also discover the styles that seem to work best with a specific topic or activity. All you must do is ask your students. Seems simple, and it is, except that many students do not think about the way they receive input, and therefore this will most likely make for a very interesting and informative class session. We suggest you ask students during your first class session how they learn best. It is most helpful to have them fill out a card with pertinent information for your records. Include "How do you learn best?" (seeing, listening and talking about it, or doing).

> *Practice yourself, for heavens sake, in little things; thence proceed to greater.*
>
> —Epictetus

By matching your teaching style to student learning styles you build rapport, and students learn better. This contributes to their feeling more comfortable in your class and being more motivated to perform. Remember relaxed interaction? This is another piece of it.

As you think about how you can make your teaching style and classes learner-friendly, consider what you are really good at. Do you tell great stories, can you create metaphors and analogies easily, and are others impressed with your enthusiasm? As you reflect, remember that the more you offer of yourself on a personal level the better students will relate to you as a real person. It's a matter of being comfortable enough with yourself that you can be real with your students.

Encouraging Better Participation and Retention: Some Quick Tips

How can you influence students to be prepared and ready to participate in your classes for every session? Just about everything we already have discussed in this chapter will contribute to greater student

Refer to Field Guide

engagement and persistence. Here are some additional ways to be sure that students are motivated to show up ready to learn at their highest level. (Many of these ideas are elaborated on elsewhere in this text as well as in the Field Guide.)

Set High Expectations

Closely related to the issue of the emotional climate is the setting of your expectations, High expectations result in higher achievement. When you plan your course and each lesson, be specific about your expectations, and set them a bit higher than you think can be accomplished. You will be surprised at how students perform based on a high standard. Students accomplish more when teachers challenge them to reach beyond their own sights. Students will do just as much as you expect. Set your sights higher, plan for less time rather than more because they will take the exact amount of time you give them.

In many workshops, one of the activities I do is have groups create a skit, rap, poem, song, chant, or model of something we're studying. I discovered, much to my pleasure and totally by mistake rather than design, how little time it really takes to do the activity. I had originally planned on about 30 minutes for a group of about 70 teachers. As sometimes happens, we were behind schedule and I figured there was less than 20 minutes to complete the activity. My thought was that everyone would create and that only a few of the 12 or 15 groups would perform. Much to my own surprise, I set up the activity and said that they only had 5 minutes to prepare and that each presentation would be no more than a minute. At the end of 5 minutes, after pacing reminders, I called on the first group. Amazing energy had already come in the room. It was very fast-paced and at the end of a total 18 minutes every group had created and performed. What a great learning for all of us. In our debrief of the activity they noted how much time we lose because we give students too much time to complete an activity.

Create Curiosity

Curiosity may have "killed the cat," but an absence of curiosity will also kill a lot of learning. There are many ways to generate interest. For example, provide an intriguing question that will be answered in the next class. You have to determine what will be novel or intriguing for your students. This might be based on the discussion in the class session you are just finishing, or you might anticipate and plan for this ahead of the class. You should offer some sort of incentive for discovering the answer before the next class. You decide. Have students e-mail their answers to you and reinforce the responses with acknowledgments for each person who responded. You should do this by e-mail and in class. But be careful; you do not want to make this activity seem more important than the content. Your goal is to motivate students to think about the content out of class and to solve a problem that will help them cement the learning that they already have.

Offer Choices

You can further the sense of "ownership" of learning in many ways. One is to offer several options for activities in the next class session and have students vote on the one that they want to experience. The activities should be part of your plan, designed when you planned your course. Describe each activity and the expected outcomes for each. If you offer the options with enthusiasm and excitement, the students will also be enthusiastic. Of course, any one of the activities should fulfill the need to reinforce concepts and learning. And you may find that you will use the others in the future.

Announce Coming "Attractions"

Create a sense of anticipation by letting students know what is coming up. Be sure to offer some excitement and not just information. For instance, announce a guest speaker who will provide an interesting presentation and answer questions about the real world of your topic. Their expertise should be acknowledged. Students may have some recognition of the person because of their being well known in the field of study. Build up a guest over a couple of classes to recognize their value. By building up the event you will motivate the students to be present. To make it more enticing, ask the students to prepare questions that they might want answered by the expert. You can take time in the current class to record the questions and add some of your own to the mix.

Offer Student-Generated Tests

Some teachers may be reluctant to have students create their own tests. But with proper guidance, they can be a very powerful way of motivating and focusing student learning. Moreover, the process of creating assessments actually reinforces their learning and facilitates

Chapter 9

their thinking about the content at a deeper level. Suggest, for example, that during the next class they will be working on a rubric for their final class project or exam. By suggesting that students will be involved in determining the criteria for grading a successful project, you give them greater motivation to participate. They have a degree of self-determination, and we all like choices. In your announcement about the rubric, you should describe how a rubric works and why you have decided to use their input to create one. The main reason you would want to do that is to tap their expertise and interest. You could also note that because it is their project they should be able to distinguish from the beginning the difference between a good and a great project result.

Share Your Passion

Let students know how you feel about the topics you teach. You are teaching the subject because of your real-world experience and passion about it. This will naturally come out in your classes, and you can take it one step further by noting how strongly you feel about your students learning the subject. Share your desire that they also come away with a greater degree of interest and passion about the subject.

Make Learning Fun

Students return to certain classes because of humor, relevance, and the fun factor. You cannot force fun; it has to be real and spontaneous, just like humor. Telling jokes is different from playing on the natural humor that occurs in everyday experiences. As you gain more experience in teaching, you will develop this important talent. A good place to start is to carefully craft each class session and then do not take it so seriously that you squash humorous situations. Students can be very funny, and they often make observations that we should appreciate. You have probably experienced that person who takes themselves and everything around them too seriously. It is not fun to be around them and you do not get as much accomplished. The same is true of your students. This is not to say that you should not take the course seriously, just do not make it too solemn.

Make Every Class Count

Finally, remember that today is really the most important key. This class at this time is what will be remembered best when students think of your classes. There is nothing more crucial to students being motivated to return to a class than what happens every class session. Your design and execution of the plan is the real key to students being motivated to be in your class. The degree of student interaction with each other and you and the subject is key as well. Having students do a minute paper at the end of a class, having them record "ahas" in a victory log, or having them map the content process for that class all help them find value in your classes.

CHAPTER WRAP-UP

There is a lot to consider in preparing for learning. Each of the topics can take many classes to develop your competence. It is our hope that you will start by using the things that make the most sense to you and are easiest for you to try, modify, and use regularly. As you become comfortable with each new idea you will become more proficient with it each time you use it. Do not give up on an idea just because it did not work the way you expected it to. Habits take time to form. It takes many repetitions just to remember something (some research says as many as six) and many more to make it happen naturally. If your intention is to become a masterful instructor, you have to keep doing the same thing over and over until you know how it plays out in many circumstances and with different groups. Here are six things to think about:

1. Start with what you are comfortable with.
2. Use it at least 10 times in different circumstances (28 times to form a habit).
3. Reflect on your practice using it (what worked, what did not work, and how you should do it differently next time).
4. Keep a record of what you try.
5. Adjust each technique to better match your style and the students' needs.
6. Do it one more time than you want to.

There is a truckload of information in this chapter. Each section makes you think carefully about your practice. Once you filter through it all, you will discover the things that you want to use. As stated above, do not try to do it all. Choose what you are comfortable with and do those things. Once you see the results, add more ideas. This chapter does not include everything that can make a classroom more learner-centered; however, in our experience these are keys to success in creating an inviting and exciting classroom. Fear not. Even though you will fail at some of these ideas, the faster you fail the sooner you will find success. Go for it!

SPRINGBOARDS FOR FURTHER LEARNING

Key Names

Bobbi DePorter   Muhammad A. Sharaf
Georgi Lozanov   Gordon Shaw

Key Terms

learning environment   self-confidence
music   self-esteem
Quantum Learning Network (QLN)   Suggestopedia
relaxed interaction   Supercamp

CHAPTER 6

The Traditional Lecture: "The Good, the Bad, and the Ugly"

I like a teacher who gives you something to take home to think about besides homework.

—Lily Tomlin

Do You Know:

- The strengths and limitations of a traditional lecture?

- The essential qualities of a good lecture presentation?

- Some of the most common mistakes lecturers make?

- The different and best ways to organize your lectures?

- How to make abstract and complex ideas clear to your students?

Introduction

Lectures are the default teaching method for much instruction in postsecondary education. In its most common form, a lecture is basically an informative talk intended to provide listeners with a body of information.

There are many teachers who are convinced that lecturing is an appropriate teaching approach in almost every situation. Lectures have the potential to convey a large body of information quickly and to cover and organize material in the ways best suited for the needs or interests of a specific group.

173

They can communicate and therefore generate interest in a topic, give an instructor a maximum degree of control while posing little threat to students, and provide a platform for instructors to model how professionals in a discipline think about and approach a question or issue. On the other hand, there are others who see lectures as rarely appropriate or effective. They contend that a lecture, at least in its traditional and common forms, leaves students largely as passive receivers rather than active learners. The format does not teach deep understanding or higher levels of thinking, fails to effectively account for learner differences, and permits students' attention to wander and wane easily, with the information often quickly forgotten.

Arguably, each position has its merits, and the question of which side is right is not one for us to answer. A theme of this book is that it is not possible to decide on what is or is not an effective teaching method without first deciding on instructional goals. Clearly, lecturing can be suitable for some and not for others. We must leave the decision up to you as you consider the particulars of each of your classes, hopefully applying some of the knowledge and considerations offered in Unit 1 and throughout other parts of this text.

What we can help you directly with, though, is how to use lectures more effectively. There are many resources on college teaching, as well as public speaking, which provide suggestions for constructing and delivering a good lecture. We have made an effort to pull the best ideas from these many sources to give you a guide to three versions of this almost universal instructional tool:

> *Teaching is not a lost art, but the regard for it is a lost tradition.*
>
> —Jacques Barzun

1. the traditional lecture,

2. the enhanced lecture, and

3. the interactive lecture—the latter two offering valuable modifications and enhancements that address the limitations of more traditional lectures.

In this chapter we discuss the traditional lecture. Our advice mostly focuses on the two basic components of a lecture, content and delivery. It is how these elements come together that determines the quality and, therefore, the success or failure of such a presentation. With all due respect and our apologies to the makers of the classic film, *The Good, The Bad, and The Ugly,* we provide here several illustrations of lectures in ascending order of quality.

The Ugly

These are the forgettable ones. The lectures that induce a mental haze within minutes of the beginning of a class, with most of the experience lost within seconds after its end. Regrettably common despite their different settings, such lectures over time simply dissolve into recollections more sensed than actually recalled. This may seem to be an exaggeration. But just take a moment to think back on some of your own experiences as a student, and you will know what we mean. Weren't they largely dull, gray experiences seated before now nameless, faceless instructors in nondescript rooms, with you and your classmates constantly shifting uneasily and doodling in your notebooks as you struggled to stay alert? Wasn't the lecture a seemingly interminable hour or so, filled with little more than shapeless sounds trying to masquerade as intelligent discourse, words that drifted aimlessly in the still air and then evaporated into nothingness, like a wisps of thin clouds burned away under a hot sun?

The Content

Who knows what the ugly lecture is all about. It seems that this sort of presentation has little purpose other than to consume the allotted class time. There is no apparent direction, and perhaps lots of digressions of little interest to anyone other than the instructor. In the end, at best, most students are left with only a few random notes that have no meaning upon review; at worst they have notebooks filled with idle doodles.

The Delivery

Delivery is, too frequently, a verbal form of the old Chinese water torture. Students are slowly worn down to gelatinous masses of protoplasm by broken bits of ideas that lifelessly drift and fall from the air one by one as the instructor drones on. Perhaps, mercifully, the monotonous tone induces a hypnotic state that sends everyone off into idle reveries and pleasant daydreams. Or perhaps a more animated instructor, one with a gift for gab, gives the lecture. However, what is delivered are mostly irrelevant stories and clever jokes that merely serve to entertain rather than to instruct and challenge.

The Bad

Perhaps bad lectures are not completely forgotten, just mostly forgettable. Here, there are a few redeeming elements, such as relevant content and an occasional helpful insight. However, it is still a mostly poor presentation with information that lacks coherence and a tone and manner that leave learners either confused or disengaged or both.

The Content

Unlike the prior example, there is some sense of direction to the presentation; however, it does not seem to include much of any obvious importance. Often, it merely repeats the content of assigned readings. Where there are some additional ideas embedded (or should we say

> The authority of those who teach is often an obstacle to those who want to learn.
>
> —Cicero

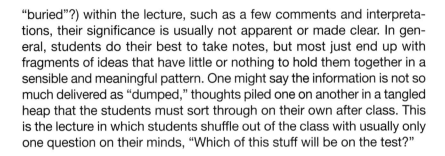

A good teacher is a good student first. By repeating his lessons, he acquires excellence.

—M.K. Soni

Refer to Field Guide

"buried"?) within the lecture, such as a few comments and interpretations, their significance is usually not apparent or made clear. In general, students do their best to take notes, but most just end up with fragments of ideas that have little or nothing to hold them together in a sensible and meaningful pattern. One might say the information is not so much delivered as "dumped," thoughts piled one on another in a tangled heap that the students must sort through on their own after class. This is the lecture in which students shuffle out of the class with usually only one question on their minds, "Which of this stuff will be on the test?"

The Delivery

Perhaps, rather than just a steady current of words that wash over the mind, the teacher's tone may exhibit some feeling, rising and falling in rolling waves that reach the shore of the students' consciousness, catching their attention now and then. The learners do manage to keep somewhat engaged, though mostly only with great effort. The teacher is generally motionless at the podium, rarely making eye contact, often fumbling with notes, or turning to a whiteboard to jot down some ideas.

The Good

Finally, the memorable one. This is the kind of lecture often described as the model for how to do a good presentation. A lecture done well is one that is organized and presented clearly to aid comprehension and promote retention and is delivered in an enthusiastic and engaging manner that maintains interest. If we think of a traditional lecture as primarily a vehicle for the delivery of information and extend this metaphor a little, an effective standard lecture can be considered your "no-frills" instructional model or method (in contrast to enhanced and interactive lectures discussed in the next chapter). It is economical, reliable, and delivers course content expeditiously from A to B. It moves at a good pace with a clear sense of direction and without "breakdowns" or notable problems. It also includes a few features that add variety and create interest to gain and keep students' attention. (The Field Guide explains more on how to enhance the delivery of your lectures.) Here are the essential features and suggestions for effectively planning and delivering a quality lecture.

The Content

This lecture is structured into three basic segments and heeds the old maxim—*Tell them what you are going to tell them; Tell them; and Tell them what you told them.* As discussed in Chapter 4, the selection of content will have been determined by the learning goals you have

Chapter 4

established when planning the lesson/course. This should take into consideration the objectives of the program and the relationship of the course to others in the curriculum, along with your own expectations and values. It is important to balance breadth of coverage with depth and to highlight a few core concepts and ideas that are critical for student understanding and that can be assimilated and recalled or reconstructed after the class.

Your Introduction: Tell Them What You Are Going to Tell Them

The opening provides a quick overview that creates student interest, creates structure for the students by letting them know what will be covered, and sets expectations that prepare them to deal with what is to come, especially possibly difficult concepts.

Preview. Consider it a map of the conceptual territory that helps students know where they are going. A simple statement of the objective(s) of the lecture and the key points that will be covered can suffice. However, putting these on the board or in a handout will be better, so students can more easily pick up the thread of the lecture if their attention wanders.

Interest. Creating interest in the topic and helping students appreciate its importance are essential qualities of a good presentation. This interest can be generated in a variety of ways, For example, you can directly tell them the significance of the lecture by indicating its connection to other course subject matter or perhaps real-life problems or current events, or you might inform them of its benefits by telling them what they will learn. (Additional ways of arousing their curiosity and interest are explained in the next section.)

Expectations. There may be particularly difficult ideas or procedures to be learned about which you will want to give your students a heads-up. You can reduce student frustration by letting them know that you are aware that some points will be more challenging than others and invite them to ask questions if they need clarification.

Your Body: Tell Them

An effective lecture should consist of much more than a lot of information readily available from your course text or other sources, unless there is a very good reason to so. And, to be honest, there is rarely such a reason. Your lectures should be about giving students knowledge and insight they cannot acquire, or do so easily, for themselves. For instance, your focus should be on helping students grasp complex concepts or see relationships among diverse and seemingly disparate ideas, or appreciate the significance of critical knowledge. This is where your subject-matter expertise best comes. To achieve this within the limited

The best teacher is the one who suggests rather than dogmatizes, and inspires his listener with the wish to teach himself.

—Edward Bulwer-Lytton

time of your class, your lecture needs careful preparation and organization and thoughtful development.

Identifying Your Key Ideas. It is here where your course and class lesson planning can mean all the difference between a good and a bad presentation. Every good lecture, just like every class, needs to find a balance between breadth of coverage and depth of development of ideas. It is commonly recommended that an hour lecture be constructed around no more three to five main ideas. The complexity and difficulty of the ideas themselves will ultimately determine what your students can best handle and, in some cases, this may mean only one idea is best. Most material will be forgotten within moments or a few hours after the class, and one way to come up with your select ideas is to ask, "What information do I want students to understand and still recall the next day?" If your goal is understanding and not the mere short-term absorption of information, you will generally need to limit your main points to allow time and opportunity for sufficient elaboration and development.

Organizing Your Ideas. Obviously, you cannot just string these ideas together. They need to be organized into logical patterns, either as a unified whole that carries throughout the entire lecture, or with each topic developed in its own "mini-lecture" that has clear delineations as you move from one part to another. There are a number of common rhetorical patterns that can make it easy for you to organize the body of your ideas. These should be chosen according to your topic and purpose. Regardless of which strategy is used, the flow of the talk and the transitions from one point to the next should make the relationship between main points clear. Even the most straightforward presentation can leave students lost, especially if their attention wanders, if there are not enough signals that show direction and the relationship of ideas. (See more in the sidebar on "Linking Your Ideas with Transitions.")

Time Pattern. Processes, procedures, or historical developments can often be explained best with a time-sequence pattern. You may go forward in time, or the strategy might be to look backward from the most recent or last event or step. (Time order may seem straightforward. However, be sure you regularly use clear signals that reveal the connections of ideas or events. Otherwise, your students can easily get lost, especially if their attention wanders a bit.)

Space Pattern. A spatial format is very effective in describing relationships. Among its uses are to describe objects or processes or functions that correlate with specific parts of objects (top-bottom, side-to-center, left-to-right, etc.) or to sort things out geographically

> *A good teacher is a master of simplification and an enemy of simplism.*
>
> —Louis A. Berman

(global economic developments) or for hierarchical structures (a company's departmental chart).

Cause/Effect Pattern. In a causal arrangement, two basic strategies may be used to arrange main points. With a cause/effect strategy you begin with a given set of conditions and explain how these will produce or have already produced certain results; with an effect/cause strategy you take a certain set of conditions as the effects and show that they resulted from certain causes.

Problem/Solution Pattern. A problem/solution design may use different strategies. If the listeners are not aware or are only slightly aware of the problem, you will probably need to describe in detail the exact nature of the problem. Sometimes, when listeners become aware of the problem, the solution becomes evident, and little time is needed to develop the solution in the lesson. If your students are already aware of the problem and the possible solutions, you may need only to briefly mention the solutions and spend most of the time showing why one solution is better than others. At other times, you may need to spend time developing both the problem and the solution(s). Still another strategy is to alternate components of the problem with portions of the solution.

Pro/Con Pattern. The pro/con pattern, sometimes called the advantages/ disadvantages pattern, is similar to a problem/solution pattern in that it is usually planned to lead to a conclusion. A major difference with a pro/con pattern, however, is that in the interest of objectivity equal attention is usually given to both sides of an issue. When using the pro/con pattern, you will need to consider whether to present the pro or con first and whether to present both sides and let listeners draw their own conclusions or to present the material in such a way that listeners are led to accept a certain position.

Classification Pattern. A topical division of the main points of a lecture involves determining the categories naturally present within the subject itself. For example, a discussion of learning strategies could break down into perceptual, cognitive, and personality preferences. There are many strategies for arranging topical main points, and the material itself will often suggest the best way for ordering the main points. Your talk can follow a simple-to-complex strategy or move from known to unknown, general to specific, or specific to general. Select the arrangement that both best presents the ideas and best facilitates student understanding of these ideas.

Combination Patterns. A single pattern of organization may make your lecture easier to plan and follow. However, it is possible that none of the

> *The best learners . . . often make the worst teachers. They are, in a very real sense perceptually challenged. They cannot imagine what it must be like to struggle to learn something that comes so naturally to them.*
>
> —Stephen Brookfield

formal patterns just discussed adequately fits your topic, content, or length of time available. In this case you may find it helpful or even necessary to use a combination of strategies—for example, choosing one organizational style for the main points and different ones for subpoints. The important thing is to be sure that each set of main points or subpoints follows an organization appropriate to your specific instructional goals.

Linking Your Ideas with Transitions

Your pattern of development needs not only to be logical, but this logic needs to be readily apparent to your students. A lack of *evident* coherence can be an enormous obstacle to student comprehension of oral presentations no matter how well they are otherwise presented. Students can easily become lost in the "forest" because of the "trees." A good lecture makes apparent both the overarching ideas (the proverbial forest) and their supporting points (the trees) *plus* offers frequent directional signs that map out the path. These signs make explicit any shifts in direction that help students know where they stand at any point in the lecture, as well as reveal the connections between ideas. Your signals should include letting your students know when you are:

1. providing an overview or outline of your lecture,

2. beginning and ending a topic,

3. emphasizing general ideas or providing specific illustrations and other supporting details, and

4. referencing and connecting new content with prior knowledge.

You can easily achieve of all this using simple verbal cues such as "first," "next," or "in contrast," etc. Which ones you use will, of course, depend on your topic and the pattern of organization you are using. (Some new to teaching may find it necessary to be rather deliberate about the use of organizational markers and transitional expressions. Yet these signals do not need to be labored or overused, which can make a presentation overly formal. In time and with experience, they will come naturally.

Supporting Your Ideas: Establishing Their Significance and Meaning. Selecting the most important subject matter for your lecture and then organizing it in a comprehensible flow creates the skeletal structure of your lecture. You will also need to add some "meat to the bones" if you want to avoid falling into a common pitfall of the weak lecture—a lack of adequate support for your ideas. This problem becomes especially apparent when trying to explain complex or abstract concepts or offering a proof or arguing a position. Remember, what is obvious to you as a subject-matter expert can be completely obtuse to your students. It is critical that your presentations include enough specific illustrations or give substance and clarity to the big, yet often general, ideas around which your lecture is arranged. In other words, a good lecture is not a matter of the forest *or* the trees but the forest *and* the trees. Having sufficient substance demands sufficient preparation.

Refer to Field Guide

A teacher is one who makes himself progressively unnecessary.

—Thomas Carruthers

Chapter 7

Connect Your Lecture to Assigned Readings. You may know that you do not want to just read from written materials at length in your lecture. But this does not mean that you should not try and connect the lecture to the course readings when you are explaining any ideas that students may have trouble grasping. If you do this on a regular basis, you may find that your students will actually read what you have assigned prior to class.

Use Lots of Illustrations to Explain and Clarify. Definitions, examples, comparisons, statistics, quotes, and testimony are among the many different kinds of supporting points you can use. Definitions are not only needed for unfamiliar terms, concepts, or principles, but may be useful with familiar ones that may be loosely and possibly incorrectly understood. (It is also possible for an entire lecture to be a definition of a broad and complex idea.) And be generous with your examples. Just be sure they accurately represent the point you are trying to illustrate and fit the content. Also consider whether or not one long illustration or a series of short ones clustered together would be more suitable. Comparisons, such as analogies and metaphors, will make some concepts clearer by placing an unknown or little understood item beside a similar but better known item. Finally, quotes, both informative and inspirational, can add authority and credibility to points as needed, as well as trigger student reflection and be a refreshing break from the possible tedium of many facts and abstract ideas.

Provide Visual Support for Your Ideas. Visual aids are "worth a thousand words"—and more. They can help you reach your audience and direct their attention, reinforce and illustrate ideas to improve comprehension, as well as help you keep on topic and even keep on time, and they should be a standard complement for most presentations. (There are many kinds of visual tools you can use besides simple tables or charts, such as conceptual maps. This topic is presented in more detail in the Field Guide.)

There are a variety of media you can use to present visual support. The most traditional media used are overhead projectors and transparencies. These should be available to just about anyone, and are easy to use. You can prepare your own visuals or possibly your textbook may have supplemental materials, including ready-made transparencies or other materials. You may even be able to copy or cut and past content from third-party sources (depending on copyright restrictions).

Refer to Field Guide

You can also go a little more high-tech if the technology is available (computer and projector) and use PowerPoint or other software to add visual complements to the verbal content of your lecture. These can include simple highlights, such as bulleted points, or more graphic elements, such as pictures, graphs, diagrams, etc.

When using visual media, keep in mind the following:

1. Be clear about which information is best presented visually or needs graphic support. Visual tools are extremely powerful, but not everything benefits from graphic representation.

2. Consider how best to lay out your visual on your transparency or slide to make it easy for your students to read wherever they may be in the room. Also, be sure to set a proper pace that allows time for your students to read and absorb the information. This may require practice.

3. Keep in mind that you are the central driver of your presentation, not the slides or other visuals.

How artfully you deliver your visuals is as important is how well you design them. It can be tempting to focus on your slides and not your audience. Do not bore your students by reading your slides or by talking to them and not your students.

Use Handouts. Handouts can support your presentations in a number of ways. They can help you grab students' attention, focus your students on the key thematic issues and information for the class, and help you clarify or elaborate complex ideas. Even a simple written outline of your lecture not only can reinforce your oral presentation but will give students something to refer to if they lose the thread of the discussion.

An important consideration, one not often appreciated, is when to distribute handouts. The flow of a presentation is important. Often handouts are passed around without much thought. This can easily interrupt and disrupt student focus as they are passed out or when students read them. Obviously, a handout of your lecture outline should be available at the start of class, but when to pass out those with other content can be somewhat problematic. If the handout is not needed to support or elaborate on points in the presentation during the lecture itself but is used as an adjunct to be read after class, then consider holding off on passing them out until the end of the class. On the other hand, occasionally taking a few moments to give handouts to your students can provide a needed break or allow you to regroup at a lagging point, especially when students' attention may already be fading. The bottom line is to consider the purpose and timing as tools that can strategically help or disrupt your lecture.

> *What the teacher is is more important than what he teaches.*
>
> —Karl Menninger

Refer to Field Guide

Your Conclusion: Tell Them What You Told Them

How a class ends is rarely given the same thought given to how it might begin. Too often classes come to their end for one reason and one reason only—you run out of time. (Of course, there are also those who sometimes dismiss class to rescue themselves because they ran out of things to say or lost their students' attention.) However, how you close is just as important as how you start off your presentation. What your students walk out of your classroom with is more important than what you tried to give them. Thus, plan your endings as well as you plan your beginnings, to create a needed, but often missing, sense of completeness and closure. Essentially, a proper conclusion should help your students consolidate what they have acquired and leave them in a positive frame of mind about the lecture and the material.

A Brief Review. Remind the students of the key points presented and leave some time for a few questions. Avoid the temptation to just ask, "Are there any questions?" Be specific, and guide this process with a reference to particular parts of the presentation, again highlighting the most important ideas. For more details, see suggestions in Chapter 7, as well as in Field Guide.

Chapter 7

Refer to Field Guide

A Quick Preview. Consider also creating a sense of movement and generating interest for upcoming lectures with a "preview of coming attractions." In particular, if outside class readings are relevant and provide a foundation for your next class, let the students know this, so they come prepared for new material.

Your Delivery

The quality of your delivery is measured primarily in terms of how well you are able to get your listeners' attention and keep them engaged. In a traditional lecture (as opposed to the enhanced and interactive forms described in the next chapter) this almost completely depends on you—your personality and presentation skills.

You Teach Who You Are

As far as personality goes, clearly you are who you are. Good teaching does not require changing your basic character, nor can anyone expect you to. However, students value instructors and often believe they learn more from those they consider to be enthusiastic, accessible, and caring. By enthusiastic, we mean a demonstrated love of your discipline and teaching. Being accessible means being friendly and available to students when they need help, and caring is a matter of you genuinely expressing your concern about what your students are learning by challenging them and consistently doing your best. The bottom line is: How can you expect your students to be

> *A teacher who is attempting to teach without inspiring the pupil with a desire to learn is hammering on cold iron.*
>
> —Horace Mann

interested in what you are teaching if you do not express a sincere interest yourself?

Adding a Little Pizzazz to Your Delivery

It is common for new instructors, as well as experienced ones who may fall victim to their own routines, to be unconscious of their delivery style and behaviors as they stand in front of their classes. Even the best among us can become nervous and too focused on the content of our message and lose sight of its medium, or the way it is being communicated. But one of the great adages of the information age is "the medium *is* the message." Despite the availability of high-tech teaching tools today, when it comes to a traditional lecture, you are and will likely always be the primary "medium."

Refer to Field Guide

Many excellent resources (books, journals, professional societies and magazines, etc.) offer guidelines for presenters to follow to improve their public speaking skills. They generally focus on the effective use of voice, mannerisms, and movement in the delivery of a presentation. Here are some basic suggestions.

A Little Attention Helps

It is often recommended that you videotape yourself or have a colleague observe you. Although we would encourage you to do so, for most of us this can be awkward and even intimidating. A less daunting and easier approach is to develop the practice of being more and more mindful of what you do when delivering your lectures. Your self-monitoring can begin very simply by identifying one particular element you want to improve on. Limit your observations to just a few moments during a class so as not to become overly self-conscious or distracted from your lecture. Using the guidelines and suggestions we include here (as well as those that can be found in the Field Guide), you should be able to recognize some of your strengths and weaknesses. After you have a handle on what you may want to improve, move on to another quality and do the same. Over time, you will gain confidence and become a much more effective presenter without having to formally train to do so.

Your Voice Quality

Refer to Field Guide

Tone and Inflection. You want to mesmerize your students, not put them into an hypnotic state. Your ability to modulate your tone and volume for emphasis and effect are critical to your ability to get and maintain your students' attention and interest. (If you do not show interest in your talk, why should you expect your students to?) Most often, a relaxed, natural conversational style works best. This will come automatically if you care about and are enthusiastic about what teach.

(Remember, a teacher's genuine passion for the subject matter is a highly regarded quality of what students believe is good teacher.) However, there will be times when you are just not feeling up to things. Then you may have to be more conscious of your effort.

Volume. It is common for instructors to focus their attention on those closest to them. However, it is important to make all students feel they are a part of what is going on and to include all students in your presentation by projecting your voice and presence through all parts of the room. This is especially true in a large classroom, where you have students inclined to sit at the back or sides of the room. Even though there will be those who prefer be "invisible" by sitting at a distance from you in the rear of the class (or maybe near the door for a quick escape), you want to do your best to include everyone and make them feel they are part of what is going on. To keep your voice strong, keep your chin up when talking; avoid speaking while looking down at your notes or at transparencies on a projector. And (do we really need to say this?) definitely avoid talking to the board or slides on a screen. If your voice does not have a natural strength to maintain a mostly conversational tone, then consider using a microphone. Even an inexpensive set-up can make a big difference.

Pacing and Pauses. Pacing is a critical skill in public speaking. Students need time to take notes and assimilate information. Speaking too quickly will make this difficult. Going too slowly, however, may leave them bored. Therefore, you need to try to vary the pace to suit your own style, your message, and your audience. For example, deliver important points more emphatically and slowly than anecdotal examples. If you tend to speak quickly, like many of us sometimes do, especially when nervous, repeat your major points so that students can absorb them. Your pauses can also have an important role in your presentation. A pause can gain attention and be used for emphasis to highlight a thought. You can also give yourself and your audience a short rest—for example, by sipping a drink. This can help you gather your thoughts and allow your students to finish taking notes before you move on to the next topic.

Your Body Language. Your nonverbal communications are about both making sure you communicate what you intend to communicate and making personal connections with your listeners. There is a vast amount of research on nonverbal communication that tells us that *how* you communicate what you are saying greatly overrides *what* you are saying and the message you intend to convey. Many studies on the relative influence of visual signals with a speaker's words have concluded that more than 50 percent of a speaker's impact on an audience actually comes from visual cues and body language; only about 10 percent comes from words, with 40 percent from tone and quality of the voice. Listeners do not always consciously recognize these

> *A good teacher is like a candle—it consumes itself to light the way for others.*
>
> —Author Unknown

signals; nevertheless, they will have a significant influence on your students' feelings about you and your presentation.

The "Eyes" Have It. Maintaining eye contact is an extremely powerful way to establish rapport and maintain the attention of your listeners. If you initially find this difficult to do, begin by making occasional eye contact with one or two students (without becoming fixated on anyone in particular—you know what we mean!); then begin to shift to others, as this becomes part of your routine. Over time, you can expect to feel more at ease and find eye contact to be a natural way to connect with your students.

Gestures. Many speakers do not know what to do with their hands while they lecture. To avoid making nervous gestures, they will seek to maintain control by clutching a podium or holding a marker or pen, or keep their hands in their pocket. Doing these things can be okay, but your hand movements can also become an asset rather than a liability if you learn to use them consciously and deliberately for effect. This does not mean you need to act in ways that are not natural for you. But it is good to let your enthusiasm show or to use gestures to highlight important points you want to make.

Posture and Movement. Your posture and movement are other forms of body language that can also be either liabilities or assets.

- *Posture:* Good posture is not necessarily what your mom told you or what you may have learned in the military. Being erect is good; being stiff is bad. You want to be upright and yet relaxed. Unless you are comfortable watching a video of yourself in action, this will be a matter of feel. You want to have a "presence" that projects a sense of confidence (even if you do not always feel this) evident through your posture. This presence needs to be balanced. It should reinforce your credibility as a subject-matter authority while also communicating your accessibility as a teacher.

- *Movement:* Movement is another effective way to create connections with your listeners. You can do this by just moving around the room during a presentation rather than remaining in the front of the class. At first you may find this difficult to do, particularly if you need to keep referring to your notes or feel more comfortable staying close to a podium. (Yes, it is okay to have a "security blanket.") At the same time, be willing to be a bit adventuresome. Remember, students like best those teachers they feel a connection with. Creating this link can be as easy as moving closer to a student in a nonthreatening manner when you are speaking. Also, since the eye naturally follows movement, you will get and keep their attention more easily and often.)

Professors known as outstanding lecturers do two thing; they use a simple plan and many examples.

—W. McKeachie

A Word on Humor

The use of humor is consistently rated high among desirable teacher characteristics. You may want to consider, therefore, incorporating a little laughter into your lectures. Just be aware that it can be a two-edged sword. A touch of relevant humor can perk up even the dullest topics and keep a lecture fresh, and build a feeling of unity in the classroom. Or, if not appropriate, it can distract or offend students and stop your lecture dead in its tracks. What works will depend on the circumstances plus the gender, race, and sociocultural background of your students. If you use humor, keep these points in mind:

- To be perceived as effective by students, your humor needs to add to the content of the presentation or contribute to a point you are trying make. Humorous examples are one way to do this.

- Be careful about using humor in tests or other anxiety-producing situations, for it can be detrimental when pressure to perform makes students anxious.

- Do not make any specific student the target of the humor, and avoid self-disparaging humor because it can undermine your credibility.

- Humor that has female targets is perceived as funnier than humor with male targets, but can easily come across as sexist.

- It has been shown that students appreciate humor used by male instructors more than by female instructors. Thus, female instructors may need to be a little more cautious or experienced to pull humor off successfully.

> *Good teaching is one-fourth preparation and three-fourths theater.*
>
> —Gail Godwin

CHAPTER WRAP-UP

There is no simple formula for transforming poor lectures into good or great ones. There are many parameters involved that range from the organization and quality of the content to the presentation style. If you are an inexperienced instructor, the implementation of these may take time and practice. The best way to develop your mastery is to incorporate one or two new ideas at a time, see how they work, and modify as you go along.

At the same time, remember that the ultimate criterion for determining the effectiveness of your presentations is not determined by the content covered or your performance or how your students or you might feel about them. What counts are the outcomes—what your students learn. Keeping a focus on learning can be the best guide for

Refer to Field Guide

improving the quality of your lectures and reducing any performance anxiety you may feel. Good lectures will come naturally when you start to incorporate practices that facilitate learning as explained throughout this book and the companion Field Guide.

SPRINGBOARDS FOR FURTHER LEARNING

Key Terms

effective lectures	presentation tools
lecture styles	public speaking
lecture delivery	speech communication
nonverbal communication	visual aids
presentation skills	

INTERNET ACTIVITY

With the wide selection of resources on presenting effective lectures and developing public speaking skills available on the Internet, your key term search will lead you to the information you will need to take the next steps in improving your ability to give great lectures.

...knowledge your students ultimately acquire and comprehend and what you transmit to them, no matter how efficiently you do so, is the final measure of the success of your presentation. Even if you faithfully follow best guide[lines for] deliv[e]ry of a quality tradi[tional lecture], this mode of presentation can carry you and your learners only so far. If you desire to take your instruction to the next level...

...want to consider two expanded formats for your lectures, the enhanced and the interactive lecture. Each of these designs incorporates additional instructional elements and modifies the teacher/student roles that can promote deeper and more enduring learning. They are distinguished by a shift along the teacher-centered/learner-centered continuum, with the enhanced lecture toward the middle of the spectrum and the interactive lecture...

CHAPTER 7

Presentation: The Better and the Best—Enhanced and Interactive Lectures

One day a mother comes home from work and asks her son, "What did you do today?" The son replies, "I taught our dog how to play the piano." The mother, incredulous, asks, "Our dog can play the piano?" to which the son laughed and replied, "Of course not mom. I said that I taught him; I didn't say that he learned how."

—Anonymous

Do You Know:

- Different ways to stimulate student interest?
- How to add "body" to the body of your presentations?
- How graphic tools can make a difference in what students understand?
- Simple things you can do to create interactivity during lectures?
- What you can do to get your students thinking about what they are hearing?
- How to end your class on a high note?

189

Introduction

The knowledge your students ultimately acquire and comprehend and not what you transmit to them, no matter how efficiently you do so, is the final measure of the success of your presentation. Even if you faithfully follow the best guidelines for the delivery of a quality traditional lecture, this mode of presentation can carry you and your learners only so far. If you desire to take your instruction to the next level, then you will want to consider two expanded formats for your lectures, the enhanced and the interactive lecture. Each of these designs incorporates additional instructional elements and modifies teacher/student roles that can promote deeper and more enduring learning. They are distinguished by a shift along the teacher-centered/learner-centered continuum, with the enhanced lecture toward the middle of the spectrum and the interactive lecture strongly favoring a more learner-centered orientation.

> *If you're not failing every now and again, it's a sign you're not doing anything very innovative.*
>
> —Woody Allen

Teaching-Learning Continuum: Shifting from Teacher-Centered Instruction to Learner-Centered Instruction

Teacher-Centered Instruction   →   Learner-Centered Instruction

←——————————————————————————→

Traditional Lectures	→	Enhanced Lectures	→	Interactive Lectures
Content Focus		→		Learning Process Focus
Teacher Control		→		Learner Interaction
Information Acquisition		→		Knowledge Construction

From Good to Better: Enhanced Lectures

If we extend the metaphor of a traditional lecture as a "vehicle" for delivering information, the enhanced lecture can be considered as an improved delivery system that goes beyond the "no-frills, standard model" to include added features to present content. Both the traditional and the enhanced lecture fit into the simple matrix suggested by the maxim "tell them what you are going to tell them, tell them, and tell them what you told them." However, the content of an enhanced lecture is "packaged" for delivery with greater variety and creativity. Rather than just structuring content into units of size and shape that make "for ease of handling," as one might to in the standard version, an enhanced lecture presents and "shapes" content into a range of forms to increase student interest in and engagement with the subject matter. In general, the purpose here is to develop a broader repertoire of teaching tools and techniques that add more variety and more substance to your presentations.

Openings with Impact

An enhanced lecture seeks to go beyond the perfunctory preview of the content used to open a class to generate more interest, better understanding, and even a bit of intrigue and pathos to your presentation. Over time it will become relatively easy to come up with many different ideas for your opening routines.

Refer to Field Guide

Creating More Interest

Opening Question(s). A single provocative question, whether rhetorical or one to be answered later in the lecture, can compel student attention and arouse thinking. A series of questions, perhaps written out on a board or given as handout for reference, can be used as an alternative to a preview or a lecture outline given as bullet points or statements.

Startling Statement. This also can provoke students' involvement by getting them engaged early on. Examples are an intriguing fact or authoritative opinion that stimulates thoughtful consideration or debate.

Measure twice,
Cut once.

—Carpenter's adage

Interesting or Famous Quotation. You probably already have some of your own favorites. If not, there is an enormous variety of quotes on a wide range of topics available on the Internet. Just do a search with "Quotes" and your topic as the key terms.

Problem or Paradox. This may be a brief problem, which, like a question to be answered, is posed up front and then solved later in the lecture. You may also want to present a puzzling paradox that defies common sense and may not have any apparent solution (often found in math and the sciences) that gets your students' mental juices flowing. An entire curricular design model known as "problem-based learning" is found in Chapter 14.

Chapter 14

Short Story or Personal Experience. Appeal to your students with a human interest story from your or someone else's life. It may be about a noted figure in the discipline being studied or an account of a scientific discovery and study that tells personal story behind otherwise bare-bone facts of course material that will make them more meaning-ful and memorable.

Demonstration. Depending on your subject matter, a demonstration can do as much to create interest as an opening. It can be rather straightforward or, better yet, open-ended, thus raising a question or posing a problem that piques curiosity or directs student attention throughout a lesson in search of a solution.

Current Event or Topical Issue. Connect the content of the lecture to a relevant news story or a long-standing issue that can create a context for and establish the importance of your topic.

Mapping Out the Learning Territory

As discussed previously, we learn and remember new things better by relating them to concepts and skills with which we are already familiar. Here are some suggestions to help make these important connections for your students.

Rapid Review. In addition to the perfunctory *preview* of a traditional lecture, offer a "snap shot" *review* of the specific content of a prior les-son or outside class reading that links to and/or provides a foundation for new material to be presented. The goal is to highlight significant material and help direct your students' attention to the most important features of the upcoming presentation.

Prior Knowledge Probe. A prior knowledge probe goes beyond a "snapshot" review that refreshes earlier learning. Consider it a wide-angle scan of the "learning landscape." It is intended is to generate a mental "map" so that learners can "locate" themselves and the con-tent of the current lesson in relation to the overall "territory" covered by the course and discipline. You can achieve this is a number of ways, some more involved than others. For the purposes here, a few state-ments of significant ideas or questions that key in on such ideas can suffice. An elaboration of this technique is presented below.

Advanced Organizer. The use of advanced organizers bring together the best elements of effective reviews, previews, and prior knowledge probes. These powerful learning tools clarify what your students already know, introduce new ideas, and reveal the relationships, or organization, of ideas, plus develop important links between old and new information. These organizers may be verbal explanations but more preferably, you should consider the use of charts, diagrams, and other visual representations that can make easily evident how ideas relate to one another.

A wisely chosen illustration is almost essential to fasten the truth upon the ordinary mind, and no teacher can afford to neglect this part of his preparation.

—Howard Crosby

Chapter 2

Refer to Field Guide

A Better Body

No, we are not suggesting you need to become a member of your local gym. This is about different enhancements to the delivery of your lectures that add impact, substance, and variety.

Learning Is in the Eye of the Beholder

As we have already emphasized, visual aids are valuable and at times indispensable tools for facilitating learning. Dual encoding postulates that knowledge is stored in two forms, verbal (words) and visual (images). The more you use visual representations to support verbal explanation the better your students will be able to think about and recall what you want them to learn. Such visual aids allow for deeper understanding by going beyond presenting facts in isolation to making more evident the patterns or links among facts and ideas. Moreover, at times a picture may be even be worth more than a thousand words, for there are occasions when there may be no words to effectively convey or clarify an abstract or complex concept. Some specific kinds of visual tools are discussed below.

Chapter 2

Process Organizers. Under this label come a host of tools that can be used to describe various processes. Many of these correspond to the various organizational patterns you can use for your lectures (explained in the previous section), such as time, cause/effect, problem/solutions, etc. Here are three examples:

Venn Diagrams. These are used for categorizing information or to compare and contrast.

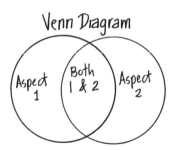

Good teaching is more a giving of right questions than a giving of right answers.

—Josef Albers

Comparison Matrix. As the name suggests, comparisons matrixes are another way to show the similarities and differences between two or more objects of learning.

Concept Maps. These are topical web-like arrangements for gathering or exploring knowledge and representing complex ideas or systems that have many component elements.

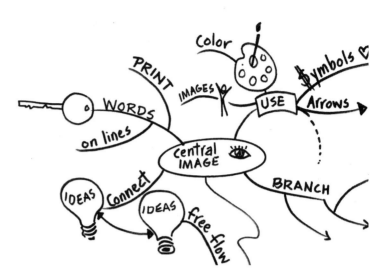

A creative variation of the concept map is the Mind Map©, which uses images and drawings in addition to words to present information.

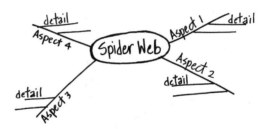

More on Analogies. Though a proven thinking and learning tool, analogies are largely underappreciated, and are worth a brief elaboration. Analogies as a type of comparison can do more than simply reveal the feature or qualities of different things by showing how they are alike or different. Analogies can help students easily grasp unfamiliar or complex ideas by relating them to something they understand. They are especially useful when using concrete illustrations to help convey abstract concepts and principles, such as those frequently found in the sciences; consider the abstract idea of invisible electrical currents. One could explain this using an analogy, describing how an electrical current is much like the flow of water in a stream moving across a fixed point in time. Or consider how one might explain the activity within a cell as like a factory with many different functions and processes. A model for teaching with analogies would follow these simple steps:

1. the introduction of the concept,
2. the introduction of the analog concept,

3. the identification of the shared features of the two,

4. the mapping/charting of these similarities (with an explanation of any possible places where the comparison may fall short, and

5. the drawing of conclusions.

Stories

"Once upon a time there was. . . ." Who doesn't love a good story? We have already suggested using a brief story to open a lecture on occasion. You can use a story, however, to do more, and can organize and present your entire presentation using a story structure, or narrative. Stories are suitable for information that can be told as a string of events or the description of processes and procedures that operate in an orderly manner. Also, a classroom narrative may be linked to a major discovery, study, experiment, or figure in the field that can give life to and provide the context for otherwise dry facts.

With a little ingenuity narratives can be used for many kinds of subject matter, even something as mundane as teaching accounting techniques, for example. Rather than lecture on how to set up a bookkeeping system, lessons can be taught through scenarios that involve the real-life operations of a new business that students must start and run. This approach can make otherwise dry facts and old ideas fresh and unforgettable over the years. In essence, a story or narrative raises unanswered questions or unresolved conflicts that characters encounter and then answer or resolve. The story line will have a beginning, middle, and end and puts general principles or abstract ideas into the particulars of experiences that are situated in time and place, thus giving concrete form to generalities. It is true that we often learn best from experience. Although you cannot always give students direct experience with important concepts, with stories you might come close.

Variety—Don't Forget the Spice

The advice is simple—do not do the same thing in the same way in every class. Not only do students need variety to accommodate their learning styles, they need variety to sustain their interest. There are so many ideas that we offer in this text and the companion Field Guide, you should have no problem expanding over time your repertoire of teaching practices and keeping yourself out of the rut of repeated and dull routines.

All Good Things Must Come to an End

How you end your class is no less important than how you conduct the rest of it. Indeed, much of the value of what you and your students have

Grown-ups never understand anything for themselves, and it is tiresome for children to be always and forever explaining things to them.

—Antoine de Saint-Exupóry

done can be lost or at least greatly diminished if your classes consistently have a weak close.

Creating Closure

Always plan your time well enough to leave a few a minutes at the end of class for reflection and tying up loose ends. If you make this a ritual, your students will anticipate it. It will also encourage them to stay focused on important learning points throughout the class.

An easy and quick technique to end a class is called "ticket to leave." It can provide feedback to you about the success of your class, help students pull together what they learned, or challenge them to extend their understanding through a question requiring some application. The exercise involves a prompt or question that requires only a brief time to respond, certainly no more than 5 minutes, but perhaps only 1 to 2 minutes. These can be shared orally by a few students, or written on an index card that you collect for you to review after class. Some possible prompts or questions to use for the ticket to leave are the following:

- Name one important thing you learned in class today.
- Ask one question about today's content—something that has left you puzzled.
- Today's lesson had three objectives. (These would have been shared at the start of class and should still be available for referencing.) Which of the three do you think was most successfully reached? Explain. Which was not attained? Why do you think it was not?
- Read this problem: [insert problem]. Tell me what your first step would be in solving it.
- Do you have any suggestions for how today's class could have been improved?
- I used overheads extensively today. Were they helpful to you in learning? Why or why not?
- Which of the readings you did for class today was most helpful in preparing you for the lesson? Why?
- We did a concept map activity in class today. Was this a useful learning activity for you? Why or why not?

End on a High Note

Finally, consider the emotional level of the class at its conclusion and how you can end on a positive note. Too often classes end with the energy level at a low point, even the lowest point of the class, rather than at a peak. This may seem natural, especially for a long class. However, if you think of the finish of one class not just as an end but as a

> *Given the recent invention of the printing press, why do college professors continue to lecture so much?*
>
> —Anonymous

transition and introduction to the next class, then you can appreciate the importance of concluding each session on a high note. For example, you can invite students to give their neighbors high-fives and/or or have upbeat music playing as they leave the room. Obviously, what you choose to do is up to you and should reflect who you are and what you are comfortable with. Anything less than an expression of your genuine feelings will come across as just an act, something your students will easily recognize. The important point is to appreciate that your endings are as important as your beginnings and are worthy of your attention.

From Better to Best: The Interactive Lecture—"When Less Is More"

An interactive lecture incorporates the best of both what a traditional and an enhanced lecture can offer, but it goes further. These features are more than just a few added "options." An interactive lecture is based on a much different conceptualization of instruction and teacher and learner roles and takes a presentation one significant step further along the teacher-centered/learner-centered continuum.

Teach to the problems, not to the text.

—E. Kim Nebeuts

To revisit our earlier metaphor, in the traditional lecture, the teacher can be viewed mostly as a "deliverer" of information, students passively receiving content, and in the enhanced lecture as a "driver" of learning, with students along for the "ride" as you identify and describe points of interest. When it comes to an interactive lecture, however, things are quite different. On this "ride," both you and your students share the driving, with frequent stops along the way as you actively explore the learning landscape. Not only is there a dramatic shift in student involvement; teaching goals are also different here. Through its interactivity, this format encourages students to interactively process knowledge rather than to passively absorb it to construct a personal and deeper understanding of what you want them to learn. Thus, in the interactive lecture less becomes more—the less you do, the more your students can learn.

General Considerations for Using Interactive Teaching Techniques

Many interactive lecture techniques take some of the previous suggestions for presenting the three segments of a lecture—the opening, body, and closing—and add an active, learner-centered spin to them. You can think of these teaching tools as the educative equivalent of a good Swiss Army knife. With a little planning, creativity, and experience, many of them have multiple applications that can be plugged in at different points in your lecture to serve different purposes based on their timing and content.

For example, the same technique when involving personal student information may be used as an icebreaker for introductions at the start of a class, when used with information related to the lecture topic as a lead-in before a lecture segment, and also provide opportunity for review when used afterward. Moreover, these techniques can be used in different configurations, such as in pairs, small groups, or the whole class, with the configuration influencing what they achieve. Lead-ins done in pairs or small groups, for instance, are great for activating prior knowledge, while if done with the whole class they can also work as an introduction to a topic and as an opportunity for you to discover what students already know. Many of these teaching tools are explained in detail in the Field Guide. Two fundamental considerations that apply to the use of any of these interactive techniques are discussed below.

Refer to Field Guide

To teach well, we need not say all that we know, only what is useful for the pupil to hear.

—Anonymous

Always Have a Clear Purpose

When you plan your classes, you will want to decide what activity to use and how often to use it. In general, these techniques can be mixed and matched to achieve different purposes:

1. to preview a topic,
2. to activate your students' prior knowledge of the topic,
3. to get feedback on what they are getting during the course of your presentation, or
4. for a quick review.

By planning exactly when to insert an activity, you can make sure that your students pay the most attention to the issues that you feel are most important. Do not do activities for their own sake; they should be integrally related to giving students practice with the most important concepts in that day's class. Also, remember that variety is a powerful force. Using a handful of activities you can draw on comfortably will keep students on their toes, wondering what you will do next.

Carefully Consider Their Timing and Duration

Learner attention waxes and wanes in approximately 20-minute cycles; therefore, use the 20-minute attention span as a rule of thumb: In a 50-minute class, insert one interactive activity in the middle; in a 75-minute class, try two, at roughly one-third and two-thirds of the way through the class period. But do not follow this slavishly; anything that becomes predictable will have less impact. How long each activity takes will depend on your topics, your students, the size of the class, and the activity itself. In most cases many of the ones suggested below can be done in somewhere between 1 and 2 minutes and perhaps 10 minutes. Be sure to save at least one-third of the time you allow for debriefing for activities that call for it.

Some Multipurpose Interactive Lecture Practices

Whichever ones of these you try out and for whatever purpose, all of them are great ways to lift the energy of the room any time student attention may be lagging. Use them liberally and have fun with them. If you are enthusiastic about them, your students will likely feel the same.

Everyone's a Liar

Purpose: Icebreaker, lead-in, prior knowledge activator, or review

Configuration: Pairs, small groups, or whole class

Description: For a lead-in, prior knowledge activator, or review of a topic, write on the board three statements concerning the subject, two of them true and one false. As an icebreaker, have the students make these statements about themselves. Participants then ask "lie detector" questions to get additional information in order to determine which statement is false. Participants decide (or vote on in a large group) which statement is a lie.

Close/Debrief: Reveal which are truths and which are lies.

> *It is not the answer that enlightens, but the question.*
>
> —Eugene Ionesco

What's the Question?

Purpose: Lead-in, prior knowledge activator, get feedback, or review

Configuration: Individual, pairs, small groups, or whole class

Description: Write some facts on the board and have the students try to find the question that matches each fact.

Close/Debrief: When they have come up with a good number of questions, tell them which are correct or have them vote and justify their responses.

Word Tree

Purpose: Topic lead-in, prior knowledge activation, or review

Configuration: Individual, pairs, small groups, or whole class

Description: Generate a list of words related to the topic. You can provide these yourself or ask students to do so. Write all suggestions on the board and then, depending on the time you want to allot to the activity, cluster them by theme where possible, either yourself or with input from your students.

Close/Debrief: If important terms and concepts are missing, you can introduce these here.

Quick Quiz (ungraded)

Purpose: Topic lead-in, prior knowledge activation, or review

Configuration: Individual, pairs, small groups, or whole class

Description: You can use multiple-choice, true/false, or complete-a-phrase quizzes. Make clear that this is not for a grade, but to help students learn more and to get feedback on what they know and understand about the topic. If given at the beginning or in the course of your presentation, you can walk around and discretely scan participants' responses to help you to identify where to focus your attention during the class.

Close/Debrief: You can also check the answers with the group at the end of the session.

One-Minute Paper

Purpose: Topic lead-in, prior knowledge activation, review, or deeper thought

Configuration: Individual

Directions: Give students 1 minute to write as much as they can, without editing, about what they know regarding a topic (lead-in and knowledge activation), what they just learned (review and deeper understanding), or what they may not understand or be confused about (clarification)

Close/Debrief: Let students keep for themselves as a personal review, or take a few moments to have them share in pairs what they wrote. You may also collect them to get feedback on what they have learned.

Think/Pair/Share

Purpose: Topic lead-in, prior knowledge activation, review, or deeper thought

Configuration: Pairs

Directions: You can ask a question for students to discuss or answer or pose a problem to solve. Rather than just give students examples to illustrate a concept, an abstract idea, or a principle, ask students to provide their own. This will get them thinking much more deeply about the topic.

Close/Debrief: Have students share what they came up with in the activity. This will give you feedback on where they are at and provide other students with new insights that can support their understanding.

Muddiest Point

Purpose: Topic lead-in, prior knowledge activation, or clarification

Configuration: Individual, pairs

Directions: Ask students to share something they do not understand, are confused about, or just about which they would like more information. This can be done orally, which can save a little time and help

---

Learning is a treasure that will follow its owner everywhere.

—Chinese Proverb

individual students appreciate that they may not be the only one who may need clarification. However, consider having them write this down on index cards and collect them at a break or the end of class.

Close/Debrief: You can share some of the responses for the benefit of all, or keep them as feedback for yourself alone.

Do Not Forget Individual Questions

All the above have been suggested for use with groups, small or large, as well as individually. For the sake of time, you will probably be inclined to use the pair or group formats frequently. There are times, however, when you may find it particularly helpful when practical (e.g., a small class) to use questions students respond to individually. At the open of a lecture or before a new segment, these can identify individual student learning needs and goals, encourage the sharing of information and resources, and/or bring to the surface resistance to learning. After a lecture or important topic, it will allow you to assess individual student understanding. Students can respond to questions in a predetermined order (e.g., left to right, front to back), or randomly in popcorn-style, by volunteering responses. If you let participants speak in random order, remember that one of the purposes of this activity is to get people talking, so try to ensure that everyone in the group makes a contribution. To encourage free-flow participation, ask participants to listen to all contributions, but reserve their comments for discussion later in the session.

A Final Word—Alternative Forms of Presentation

Lectures are the default form for conveying information to students. However, at certain times or for specific subjects (e.g., those that need to teach procedures or manual skills or where there is no way to communicate something verbally), other forms are called for. These include lab classes and the use of demonstrations. You may also be using computer-mediated instruction in your classroom or as the entire context of instruction, as in distance learning. Given the more general purposes of this text, we are not able to explore these here. However, we have included valuable tips on how to effectively use technology in the classroom or for distant learning in.

Chapter 16

CHAPTER WRAP-UP

The word *lecture* is derived from Latin with the root meaning of "to read." Clearly, no teacher today believes that standing before a class to read material is an effective way to instruct. However, many teachers still rely on the lecture as their default method of teaching to convey information in a time-efficient manner. We have suggested that there is nothing inherently wrong with lectures and, when done well, lectures can be used effectively for many topics and in certain settings—for example, large classes. Therefore, we have provided basic guidelines on how to conduct a quality lecture in its traditional form. But we have also suggested that you consider expanded formats, especially interactive presentations, to improve student learning. Your students will appreciate it, and so will you if you take the time to try them out. As always, experiment with them in a managed and mindful manner. Add new ideas or techniques one at a time, observe how they work, get feedback from your students when appropriate, and modify and refine if necessary.

SPRINGBOARDS FOR FURTHER LEARNING

Key Terms

active learning
advanced organizers
classroom assessment
  techniques
graphic teaching aids
interactive lectures

story telling
teaching with analogies
visual learning tools
visual thinking tools

Key Names

Patricia Cross and Angelo Thomas are commonly associated with many of the interactive teaching tools we have introduced here in their book, *Classroom Assessment Techniques.*

CHAPTER 8

Personalizing Knowledge: Taking a Deep Approach to Teaching and Learning

Teachers need to know more than their subject. They need to know the ways it can be understood, what ways it came to be understood, what counts as understanding: they need to know how individuals experience the subject.

—Diana Laurillard

Do You Know:

- The differences between surface and deep understanding?
- When deep learning and understanding are most needed?
- How you can encourage your students to take a deeper approach to learning?
- What skills you need to facilitate deep approaches to learning?
- How to ask questions skillfully?
- How to facilitate a good discussion?

203

Introduction

Previously we have used a number of metaphors for teaching and learning. In the previous chapter we extended the common metaphor for lectures as a system for "delivering" information. We suggested ideas for moving from the traditional format, which primarily seeks to convey information, to a more interactive one, which shifts the goals of instruction, as well as teacher and student roles, to a focus on student learning and the student's increased responsibility for learning.

With a focus on the "personalization" of knowledge or deep understanding, the activities explained in this chapter shift further along the teacher/learner-centered continuum, with the focus almost entirely on the learner side.

Instructors no longer have the primary responsibility for student learning outcomes when it comes to students' personalization of knowledge—the students do. Indeed, a deep understanding of subject matter can come only from what students do for themselves. Students now become the "driver" of their learning, with you in the passenger seat. This does not mean you are only along for the ride. Think of this situation as akin to driver training school. Students are behind the wheel, but you also have your own steering wheel and brake. This enables you to exercise control and provide direction whenever needed. Your goal is to facilitate a deeper approach to learning by your students rather than to teach. You leave as much of the "driving" as possible to your students so that they may learn from their own explorations and experience.

There is a wide assortment of learning activities that accommodate this style of instruction. In general, these activities are designed to engage learners at a deeper level of learning that elaborates on topics and helps students to integrate and apply what they know. In this chapter we examine some of the more common and valuable among these activities. Since your role here is to assist or (to return to another metaphor from an earlier chapter) "orchestrate" student learning activities and experiences, we include in this discussion some skills needed for facilitating these processes.

Deep Learning and Understanding— So, What Does It Really Mean?

Deep knowledge, deep learning, and *deep understanding* are three terms often used interchangeably to characterize what many consider to be the ideal and even ultimate goal of instruction. These concepts are intuitively appealing and powerfully suggestive. But they can also be difficult to define, and it is unlikely that any two people have the same idea of what this kind of knowledge, learning, and understanding actually look like. To fully appreciate learning activities designed to

> To grasp the meaning of a thing, an event or situation is to see it in its relations to other things; to note how it operates or functions, what uses it can be put to consequences follow from it; what causes it, what it can be put to. In contrast, what we call the brute thing, the thing without meaning to is something whose relations are not grasped.
>
> —John Dewey

promote a greater depth of student knowledge and understanding, we describe in some detail the nature of this kind of learning.

What Does It Mean to Know Something?

"What does it mean to know something?" This is a profound question. Is knowledge something you "possess," like a thing or object, stored away in the mind in an inert state, which can later be recalled and asserted as a statement or used, as behaviorists and cognitivists contend? Is it something chemically represented in networks of brain cells that become activated through some mysterious act of free will and consciousness, as neuroscience may define it? Is it a highly personal, subjective construct that each individual ultimately can determine only for himself or herself, as viewed by psychological constructivism? Or is it something that exists only by consensus among social groups that collectively agree on what something means, as social constructivists will argue? The answers may seem to have more interest to philosophers than to teachers, but they have direct relevance to understanding the goals of education. Fortunately, thinking in educational circles about the nature of knowledge is much less obtuse than the musings of philosophers, and for our purposes we do not need to become philosophers to understand how conceptions of knowledge influence the character of teaching and learning.

Kinds of Knowledge

In general, three major distinctions are made among kinds of knowledge: declarative, procedural, and conditional. A fourth, metaknowledge, is also being discussed more and more as an important kind of knowing.

Declarative Knowledge. This is the *what* of knowing—what something is or what it is meant to do. It is facts and ideas we need to commit to memory and can be asserted as statements or definitions, such as "CPR means cardiopulmonary resuscitation," or "a lecture is a method of delivering information."

Procedural Knowledge. This is *knowing the how* of things—that is, how things are done. It is performance or skills-based knowledge that improves with practice—for instance, how to perform CPR or deliver an effective lecture.

Conditional Knowledge. This is *knowing the when and why* of things. It involves using declarative and/or procedural knowledge under the right circumstances or conditions. For example, you might know what CPR is and even how to perform the procedure, but knowing why and when to use it—the conditions or circumstances of its proper administration—calls for a conditional understanding of the technique.

Chapter 2

Every truth has four corners: as a teacher I give you one corner, and it is for you to find the other three.

—Confucius

Metaknowledge. Metaknowledge is a fourth kind of knowing, as the name indicates; it is *knowledge about knowledge,* or knowledge of how to learn. Often referred to as metacognition, it is a person's understanding of the processes and strategies used in learning.

The first two forms of knowledge are the primary, if not the only, focus of much teaching and training. The last two are the kinds of knowing that reform-minded educators are most concerned about today. They are also the kinds of knowledge that much of this chapter is about.

Levels of Understanding

Chapter 2

To further appreciate the character of a "personalized" understanding, it is helpful to examine the distinction made between two levels of understanding—surface understanding and deep understanding. The use of these two terms mirrors some of the debate and controversy surrounding the different theories of learning that have influenced educational practices. However, the distinctions made here have more to do with how students gather knowledge rather than the kinds of knowledge they are taught.

Surface Understanding

Who hasn't experienced their students (or oneself) preparing hard for an exam only to forget a great deal of what was studied in a matter of days, if not hours? And who hasn't seen students (and again experienced oneself) unsuccessfully trying to use what they have learned as memorized facts or formulas to deal with unfamiliar problems or new or advanced material outside the setting of the original instruction? These observations have even led some to question whether information so readily forgotten or unsuccessfully used was really learned in the first place.

Much school learning occurs on this level. Course textbooks, manuals, lectures, and other materials are filled almost entirely with large amounts of declarative and procedural information (facts, definitions, processes, etc.) that must be committed to memory for recall and/or to perform to some degree of competence at a later date. The teaching of factual knowledge for memorization and recall is an important part of education and foundational learning. The problem is not the knowledge itself, but how learners ultimately understand it.

Memorizing a body of information or repeatedly practicing a skill does not mean something has been learned in a meaningful way. Rote recall often leads to only a superficial or "surface" level of understanding. Knowledge learned at this level may be reproduced on demand, but it is not necessarily knowledge understood for its significance. Knowledge learned at a surface level is frequently fragmented and bound to the situation in which it was first gained. Consequently, students often fail to recognize how what they have learned is part of a

Learning is something students do, not something done to students.

—Alfie Kohn

broader conceptual framework, and they fail to recognize opportunities to transfer it to new situations removed from the original instruction and study. When learners do try to apply information to new situations, they sometimes get caught up in the superficial details of these situations and miss underlying relationships that exist between the information they have learned and the situation they are in. They fail to perceive the essence of what is to be transferred and often try to inflexibly apply memorized procedures, formulas, and facts that are not necessarily relevant to a new learning task.

This is not to say that possessing factual and procedural knowledge is not essential to understanding. The point is that such knowledge, although necessary, is often insufficient. There are many occasions, and ever increasingly so in today's world of work, when learners need to go beyond a surface approach to learning. The question is not whether deep understanding is better than surface knowledge. The proper questions are, "Have my students learned what they need to know in a way that permits them to do more than reproduce facts and/or procedures?" and "Can my students explain, interpret, and apply what they know to succeed in other, possibly more advanced classes, and to perform well on their jobs in the future?" If you cannot answer these questions with an unqualified "yes," then you will gain much from what follows in this chapter.

Deep Understanding

Deeply held knowledge is not information stored inertly in memory or information "on tap," as David Perkins, a noted educational researcher, has described it. The human brain is not a recording device, but a thinking one, and building deep knowledge and understanding involves actively thinking about, discussing, and working with ideas and concepts in meaningful ways.

These are the hallmarks of a deep approach to learning, which can produce knowledge with the qualities described below.

Meaningful and Significant. Deep knowledge is information not just memorized but information appreciated for its meaning and significance. (Just think of the difference between knowing someone and understanding someone.) It is knowledge that has personal relevance to the learner. It is knowledge that yields valuable insights into the most central, defining concepts and primary principles of a field of study for which students develop relatively systematic and integrated understanding that allow them to evaluate the importance of these ideas.

Well Organized and Dynamic. How information is organized in memory determines whether it is meaningfully and deeply understood or simply "shelved" away and later mostly forgotten. Deeply held knowledge is not "compartmentalized" in the mind of the knower (like a

Some folks are wise; some are otherwise.

—Tobias George Smollett

Chapters 2 and 3

Education is the acquisition of the art of the utilization of knowledge. This is an art very difficult to impart. We must be aware of what I will call "inert ideas," that is to say, ideas that are merely received into the mind without being utilized or tested or thrown into fresh combinations.

—Alfred North Whitehead

library card catalogue as isolated bits) but is organized into complex, dynamic, and adaptive networks. Connections have been made between existing knowledge and new knowledge, as well as between the ideas that comprise a body of knowledge, so they are experienced as parts of a whole or system of thought.

Flexible and Usable. Deep knowledge is transferable. It is knowledge that consists of both the what and the how of declarative and procedural understanding and the why and the when of conditional knowledge, all supported by metacognitive awareness. It is knowledge that can be called up when needed and that is readily available for use in novel situations that exist outside the classroom or to solve unfamiliar problems. (A major, but often tacit, assumption in education is that the knowledge students learn in school will transfer to situations and problems encountered outside school. Yet, despite this assumption, as measured by research studies, most educational practices fail to effectively promote transfer. Deep understanding addresses this issue because it makes it easier to see the important relationships and thus increases the likelihood that students will see the relationships and appropriately use what they already know.)

Generative. When knowledge is deeply held, it increases the chance that what one knows will generate new understandings of what one does not know. Deep understanding in one area will not only help students apply what they learn but enable them to make broad connections and build new understandings in other areas in ways that superficial knowledge cannot. In this sense, deep understanding is extensible knowledge that helps students grasp other subject areas by providing insight beyond the particular subject matter studied, thus making comprehensible a range of ideas. And deep knowledge enables learners to approach unfamiliar ideas or solve problems in creative ways. When people possess meaningfully learned concepts, they are more likely to come up with their own useful strategies to solve problems rather than to rely solely on memorized procedures or formulas which, as already argued, may be flawed or applied in ways that do not make sense. Thus, real understanding opens the door to learning on many levels and in many different settings.

Teaching and Learning for Deep Understanding—General Considerations

Though most teachers say they prefer their students to take a deep approach, students often take surface approaches. Some teachers may even believe that a particular approach is characteristic of a student and that there are "deep" students and "surface" students.

But students' approaches are not fixed. A student who takes a deep approach to one subject, or even part of a subject, may take a surface approach to another subject. Learning approaches, in general, can vary according to the learning environment, the learning tasks students are given, and the students' perceptions of the learning environment. There are things you can do to influence the approaches that your students take by discouraging surface approaches and encouraging deeper ones.

Understanding Why Students Take a Surface Approach

There can be a number of reasons why students do not take a deep approach to how they learn. These include factors that have to with the design of your course and methods of instruction, as well as the attitudes and behaviors of your students.

Do not be too timid and squeamish about your actions. All life is an experiment.

—Ralph Waldo Emerson

- Teaching is teacher-focused and emphasizes transmission of information.
- Course content is taught in a way that does not make clear its overall structure or the connections between topics, making it harder for students to make these connections.
- Students see no personal value in learning the subject, and teaching does not help them to find the value.
- The subject matter does not take students' prior knowledge into account, so students are not able to engage meaningfully.
- Assessment and other learning activities can be successfully completed with a surface approach (e.g., exams that call only for the rote learning of facts, with no need for a deeper grasp of materials).
- Students do not get regular and adequate feedback on their progress and their areas of learning strengths and weaknesses.
- There is too much breadth and too little depth to the subject matter, with lots of topics covered but little time to engage with new material more deeply.
- Teaching fails to challenge students or encourages cynicism, anxiety, or other negative feelings about the subject;
- Students have been successful by using surface approaches in the past and have become habituated to learning in a rote, unreflective manner.
- Students have many demands on their time and other commitments and are content with doing the bare minimum necessary to pass the subject.

Teaching for Expertise

To put it into a different context, teaching and learning for deep understanding can be characterized in terms of how an individual progresses from novice learner to become an expert in a particular field of study. This process involves entering into what is considered a "community of practice." Such a community is defined not only by the knowledge that comprises a discipline but also by the ways in which those who are professional members of it think, see, interpret, and behave. (This represents the apprenticeship perspective of teaching described in Chapter 1.) Significant learning happens when our students are guided to become successful professionals themselves in this new domain, becoming acculturated in these new ways of thinking and behaving that are characteristic of those already competently working within it. This enculturation is intended to produce two kinds of changes in students' knowledge of a subject. It seeks to produce quantitative changes in knowledge, the amount of information students possess, and deeper qualitative changes that are reflected in their ability to think about this information in increasingly differentiated and elaborate ways.

We are not making any claims here that taking such an approach will turn novice learners into experts in a matter of weeks or months of study. Gaining expertise is a gradual process that occurs over many years. But it is helpful, if not necessary, to hold the most powerful vision of learning possible. Doing so creates higher expectations and encourages students to deepen their approach to learning, so their understanding progressively approximates what competent professionals in a field know, how they think, and the ways they behave.

Encouraging a Deeper Approach to Learning

Chapters 2 and 3

Many, if not most, of the instructional practices geared for the development of deeper student learning reflect what we know about how people learn best. These practices are learner-centered, authentic, generative, and social in nature and give students opportunities to think about and actively practice with the knowledge you want them to learn.

Your Course and Lesson Design and Treatment of Subject Matter

You can do many things in creating your courses and lessons that guide your students so that they assume deeper approaches to learning.

- Focus on topics that are most worth understanding. These are ideas central to the understanding and practice of a discipline.
- Establish the relevance of the material and share your passion for it.

- Explore student misconceptions that may interfere with or frustrate new understanding.
- Offer clear goals and standards for learning, with the expectation that students not just reproduce information but think about what they are learning.
- Make the structure of the subject explicit so that students can make connections between what they are learning and what they already know, as well as see the relationships among different topics and concepts.
- Match the level of the subject material and the pace at which it is presented with students' prior knowledge.
- As much as possible, teach content using questions and problems that encourage independent exploration, discovery, and knowledge seeking.
- Embed content in authentic contexts and use realistic approaches to solving problems that mirror some of the natural complexities and uncertainties of the real world.
- Offer students opportunities to make reasonable choices about what and how they will learn.
- Use multiple representations and perspectives of content that capture varying student learning preferences and styles.
- Provide regular guidance and support through scaffolding and qualitative feedback that keep student learning on track.
- Attend to the need for student development of and demonstration of metacognitive awareness.
- Align assessment tasks with the desired learning outcomes (e.g., reduce rote recall of theories and facts).
- Limit workload to a level that allows students the wider exploration of ideas and the development of interest.

Three things give the student the possibility of surpassing his teacher: ask a lot of questions, remember the answers, teach.

—Jan Amos Coménius

Student Learning Tasks for Deeper Understanding

What follows is a list of learning activities that encourage and facilitate deeper understanding. As you consider them, do not assume that your students already know how to take such an approach. Providing learning opportunities for deeper understanding can only *encourage* a deeper approach, not ensure that such an approach will be taken. You will need to be as explicit as possible and be ready to provide guidance as needed. (See the section that follows on "Promoting Metacognitive Awareness.")

- Ask students questions to help them accurately integrate new learning with old and identify similarities and differences between the two to avoid misconceptions about new learning.

- Ask students to organize, classify, compare/contrast, explain, etc. and to seek out the relationships among discrete facts, information, and new material using conceptual mapping, outlining, graphics, summaries, etc.
- Involve students in discerning and reporting contextual differences when presenting new problems to support the development of conditional knowledge.
- Have students apply new learning to an unfamiliar problem, in a new situation or within the context of a case study.
- Do not just tell students how to do something, but involve them in describing steps in an operation/procedure, *then* ask them to practice it, report results, and evaluate.
- Involve students in applying decision-making rules and being able to support their decisions with evidence and reasons.
- Have students develop questions or tasks to assess new learning.
- Ask students to explain to each other what they understand.
- Give them opportunities to informally assess the work of their peers.
- Ask students to generate their own example of a concept.
- Challenge students to think of ways new knowledge affects those outside the field.
- Ask students to evaluate their own work or that of their peers.

The lasting measure of good teaching is what the individual student learns and carries away.

—Barbara Harell Carson

Specific Facilitation Strategies for Deep Learning

The following are general strategies for facilitating a deeper approach to learning. They include teaching metacognitive awareness, using questions skillfully, conducting effective classroom discussions, and a handful of innovative teaching models that support the development of deeper understanding of course content.

Promoting Metacognitive Awareness

How people learn is highly personal and experiential. Thus, it is commonly idiosyncratic. It is important to take these individual differences into consideration when trying to facilitate deeper approaches to learning.

Consider the rather straightforward, commonplace instruction; "Please read the next chapter in the text for tomorrow's class." Because of the unique educational experiences and personality of each student,

A little learning is a dangerous thing. Drink deep, or taste not the Pierian spring.

—Alexander Pope

Unit 3

Chapter 7

how each student interprets and responds to this instruction can be quite different from what you had in mind. For some students, this might mean simply starting with the first word of the body of the first paragraph and to proceed until they have reached the end, making or seeing no distinctions between main and supporting ideas. Others may look for such distinctions and will pay attention to and possibly preview subtitles, graphs, topic sentences, or other content to get the gist of the material. Still others might take time for an even more strategic approach and underline, write notes and comments, and think critically about what they are reading as they proceed. When such a variance in approaches can be ascribed to the seemingly "simple" task of reading an assignment, imagine the different understandings and possible misunderstandings that may arise with learning tasks that call for more complex and deeper approaches to study, such as summarizing, analyzing, applying, interpreting, evaluating, or other reasoning skills.

Therefore, teaching students how to learn and reason better is one important component of any instructional designed geared for deeper understanding.

How experts approach problems in their field offers a helpful perspective on this issue. Experts possess many metacognitive skills that enable them to regulate their learning in ways that help them successfully handle many different and unfamiliar tasks. For example, their behavior is strongly driven by prior knowledge and, when faced with an unfamiliar problem, experts commonly construct a similar but simpler problem. They are able to recognize what they know about a topic or a problem, as well as what they do not yet know. They can easily call on personally preferred cognitive strategies for acquiring and using knowledge and monitoring their learning, as well as developing new strategies as needed. These and other skills possessed by practiced professionals or experts are ones that your students also will need to know how to use for deeper learning and understanding.

Your students can begin to develop these same metacognitive skills by observing you as an "expert" and by your making explicit your otherwise implicit reasoning processes. You can make your thinking "visible" by describing how you tackle, for example, a difficult reading selection or go about understanding a new concept or solving a problem. This would include any planning, regulating, and reasoning strategies such as questioning, summarizing, predicting, generating, and evaluating alternatives and how you identify important conceptual relationships and connections. The use of graphic aids or visual thinking tools is particularly helpful.

After modeling your thinking strategies, present students with their own challenges and scaffold support, progressively fading it as your students apply their learning to different learning tasks or problems. Students will also benefit from opportunities to reflect on and articulate their own reasoning methods and how they learn new ideas or solve a problem. They should be asked to discuss and explain their problem-solving processes or strategies, and to compare their processes to those of others. Doing so will not only reinforce their metacognitive abilities, but also will bring out any misconceptions that may block their development of deep understanding.

The Skilled Use of Questioning Strategies

Asking questions and answering them are critical components of effective learning and teaching in any setting, whether it is a large lecture or an interactive one or is in the context of a discussion. Asking and answering questions, however, is not just something you should do because it is commonplace. Effective questioning calls for great skill. This includes knowledge of the different kinds of questions and knowing when to use them. It also involves knowing ways to properly ask questions and respond to student inquiries that will capture and keep their attention, foster involvement and the thoughtful consideration of important ideas, as well as contribute to a positive learning climate.

Two Basic Question Types

There are a number of ways to classify questions in terms of the direction and the level of thinking they seek to produce. Two of most basic types are discussed below.

Closed Questions. Closed questions (also known as convergent questions) call for one correct answer that can often be stated in "yes" or "no" responses or with a factual response. Asking closed questions will not produce the deeper level of understanding we are talking about here. However, they can serve a purpose, such as a "warm-up" for more rigorous thinking challenges or just to shift activities and energy. Students generally need time to acclimate to the classroom and the session. Closed questions asked at the beginning of a session can help get the ball rolling and can give you an idea of how much students already know about a topic that you will be exploring in greater depth.

Open Questions. Open questions require more complicated responses than simply "yes" or "no" or a short factual answer. In general, they will push your students to delve more deeply into a topic and will call for more than a short response. There are many kinds of open questions, some convergent, with a single correct answer, and others divergent, permitting a range of possible acceptable responses, such as an opinion or problem with more than one solution. These are appropriate at any time, but you may want to begin to ask them after students have become comfortable with the session and with you as an instructor.

To be on a quest is nothing more or less than to become an asker of questions.

—Sam Keen

Chapter 13

Chapter 9

The joy of learning is as indispensable in study as breathing is in running. Where it is lacking there are no real students, but only poor caricatures of apprentices who, at the end of their apprenticeship, will not even have a trade.

—Simon Weil

A Common Question Taxonomy

To develop effective questioning skills, you need to consider not only the direction of your questions (open or closed) but the level of the knowledge your questions seek to assess and the kind of reasoning they require for a proper response. The most common knowledge taxonomy is based on Benjamin Bloom's hierarchy of cognitive skills, which progressively calls for a greater degree of critical-thinking ability as one proceeds through the hierarchy. Any of these questions can be combined as a series of probing inquiries that take students more deeply into a topic.

- **Knowledge.** These are closed questions. These call for the simple identification and recall of information and can provide a baseline for further discussion and learning. They are *"Who, what, when, where, how . . . ?"* kinds of questions.

- **Comprehension.** More than rote recall questions, comprehension questions ask students to organize and select facts and ideas that they can recall to summarize and explain their understanding of a topic or reading, etc.

- **Application.** Here learners are called on to explain, give examples of, or possibly demonstrate, the appropriate use of facts, rules, and principles. These include *why, when,* and *how to* questions that require students to engage in a discussion of the relationship of facts to their application in some suitable environment.

- **Analysis.** Questions calling for analysis ask students to break "wholes," whether a single concept or body of ideas, into component parts and understand their organization and relationships through outlines, classifications, comparisons, hierarchical structures, as well as support and evidence for findings.

- **Synthesis.** Questions at this level seek responses that involve the combination of ideas to form a new whole or idea. Elements of what students know are pulled together to make connections, inferences, and predictions, provide solutions to problems, or propose new ideas.

- **Evaluation.** These are the most open-ended or divergent questions. They call for interpretations of the significance of facts and ideas, the expression of opinions, and the making of judgments and decisions that combine factual knowledge with an assessment of these facts.

Skillful Ways to Ask Questions

Some teachers ask questions in a perfunctory manner as an afterthought at the conclusion of a presentation on a topic or with the belief that this is something they "are supposed to do." However, your use of questions must be given thoughtful consideration if they are to facilitate student learning at a deep level. The following are some important considerations.

Do Not Use Questions "Ritualistically." A common pitfall is asking, "Are there any questions?" Such inquiries are often viewed by students as a habitual exercise on the instructor's part and are usually met with silence. If you do ask the above, be sure that your request is genuine and has a clear purpose. If there is no response, follow up with a more specific question, such as "That means that if I were to ask you on an exam whether . . . you would know how to answer?" This usually will get their attention and get them to honestly reflect on whether they have any questions.

Set the Proper Tone. Let your students know that you want to create an active learning environment, are interested in their ideas, and will be posing lots of questions. Let them know that you use questions not to "put students on the spot" just to see whether they are paying attention, but because you sincerely want to know whether they are learning.

Plan Them Well. Plan your questions and strategies in advance. Most teachers rely on impromptu questions or use them casually to end a topic or class. Although there is nothing wrong with these practices, they are not a substitute for thinking ahead about the different questions that you can ask as well as different ways and times to ask them.

Wait for the Answer. Give your students a chance to respond. Research shows that teachers rarely wait more than a second or two for a student response and, if no response is given, will jump in and answer the question themselves. This lack of wait time has been shown to significantly inhibit student participation, in some cases, more so than any other factor. People need sufficient time to think about the question and formulate an answer. The silence may seem awkward and uncomfortable. But you can handle this by simply letting students know that you do not expect them to come with an immediate response and that a "thoughtful pause" is okay. Also, give them permission to ask for clarification if they do not understand the question.

Ask Only One Question at a Time. Sometimes when attempting to clarify a question by rephrasing it, teachers end up asking a different question. Be clear about what you are looking for to avoid confusion among students and reducing the chances that they will respond.

Avoid Leading Questions. These are not "real" questions at all. A leading question, such as "Don't you all think that . . . ?" will restrain student responses and discourage them from offering their opinions and views on the subject.

Conventional Curriculums reinforce the idea that knowledge is uncontroversial or self-evident, when the opposite is often true. The test for a modern Curriculum is whether it enables Students, at any level, to see how knowledge grows out of, resolves, and produces questions.

—Grant Wiggins

Handling Student Responses and Questions

How you handle student responses to your questions and answer their own questions is just as important as how you go about asking them. The nature of your responses will have a powerful influence on students' participation, the quality of their responses, and the overall classroom learning environment.

Listen. Avoid interrupting a student, even if you think the student is heading in the wrong direction. Be respectful and maintain eye contact and use nonverbal gestures, such as smiling and head nodding, to indicate your attention and interest.

Acknowledge All Contributions. It takes courage to ask a question or make a comment. Commend and compliment students with your comments, such as "That's an excellent question," or "I appreciate that thought." Make sure to offer these comments sincerely, since students usually know when an instructor's response is not genuine. To avoid sounding perfunctory, address students by name when responding ("Sara, let me make sure I understand . . ."), and vary your responses. For example, restate what they have said, ask for clarification or elaboration, expand on what a student has offered by following with your own thoughts, or acknowledge the originality of something offered.

Repeat or Paraphrase Contributions and Respond to the Whole Class. If someone in a class asks a question or makes a comment, paraphrase or repeat it back so that the whole class can hear it before you respond. This is especially important for a long or complex question or comment. Be sure to look at both the questioner as well as other students to include them in your comments. (A rule of thumb is to focus 25 percent of your eye contact on the questioner and 75 percent on the rest of the class.)

Encourage Interaction among Students. Try to structure your comments so that students interact with and pay attention to one another, "That's an interesting thought, Robert. How does it relate to what Maria said a few minutes ago?" (Of course, this means you have to have had paid attention, too!)

Be Honest. If you do not know the answer to a question, say so. It is okay to admit when you do not know the answer or might be wrong. You will lose more credibility by trying to fake an answer than by admitting you do not have one. You can handle this situation in a number of ways. Let the person know that you will find out and respond later, or suggest resources that would enable the student to find the answer.

To be able to be caught up into the world of thought—that is to be educated.

—Edith Hamilton

You can also ask if anyone knows the answer. Just be sure to verify any responses.

When you pull all the above elements together into your questioning strategies, you will have taken a major step toward facilitating deeper student learning.

Conducting Productive Classroom Discussions

The effective use of classroom discussions also provides a relatively easy bridge for shifting surface student learning approaches to deeper ones. We discuss both how to effectively facilitate whole-class, teacher-led discussions and small group ones.

Teacher-Led Discussions

Many consider a classroom discussion as a "tried and true" teaching tool that is pretty much old hat for many teachers. Well, although a discussion may be a "tried" tool, it is not necessarily a "true" one. As common and familiar as they may be, an effective discussion is pretty rare. It is not easy, as some of you may already know, to get students engaged in animated self-directed conversation about at a topic. How frequently do we have thoughtful and purposeful extended conversations with our best friends? We should not be surprised if such conversations are harder to achieve with a class of students, or that when we do achieve them, the topics sometimes drift just as aimlessly as our own conversations may or in ways that do not best serve educational goals.

A good discussion requires preparation and skillful facilitation in order for students to consider themselves to be participants in it and for them to get something meaningful out of it. (And for those of you who already may "be in love" with discussions, the needs of students and of the subject are often better served by varying the kind of discussion and the kinds of participation in class activities. So use them not only skillfully but also strategically.)

Encouraging Students to Be Prepared. Teachers often expect their students to jump into a discussion about a topic presented in class or from a reading without having set the proper expectations and conditions. However, your students will benefit from direction.

- Require each student to bring in a "good" question covering the material of the day, such as, "What was the most difficult part/concept/idea in the reading?" or "What did you like the best/what was the most exciting idea?" Or, since we know that

> *Theories and goals of education don't matter a whit if you don't consider your students to be human beings.*
>
> —Lou Ann Walker

students pay attention to what is tested, you can have them generate test and quiz questions.

● Require each student to complete and bring in a work sheet on a reading(s) for the day that you have prepared or have them prepare their own concept maps on a given reading or an idea from the reading to bring to class and compare with others.

● Require each student to take a turn as class discussion leader or play another role, such as recorder or timekeeper. (See below for developing group skills.)

● Use small-group assignments (summarize a reading, respond to a question on a reading, compare two readings) and have a group scribe or reporter from each group share with whole class.

Refer to Field Guide

Chapter 4

Creating Rapport. In addition to a lack of preparation, the absence of rapport among students is a major obstacle to good discussions. Even students who come prepared may not feel comfortable participating if the classroom climate and group dynamics do not encourage this.

Set the Norm. Prepare a good social climate for discussions beginning the first week of class. You want to get students used to talking right away. This can be accomplished with ice-breakers and "getting-to-know-you" activities as well as setting the tone for social learning by using interactive techniques in your lectures on a regular basis (in dyads and small groups).

Names. It goes without saying that you and your students need to know each other's names. If for whatever reason (large class, etc.) you and they may not already have done so, you can put a name card (3-by-5-inch index cards will do) in front of each student.

Etiquette. Proper etiquette should always be observed. If students do not know how to conduct themselves in ways that demonstrate respect for others, students will feel less inclined to participate. (More on etiquette below.)

Closing a Discussion. Like any class, a fine discussion should come to a fine ending. Do not let students end your class for you by starting to load up their backpacks. Keep track of the time and bring the session to a fitting close. One good way to conclude is with a final bit of writing: give students 5 minutes to enter an observation about the class into their notes, or to write you a brief note asking a question or commenting on the day's activities. Collect these as they leave. In general, if students observe that you structure all class activities carefully and capably bring each class to an appropriate conclusion, they will remain attentive participants until dismissed.

In almost 30 years of teaching, I have found discussions to be one of the most seductively misleading, as well as effective, teaching techniques I have used. Early in my teaching career, I believed that I was doing a lot just by getting students to talk about a topic. In many ways, this was and continues to be true. But as I became more experienced, I realized it was easy to confuse students actively doing something with students actively learning something. I realized that activity for its own sake (whether a discussion or any other kind of interactive practice) achieved little in the long run. In the moment, being active can keep students more alert and involved, but in the long run it rarely contributed to deeper learning without facilitation, structure, and predefined learning goals. The lesson learned—what I or the students did rarely translated into something they "got"—without some preparation and evaluation.

Unit 3

Refer to Field Guide

Wise sayings often fall on barren ground; but a kind word is never thrown away.

—Sir Arthur Helps

Dyads and Small-Group Discussions

In addition to teacher-led, whole-class discussions, dyads (pair interactions) and small discussions and other group activities are an obvious and common option for active learning activities. Indeed, there is an entire learning method centered on group learning, collaborative or cooperative learning, that one can use. This approach is much more formalized and uses norms and various rules to be effective. (However, for our purposes we offer just a few guidelines and suggest a handful of easy-to-implement strategies you can use to deepen your students' learning experience.)

General Considerations for Forming Small Groups. Pretty much all of the above considerations for preparing for, encouraging participation, and handling a successful whole-class discussion can and do apply here. However, there are three special considerations that need to be taken into account with group small-group discussions: group size, arrangement, and roles.

Size. A small group can work for three to six people, though four to five is generally considered the best size. Larger groups limit the opportunity for each person to contribute. In general, the less time available and the less skilled the members, the smaller the group should be.

Seating Arrangements. In general, you should make sure your students can see each other. Insist on everyone's adjusting chairs to accommodate all members of the class. Also, you may want to get to class a few minutes early to make sure that there are enough chairs, suitably arranged in a small circle or square.

If you are in a room with fixed seating, such as a theater-style lecture hall, you will not have the option to move chairs. But you still can create group interactivity. First, do not let anyone sit on the fringes, and pull in loners. Have students sitting next to each other and in adjacent rows turn to face each other to form groups of four to six people. If combinations of incompatible students develop, rearrange seating. For example, have students count off to four or five for small-group work: all 1s work together, all 2s, etc. Then keep the seating arrangement for whatever time is needed to maintain these working groups. (Students also develop rapport by shifting who they sit next to rather than clinging to one dependable friend.)

Unit 3

Roles. Depending on the group purposes and dynamics you can assign roles to promote the discussion and further the learning goals. For example, in a group of four, you may want to assign a discussion leader, recorder, reporter, and timekeeper. The discussion leader is responsible for keeping the conversation on topic, the recorder acts like a secretary to take notes, the reporter will share the outcome of the discussion with other groups or the whole class, and the time-keeper makes sure things progress within the limits established. (This structure is often a formal part of cooperative learning methods.)

Chapter 7

Suggestions for Small-Group Activities and Structure. Topics and discussion formats are limited only by your imagination and the needs of your course. Many of the ideas for promoting greater student engagement and more active learning, such as think/pair/share or 1-minute papers, can be part of a "deep learning tool box" that you can use for small-group work. These only need to be extended to by simply allowing more time or through elaborations, such as asking students to write and also share their ideas in small groups. Some additional ideas are discussed below:

Debates. Divide the class into teams for informal "debates" (teams prepare outside of class or during one class period prior to the debate).

Concentric Circles. Use concentric circles to stimulate discussion. Divide students into two circles facing each other, and have each pair of students share thoughts on a question for 3 minutes or so. Have the inner group rotate to create new pairs, and continue as time allows.

Group-Generated Graphic Tools. Have groups develop a group concept map or some other kind of visual tool to represent an important topic or idea.

Peer Teaching. Divide the material among students or groups of students. Have each study and/or write on a topic or question for 5 to 15 minutes and then teach their peers (dyads or small groups) the material they have studied.

"Pass the Folder." This involves dividing a class into small groups, with each group getting a folder. Each group takes about 5 minutes to choose a different topic from a reading or lecture to discuss, and 5 to 10 minutes to discuss it. They then write that issue on the front of their folder and their ideas in the folder and pass folders to next group, which has 5 to 10 minutes to discuss the issue. This can be repeated as needed. During the final time, the group has 10 minutes to read all the responses to the issue on the folder they have at that time and to respond and share.

Problem Solving. Small groups may look for solutions to a problem, try to reach consensus on an issue, define a term, provide data or evidence for a position, and so on. The groups then compare and evaluate their results; conflicting "facts" will be of special interest.

Text Analysis. Students may examine a text for various purposes—for example, to examine style, analyze evidence or structure, compare what two writers say on a given subject, and so on. Have them make lists, prepare written statements, and so on. Then use this material for discussion with the entire class.

Favorite Ideas. Have students select significant quotations or ideas from the text being studied; students can lead discussion of their own passages. The class can examine which passages were selected, how they fit together, and so on.

Presentations. Small groups provide an excellent situation in which to have students read aloud their outside class work, such as reports or essays, and receive comments on their work. Students in small groups can also give each other suggestions on drafts of essays; students take this work seriously, and they value advice received at this early stage. At first be sure to provide guidelines, in writing, for the work to be done.

> You learn to speak by speaking, to study by studying, to run by running, to work by working; and just so, you learn to love by loving. All those who think to learn in any other way deceive themselves.
>
> —Saint Francis De Sales

Special Considerations When Facilitating Discussions

Whether you are trying to facilitate a whole-class discussion or have put your students into small groups to work together, you will likely need to deal with some of the following challenges from time to time. These include a lack of participation, difficult or sensitive topics, and improper conduct.

Nonparticipation. Contrary to what you may first think, most students do not object to teachers insisting on participation rather than letting one or two students dominate while the rest drift off, and they generally do not mind your calling on them. What students mind more is being bored or feeling that a class was a waste of their time. (Have you ever had a student complain about being asked to participate?)

Teach the Value of Discussions. Do not just tell students about how discussions can work to make for better learning. "Walk the talk" of active learning from the start. Have your students actually discuss the nature of a good discussion. Have them consider questions such as: (a) Is it helpful to be the only person talking? (b) How can a person who talks easily encourage others to talk? (c) What role do listening and asking questions play in a conversation? (d) What kinds of responses make people feel bad?

Use Questions That Automatically Are Inclusive. Get a discussion going by first asking questions that every student can and will have to answer, either with a yes or no, with just with a show of hands, or a round-robin session. Or, if you have prepared them for the topic with an outside classroom assignment, pick some ideas from it, formulate questions, and require that each person respond.

A fool sees not the same tree that a wise man sees.

—William Blake

Work to Include Shy Students. Some students will be too shy to speak or simply have quiet dispositions and thus do not feel comfortable in possibly boisterous group settings. Still other students may think that everyone else in the room is better prepared or smarter than they are and be afraid to speak up. (And some students may indeed have weaker preparation, so this is a genuine problem.) In addition to those described above, the following are some other techniques to include reluctant participants.

- Do not always call on the easy talkers first. Keep looking around the room and call on someone who is nonverbally signaling readiness.

- When a student has talked, do not automatically be the first respondent. Wait a few moments to see who else may speak up, and let students know that they can ask someone in the room other than you to respond to their comments.

- After a discussion gets going, turn a speaker's opinion into a question. Then ask students who have not been talking what their thoughts are or if they know of evidence that supports or refutes the opinions being offered.

- Perhaps call on a shy student in a different situation, to get them gradually comfortable with verbalizing. For example, have them read aloud a handout or some instructions. Or, if you have had all students write a response to a text or problem, pick nonparticipants to read what they have written. Since the words are already

> *A good teacher feels his way, looking for response.*
>
> —Paul Goodman

formulated, many students who find speaking difficult can more easily be drawn into participation on these occasions.

- Quiet students can be good note-takers. Choose one to act as a recorder of a discussion to read aloud the notes later. If you ask for a summary of the previous class at the beginning of a session, or for a summary of the day's discussion, again try calling on the student who usually does not participate.

- You may get an entire class of quiet students. If so, discuss the situation with them and have them come up with their own ideas for increasing participation.

- Of course, it can be helpful to talk with shy students individually outside the class about methods to include them. Discuss whether the student feels comfortable talking and would like to be called on. Emphasize that this is their class too and that you would like to make sure everyone is getting the most out of the experience.

Unit 4

Dealing with Diversity. Sometimes our students and we will inadvertently trip into what, with a little hindsight, would appear to be rather obvious traps. A few dos and don'ts follow.

Don't Let Stereotypes or Surface Impressions Determine Expectations. Be careful not to quickly judge your students' talents, personality traits, or willingness to participate in class. Don't inadvertently pretailor your comments or responses because of your presumptions about students' backgrounds.

Don't Make Any Student in Your Class Responsible for Dealing with Stereotypes. Whether it be one woman/man/member of a minority, do not ask them to be or hold them somehow responsible for dealing with stereotypes by reporting on "the woman's/man's/African-American's" etc., point of view. Dealing with the group's ignorance is not any one person's responsibility.

Do Think about How You and Your Students Respond to Each Other. Perhaps have an up-front discussion of factors that can influence a classroom conversation and how you and your students can understand and respect different styles and approaches. For example, men tend to be more confrontational in conversation, while women tend to take a more cooperative approach. Men also may dominate a discussion: if this starts to happen, the class will probably need to discuss the situation and decide on ways to resolve it.

Do Be Sensitive to Different Conversational Styles of Different Cultures. For example, it is common to enter a conversation by overlapping the last speaker's words; students accustomed to waiting for a pause can be effectively excluded.

Handling Difficult Subjects and Comments. Students will benefit from advice about how to conduct themselves when they are discussing sensitive matters. Therefore, it is important to have thought these issues through before they come up in class.

Be Prepared. Consider in advance how you can respond. Situations in which a student makes an offensive or discriminatory comment, or uses an expression or behavior that is inappropriate, are never easy. Unless you have thought these situations through beforehand, you may allow yourself to express anger. However, this may weaken your effectiveness as a teacher. Therefore, it is important to have a strategy for dealing with such an episode. For example, you may choose to be direct and simply say that out of respect for others and yourself, you prefer that everyone consider what they say or do before they act. Also, it may be effective to distance the student from the comment, which you can then address. For instance, you might recast a sexist comment by beginning "It's common for people to say that." "People often say that . . ." or "I've heard other people say that." Then you can address the comment, having put it into a new context.

Involve Your Students. If you are comfortable with the kind of conversation that may ensue, you can ask the class to respond to the comment, asking them how they see or if they agree with what someone has said. You may, of course, want to preface this with the comment that you are not inviting an attack on the person, and want a thoughtful, reasoned response that respects each person's right to their own opinion.

Give Yourself a Break. If follow-through on a situation seems desirable, but you do not have an immediate strategy available, give yourself time to consult other teachers and figure out a good teaching plan. Let the students know that it is an important issue that you will bring back to the class later.

The Excessive Talker. Yes, there always seems to be one or more of these types of students in a class. Many of the above methods for including reluctant participants can control the excessive talker by simply including other students. But additional ideas are discussed below.

Talk to the Student Outside of Class. Make it clear that, like most people, you value the student who listens well, who asks good questions of other students, or who is sensitive to the needs of others in the class.

> *A great teacher never strives to explain his vision. He simply invites you to stand beside him and see for yourself.*
>
> —R. Inman

Give the Talker an Assignment. Assign the excessive talker, for example, to the role of discussion recorder to simply observe and record, with the understanding that there is no talking until handing in (or giving) the final report.

Use a "Talking Stick" (or Some Other Object). The person talking holds the object. When done, it is passed to the next person the talker wishes to have speak. No one can speak unless holding the object (including the teacher). This same procedure can be accomplished without the stick by having each speaker call on the next speaker. It has the added advantage of getting quieter students to participate and getting a discussion moving.

Conduct a Class Discussion on the Issue. Have the class discuss who is talking, who is not talking, what changes they would like, and how they might achieve them. (Be sure to not single out any particular problem students.) If the one or two students who dominate a discussion are not elbowing others into silence and are making valuable contributions, and if you are finding other activities to help the rest of the students participate each day in some way, relax. You are doing what you can; so are your students.

Alternative Strategies for Deep Learning

Unit 3

It is important to note that there are many methods for promoting deep learning. Here we briefly introduce some of these alternatives as modifications and elaborations of several ideas already suggested in this chapter.

Small-Group Learning

Discussion groups are not the only way to organize students into small groups for better learning. Regardless of subject matter, students will learn more when working in small groups and generally feel more satisfied with instruction. There are a number of forms that small-group learning can take, such as cooperative learning, collaborative learning, learning communities, peer teaching, team learning, and study groups. Among these different forms, three helpful distinctions have been made by two of the most prominent researchers in this area, D.W. Johnson and R.T. Johnson: study teams, informal learning groups, and formal learning groups.

Study Teams. These are also long-term, stable support groups whose purpose is to provide encouragement and assistance to its members. Study-team members help each other succeed in the class by working together outside the class as needed to complete assignments, inform students of assignments, and possibly share notes when one misses a class. Although such a group is not always intended to *deepen* student learning, they obviously contribute to better student learning outcomes through the support they provide.

Informal Learning Groups. These are temporary, impromptu groups that are constituted for a single class session. The dyads and small-group activities we have already suggested fall into this category and, as explained, can be quickly organized around a question to be answered or a problem to be solved, to have students clarify their understanding by constructing graphic representations, or whatever else may be serve the clarification and deepening of understanding. Though little planning is required for this kind of group, you will want to consider some of the following to improve their effectiveness:

- Establish the Purpose: Be clear about the purpose of the activity and the specific learning outcome.
- Create Balance: Balance structure and predictability that make students feel secure with flexibility and openness to student suggestions that creates interest and a willingness to become involved.
- Get Feedback: Ask for feedback on how things worked, especially on what the students got out of the activity.
- Stay Small: Keep the topic or task small enough to be meaningfully handled in the time allotted.
- Provide Learning Supports: Use handouts or other materials to provide basic information that may be needed to conduct the activity but not immediately or easily accessible to students.

Formal Learning Groups. These groups are created to complete a longer-term task, like conducting research, writing a report, and developing a project that will be completed over an extended period of time and possibly be graded. These groups require planning and thoughtful direction, similar to those needed for informal groups, plus additional considerations, such as the following:

- Prepare: Decide in advance, often when writing your syllabus, what topics or tasks and time frame will be suitable for such extended work and how they fit into the overall course design.
- Provide Resources: Consider what resources will be needed for the group work.
- Create Structure: Structure activities and learning goals that are complex enough to require a great deal of interdependence, so that each member needs to contribute and is accountable to the others.

> . . . an ordinary degree of understanding is routinely missing in many, if not most students. It is reasonable to expect a college student to be able to apply in a new context a law of physics, or a proof in geometry, or a concept in history of which she just demonstrated mastery in her class.
>
> —Howard Garnder

- Offer Support: Break down topics and learning tasks and scaffold them to accommodate the abilities of your students. (For example, start with relatively easy assignments and plenty of directions and guidance up front.)

- Organize Roles: Know how you will organize these groups and the roles students will play.

- Guide Students: Teach students how to work together and conduct themselves in appropriate and effective ways so that they can accomplish their goals (etiquette, dealing with conflict, etc.).

- Give Feedback: Consider when and how you will provide feedback through the process and how you will evaluate the work.

To assist you in the above, you may want to use written "contracts" that specify each student's responsibilities to ensure a fair workload for each, and spell out the steps and schedule for the work, along with the assessment criteria.

Chapter 9

Types of Small-Group Learning Projects and Activities

There are a variety of learning challenges that can provide the focus and structure that a learning group needs to accomplish its goals. In general, using facilitation skills, you will guide students in their work with tasks as they identify, acquire, and apply what they need to learn and develop self-directed learning and reasoning skills.

Unit 3

Problem-Based Learning Tasks. There are numerous definitions and interpretations of problem-based learning (PBL). Some see it as a way to structure and entire curriculum and others in more limited terms as a short-term process and learning activity, as we are discussing here. As a small group learning task, in problem-based learning, students are confronted with an ill-structured problem that mirrors real-world problems. Well-chosen problems encourage students to define problems; identify, acquire, and use the information that is needed; and find solutions and make decisions. A good problem has the following qualities:

> *Too often we give our children answers to remember rather than problems to solve.*
>
> —Robert Lewin

- Engaging and oriented to the real world
- Built on previous knowledge/experiences
- Develops an integrated knowledge base that is readily recalled and applied to the analysis and solution of problems
- Generates multiple hypotheses and possible solutions
- Requires team effort and self-directed learning skills
- Consistent with desired learning outcomes
- Promotes development of higher-order cognitive skills

Case Studies. This is a variation of PBL. A case is a story or narrative about an event or series of related events relevant to the course that students read or explore interactively. A case can direct students toward a conclusion or provide the resources and context to discuss and debate issues dynamically. They are best suited for teaching about realistic decision-making situations. Students work through the case, in the class or outside it, depending on its complexity, and decide what should be done. Cases can be designed with complete information provided to help students quickly understand them, or with incomplete information that requires engagement in considerable conversation and reasoning to reach an informed decision. When you consider a case for use in your class, ask yourself the following questions:

- What is the case about?
- What are some of the potential learning issues?
- Are these central enough to the case for me to use this case? Can I modify the case?
- How difficult or obscure are the issues in the case?
- Will there be issues my students will care about?
- Is the case open-ended enough for students to go beyond fact finding?
- What do I see as possible areas for investigation?
- What might I ask students to produce?
- Is the case too short or too long for the time I have available?
- What sorts of learning resources might be needed for this case? Are they accessible?
- If I use this case, what lectures/labs/discussions might I want to change, add, or eliminate?

> *. . . even when students can "think about" the subject matter, they may not be able to "think with it."*
>
> —Bill Cerbin

Debates. Controversy heightens interest. Use debates to deepen understanding of opposing facts, theories, and philosophies. The contest-like environment is engaging, while encouraging students to analyze information and synthesize well-supported positions. Use these guidelines for effective debates:

- Encourage students to research the issue prior to entering comments online.
- Direct students to spend at least as much time rebutting as building their own case.
- Provide feedback and structure to facilitate carefully composed position statements.
- Provide closure to each debate through a well-crafted summary of the process and positions.

> *The body of research on the impacts of the College academic experience is extensive. The strongest general conclusion [is that] the greater the student's involvement or engagement in academic work, the greater his or her level of knowledge acquisition.*
>
> —Pascarella & Terenzini

Team Presentations and Teaching by Learners. Sometimes the deepest learning comes through teaching others. Examples of this are discussed below.

Seminar. To take on a teaching role, two to four students might work on teams to present, moderate, and synthesize a seminar on a class topic for other students. The activities might be sequenced as follows:

1. On day 1, the work team prepares and presents an introduction to the topic based on assigned readings. Two or three questions are asked of the larger group to stimulate and focus discussion.

2. On day 2 and possibly 3 (depending on the time needed), the working group moderates the class discussion. Their task is to maintain communication flow and encourage students to deepen their analysis while staying on topic.

3. The day after the seminar has concluded, the work team posts a synthesis of the content as well as an analysis of the group process. Meanwhile, the second working group launches another topic.

Jigsaw Activity. A highly effective tool for peer teaching is known as the jigsaw technique. This activity works well when large amounts of reading must be covered or students need to review many resources. They can share the workload by becoming experts on one resource. The procedure is quite simple:

1. Divide the class into primary "home" groups of three to five students. Give assignments and provide suggested references.

2. Redivide the class into three to five secondary "expert" groups, composed of one member from each primary group. Each expert group is assigned a separate subtopic, relating to a common theme. All members in the expert groups become experts on their subtopic.

3. Once expert groups research their subtopics, they then return to their primary groups. Experts report their findings and teach their concepts to their primary groupmates, or the group can collaboratively solve a task incorporating all the subtopics.

Variations on a Theme—Online Group Learning Activities

Online learning environments offer opportunities for group learning tasks. These include some of the above activities designed for face-to-face instruction adapted for use in online classes and hybrid classes, which have both online and face-to-face sessions.

Online Case Studies. Your learning goals will help you determine how you can design a case-based project for an online class. For example,

Unit 3

if you prefer to direct students to a certain conclusion or a core set of knowledge, a Web-based or multimedia case might simply tell a story. If you prefer students to experience a case in realistic terms, you can design an interactive case by sorting through digital libraries to find information that helps to frame or "solve" a problem presented in the case. Two primary methods are possible to deliver cases. You can use a "low-tech" approach to delivering a case, simply presenting the case and discussing it, or you can use technology, which progressively increase, the possibilities for student interaction with the data (collecting it, sorting it, organizing it, evaluating it, etc.).

Online Simulations and Role Plays. Although simulations and role plays can be conducted in face-to-face class meetings, online learning environments are potentially fertile ground for these activities. Hypothetical scenarios may be established, and students can assume the personas and perspectives of others. The instructor stipulates the rules, tasks, and schedule. Outcomes may be project-oriented, such as requiring students to create a final report. As well, the goals for the activity can be process-oriented and concerned with creating an opportunity for learners to investigate diverse perspectives.

Two innovative environments are MUDs, multi-user text-based virtual realities, and MUSEs, multi-user simulation environments. In both these applications of online communications, users log on and explore a virtual world in real time by using commands that enable them to walk around the environment and interact with other characters. Participants might solve puzzles, play games, and construct new rooms or activities. Examples of this type of application include combat and fantasy games as well as those with explicitly social or educational goals, such as science labs in which participants talk to actual scientists.

Online Debating Teams. Online debates held as conferences have the distinct advantage that a transcript of each debate is automatically generated and may be used for evaluation and analysis by students and instructors. By revisiting the discussion and reworking it, students sharpen their analytic thinking.

Debates may be unstructured, allowing participants to post messages at will, or structured as dyads or teams. In small classes (fewer than 20), students may choose their sides. In larger classes, or when there are multiple sides to an issue, it is most efficient for instructors to assign students. If the team has six or fewer members, students may be asked to coordinate their arguments. This results in a comprehensive position, but adds about a week to the preparation process. You will need to allow significantly more time for online debates.

Networked Classrooms. Classes or courses within a campus or among several campuses may be networked to engage in joint activities online.

Out of intense Complexities intense simplicities emerge.

—Winston Churchill

This strategy may be used to broaden the perspective of participants through contact with other students, cultures, disciplines, and instructors who may provide differing points of view.

Online Informal Social Conferences. Virtual cafes are informal conferences that foster a sense of community. This space should be moderated by and for students for socializing and not be directly tied to curriculum.

Online Help Conferences. Students or instructors may moderate online help conferences to assist with troubleshooting problems and providing technical information. This is an efficient and effective way to respond to student needs, as several students often share the same problems during a course. By reading through the list of concerns addressed, students might resolve difficulties without requiring any additional input from the moderator.

CHAPTER WRAP-UP

Just about all teachers agree on the value of teaching for deep understanding, helping students to take a deeper approach to their learning. Still, some of you may be thinking, "But let's get real. How many teachers really have time to get students to think deeply, yet alone teach them how to do so? We can barely find the time to just give them the important information they need. And besides, it seems a lot of things they need to learn don't really need this deep kind of learning."

As long-time classroom instructors, we understand and appreciate these concerns. There is without a doubt a tension in most courses between limited time, large amounts of information to be learned, and the goal of learning this material well. "Uncovering" learning by getting students to understand topics deeply and the need to "cover" the curriculum and getting through material are often pitted against each other. Trade-offs between the two must be made constantly.

Moreover, we realize that you may not always need to teach for deeper knowledge and that, on balance, the benefits of deep understanding depend on the particular skill or subject in question. There are things that students need to know and need to be able to do that do not call for understanding at a deep level. Surface knowledge may be adequate to serve a particular purpose, say in an introductory or survey lecture. Also, many basic skills are not improved by a deep understanding. (How many of you learned to ride a bike without ever understanding the biomechanics of balance?)

So given the trade-off that will sometimes need to be made, is it really worth the effort to make sure your students achieve a deeper, personalized degree of understanding? Our answer to this question is an emphatic "yes." When students take a deep approach to their learning they develop an enriched and enduring understanding and are able to make more sense of what they are learning. They make ideas their own by focusing on the meaning of what they are learning; they are able to relate otherwise fragmented ideas and make connections with previous experiences. They ask themselves questions about what they're learning and discuss their ideas with others. And they are likely to work hard for more than good grades, freely exploring the subject beyond the immediate requirements and thus experiencing positive emotions about learning.

Clearly, teaching for deeper understanding does make a difference. With the intention, experience, and practice, you will find it easier and easier to plan and implement courses that include designs and activities that "uncover" learning even as you also "covering" content.

SPRINGBOARDS FOR FURTHER LEARNING

Key Names

John Seely Brown   David Perkins
Allan Collins   Robin Scarmadilia
Johnson and Johnson   Grant Wiggins

Key Terms

case-based learning   problem-based learning
cognitive apprenticeship   situated learning
computer-mediated   small-group learning
  instructional environments   teaching for deep understanding
effective discussions

INTERNET ACTIVITY

There are Web sites that include papers or case studies of subjects and try to encourage deep approaches to learning related to specific subjects, such as science and math. Try a Google advanced search, using phrases such as "deep approach to learning," "deep knowledge," and "teaching for understanding" along with keywords that relate to your discipline.

CHAPTER 9

Assessments *of* Learning and Assessments *for* Learning

Not everything that counts can be counted, and not everything that can be counted counts.

—Albert Einstein

Do You Know:

- What the multiple purposes of assessment are?
- How assessment can be used to facilitate rather than just measure learning?
- What the qualities of effective assessments are?
- What are some innovative assessments for measuring deep learning?
- When is the best time to plan your assessment strategies?

Introduction

For many educators, the term *assessment* has to do with teachers assigning grades to their students. Classroom assessment, however, is about much more than trying to figure out what grades to give your students. It has many other important roles and exerts powerful influences—both intentionally and incidentally—on just about every dimension of teaching and learning.

Consider the truism, "What you test is what they learn." Utter one of those feared four-letter words—"test"

or "exam" or "quiz"—and otherwise distracted or bored students will give you their attention as if you were Moses coming down the mount. Slouching students will suddenly sit erect. Ears will perk up and all eyes will be on you. Even if you do not directly use any of these words in any particular class session, you can be pretty certain your students will be regularly wondering and asking themselves or each other, "Will this be on the test?"

What we know about the power of assessment as a driver of learning is not just anecdotal. There is plenty of research to back this up. For better or worse, most students will gear almost all their studying and learning activities to focus on what you communicate through your assessments. What you test tells students—more than just about anything else you say or do—what you consider to be important and what you believe they need to learn. Moreover, assessment in many respects is the primary link in all the major components of a course—its content, instructional methods, and skills development. The final results your students and you achieve will largely be a reflection of the decisions you have made about how and when to measure learning.

Unfortunately, the testing methods you use can be narrow measures of student learning and of limited value for directing this learning. There are several reasons for this. Your assessments may be improperly constructed and poorly implemented and, therefore, fail to measure course content appropriately or reflect student mastery accurately. Also, many customary assessment methods are inconsistent with the shifting vision of learning emerging in education today. This vision recognizes the need for students to acquire personally meaningful understanding, to reason critically and understand and communicate at deep conceptual levels, and to acquire lifelong skills that permit continuous adaptation to workplaces that are in constant flux. Moreover, the ways assessments are designed and administered could actually inhibit learning rather than support it, by adversely impacting student motivation and perceptions of their competence. With these considerations in mind, this chapter will guide you through the multiple roles of classroom assessment and help you learn the basics of designing and implementing quality traditional, as well as innovative, assessment measures. We focus on three kinds of measures:

1. summative assessment,

2. formative assessment, and

3. innovative assessment techniques. (In Chapter 10 we carry the topic of assessment to its logical conclusion and discuss two related topics, developing reliable and fair grading policies and ways to evaluate your teaching effectiveness.)

Chapter 10

A man would do nothing if he waited until he could do it so well that no one could find fault.

—John Henry Newman

A Few Initial Considerations

Before getting into the nitty-gritty of each of the above measures, here are some foundational ideas to keep in mind.

Assessment versus Evaluation

The terms *assessment* and *evaluation* are often used interchangeably. However, they have different meanings. *Assessment* is the gathering of data to inform both instructor and student about the progress of learning. *Evaluation* is what we do with this information to judge the effectiveness of our instructional methods, the course content, and the achievement of course goals.

Classroom Assessment versus Standardized Tests

When we speak of assessment in this chapter, we are referring to tests that instructors design for the purposes of measuring what their students have learned in a particular class. These kinds of measures are distinguished from standardized tests. Standardized exams are generally professionally constructed by testing experts and are used to compare student performance across a large population of learners, and not to measure individual student performance against standards set by you as their personal instructor.

Multipurpose Assessments

Summative and formative assessments, as mentioned, are the two forms of classroom assessment. Summative assessments are primarily for grading purposes, while formative assessments are more informal day-to-day feedback techniques used to guide learning. (These are both explained at length later.) What is important to understand at this point is that each form does not necessarily describe a different gauge of learning, and the same assessment might be used either formatively or summatively. Within the past decade or so, the need to integrate, or at least to align, the routines of formative feedback with formal summative assessment practices has been recognized. The terms *summative* and *formative* are, therefore, descriptions of how the information generated by a particular indicator of student progress is used and not the customary intent of the assessment.

Assessment and the Issue of Accountability

Assessment has become an important means of addressing many public concerns about education today. As used in today's debates about educational reform, assessment means much more than classroom-based methods for getting information and feedback to our students and

> People always seem to know half of history, and to get confused with the other half.
>
> —Jane Haddam

Unit 5

Chapters 1 and 2

Three minutes thought would suffice to find this out; but thought is irksome and three minutes is a long time.

—A.E. Houseman

methods we can use to improve the results of learning and teaching. As such, different kinds of measures are and may be used as indicators of the quality of our work as teachers, which may be communicated to administrators. These are also a means to communicate the overall effectiveness of a school to external interests and agencies, such as prospective students, employers, educational policy makers, and government officials. Within the scope of this chapter we cannot address concerns at these levels. However, these accountability issues may have a significant bearing on you and your students' success, and it is important to consider your uses and methods of classroom assessment in the larger context of these issues.

The Role of Your Teaching Philosophy

Finally, as you read through this chapter, we encourage you to keep in the forefront of your awareness your fundamental teaching philosophy and course learning goals. How you approach assessment, as all your instructional decisions and practices, directly or indirectly emerge from your personal teaching philosophy and perspective on learning. Indeed, in some respects your views on the purposes and best designs for assessment may say more about your beliefs about learning and teaching than any other classroom practice.

Assessments *of* Learning—Summative Classroom Assessment

Summative assessments "summarize" student progress at particular points during a course so that we can assign marks. When most instructors think of *assessment,* it is this kind of measure that probably comes to mind. They basically answer the question, "Which grades do I assign my students and how will I determine these grades?" Yet, as emphasized, summative assessments can and often do much more by telling your students, whether you intend to or not, your fundamental vision of learning and what you believe is important about your subject matter. This incidental influence is so powerful that it deserves elaboration.

Consider the multiple-choice test, the most commonly used assessment. When designed properly, these are effective measures of fact-based knowledge and a student's ability to perform fixed, routine procedures. If your goal is for students to be able to recall facts or solve simple, routine problems, then this assessment technique is well aligned with your purposes. However, if throughout your course you only or mostly test for facts and factual recall, what you are telling your students is that this type of knowledge is what is most important; it will seem you assign less value to their deeper understanding of the critical concepts and main principles of your discipline. Your students will likely be motivated to study only to the degree needed to succeed on such assessments. This may result in a superficial learning that does not yield

Chapter 8

Nothing in education is so astonishing as the amount of ignorance it accumulates in the form of inert facts.

—Henry Adams

Chapters 4 and 5

Chapters 6, 7 and 8

a meaningful grasp of the course content, as discussed in Chapter 8. But if your goals also include different student outcomes, such as more expert-like understanding, a lifelong interest in the subject, and the ability to critically analyze and solve problems and apply what they have learned outside the classroom, then a multiple-choice test will not necessarily provide useful feedback about the attainment of these goals. For this reason, we cannot overstate the importance of setting course goals and being clear about the purposes and character of your tests so that your choice of classroom assessments suitably guides what your students learn and how well they learn it.

Planning for Summative Assessment—Linking Course Goals and Assessments

The three most fundamental elements of any course are

1. its content,
2. the instructional methods used to present this content, and
3. the assessment techniques with which student progress and our success in attaining course goals are determined.

A good deal of the work for designing your assessments will already have been done, if you have done your job of:

1. articulating your goals in your course design,
2. preparing the proper learning environment, and
3. carefully considering and implementing your instructional methods.

Once you have done these three things, with your goals as your learning standards, you are ready to select the assessment techniques you need to judge whether your students have attained these standards. The process begins with translating your goals into outcomes that you can quantitatively measure or qualitatively benchmark in some fashion. (Of course, identifying outcomes that are measurable requires knowledge of the different assessment techniques that can be used, and what each technique is a good measure of—something that we will cover in the section that follows.)

From Course Goals to Measurable Learning Outcomes

The overarching course goals you specify in your initial planning are generally going to be too broad to measure concretely. As a representative example, let's look at the subject of math. Experts consider the learning of mathematics to involve all the following:

1. being able to explain mathematical concepts and facts in terms of simpler concepts and facts,
2. easily making logical connections between different facts and concepts,

3. recognizing the connection between something new (inside or outside of mathematics) to what has been learned, and

4. identifying the principles in a given math operation or problem that make everything work (i.e., being able see past the details of the problem to see the fundamental principles).

These are all valuable goals, yet they are abstractions that cannot be directly measured, and it is difficult to know what this kind of understanding "looks like." Desired student outcomes need to have specific and observable characteristics that will allow you to evaluate the extent to which they have been achieved. In order to select the proper assessment technique for each of your course goals, you will need to identify and describe the specific performance you would expect from a student who has achieved that goal and at the relative degree of mastery. This means that your summative classroom-assessment techniques should be capable of distinguishing and assessing a variety of types and levels of learning and proficiency.

Bloom's Taxonomy of Educational Goals as an Assessment Tool

Bloom's Taxonomy of Educational Objectives, introduced in Chapter 8, is not useful just as a typology for organizing levels of knowledge for the specification of learning objectives. It can also be used for measuring the attainment of these objectives by expressing the level of mastery required to achieve desired student outcomes. Below are two systems, one for knowledge-based goals and another for performance or skill-based goals. Each lists levels of understanding in order of increasing complexity, with subsequent levels incorporating the preceding ones. Student achievement requiring higher levels of understanding will call for more sophisticated classroom-assessment techniques at each level. Which of these two you use will depend on the original goal to which outcome is connected.

Bloom's Taxonomy for Assessing Knowledge-Based Goals

Knowledge: Simple recall or recognition of terms, ideas, procedure, theories, etc.

- Assessment: tasks that require student to define, describe, identify, label, list, match, name, outline, select, state, etc.

Comprehension: Understanding without the ability to grasp the deeper significance or transfer knowledge.

- Assessment: Tasks that require students to convert, distinguish, estimate, explain, give examples, summarize, etc.

Application: Use of abstractions, general principles, or methods in specific concrete situations.

- Assessment: Tasks that require students to demonstrate, modify, operate, prepare, produce, relate, show, solve, use, etc.

Chapter 8

Ignorance is preferable to error, and he is less remote from the truth who believes nothing than he who believes what is wrong.

—Thomas Jefferson

Analysis: Separation of a complex idea into its component parts and an understanding of the organization and relationship among the parts.

- Assessment: tasks that require students to diagram, differentiate, distinguish, illustrate, infer, relate, separate, subdivide, etc.

Synthesis: Pulling together of ideas and concepts from multiple sources to form complex ideas into a new, integrated, and meaningful pattern.

- Assessment: Tasks that require students to categorize, combine, compile, design, organize, plan, rearrange, reconstruct, revise, etc.

Evaluation: Making judgments about ideas or methods substantiated by observations, evidence, or informed rationalizations.

- Assessment: tasks that require students to appraise, compare, conclude, contrast, criticize, discriminate, justify, interpret, support, etc.

You may want to simplify and collapse this system into three more general levels: The first category would be to assess knowledge (recall or recognition of specific information), the second category would combine comprehension and application, and the third would look at problem solving as the transfer of existing knowledge and skills into new situations.

Bloom's Taxonomy for Skills-Based Goals. Here is an adaptation of Bloom's classification system for the assessment of learning that calls for the demonstration or performance of skills. Again, these progress from the simple to the complex.

Observation: The ability to describe the actions that guide an observed process or procedure.

- Assessment: Students report what they observe. (e.g., based on your observation . . .).

Preparation: A general readiness to take action to perform a task.

- Assessment: Students describe in general terms how they would go about performing the task (e.g., What general actions does one need to take to . . .).

Response: Knowledge of and ability to explain the precise sequence of steps required to complete a task.

- Assessment: Students explain the exact steps of a procedure or process that must be followed to perform it correctly (e.g., Determine the next three steps of the following procedure . . .).

Basic Performance: Performance of a task in a routine or rudimentary manner with at least minimal proficiency.

- Assessment: Students perform the required task satisfactorily (e.g., Use the procedure for. . . . Determine the . . .).

Education is a progressive discovery of your own ignorance.

—Will Durant

Complex Performance: Performance of a task with greater confidence and proficiency than demonstrated at basic level.

- Assessment: Performance with the expectation of greater skill and fluency than in the prior task level.

Adaptation: Performance of a task with the ability to modify actions to account for new or problematic situations.

- Assessment: Students face an unfamiliar situation they must deal with to perform a task successfully (e.g., You are performing . . . , when . . . occurs. What would you do?).

Innovation: Performs new, original tasks that incorporate learned skills.

- Assessment: Students must apply what they have learned to the successful performance of a new skill (e.g., Based on what you know about . . . , develop a new strategy for . . .).

After matching course goals with specific student learning tasks, you can proceed to the design and the selection of the particular assessment tools you will want to use.

The Design and Administration of Effective Summative Assessments: Preliminary Considerations

Two Characteristics of Effective Summative Assessments

In general, the information generated by good summative assessments provides accurate estimates of student performance and will enable you or others (supervisors or administrators) to make appropriate

A Note on Terminology

Instructors often use the terms *tests, exams,* and even *quizzes* interchangeably. Test experts, however, make distinctions among these based on the scope of content covered and their weight or importance in calculating the final grade for a course. An *examination* is the most comprehensive form of testing, typically given at the end of the term (as a final) and one or two times during the semester (as midterms). A test is more limited in scope, focusing on particular topics or aspects of course material; a typical course might have three or four tests. A quiz, as you probably know, is even more limited and usually is administered in 15 minutes or less. Though these distinctions are useful, the terms *test* and *exam* will be used interchangeably throughout the rest of this section because the principles in planning, constructing, and administering them are similar.

decisions. To understand how you can properly gauge the effectiveness of any kind of assessment (self- or professionally constructed), you need to have a basic grasp of two very elementary statistical concepts. They are not well appreciated by many classroom teachers, yet are important criteria for determining the quality of a specific test.

Validity. Test validity is that extent to which an assessment actually measures what it is intended to measure and permits generalizations about students' skills and abilities. By way of analogy, imagine you have a cloth tape measure. You measure some fabric with it and get a certain length. However, when you measure the piece again using a wooden yardstick, for example, you get a different measure because the cloth tape had become stretched and no longer yields standard units; therefore, it cannot provide a valid measure. Likewise, if you give a test on a number of items, the test is valid only if you can safely generalize that students will likely do as well on similar items included in another test designed to measure the same objectives. Validity is also tied to the purposes for which an assessment is used. A test might be valid for one purpose but inappropriate for others. For example, a test designed to measure a student's ability to *recall* the sequence of steps in a procedure does not necessarily mean that the student could also accurately *perform* these steps if asked to do so. Therefore, the validity of a test needs to be determined for each purpose for which the assessment is used.

Reliability. A second characteristic of good assessment information is its reliability. Reliability is the ability of a test to consistently yield a stable score over time. Think of a weight scale. If you weigh the same object three times on three different occasions and get three different measures, the scale cannot be considered reliable. The same holds true for assessments. You cannot have much confidence in the scores generated by tests that do not consistently measure what you want to measure. The most direct indicator of reliability would be having a group of students take the same test twice and get the same scores (assuming they would not remember the test items from the first administration). This would not be practical, of course, but there are other procedures for determining reliability.

The Bottom Line. Creating summative tests that are both valid and reliable can be challenging. Even exams produced by publishers under the guidance of experts will never be perfect. Test publishers try to minimize error by studying and reporting, then improving the reliability and validity of their tests. Doing the same as a classroom instructor is neither practical nor reasonable, especially for those not trained do so.

> *The dumbest people I know are those who know it all.*
>
> —Malcolm Forbes

Still, we must assess. Here are some suggestions for ensuring the validity and reliability of tests you devise yourself:

- Before you design an assessment, carefully review your syllabus and lesson plans for what you covered in class and/or assigned for student study. You need to be sure the content of the test represents an adequate sampling of the covered knowledge and skills.

- Write your test questions as you plan each lesson or at the end of each class session. (You can place them on index cards or computer files for later sorting.) This way you will not end up throwing into your assessments items that you may have planned to cover but never did. It is also important for a test to be balanced, which means it should cover most of the main ideas and important concepts in proportion to the emphasis they received in class. This will be easier to figure out if you do so right before or after a class meeting.

- When grading your assessments, analyze student errors to identify possible patterns of difficulty on specific items. Any item with a high percentage of wrong or incomplete responses may indicate that the question was too difficult, may have dealt with content that you actually failed to cover or inadvertently failed to assign for study, or perhaps did not explain clearly in class. Whatever the case, consider revising student grades to account for any problems in the test design.

- Be sure to carefully consider the guidelines for test design and administration given in the following section. In general, an inadequate variety of tests, ambiguous questions, unclear directions, improper length, and vague scoring criteria all can undermine both validity and reliability.

(*A final caution:* It is tempting to recycle exams or quizzes used in previous terms of the same course. Though it is time consuming to develop tests, a past exam may not reflect changes in how you have presented the material or in which topics you have emphasized in the current class.)

Basic Considerations in the Design and Administration of Summative Assessments

Once you are clear about your learning goals and what exactly you wish to measure, you will then need to consider other important factors when planning and giving your assessments. These include:

1. how to use different type of tests,
2. the most suitable format and layout of tests,
3. the range of difficulty of items,
4. when and how often to give tests,
5. the length and time limits for the test,

Nobody notices it when your zipper is up, but everyone notices when it's down.

—Cynthia Copeland Lewis

Chapter 10

Tradition is what you resort to when you don't have the time or the money to do it right.

—Kurt Herber Adler

6. test instructions, and

7. the testing environment. (A final important consideration, your scoring procedures, is discussed in Chapter 10.)

The Variety of Testing Formats and Methods. Given the potential weaknesses of any particular assessment, you should use multiple sources of information on student learning so that you can triangulate the results. Just as the use of several devices can determine the precise location of a communication signal, using a wide range of indicators to gather data helps pinpoint where your students are in their learning. These include not only the use of a variety of summative assessments at different times throughout your course, but also the frequent and regular use of formative indicators and alternative assessment approaches (explained below).

We know from research that students vary in their preferences for different test formats, so using an assortment of methods will not only help you achieve your course goals but also help your students do their best. A single test can combine several formats—for example, multiple-choice items with short-answer questions. But in using variations, try to avoid introducing a new format on a final exam (such as giving an essay exam when all others have been multiple-choice), which may leave students at a disadvantage. Also, consider making your tests cumulative. These require students to review material they have already studied, thus reinforcing what they have learned and giving them a chance to integrate and synthesize course content.

Test Layout. Here are some pointers to make your assessments both effective and user-friendly:

- Use ample margins and line spacing for easy reading. This will help students easily survey the test items, a good test-taking strategy that you want your students to use.

- Indicate the point value next to each item if items are worth different points, so students can allocate their time effectively.

- Group similar types of items, such as all true–false questions, together. This will make it easier for students to complete these more quickly.

- Use proper spacing for fill-in-the-blank short-answer questions. The amount of space given for short-answer questions often signifies the length of the answer expected.

- Consider the level of difficulty of each item.

- Put some easy items first. Place several questions all your students can answer near the beginning of the exam. Answering easier questions helps students overcome their nervousness and may help them feel confident that they can succeed on the exam.

- Challenge your better students. Consider at least one very difficult question—though not a trick question or a trivial one—to challenge the interest of the best students. Place that question at or near the end of the exam. This is because many students, as you probably know, do not have good test-taking skills. When under the stress of an exam, these students may get hung up on a difficult question and end up spending too much time on it and thus fail to move on to easier ones that they could answer.

When and How Often to Give Tests. Consider using assessments early on and frequently in your courses. Many instructors will assess only after they have progressed a good way into a term. Some instructors will even assign only a midterm and a final exam. Although this may make things easier on you, it can be a great burden for students. Your students need to understand and will appreciate knowing your testing methods and grading style, so they can study properly for the kind of tests you give. Moreover, testing sooner rather than later gives them feedback early enough in a term to make adjustments in their learning approach that may be necessary based on their performance. This will also permit you to make modifications in your assessments to accommodate your students' needs.

Allotted Test Time. A common complaint of students is that they did not have enough time. This may be an excuse for poor preparation or performance. But it also may be because you did not allow the proper amount of time given the length and difficulty of the assessment. If your test it too long for even well-prepared students to finish and review before turning it in, it will have failed to provide an accurate measure of student learning. Here are some simple guidelines that will allow most students to complete an assessment in the time provided:

- 30 seconds per item for true–false tests
- 30 seconds to 1 minute per item for multiple-choice tests
- 2 to 3 minutes per short-answer requiring a few sentences
- 10 to 15 minutes for a limited essay question, and possibly about 30 minutes for a broader essay question
- 5 to 10 minutes for students to review their work
- A few minutes for you to explain directions and to distribute and collect the tests

A good way to see whether the time allowed is appropriate is to take the test yourself and then allow students about four times as long as it took you to complete it.

Your Test Instructions. You will be surprised—or maybe not, from your own experience as a student—how often students do poorly on tests

> *Mistakes are the usual bridge between inexperience and wisdom.*
>
> —Phyllis Theroux

simply because they did not correctly follow directions or did not clearly understand what the expectations were. You might feel inclined to dismiss student complaints about unclear instructions as another excuse. However, it may be true, especially if a significant number of your students have similar problems. Therefore, be certain your instructions are clear. If you are at all concerned that there may be some confusion, go over the directions before students start the assessment. You may even want to test your instructions by asking a colleague to read them.

The Testing Environment. Test-taking is inherently anxiety-producing for just about everyone, even the best-prepared students. You may be able to help reduce the tension for some with a few words of encouragement and advice. Remind students of some good test-taking strategies, like reviewing the entire exam before they begin, determining which questions are harder than others and which have higher point values, and leaving a little time to review. Also, you can help students keep track of time throughout the test so they pace themselves properly, though you may want to gauge their reactions, since some students may find this more stressful.

Types of Summative Classroom Assessment

As you read the following description of the common kinds of assessments you can choose for use in your instruction, remember two things:

1. most of your students will use your assessment techniques as the means for gauging what you expect them to learn, and

2. they will generally adopt the easiest course of action, adapting their learning approach to meet the minimum requirements of your assessment techniques.

So choose carefully and thoughtfully. If you want to promote higher-quality learning, be ready to use a mix of assessment formats to encourage a mix of learning approaches.

The formats described here are arranged in the order of the levels of learning they best assess, as classified by Bloom's taxonomy. (The "nuts and bolts" of constructing these various kinds of tests comes in the section that follows.)

True–False Tests

Advantages: These are good for measuring the grasp of basic knowledge, evaluating student understanding of popular misconceptions, and fundamental ideas that have only two logical responses. They can quickly test large amounts of content in a short time, taking about a minute per two to three questions.

Disadvantages: True–false tests can be too easy, allowing random guessing that can produce a correct answer half the time, and are less reliable than other types of exams. We suggest using these items only

Examinations are formidable even to the best prepared, for the greatest fool may ask more than the wisest man can answer.

—Charles Caleb Colton

occasionally. (At the same time, you can add a deeper dimension to them, by including an "explain" component, in which students are called on to write one or two sentences justifying each response.)

Matching Tests

Advantages: The matching format is valuable in content areas that have a lot of facts, and is an effective way to test both knowledge level and some comprehension-level learning when constructed well. This includes students' recognition of the relationships between words and definitions, events and dates, categories and examples, causes and effects, problems and solutions, parts and wholes, and so on. They are also relatively easy to construct and score.

Disadvantages: Matching tests are weak indicators of higher levels of learning. Also, it can be a challenge to select options for answers that include both correct responses and reasonable incorrect wrongs.

Multiple-Choice Tests

Advantages: Multiple-choice items have a number of distinct advantages that make them the default assessment for many teachers. Depending on their design, they can be used to measure simple knowledge, as well as complex concepts and higher-order knowledge, such as application, synthesis, analysis, and evaluation. They are suitable for many kinds of courses and subject matter, enable an efficient sampling of a broad range of content, reduce guessing, and can be scored quickly. They are also versatile, with several types available: question/right answer, incomplete statement, and best answer.

Disadvantages: Multiple-choice tests may be a well "tried" format but they are not always "true." Contrary to what many believe, good multiple-choice questions can be quite difficult to write. Unless the items are very carefully constructed, they will not necessarily measure what you think they are assessing, especially the understanding of concepts and principles and other higher-order knowledge. Also, if poorly written, they can easily be misleading and confusing for students.

Completion/Open Short-Answer Tests

Advantages: There are two variations. The first is the completion type, in which one word or a phrase inserted in a blank is required for the answer. This type is usually used to test recall. The second calls for a sentence or several-sentence response. This format is good for more advanced levels of understanding, such as application, synthesis, analysis, and evaluation levels. Depending on your objectives, short-answer questions can call for one or two sentences or a long paragraph response. They give you some opportunity to see how well students can express their thoughts and encourage more intensive study, since

> *Experience is that marvelous thing that enables you recognize a mistake when you make it again.*
>
> —F.P. Jones

students must know the answer versus recognizing the answer. They are relatively easy to construct.

Disadvantages: Completion/open short-answer tests take time to score and can have more than one correct answer. Evaluating answers will call for subjective judgments, reducing their reliability.

Essay Tests

Advantages: Essay-type exams can assess understanding and encourage a deep approach to learning. Thoughtfully crafted essay exams require that students be able to incorporate all levels of knowledge into their responses. They enable you to judge students' abilities to organize, integrate, interpret material, and express themselves in their own words. Essay tests also give you an opportunity to comment on students' progress, the quality of their thinking, the depth of their understanding, and the difficulties they may be having. These exams motivate students to study more than do tests requiring only the recognition and selection of correct responses (multiple-choice, true–false, etc.). To prepare adequately for essay tests students will need to focus on broad issues, general concepts, and relationships rather than on specific details.

Disadvantages: Because essay tests pose only a few questions, they can limit the amount of material tested, which reduces their validity. In addition, they are time-consuming to correct and administer, and because of subjectivity and inconsistency in grading, they are not as reliable as other measures, unless several independent raters are involved in their evaluation.

The color of truth is gray.

—André Gide

Oral Exams

Advantages: You can probe students' level of understanding of complex constructs. They are also useful as an instructional tool, given that they allow students to learn at the same time as they are being tested, through instructor feedback and coaching.

Disadvantages: Most common at the graduate level, aside from foreign language classes, oral exams are rarely used, since they can be time-consuming, too anxiety-provoking for students, and difficult to score unless you tape-record the answers, have a performance checklist, or have a panel of raters.

Performance Tests

Advantages: Performance tests are an excellent means to assess application of knowledge and skills and certain abilities that cannot be measured in other ways. They call for questions, tasks, or activities that require students to perform an action, and can vary in their scope of the response required. They may involve students' conducting a demonstration, executing a series of steps in a reasonable amount of time, following instructions, manipulating materials or equipment, or reacting to real or simulated situations. Or, rather than actual demonstrations or presentations, they may call for students to explain how they would perform a task or solve a problem by writing a few sentences or paragraphs, or possibly by drawing or explaining a diagram to reveal how they would do so. Performance tests can be administered individually or in groups. When involving work with a group of students, they may think through the responses together and later provide their own individually written answers.

Disadvantages: Performance tests cannot be used in some fields of study and are seldom used in colleges and universities. The content of many courses does not necessarily lend itself to this type of testing, and these tests may be logistically difficult to set up. They can be time-consuming to take and difficult to score.

Problem Sets

Advantages: These are effective assessments for evaluating higher-order learning in certain courses, such as mathematics, the sciences, engineering, and health-related fields.

Disadvantages: Writing or selecting problems that can be addressed in the time available can be a challenge. Also, they call for very clear directions that define your expectations, the format for student responses, and the criteria to be used to assess their performance. Properly specifying all these elements to avoid student confusion can be demanding.

Take-Home Exams

Advantages: Take-home tests allow students to work at their own pace with access to books and materials. They permit longer and more involved questions, without sacrificing valuable class time for exams. Problem sets, short answers, and essays are the most appropriate kinds of take-home exams. A variation of a take-home test is to give the topics in advance but ask the students to write their answers in class. Some faculty hand out short lists of questions the week before an exam and announce that several of these will appear on the exam.

Disadvantages: You need to be wary of designing a take-home exam that is too difficult or an exam that does not include limits on the number of words or time spent. Also, it is difficult to guide and monitor the manner in which the test is completed. You will need to give students very explicit instructions on what they can and cannot do (e.g., will you allow students to talk to other students about their answers?).

Open-Book Tests

Advantages: Open-book tests can simulate the situations professionals face every day, such as tasks that call for the proper use of

> *It is easier to perceive error than to find truth, for the former lies on the surface and is easily seen, while the latter lies in the depth, where few are willing to search for it.*
>
> —Johann von Goethe

resources to solve problems, preparation of reports, or writing memos for a specific purpose and audience. Open-book tests also appear to reduce stress.

Disadvantages: Open-book tests tend to be inappropriate in introductory courses, in which facts must be learned or skills thoroughly mastered if the student is to progress to more complicated concepts and techniques in advanced courses. On an open-book test, students who are lacking basic knowledge may waste too much of their time consulting their references rather than writing. Also, some research shows that students do not necessarily perform significantly better on open-book tests and that these tests may reduce students' motivation to study. An effective compromise between open- and closed-book testing is to let students bring an index card or one page of notes to the exam or to distribute appropriate reference material such as equations or formulas as part of the test.

Group Exams

Advantages: Group exams can be used either in class or as take-home projects. There is evidence that groups outperform individuals and that students respond positively to group exams. You can group students randomly, or by ability based on students' performance on individual tests to minimize differences between group scores, or to balance talkative and quiet students.

Disadvantages: The biggest challenge is how to assess group work. There are several options, such as each student receiving the score of the group; however, some students may not feel this is fair if all members of the group did not contribute equally. Those not experienced with group tests and grading may want to use them initially as ungraded formative learning tools. (A brief guide for handling the grading of group work is explained in the section on "Authentic Assessments" below.)

Tips for Construction of Effective Summative Assessments

In general, no matter what its format, a good test should do the following:

- Assess achievement of your instructional objectives
- Measure both elementary elements (facts, formulas, etc.) and higher-level aspects (concepts and conceptual relations) of the subject taught
- Accurately reflect the relative emphasis you have placed on different aspects of instruction
- Measure appropriate levels of student knowledge
- Vary in their levels of difficulty

> *Human beings learn and progress by making—and correcting—mistakes. Why, then, do schools teach students to avoid and fear them?*
>
> Neil Postman

True–False Tests

- Make items simple and clear and avoid long/complex sentences that can cause confusion.
- Select wording carefully and consider how students will interpret word meaning.
- Make positive statements, and especially avoid double negatives.
- Make sure the statements are entirely true or entirely false.
- Use qualifiers with caution: "never," "only," "all," "none," and "always" will usually be false; "could," "might," "can," "may," "sometimes," "generally," "some," and "few" are often interpreted as true.
- Use only one central idea in each item so what you are assessing is clear.
- Use precise quantitative language (e.g., "more than 50%," rather than "frequently," "many," etc).
- Avoid taking items directly from text materials.
- Use more false items, since they tend to discriminate more than true ones.

Matching Tests

- Use 15 items or less.
- Put all items on a single page.
- Use more responses (possible answers) than stems (left-hand column) to minimize guessing.
- Make directions clear for the basis of matching. For example, can responses be used more than once? Where will each go?
- Place most of the information in the stem, and keep responses short.
- Arrange the response column in a logical order (alphabetical, etc.) so students can find them quickly and easily.
- Do not let grammatical cues (such as verb tense) signal the correct response.
- Make all responses plausible.

Multiple-Choice Tests

We provide more details on how to construct multiple-choice tests than other test formats. This is not just because they are probably the most common type of assessment used. Despite their common use, many instructors do not realize that they are generally more difficult and

The trouble with the world is that the stupid are cocksure and the intelligent are full of doubt.

—Bertrand Russell

time-consuming to write than most other kinds of tests and require careful consideration to construct properly.

Multiple-Choice Test Item Anatomy. A standard multiple-choice test item consists of two basic parts: a problem or question, known as the *stem,* and a list of suggested solutions, the *alternatives.*

- The stem may be in the form of either a question or an incomplete statement.

- The list of alternatives contains one correct or best choice, which is the *answer,* and a number of incorrect or inferior alternatives, know as *distracters.*

- Distracters serve as possible answers to challenge students' recall and understanding. The distracters must appear as *im*plausible solutions for those students who have achieved the learning objective; only one possible answer should appear plausible to these students. Here is an example:

1. When writing multiple-choice exams
   the first consideration is the: ← STEM
   a. Number of questions to include. ← Distracter
   b. The learning objectives you wish
      to assess. ← Answer
   c. The amount of time you need to
      allow for completion. ← Distracter
   d. Your students' learning level ← Distracter

Most poorly written multiple-choice test questions are characterized by at least one of the following weaknesses:

1. they attempt to measure an objective for which they are not well suited,

2. they contain clues to the correct answer,

3. they are worded ambiguously, and/or

4. they have poorly written distracters.

Coming up with good questions and acceptable distracters requires a fair amount of skill, which may be increased through experience.

Special Note: Negatively worded items are those in which the student is instructed to identify the exception, that is, the incorrect answer, or the least correct answer rather than the correct one. Instructors often use these kinds of items because they are relatively easy to construct; you need only come up with one distracter, rather than the two to four required for a positively worded item. Positive items, however, are more

> *The greatest obstacle to discovering the shape of the earth, the continents, and the oceans was not ignorance but the illusion of knowledge.*
>
> —D. Boorstin

appropriate to use for measuring the attainment of most educational objectives; therefore, you should avoid using negatively stated items.

Types of Multiple-Choice Items

- *Single Correct Answer:* All of the alternatives are incorrect except one.
- *Best Answer:* The alternatives differ in their degree of correctness. Some may be completely incorrect and some correct, but one is clearly more correct than the others.
- *Multiple Response:* These items have two or more possible correct answers among the alternatives; the remaining alternatives serve as distracters. The student is directed to identify *each* correct answer. This kind of item can be a difficult to score and can be scored in several different ways. Scoring on an all-or-none basis (one point if all the correct answers and none of the distracters are selected, and zero points otherwise) and scoring each alternative independently (one point for each correct answer chosen and one point for each distracter not chosen) are commonly used methods. Both methods, however, have distinct disadvantages, though the second is preferable. With the first method a student who correctly identifies all but one of the answers receives the same score as a student who cannot identify any of the answers; the second method produces scores more representative of each student.

Specific Tips for Multiple-Choice Tests

- The stem should present a single, clearly formulated problem or question.
- The stem should be simple and direct, with no unnecessary words.
- A good stem permits good students to anticipate the answer before reading the alternatives.
- Avoid "all of the above." These can often be answered correctly based on partial knowledge.
- Avoid "none of the above." This does not accurately assess what students know.
- Make all distracters equally plausible.
- Do not use double negatives.
- Present alternatives in logical or numerical order.
- Make all alternatives approximately the same length.
- Place correct answer at random.
- Make each item independent of others on the test.

> To be conscious that you are ignorant is a great step to knowledge.
>
> —Benjamin Disraeli

- List alternatives on separate lines, indent, separate by blank line, and use letters versus numbers for alternative answers.
- These tests need more than three alternatives; four is best.

Completion/Closed-Short-Answer Tests

- Arrange for a variety of items in your test. These can range from those that call for one-word responses to paragraph answers.
- If your short-answer question will be of the completion type, try not to simply leave out words from sentences taken from the resource materials you have used for instruction.
- Make sure that enough detail is provided so that the item is unambiguous.
- If the question is in the form of filling in the blank, arrange for the blank to come at the end of the item. This allows the student answering to absorb all the information before being faced with the unknown.
- For completion items, tell your students whether the length of the blank reflects the length of the intended answer. The item is somewhat easier when the length of the blank does reflect the length of the intended item.
- Provide grading criteria in advance so students will understand what you are looking for in each item. If your item requires students to write sentences rather than fill in a blank, tell them how much you want them to write (a sentence or two, short paragraph, etc.).
- When using with definitions, supply the term to be defined, not the definition, as this provides for a better judgment of what students know.
- If you do use incomplete statements, do not use more than two blanks within an item.
- Try to each item so that there is only one answer possible.
- Provide enough context so that only one word fits in each blank, and use concise clues and familiar vocabulary.

Open-Short-Answer and Essay Tests

The most common problem with open-short-answer and essay questions is that they are too open and do not indicate what the teacher is looking for. A good short-answer or essay question indicates:

1. what the scope of the answer should be, and

2. the criteria that will be used to assess the quality of the answer.

In addition, consider the following:

- Provide reasonable time limits for thinking and writing.

> *The longer the test the better you feel when it's over.*
>
> —Cynthia Copeland

- Avoid letting students answer a choice of questions. (You will not get a good idea of the breadth of student achievement when they answer only a set of questions.)
- Give a definitive task—to compare, analyze, evaluate, etc. different topics or ideas
- Use a checklist point system to score with a model answer—write an outline, determine how many points to assign to each part.
- Score one question at a time.

Performance Exams

These are customary in programs for hands-on skills training. They are also associated with what are considered "authentic" assessments (explained later, in the section on "Innovative Classroom Assessment"). When administering a performance test, be sure do to the following:

- Specify the criteria to be used for rating or scoring (e.g., the level of accuracy in performing the steps in sequence or completing the task within a specified time limit).
- State the problem so that students know exactly what they are supposed to do. (If possible, conditions of a performance test should mirror a real-life situation.)
- Give students a chance to perform the task more than once or to perform several task samples.

Oral Exams

An alternative to a written exam may be an oral exam. Oral exams may be frightening for some students, but they may also be a blessing for the student who feels more comfortable speaking than writing. But be prepared to deal with these with fairness. Because an oral exam tends to be less objective than a written exam students may raise legitimate questions about how you will evaluate the responses. You may want to talk this issue over with the students before the exam. Here are some other things to consider when administering an oral exam:

- Will you ask all the same questions or different questions of each student? There are benefits to each approach, but carefully weigh the difficulty level of the questions if you choose to use different questions with each student.
- Who will ask the questions? It does not have to be you. Some students may feel intimidated being asked test questions by the instructor. You may want to consider having students ask each other the questions while you listen to the responses. Students may also have a good time asking each other the questions (be sure the students are comfortable with this arrangement).

> *If anything concerns me, it's the oversimplification of something as complex as assessment. My fear is that learning is becoming standardized. Learning is idiosyncratic. Learning and teaching is messy stuff. It doesn't fit into bubbles.*
>
> —Michele Forman

- Will you provide the questions before the exam? Presenting the questions before the exam will give the students time to prepare. You may also want to allow students to prepare talking over points of information they want to cover in their response. In addition, you may choose to ask all of the provided questions or only a few of them.

- What ground rules will you set? For example, you probably will want to let students know before the exam that it is all right to ask for clarification of a question if they do not understand it. In general, it is a good idea to make statements that will help put the students at ease. The more comfortable they are the better their responses will be.

Group Exams

There are a number of approaches to giving group exams. For instance, for a 50-minute in-class exam, you can use a multiple-choice test of about 20 to 25 items, dividing the students randomly into groups of three to five students. You may have the students complete the test individually before meeting as a group, or let the groups discuss the test item by item in class. A variation of this would be to have students first work on an exam in groups outside class; students then complete the exam individually during class time and receive their own score. Here are some more specific guidelines and suggestions:

- Ask students to discuss each question fully and weigh the merits of each answer rather than simply vote on an answer.

- Let students know in advance you will be asking them to justify a few of their responses. (This will keep students from relying on their work group for all the answers.)

- If you assign problems, have each student work a problem and then compare results with the others in the group.

- If you want students to take the exam individually first, consider devoting two class periods to tests, one for individual work and the other for group.

- Show students the distribution of their scores as individuals and as groups; in most cases group scores will be higher than any single individual score.

Assessments *for* Learning—Formative Assessment

Any activity undertaken by you and your students can be a source of insight into the teaching and learning activities in which you are engaged. What distinguishes summative and formative assessments are the purposes of each assessment. Whereas summative assessments are intended to measure student attainment at a particular time

> *We don't know who we are until we see what we can do.*
>
> —Martha Grimes

for assigning a grade, formative assessments are intended to "form" or direct learning to promote further student improvement. Activities become formative assessments when the evidence gathered from them provides feedback used to:

1. help your students modify and improve their approach to learning and

2. help you adapt your teaching to meet their needs.

Consider formative assessment as a kind of coaching. Good coaches carefully monitor their players' performance, make suggestions for improvement, provide opportunities for practice, monitor again, and so on, in what is ideally an ongoing spiral of improvement. Within this model, classroom instruction and feedback become intimately connected in a seamless interaction between teachers and their students. With the support of the instructor, students become increasingly responsible for their own learning as they come to understand their strengths and weaknesses, and how they may deal with them to progress.

These assessments are generally informal in character and can include a wide range of procedures in addition to tests. They are also ungraded activities. Numerous research studies show that formative assessments can lead to dramatic gains in learning, especially for weaker students. On the one hand, marks or grades alone provided by summative measures rarely produce significant learning gains. Indeed, there is some evidence that students attain the highest achievement from assessment when the feedback is provided without marks or grades. When marks are provided, they often seem to dominate students' thinking and are seen as the only purpose of assessments, obscuring the other valuable roles they can serve.

The feedback generated by formative assessments can do the following:

● Increase students' motivation to learn by giving them a sense of success in the subject and self-confidence as a learner.

● Encourage ongoing teacher and peer dialogue around learning that yields high-quality information to students about their learning and to teachers about their teaching.

● Clarify what good performance is (goals, criteria, expected standards) and provide opportunities for students to close the gap between current and desired performance.

● Help students decide what to learn by highlighting what is important based on what is taught and through an understanding and recognition of the desired standards.

● Help students learn how to learn by influencing their choice of learning strategies and by inculcating self-monitoring skills that assist them in judging the effectiveness of their learning.

> The only Completely Consistent people are dead.
>
> —Aldous Huxley

- Improve students' achievement by enhancing their abilities to understand and retain knowledge, as well as to evaluate and consolidate their present level of learning, and by reinforcing new learning.

Quality feedback via formative assessment can be the single most powerful instructional influence on student achievement and should become an integral and inseparable part of the teaching and learning process in every class. (How formative assessment can be used to modify and improve your teaching as well as your students' learning is discussed below.)

Assessing While You Teach/Teaching While You Assess

The most common classroom cycle for many instructors is Teach → Assess → Evaluate → Grade → Teach New Topic. In this cycle, teaching and assessment are treated as independent processes. When you use formative assessments, on the other hand, assessment becomes woven throughout the teaching and learning process: Teach → Assess → Teach → Assess and so on, as a regular support for your students' learning.

There are three kinds of activities for formative assessments that can be used within this process:

1. unplanned or impromptu feedback activities,

2. planned lesson-specific feedback activities, and

3. longer-term, comprehensive assignments.

The main thing is to keep the main thing the main thing.

—Unknown

Informal		Formal
Unplanned		Planned
←		→
Impromptu "Spot Checks" Intra-Lesson Feedback		Comprehensive Evaluations

Unplanned Formative Assessment

These arise spontaneously at what some identify as "teachable moments." A teachable moment is an unexpected point during a class that offers a unique opportunity to help a student or group of students learn something in a significant way. These spontaneous interventions are not always obvious. Recognition of these moments is often intuitive, but can become more apparent based on a cumulative wisdom of practice. Identifying these moments is, of course, not enough to take advantage of them. You must also possess the necessary techniques or content knowledge to sufficiently challenge and respond to the students in a suitable manner at these times.

Chapter 6

Things are seldom what they seem, skim milk masquerades as cream.

—Sir William Schwenck Gilbert

Impromptu feedback can also come from spontaneous "spot checks" on where students are when you may sense some of them may not be getting what you are trying to teach at a particular point in a class presentation. (You can get this feedback with a good question or other interactive technique, as explained below.)

Planned Intra-Lesson Activities

This kind of feedback activity is prepared in advance of a particular lesson. Good examples are found among the components of interactive lectures and elaborated below. For instance, whereas a 1-minute paper might be used as an exercise to consolidate information, the same exercise can become a tool for formative assessment when feedback (either from you or a fellow student) is given on student responses. This feedback then becomes something the students can use as insight into their understanding of the lesson and what they may need clarification on before the class moves to another topic.

Teacher questioning also plays a role here. Even a simple question can become formative in character when used with the proper intention and planning. You no longer question students, for example, just to get a correct answer but plan your questions to maximize their learning and close the gap between where they are and where they need to go. Such questions are structured to prompt deeper reflection and study of a particular topic or point and to help students monitor what they understand or do not understand outside class.

Comprehensive Formative Assessments

Comprehensive assessments are embedded in course design as part of your overall teaching method. They are used to build a more complete and broader picture of student learning than can be gleaned just from the use of occasional graded summative measures. Less narrowly focused and used less frequently than either impromptu and lesson-level feedback designs, comprehensive assessments cover more than a single or short series of class sessions and can be used (depending on the length of your course) weekly, monthly, midterm, and/or end of term.

Comprehensive formative measures may be as simple as a student self-report done weekly or embedded intermittently into instruction after every few lessons as indicators of student progress. In a more sophisticated approach, they can be administered as ungraded summative assessments. These can be given at critical junctures in a large unit of instruction to signal student achievement of intermediate objectives needed to meet the goals of the larger unit. Feedback on performance is focused on areas of difficulty revealed by the assessments. These comprehensive evaluations may also consist of general reflective activities. These are composed of a sequence of investigations that enable you to step back at key points during instruction to check student understanding and consider the next steps you must take to move forward. Ideally, as with any type of formative assessment, the feedback given should be immediate and crafted to lead to effective teaching interventions, as well as lead to shifts in your students' approach to their study to close any learning gaps.

It may be helpful to think of the complete process involved in this kind of evaluation in terms of a medical analogy:

1. *Student Performance (identify symptoms of problems):* Simply ask, "What are students doing well or doing poorly?"

2. *Problem Diagnosis (identify cause of problems):* Work with students to figure out specifically where they are having trouble. What material do they find most difficult? Where did they get an answer wrong and why? What ideas/concepts/theories do they have difficulty understanding? In short, what led them to perform poorly on a test or assignment?

3. *Prescription (determine the solution to the problems):* Given student performance so far and the problem areas you have identified, now work with them to design a plan of action for improvement. Are there additional readings the students might consider? Are there some practice problems the students can work on? Do you simply need to talk through some concepts more slowly so the students can ask questions and clarify ideas? Try to give students specific suggestions for improvement rather than generic ones like "study harder next time."

Guidelines for Implementing Formative Assessments

The informal character of formative assessments allows for a wide range of methods in addition to tests and quizzes (though you can use your formal summative indicators for formative purposes). Below is a summary of some basic guidelines for developing and using your own formative feedback devices. These (and the specific techniques that follow) are largely based on the work of K. Patricia Cross and Thomas Angelo, who have developed excellent resources on the purposes, design, and implementation of many kinds of formative classroom-assessment techniques. (We strongly encourage you to explore their work in greater depth.)

1. *Gather pertinent, general information.* This will focus on and generate a brief description of the instructional context. It can include background information on your students (majors, motivation level, skill levels, etc.) plus core goals of the course.

2. *Develop central questions.* You do this based on both your and your students' needs. Central questions specify what you would

---

To teachers, students are the end products—all else is a means. Hence there is but one interpretation of high standards in teaching: standards are highest where the maximum number of students—slow learners and fast learners alike—develop to their maximal capacity.

—Joseph Seidlin

like to find out through an assessment by identifying what is most essential for students to learn and accomplish in your course, and your most pressing instructional needs.

3. *Determine the purpose of your assessment.* You want to be sure you do not attempt to accomplish too much with one assessment. (A focused feedback device, for example, would be one that identifies student prior knowledge or misconceptions on a particular topic.) Decide whether you are primarily interested in gaining insight, changing a course practice, or measuring the effects of a change you have already implemented. (The work of Angelo and Cross identifies and explains many different kinds of assessments for very specific purposes.)

4. *Determine how you will use the assessment results.* This is linked to your central questions and takes into consideration the resources available to implement changes. It also will help guide the content of your assessment. If you are unsure how an assessment could potentially improve learning or instruction, it is probably best not to conduct it until you have determined this.

5. *Choose your specific feedback technique.* This should be appropriate to your context and purpose, answer your central questions, and be something you can implement given your resources. (A number of common ones are presented below.)

6. *Administer the feedback measure.* This may be before, during, or after an instructional activity. Inform students beforehand what you are going to do and why you are doing it. Let them know it will not be graded. Allow them to make the exercise anonymous (if suitable for your purposes). Clearly explain the procedure for completing the exercise, and collect student responses.

7. *Analyze the student feedback.* You can do this by simply reading the responses and categorizing them. It is helpful to use your central questions as a starting point to develop categories. Initially, try to get the "big picture" and focus on how the whole class is learning rather than on the performance of individual students.

8. *Draw conclusions based on your analysis.* How do the results answer the central questions on which the assessment was based? What can you do to improve learning based on the feedback results? What changes in student behavior do the results suggest? What changes in instruction do the results suggest?

9. *Disseminate results.* A key component of this method is completing the feedback loop by sharing results with students. Let students know what you have learned and how you will use the results. Discuss with students what they can do to improve their learning.

> *The most important knowledge teachers need to do good work is a knowledge of how students are experiencing learning and perceiving their teacher's actions.*
>
> —Stephen Brookfield

Chapter 7

Examples of Formative Assessments

Any activity that provides information to our students can serve as a formative assessment. As we have mentioned, some formal methods that are summative and for which we assign grades can be used formatively if specific feedback on a student's performance is given. Many of the techniques suggested for promoting interaction during lectures suggested in Chapter 7 are included here. The key difference is you need to collect and analyze the student responses to activities to adjust learning or teaching practices. Most require relatively little time to prepare, administer, and evaluate.

Impromptu and Lesson-Designed Feedback

The tables below provide an overview of both unplanned, impromptu, and planned, comprehensive formative assessments for a broad range of learning goals.

Assessment of Prior Knowledge, Recall, and Understanding

TECHNIQUE	DESCRIPTION
Background knowledge probe	Examine students' prior knowledge of subject matter through a short questionnaire or checklist to determine where to begin new instruction.
Misconception/ preconception check	Use a short questionnaire, multiple choice test, true-false quiz, etc. to assess prior knowledge and beliefs that can interfere with the ability to learn new information so instruction can be modified to facilitate acquisition.
Focused listening	Give students a term and have them list or map out all related ideas to discover what learners recall as important points and focus student attention on a topic and/or concept.
Empty outlines	Provide students with a blank or partially completed outline of course material and have them fill in the missing components in a limited amount of time. Assesses not only recall but also ability to organize what they know.

(continues)

One-minute paper	Ask class to answer in one minute "what was the most important thing you learned during this class?" or "what important question remains unanswered?" to quickly assess the learning attained during a class.
Memory matrix	Provide students with a 2-dimensional matrix consisting only of row and column headings that they need to fill in. Promotes the organization of ideas and illustrates relationships.
Muddiest point	Variation of one-minute paper. Determines conceptual errors by asking questions such as "what was the muddiest point in _____?"
Chain notes	Have students pass around an envelope on which the teacher has written one question about the class. When the envelope reaches a student he/she spends a moment to respond to the question and then places the response in the envelope. Go through to detect response patterns (correct vs. incorrect, shallow vs. deep understanding, etc.).

Assessing Skill in Analysis and Critical Thinking

TECHNIQUE	DESCRIPTION
Categorization grid	Give students a grid containing 2 or 3 important categories and require them to sort a scrambled list of terms, equations, etc. into these categories.
Pro and con grid	Have students list pros/cons, costs/benefits, advantages/disadvantages, etc. in relationship to a specific concept, theory, or idea.
Defining features matrix	Learners determine whether concepts have a presence or absence of a list of important defining features to judge how well they can distinguish between similar concepts.

(continues)

Analytic memos	Learners write a structured 1–2 page analysis of and response to a specific problem or issue using specific problem solving methods.
Content, form, and function outlines	Give a short presentation and ask students to identify the what (content), how (form), and why (function) to help students focus on important elements and analyze new information.

Assessing Skill in Synthesis and Creative Writing

TECHNIQUE	DESCRIPTION
One-sentence summary	Students synthesize information about a given topic into one long, grammatically correct summary sentence that answers the questions "Who, what, when, where, how, and why?" to assess how effectively they can summarize a large body of information by selecting only the defining features of an idea.
Word journal	Learners summarize information into a single word, then write a short paragraph explaining the word selection to examine the depth of comprehension.
Concept map	This is a graphic tool that students construct to focus their attention on associations between a major concept and other learning by requiring them to diagram relationships.
Approximate analogies	Provide the first half of an analogy which students complete to help them connect new ideas to more familiar ones.
Invented dialogues	Learners are required to either weave together original quotes or invent their own dialogue based on a specific theory or historical period that requires them to creatively adapt what they have learned.

Assessing Skill in Problem Solving

TECHNIQUE	DESCRIPTION
What's the principle?	Give examples of problems from which they must identify what principle or theory is at work to assess their ability to connect problems with appropriate solution strategies.
Documented problem solutions	Ask learners to document the steps in the problem-solving process as they work through real-world type issues to encourage self-monitoring.
Problem recognition tasks	Provide students with a range of problems from which they must identify the type of problem that each example represents to determine how well they can identify types of problems and corresponding solution strategies.

Assessing Skill in Application and Performance

TECHNIQUE	DESCRIPTION
Application cards	Students are called upon to generate a real-world application after learning a new theory, principle, or concept.
Directed paraphrasing	Ask learners to write a layman's "translation" of something they have just learned—geared to a specified individual or audience—to assess their ability to comprehend and transfer concepts and their ability to communicate what they know.
Student-generated test questions	Students must write test questions based on the material they have learned to determine what they judge to be most important and how well they have grasped related information.

Comprehensive Formative Assessments

TECHNIQUE	DESCRIPTION
Student learning logs	These can be used weekly or at longer intervals. Reports are papers written by students in which they address 3 questions: (1) What did I learn this week? (2) What questions remain unclear? and (3) What do I need to do to improve my understanding? These reports provide an easy way for students to develop the habit of reflecting on knowledge and learning and improve their self-assessment skills and, when collected, give you a clear picture about what they think they are learning and what conceptual difficulties they are experiencing.
Exam evaluations	Select a type of test that you are likely to give more than once or that has a significant impact on student performance. Create a few questions that evaluate the quality of the test. Add these questions to the exam or administer a separate, follow-up evaluation. Try to distinguish student comments that address the fairness of your grading from those that address the fairness of the test as an assessment instrument. Respond to the general ideas represented by student comments.
Group or paired exams	For paired exams, pairs of students might work on a single essay exam, and the two students turn in one paper. Pairs can be self-selected or assigned. For example, pairing a student who is doing well in the course with one not doing well allows for some peer teaching. A variation is to have students work in teams but submit individual answer sheets. Groups can work in the same way, though you may want to use mostly objective tests, such as multiple-choice exams, since group essays are cumbersome. Students can complete the tests outside of class, in class, or partly outside and the rest in class. You can also group students by ability so weaker students can benefit from working with some more capable.

(continues)

| Annotated portfolios | Students select a few assignments that they believe highlight their work and provide a short written explanation why each piece was selected to encourage critical self-evaluation. [More on the use of portfolios follows in the section on "Innovative Assessments."] |

A Final Word on Formative Assessments: Providing Constructive Feedback

Since we know assessment is a major influence on student motivation, it is essential to anticipate and optimize the motivational effects of feedback on assessment. One way to achieve this is to think of your feedback as a conversation with your students. This dialogue should be thoughtful, reflective, focused to evoke and explore understanding, and conducted so that all students have an opportunity to think and to express their ideas.

The research evidence available suggests that the greatest benefits will come from focusing feedback on the following:

- The quality of a student's work, and not on comparisons with other students
- Specific ways in which the student's work can be improved by identifying the next steps and how to take them
- Improvements that the student has made compared with his or her earlier work
- Learning goals understood and shared by both teachers and students
- Building students' confidence that they can improve their work

Formative assessment should lead to appropriate and effective action students can take. If you give feedback to students indicating what they need to do to improve, it is not formative unless they can understand and act on that information. If, for example, you tell a student to "be more thorough," it is not feedback unless the student knows what "being thorough" specifically means. If learners understood what "being thorough" meant, they would probably have been able to be more thorough in the first place. Just consider how helpful it is for you to be told by an administrator to "teach better." Teachers often believe that the advice they are giving is helpful, not realizing that what is obvious to them is not so obvious to their students. Therefore, you cannot assume your communications—no matter how carefully worded they are—will have the same meaning for your students as they do for you. Learners will come to understand your evaluative statements only by developing their own notions of quality; your feedback can at best provide a basis for them to figure this out. This objective of helping students understand expected standards and how to achieve them unifies summative and formative functions of assessment and are at the heart of quality learning and teaching.

Innovative Classroom Assessment: Alternative Strategies for Measuring Student Learning

Shifting Views of Assessment

We have argued throughout this text that learning is not just about absorbing information, but also about building meaningful understanding, and that it is important for each of us to broaden our customary teaching strategies to engage learning and to promote thinking on deeper and more complex levels. Here is a quick review of some key points that are relevant to your assessment strategies:

- Deep conceptual learning is not something delayed until all the basic facts have been memorized and mastered. People have the ability to learn complex ideas even as they learn more fundamental ones.

- There is tremendous variety in the modes and speed with which people learn, and instruction needs to address and accommodate these differences.

- Instruction that calls for the application of knowledge and skills to solve real-world problems after the completion of instruction make these tasks much more difficult. Most students need to be given the opportunity to use and develop higher-order thinking skills during instruction.

- Studies of motivation have highlighted the importance of affective and metacognitive skills. Acquisition of knowledge or basic skills is not sufficient to make someone a competent thinker or problem solver. People also need to acquire the disposition to use these skills and strategies, as well as the knowledge of when and how to apply them.

- Attention to the role of the social context of learning in shaping higher-order cognitive abilities and dispositions points to the fact that real-life problems often require people to work together as a group in problem-solving situations.

- Changing notions of intelligence suggest that intelligence is no longer unitary in nature but multidimensional and capable of being

There are some who operate largely from a constructivist and/or humanistic perspective and question the validity of customary assessment procedures. We do not believe you should or even can abandon the use of traditional summative assessments. Indeed, some summative assessment instruments can effectively measure the deeper kind of learning we are looking for. However, they are still generally limited in many ways when conceived of as mostly paper-and-pencil exercises. In this form, they can describe only a limited number of knowledge and cognitive skills and thus do not adequately reflect this new vision of learning. Although formative approaches to assessment do serve this new vision, as we have described them, they are not always adequate for the purposes of *summative* assessment, since they are mostly informal and ungraded. Consequently, we need to consider additional quantitative and qualitative instruments that can gather the information both as a source of helpful feedback toward the achievement of these expanded learning goals on student progress, as well as for the purpose of assigning grades. This expanded alternative approach is commonly known as "authentic assessment."

expressed in many different ways that go beyond the traditional emphasis on logical–mathematical and verbal–linguistic abilities.

To evaluate learning in these dimensions, you need to broaden your assessment strategies. In addition to traditional assessments that focus on knowledge acquisition and recall, we need measures that can describe your students' learning at more complex, meaningful levels and in all the diversity they bring to the learning situation.

From Testing to Authentic, Multidimensional Assessments

In the standard educational experience, student learning is most frequently measured by tests that have the following characteristics:

1. they use limited, specific questions with a single correct response,

2. they are designed to be administered within a limited time period, and

3. they are narrowly focused to tap into a small set of knowledge and skills.

Based on a new vision of learning, an expanded perspective of evaluation views assessment as "authentic and multidimensional," to better capture more significant learning outcomes and match the kinds of tasks that students will need to accomplish once they leave school. Authentic assessments share the following qualities:

- They are broad-based, relevant to real life, process-oriented, and based on multiple measures that provide a rich portrayal of student learning over extended periods of time.

- They attempt to include visual, auditory, kinesthetic, intrapersonal, and interpersonal abilities (even as they assess logical and verbal abilities).

- They assess students' repertoires of learning strategies, skills in communicating with others, and knowledge as it is applied to day-to-day and diverse contexts.

- They draw on and integrate many kinds of evaluation procedures in addition to customary paper-and-pencil testing involving a range of methods and different media, as described below.

Multi-dimensional, Authentic Assessments

On the whole, an innovative approach to assessment adopts a more positive approach to education. By spreading the assessment net more widely, it provides students with a range of opportunities to demonstrate how much they understand, rather than how little. Innovative assessments also encourage the assessment of learners not just as individuals but also as individuals working in groups, and as groups of individuals.

Student performances and presentations	Interviews
Computer simulations	Classroom simulations and scenarios
Projects and student products	Role plays
Seminars	Group work
Problem solving tasks and case studies	Portfolios and reflective diaries

In the figure on the next page, we characterize some of the distinctions between traditional and more innovative assessments.

Traditional Assessments		Authentic Assessments
←		→
Knowledge and Skills Tested in Isolation		Knowledge and Skills Embedded in Authentic Settings, Applied
Single Measures of Learning, Limited Knowledge Sets		Multiple Measures of Learning, Broad Knowledge Sets
Focus on Single, Low-Level Learning Dimensions		Focus on Complex, Higher-Order Learning
Focus on Single Dimensions of Intelligence		Focus on Multiple Dimensions of Intelligence
Emphasis of Assessment	Traditional Assessment	Authentic, Multidimensional Assessment
Student Task	Selecting, choosing, identifying correct answers	Actively constructing own responses
Scope	Discrete, isolated information that calls for recall and recognition of correct answers	Integrated approach—calls for understanding of relationships, overarching concepts and principles and application and use of knowledge and skills. Tasks often provide measures of metacognitive skills and attitudes, collaborative skills, and intrapersonal skills as well as the more usual intellectual products
Characteristics	Paper-pencil, objective items	Contextualized with problems that are open-ended, relevant and meaningful, emphasize higher-level thinking, do not have a single correct answer, and have public standards known in advance
Frequency	Single occasion	Samples over time (portfolios) which provides basis for evaluation by both teacher and students
Who Assessed	Individual assessment	Include group process skills on collaborative tasks
What Assessed	Single attribute	Multidimensional and recognizes the variety of human abilities and talents, fluidity of student ability and intelligence

Different Types of Authentic Assessments

Here is a brief description of a few common alternatives to customary "pencil-and-paper" tests.

Performance and Project-Based Assessments. A performance assessment is not necessarily an innovative or alternative way of measuring student progress. Career-specific training courses, for example, commonly call for the learning of hands-on skills and performance abilities and performance assessments are a regular practice. The demonstration of a knowledge and skill becomes innovative or authentic when students are required to exhibit their knowledge of a discipline in realistic contexts or in other ways not traditionally called for. An example would be math students being asked to apply math knowledge to analyze an engineering problem. In these nontraditional settings, performance assessments can be brief, for instance, conducting an experiment in a lab class or dealing with short problem sets. Or they may involve more extended tasks common in problem-based learning approaches, such as students in an engineering class working in teams to devise alternative designs for a mechanical system, which may take several days or even several weeks to complete. In general, these tasks require that students generate problems, consider options, and propose and then demonstrate their solutions. Students may also work in groups at certain times to collectively analyze options, as well as to present their thinking and conclusions to each other.

Portfolios. A portfolio is not a specific test but a cumulative collection of a student's work that shows you (and others who may evaluate them) the range and quality of student work across a period of time and topic areas. Whereas many summative tests are designed to determine what a student *does not* know, portfolio assessments emphasize what a student *does* know. Their overall goal is for learners to demonstrate and provide evidence that they have mastered a given set of objectives. Students decide what examples to include that characterize their growth and accomplishment over the term. Although they are common in writing and art courses, portfolios are more frequently being used in other disciplines to provide a fuller picture of student achievements. More than just thick folders containing student work, portfolios are typically personalized, long-term representations of a student's own efforts and achievements.

To prepare a portfolio, students must organize, synthesize, and clearly describe their achievements and effectively communicate what they have learned. There are almost as many approaches to compiling and evaluating portfolios as there are proponents of this form of assessment. The evidence can be presented in a three-ring binder, as a multimedia tour, or as a series of short papers, such as sample papers (first drafts and revisions), journal entries, essay exams, and other work representative of the student's progress. Portfolios can be used both formally and informally; ideally, portfolios capture the evolution of a student's ideas and act as progress markers for the students themselves, as well as for you and possibly program evaluators. You can assign portfolios a letter grade or a pass/not pass. If you do grade portfolios, you will need to establish clear criteria. (See discussion below for grading portfolio and other multidimensional assessments.)

A unique aspect of a successful portfolio is the inclusion of explicit statements of self-reflection. These are statements accompanying each item about how the student went about mastering the material, why a specific piece of evidence demonstrates mastery, and why mastery of such material is relevant to the overall course goals and perhaps to contexts outside the classroom. Self-reflection makes clear to you the processes of integration that have occurred during the learning process. Often, this is achieved with an introductory letter or as a summary at the end of each section. Such reflections ensure that the student has personally recognized the relevance and level of achievement acquired during creation and presentation of the portfolio. It is this self-reflection that makes a portfolio much more valuable than a simple folder of student-selected work.

Public Exhibitions. Some teachers may occasionally have students "publish" their work in exhibitions. These exhibitions focus on the student's ability to use and display knowledge intelligently and ensure that essential skills have been taught and learned. Exhibitions can yield an authentic measure of students' abilities to engage in inquiry and skillful expression, and they can motivate and engage students by involving them in a public challenge, such as a science competition or an in-class presentation. Exhibitions require reading, writing, questioning, speaking, and listening. They are generally a final class project, designed to bring together a number of strands in a unit. As comprehensive tasks, projects call for higher-order objectives, which are integrative in nature. Credit is given on the basis of what students can actually do in demonstrating their knowledge and know-how.

Group-Based Projects. The role of the social context of learning in shaping higher-order cognitive abilities and dispositions has received much attention in recent years. Groups facilitate learning in several ways: modeling effective thinking strategies, scaffolding complicated performances, providing mutual constructive feedback, and valuing the elements of critical thought. It has also been noted that real-life problems often require people to work together as a group in problem-solving situations. However, most traditional instruction and assessment have involved independent rather than small-group work.

Assessing Group Work/Projects

Most work situations require people to be able to work in groups/teams. There has been recognition of the importance of this generic skill. Aside from the course content, the skills and process of working in a group itself is an aspect that many academic programs wish to assess. The issue of assessment in groups, therefore, is twofold:

1. assessment of participation in the group—the group process, and

2. assessment of the content covered by the activity—the product of the group.

Groups can come in very different sizes, shapes, and forms (e.g. small groups within a large group, seminars, tutorials, task groups, problem-based learning groups, etc.), and each may require very different methods of assessment. Here are a number of suggestions for assessing students in groups:

- Tasks to Isolate and Assess as Part of Group Processes:
  - o Understanding of concepts
  - o Development of relevant concepts
  - o Contribution to the development of discussion
  - o Awareness of others in the group and listening skills
  - o Reference to literature/other sources
- Options for Assigning Grades:
  - o All students get the same mark for group project.
  - o All students get separate tasks within a group project, which are assessed separately.
  - o All students get the same mark. These are then aggregated (e.g., 75 for a group of three students. They can negotiate individual marks based on their individual contributions, as long as they total 75.).
  - o All students get the same mark for the product of the group and then peers assess contributions to the process and assign additional scores to each student according to the quality of their participation.
  - o All students get the same mark for original task and then get different marks for an additional task.
  - o All get the same group mark for the product, and then you assign individual marks for personal performance in the group
  - o All get the same mark for the original task, but differentiations are made in an additional exam task based on the group work, where those who worked hard at the first task would be better placed to answer well in the exam.

Group assessments, therefore, can serve as a way of evaluating group-based learning. Just about any project-based authentic assessment designed for individual learning and assessment can be modified to serve as a group activity.

Rubrics—An All-Purpose Tool for Grading and Evaluating Authentic Assessments

Rubrics are powerful, versatile designs that can come in handy in many assessment situations, not just authentic ones. Just about every teacher should learn how to develop a rubric.

What Is a Rubric? A rubric is an assessment tool useful for complex and subjective assessment criteria. Rubrics are rating scales or scoring guides consisting of specific preestablished performance criteria used for various multidimensional assessments, including those designed to simulate real-life activity to solve real-life problems. They can serve both as summative and formative assessments as an ongoing part of the teaching and learning process. Using rubrics, students themselves can become involved in the assessment process through both peer and self-assessment. Moreover, as students become familiar with rubrics, they can even assist in their design by helping to construct the performance criteria.

Rubrics can be constructed in a variety of forms and with various levels of complexity. When designed properly, they all allow subjective assessments to be more objective and reliable. They achieve this through three features:

1. the use of specific criteria that clarify the learning standards, show students what is expected, and show students how their work will be evaluated,

2. the organization of these criteria into levels that indicate the degree to which a standard has been met, and

3. providing feedback regarding the effectiveness of the instruction against explicit benchmarks.

Types of Rubrics. There are two basic types of rubrics: holistic and analytic.

Holistic Rubrics. Using a holistic rubric you rate the overall performance or product as a whole, without evaluating the component parts separately. With an analytic rubric, you score individual parts of the product or performance first, and then combine the individual scores to obtain a total score.

Holistic rubrics are most suitable when:

1. the focus of the assessment is on overall understanding or proficiency,

2. tasks require students to respond to a question or task for which there is no definitive correct answer, and

3. errors in some part of the process can be tolerated as long as the final quality is acceptable.

With attention to the overall performance, holistic rubrics are also typically, though not exclusively, used when the purpose of the performance assessment is summative in nature. At most, only limited feedback is provided to the student as a result of scoring performance tasks in this manner.

Analytic Rubrics. Analytic rubrics are usually preferred when the assessment is concerned with the separate elements of a learning task and a specific type of response is required. Analytic rubrics are also multidimensional and generate separate scores for each element of the response, followed by a summed total score. Analytic rubrics are more demanding to construct, use, and score than holistic rubrics, though they offer distinct benefits over the latter:

1. the quality of feedback offered is significantly greater and more meaningful,

2. students receive feedback regarding individual scoring criteria, and

3. it is also possible to create a profile of specific student strengths and weaknesses.

Basic Rubric Design Considerations. Your most important consideration is whether the performance or product to be assessed will be scored holistically or analytically. Since one type of rubric is not inherently better than the other, you will need to decide on the format that works best for your purposes. This decision will be based on several considerations with several possible implications. The most important of these is how you intend to use the results. If an overall, summative score is desired, a holistic scoring approach would be more desirable. In contrast, if formative feedback is the goal, an analytic scoring rubric should be used. Other implications include the time requirements, the nature of the task itself, and the specific performance criteria being observed. Whichever type of rubric is selected, specific performance criteria and observable indicators must be identified in the initial development. More information on how to design rubrics can be found in the companion Field Guide.

Refer to Field Guide

　　　　The levels of student performance can be defined using either quantitative (i.e., numerical) or qualitative (i.e., descriptive) labels. The traditional quantitative Likert scale, using ratings of 1 to 5, offers gradations that are familiar and make sense to most students. Qualitative scales need not be just labels; they also can be descriptions that are quite specific in order to be clear. The labels might be as simple as Unsatisfactory to Exceptional, with Acceptable, Satisfactory, and Outstanding rounding out a five-part scale.

One valuable aspect of rubrics is having students participate in creating the measure for their work. Starting with a simple question such as: "What does a good job look like?" can get a group started on determining the details and gradations that offer a final tool for assessment. When students say what they think a good job is and then have to abide by the rules they have agreed to, performance usually is better. This process takes more time than the instructor simply making the final decision on what criteria will be used to measure work, but it is more powerful. Students become engaged in a thinking process that can influence their ownership of projects and assignments. If nothing else, it is different from students usual experience in school and will provide an opportunity to think about things they may not have thought of before.

One potentially frustrating aspect of scoring student work with rubrics is the issue of converting them to grades. The process of converting rubric scores to grades or categories is a somewhat subjective and qualitative rather than quantitative process. You will need to come up with a system of conversion that works for you and fits comfortably into your system of reporting student performance. Again, you should consider asking for student input on how to convert rubric assessments to letter grades.

A Final Word: Innovative Assessments—Challenges and Conclusions

Innovative assessment is not just some trendy technique dreamed up purely to save time teachers spend on marking. It is a genuine attempt to improve the quality of learning. However, authentic, multidimensional assessment practices are not without their challenges and critics and do require careful and considered application if they are to be used successfully. Also, some of you may have nagging questions about their efficacy and ultimate value. Therefore, we briefly address some of the common criticisms and concerns to encourage you to try some of these alternatives out if you have yet to do so.

Are Innovative Assessment Too Demanding and Stressful for Students?

The same concern probably holds true for traditional comprehensive exams, such as midterms and finals. Any kind of test will favor some students and disadvantage those who are less able to perform under the circumstances of a particular kind of test. One benefit of some forms of innovative assessment, such as self-assessment, is that they enable students to set their own learning goals and make their own decisions about whether these goals have been achieved. In this way, they create their own level of pressure; it is not imposed on them externally.

Still, it can be argued that many students will feel burdened by the demands of more innovative and authentic assessments and will likely prefer to take a traditional test to "just get it over with." For these students, the exam is preferable to more varied and continuous forms of assessment. They are possibly good at exams and quite happy to get away with doing as little as possible for most of the year and then just cramming for a few weeks before the exams. But is this really what we want? And what about those students who are not as good at exams, who show up to every class and retain more from the course than the crammers, but simply cannot reproduce their ideas under exam conditions? Should we have a system that discriminates against these students or one that rewards effort and understanding?

Are Innovative Assessments Too Time-Consuming for Instructors?

Any potential changes that may involve a greater investment of your time are, understandably, treated with suspicion. Indeed, most instructors will need to work hard at just developing quality traditional summative tests plus experimenting with and build a repertoire of formative techniques. We believe these efforts should be your first priority. Still, in the end, most forms of innovative assessment are potentially labor-saving once designed and put in place.

Are Innovative Assessments Less "Rigorous" Than Traditional Assessments?

On the contrary, these assessments are about valuing a range of different skills, and it could be argued they are more rigorous than traditional forms of assessment. Using a system of innovative assessments means students have to perform consistently in a number of different skill areas and over a longer period of time. And they do not assess a student's performance only when under considerable pressure—possibly first thing in the morning after an argument with a spouse or some evening after a tiring day of work and a stressful rush-hour commute. In this regard, they can be more rigorous and fairer at the same time.

How Can Authentic Assessment Be Reliable?

Many traditional teacher-developed assessments are unreliable—the results of these tests are not consistent with repeated administration. In fact, one of the major arguments for using more authentic assessment is the very unreliability of some traditional assessment practices. Innovative assessment is considered a highly reliable indicator of student learning because it is not dependent on any one method. It allows for the fact that all individuals have strengths and weaknesses. By assessing an individual's performance and/or demonstration across a range of skills, a more balanced and trustworthy assessment can be obtained.

Are Real-World Applications Beyond the Scope of Classroom Instruction?

Most traditional assessment methods tend to discourage critical thinking and incline students toward a more superficial approach to learning. Innovative assessment, on the other hand, is designed to develop critical thinking, including the ability to be self-critical. Also, with an increasingly competitive market for employment, most students are very keen on getting some valuable work experience or at least developing job-related skills during their degree or certificate courses. Furthermore, whether we like it or not, the government and business now put considerable pressure on institutions to produce graduates who are not just educated but are also employable. Authentic, real-world challenges are exactly what students need today.

So, What's the Bottom Line?

The arguments in favor of changing the way we assess more than outweigh the potential challenges. The measurement and evaluation of learning should not be viewed as something separate and distinct from the learning process itself. Students should learn through assessment, not learn to be assessed. When included in your overall assessment plan, innovative assessment can be an integral part of this process.

CHAPTER WRAP-UP

Assessment has multiple roles and influences in the classroom, and we trust you appreciate how it can impact your students in many powerful ways. Assessments guide students' judgment of what is important to learn. They affect students' motivation, impact their perceptions of their competence, structure their approaches to how they study, consolidate their learning, and can encourage the development of enduring learning strategies and skills. All in all, assessments are among the most potent tools in your teaching practices for influencing the character of student learning.

Implementing a balanced assessment program to capture all these purposes necessitates a full range of assessment techniques suited for each of your specific learning objectives. Not every strategy will work well or work in the same way with different students and courses. You need to be flexible and ready to mix and match. As with almost every instructional practice that supports learning in its fullest scope, this calls for thoughtful planning, and much practice, patience, and persistent effort. Below is an outline that summarizes what we have discussed and covers the primary considerations you need to make a proper assessment plan.

Assessment Planning Guide

In the final analysis, the quality of your assessment is more important than the quantity. If learners are overburdened by seemingly meaningless assessments over which they have very little control, then it is likely that they will take a surface approach to their learning. If, on the other hand, learners understand the rationale for your use of assessments, they will experience a sense of control over what they need to learn, and have more appreciation of what they actually have learned and how they gained this understanding. They will then likely take a consistently deep and meaningful approach to their studies. All this will produce not only a more fertile learning environment but also a more rewarding experience for both you and your students.

Prior to Course	Analyze curriculum and course objectives to establish clear learning outcomes and performance criteria.
	Design assessments based on desired outcomes and plan timing for administration of measures.
Beginning of Course	Assess previous knowledge and possible misconceptions.
	Give pre-class student attitude survey.
During a Course	Regularly use formative feedback strategies and tools to assess student progress and learning strategies skills and the effectiveness of your teaching practices.
	Administer appropriate summative assessments linked to student learning goals at suitable intervals.
End of Course	Administer summative student assessment and course/instructor evaluation instruments.
	Give student post-attitude survey.

SPRINGBOARDS FOR FURTHER LEARNING

Key Names

Patricia Cross and T.A. Angelo
Black and William
Grant Wiggins

Key Terms

assessment types

classroom-assessment
  techniques

course evaluation

formative assessment

learner and student feedback

student assessment

summative assessment

CHAPTER 10

Making the Grade: Determining Your Grading Policies and Gauging Your Teaching Effectiveness

Blessed are those who are flexible for they shall not be bent out of shape.

—Unknown

Do You Know:

- How to develop fair and consistent grading policies?
- The different kinds of grading systems you can use?
- How to deal with "grader's guilt" and other subjective factors involved in giving marks?
- How to use your student assessments as feedback on the quality of your teaching?
- Other sources of information you can use to document your teaching effectiveness?

Introduction

The two topics of this chapter, policies and practices of assigning student grades and evaluating the effectiveness of your teaching practices, follow closely from the previous chapter. Much of the information you use to assign grades will logically come from student performance on your assessments and other class assignments. However, assigning grades to student work is not as straightforward as it may seem at first. There are many factors involved in determining the marks you give for student work. If you are an experienced instructor you may already understand this and be already familiar with some of the issues and challenges involved in establishing accurate, consistent, and fair grading polices and practices. If you are new to teaching and have yet to teach your first course, you may believe you have covered your "bases," so to speak, when it comes to grading policies by articulating your grading policy in your syllabus. However, stating your policies and actually implementing them can be entirely different matters. Making decisions about how to give students grades, especially their final course grades, can be a complex, highly nuanced, and subjective process.

Similarly, much of the of the information generated by your summative and formative assessments of student learning as discussed in Chapter 9 can also provide critical feedback on your own teaching performance and the overall success of your course. However, this information is meaningful and of value only when you know how to properly interpret it and use it. Also, in addition to student assessments, there are indicators of the quality of your course and teaching that you will want to use as feedback. This chapter introduces some of these additional sources.

Making the Grade—Establishing Your Grading Policies and Procedures

Assigning appropriate grades can be one of the more difficult tasks you will face. For one thing, you will need to combine a variety of indicators of student performance into a single course grade. It can be a challenge to devise a grading method in which the final grade fairly reflects all these diverse elements of a student's performance. Furthermore, most institutions allow teachers (within certain limits) to develop their own grading systems. Because the standards used can be idiosyncratic, grades rarely have a uniform value. "A" from one teacher, for example, may be the equivalent of a "C" from another, so what a specific grade actually means can be open to interpretation and even argument. Another problem with grading arises from the fallibility of the tests we use to measure student performance. The effectiveness of any grading system is highly dependent on the accuracy of the tests on which it is based, and many teachers lack confidence that they can accurately and consistently use assessments to gauge student achievement. Still, despite these concerns, there are some reliable guidelines you can use to devise a fair and reasonably accurate system of grading.

Where to Begin—Your Grading Philosophy

Many experienced instructors know that giving grades can be just as involved as other essential teaching practices and poses many questions,

> *I don't divide the world into the weak and the strong, or the successes and the failures, those who make it or those who don't. I divide the world into learners and non-learners.*
>
> —Benjamin Barber

such as the following:

- What are my goals with regard to grading?
- Who is the audience for my grades or other forms of feedback? Will it be my students and myself only, or will others want and need this information, such as administrators, counselors, and employers?
- What is the impact of my grading policies and practices on student performance?
- How do I keep subjective feelings and personal biases from influencing my decisions?
- What does it mean to give a "B+" versus an "A−"? How can I tell the difference?

There are no hard-and-fast rules that can be universally applied to help you answer these and other questions that arise when considering grades. Assigning grades, like your other teaching policies and practices, depends a great deal on your values, assumptions, and other components of your teaching philosophy.

Consider the cases of two teachers who teach the same introductory course. If one instructor views student performance as 100 percent the students' own responsibility and academic success or failure a matter of "sink or swim," this instructor may believe grades are a good means of "weeding" out students who lack the potential for future success in the field of study. The other instructor might see learning as a shared responsibility and the course as teaching important skills that all students need to master. Because of these different perspectives, each would likely interpret and evaluate the same level of performance of a particular student in entirely different ways, assigning very different grades for the same work.

Since grades are a core component of your overall assessment strategy, you need to keep in mind the multiple influences and purposes of classroom assessment as discussed in Chapter 9. Thus, having an explicit understanding of your beliefs and values is a necessary first step in establishing your grading policies. Moreover, once you have clarified your grading philosophy, you also need to communicate to your students this rationale for your grading. This can reduce the number of student complaints and the need to defend a grade. (See more below on dealing with these issues.)

Operating with good, objective guidelines, you will find the grading process more efficient, and communicating to students their level of achievement will be easier. The suggestions that follow are designed to help you develop clear and fair grading policies.

(*Note:* Investigate your department's policies on grading practices. Even if there is no written policy, there may be traditions and

> *Junior was being chided for his low grades. Little Robert, who lived a few doors away, was held up as an example. "Robert doesn't get C's and D's does he?" asked his father. "No," Junior admitted, "but he's different. He has very bright parents."*
>
> —Jacob M. Braude

unwritten rules regarding grading, and your grading system will probably need to conform to these rules.)

A Grading Primer

This primer covers six topics:

1. the basic elements of a good grading system,
2. how to go about setting your performance standards,
3. the different kinds of grading systems among which you can choose,
4. dealing with subjective factors that can influence how you grade,
5. handling student complaints and dishonesty, and
6. assigning your marks.

Essential Qualities of Good Grading Systems

A good grading system should meet three criteria, as described below.

Accuracy: It should accurately reflect differences in student performance. This performance can be defined either in relative terms (comparing students with each other—grading on a curve) or absolute terms (measuring students' achievement against a set scale). Each system has its defenders.

Clarity: It should be clear to students, so they can chart their own progress. Whatever grading scheme you use, students should be able to calculate (at least roughly) how they are doing in the course at any point in the semester. Some relative grading schemes make it impossible for students to estimate their final grades because the cutoff points in the final distribution are not determined until the end of the course. A complete description of the grading system should appear in the course syllabus, including the amount of credit for each assignment, how the final grades will be calculated, and the grade equivalents for the final scores.

Fairness: Students should perceive the grading system as equitable, rewarding them proportionately for their achievements. From the standpoint of measurement, many different kinds of assignments that are spread over the entire semester provide a fairer estimate of student learning than one or two large tests or papers.

Establishing Your Performance Criteria

You need to decide before you start your class what your precise grading criteria will be. These criteria are both specific (for a single task) and global (overall course grade, for example) and will vary according to your teaching perspective, your subject, and the kinds of assessments you give. The following are some examples of the kinds

> *I just read about a schoolteacher who got hurt. She was grading papers on a curve!*
>
> —Milton Berle

of questions to ask yourself:

- How will you weigh different kinds of assignments in calculating grades? Which are more important? Outside class work? In-class tests?
- What formula will you use to balance the value of all assignments in calculating a final course grade?
- Will you be grading the students on the process they went through in completing an assignment or just the finished product?
- Is getting the problem right as important as making a good case for the answer?
- Will there be credit for partially correct responses to test questions?
- When grading written work, will you be concerned with grammatical errors and writing style as much as content?

If you have answered these and other important questions at the beginning of a course, you will likely be more consistent with your grading, avoiding the problem of unequal treatment and correction of different students' work.

Choosing Your Grading System

There are three customary options to choose among for designing a grading system (although, again, you may have some limits given department and/or school policies).

Option 1—Absolute Grading: In absolute grading, instructors set hard limits for a given letter grade no matter how a student performs relative to others; thus, if a student collects 90 percent of the available points, they get an A, and so on. There is the problem, of course, that all students might do extremely well or extremely poorly in your course. Then you will need to ask: Is it OK to give A's to everyone in a class? or Is it OK to give everyone a failing grade? Grading on an absolute scale can do a good job of identifying a poorly designed test or course and you may have to wrestle with some bigger issues if you find either of these cases to be true.

Option 2—Relative or Normative Grading: Relative grading is known commonly as grading on a curve. In this system students are graded according to their performance relative to each other. For example, you may give the top 10 percent of students an A and so on. Relative grading is based on two assumptions:

1. one of the purposes of grading is to identify students who perform best against their peers and to weed out the "unworthy," and

2. student performance more or less follows a normal distribution pattern—the famous bell-shaped curve of elementary statistics. Teachers who use relative grading feel these systems can

> *It's easier to see the mistake on someone else's paper.*
>
> —Cynthia Copeland Lewis

accommodate and correct for unanticipated problems (e.g., widespread absences due to flu season, tests that are too hard or too easy, or poor teaching) because the scale automatically moves up or down. Students like relative grading for the same reason.

The risk with grading on a curve is that you could get a class of students who perform poorly overall, with "A" students representing the best of a generally bad bunch of students. Giving high grades for what is really mediocre achievement is both difficult and questionable. In addition, relative grading puts students in competition with their classmates. Grading on the curve could work against collaborative learning strategies shown to be effective in promoting student learning. In general, relative grading produces undesirable consequences for many students, such as reducing motivation, producing greater test anxiety (since the performance standards are not always clear), and decreasing your ability to use feedback to improve learning.

Option 3—Gap Grading: An alternative form of relative grading is gap grading. Rather then specifying hard limits within a curve system (such as the top 10 percent get A's), an instructor would look for natural breaks in the distribution of scores from students. For example, if there are 10 students who all score above 92 percent and the next student on the list achieves only 84 percent, then the large gap between 92 and 84 would define the difference between an "A−" and a "B+". It is the large gaps that define grade boundaries rather than discrete rankings of students.

Being Aware of Subjective Factors in Grading

When it comes to your grading, subjective factors can come into play possibly more than in just about any other area of teaching. This influences not only how you assign grades but also your students' reactions to your grading policies and practices. Here are some ideas to help you deal with these factors and hopefully minimize any negative impact.

Grading Bias and Unfair Treatment. You will need to do your best to keep personal feelings about students from biasing your grading (in either direction). Unfortunately, this is not always easy to do. Although these biases may include obvious prejudice in some cases, such as racial or gender biases, they can also be quite subtle. Personal feelings and attitudes about individual students can come to play in your grading in many ways, such as an affinity for attractive students or those who get themselves noticed by always sitting up front. You can deal with this in part by having students type their work as much as possible (so you do not recognize handwriting) or read work without looking at names until you have finished grading it. If you cannot help recognizing a student's handwriting, you might try grading one question, page, or section at a time across everyone's assignment/exam. Even for objective tests that require no writing, you may need to insulate yourself

Old teachers never die, they just grade away.

—Henny Youngman

from possible biases by having students use ID numbers rather than names on their exams.

A lack of equitable treatment may also be circumstantial rather than personal. In particular, fatigue can cause you to be uneven in your evaluation; you may just be more tired on one occasion than on another and thus grade differently. Or at one sitting you may become progressively exhausted as you proceed through a large number of exams that need to be corrected by hand. You may be a little more rigorous, and therefore harder, at the beginning of the grading session than at the end, when you just "want to get through them." Conversely, you may grade later work according to more stringent standards as you see the quality and range of student performance on the earlier work you have corrected. Or you just might get more careless as you go along, and fail to mark errors or give proper credit to correct responses. If these or other circumstances come into play (did you just have a fight with your spouse or get stuck in traffic?) that could affect how you judge your students' work, you may need to go back and check each for accuracy and fairness, or just put aside the correction for another time when you are in a better frame of mind.

Tone. Your grading policy should be a part of your syllabus. Once you have explained your policies, avoid stressing grades or excessively talking about grades. This only increases students' anxieties and may decrease their motivation to do work for its own sake rather than to obtain the external reward of a good grade.

Grading should also not just be a catalogue of what the student failed to do. In order to be constructive, grading and evaluation should also convey to your students what they have done well and what needs improvement. You may want to give students a concrete incentive to actually read your feedback by offering credit for review or revision, when this is appropriate and suitable. The portfolio system, in which no grades are fixed until the end of the quarter, is the logical extension of this approach. Over a fixed period students assemble a portfolio of projects and materials that they complete during the course. No summative grading is completed until the entire portfolio is submitted. This allows instructors to focus largely on formative feedback during the course.

"Grader Guilt." Some instructors feel badly about burdening diligent students with low grades and may sometimes grade "on improvement"; unfortunately, this seldom works well. This matter is complex and ties directly to your teaching philosophy and personal values; whether students should be graded on effort, on the quality of what they produce, or both is not easily resolved. In general, if you feel you need to reward as well as encourage improvement, find ways of building revision into

> *The Great Cliché: Don't worry about it. It won't be on the exam. The Truth: I Can't do this problem either.*
>
> —Art Peterson

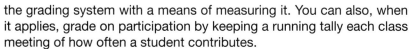

> *I was thrown out of College for Cheating On the metaphysics exam; I looked into the soul of the boy next to me.*
>
> —Woody Allen

Chapter 9

the grading system with a means of measuring it. You can also, when it applies, grade on participation by keeping a running tally each class meeting of how often a student contributes.

Still, it is generally advised that you limit your evaluations to academic performance and eliminate considerations not directly tied to the course goals. These include things such as classroom behavior, effort, classroom participation, attendance, punctuality, attitude, personality traits, or student interest in the course material. By not including these nonacademic factors, you may can keep the primary meaning of the grade clear and also avoid the pitfalls of possible unconscious personal biases. Still, the final decision must be yours and must be in alignment with your teaching values and beliefs.

Grading Essays and Performance Tests. How often have you attempted to grade your students' work only to find that the assessment criteria were vague and the performance behavior was overly subjective? Would you be able to justify the assessment or grade if you had to defend it? These questions reflect a common concern about and issue with essays, performance tests, and other forms of subjective assessments that try to capture more complex learning outcomes.

Basic Guidelines for Subjective Assessments. Being clear about and maintaining your grading standards are critical when assigning marks for student work that calls for qualitative rather than quantitative judgments.

Create clear standards: It is necessary to identify clear criteria when designing and evaluating any kind of assessment. However, this is especially true for subjective tests or student performances. The development and use of rubrics is a valuable assessment tool for grading criteria that are complex and subjective, since they describe levels of understanding and competence that will count in the scoring of an assessment and build on a scale for determining the score. If you develop them properly, rubrics communicate to students exactly what is expected and what you will look for when gauging their work, keeping you and them on track. This will increase both the reliability of your assessment and provide a check on its validity.

Maintain your standards: Imagine having to read 25 or 30 (or possibly more) short-answer or essay exams, especially when all the responses are on the same topic or question, each of which takes 10 minutes or more to carefully read and comment on. How would you maintain consistency? You probably will more likely be thorough with the first few papers you read than with the rest and less likely to be careful with the comments at the end. The following are two suggestions on how to handle this kind of situation:

- *Work for short intervals:* Read five or six papers before you start grading to get an idea of the range of quality (some instructors rank-order the papers in groups before they assign grades), and stop grading when they get tired, irritable, or bored. When you start again, read over the last couple of papers you graded to make sure you were fair. Some instructors select "range finder" papers—middle range "A", "B", "C", and "D" papers to which they refer for comparison.

- *Be selective:* Try to select only the most insightful passages for praise and only the most shallow responses or repeated errors for comment; in others words, avoid the tendency to edit the paper for the student and do not hack away at a neatly typed paper. If you comment on and correct everything, a student loses a sense of where priorities lie. Do not give the impression that a run-on sentence is as important to good writing and to a grade as, say, adequate support for an argument.

> *Inside every C+ student is a B- student trying to get out.*
>
> —Art Peterson

Grading Essay Exams. In assigning grades to essay questions you may want to use one of the following methods:

Analytic method: In this method the ideal or model answer is broken down into several specific points regarding content. A specific subtotal value is assigned to each of these points. When reading the exam, you decide how much of each maximum subtotal you judge the student's answer to have earned. When using this method, you may want to outline a model acceptable answer before you begin.

Global method: In this method you read the entire essay and make an overall judgment about how successfully a student has covered everything that was expected in the answer and assign the paper to a category that reflects a particular level of performance. Ideally, you should read all the essays quickly and sort them into four or five piles; then you should reread each group to check that every essay has been accurately (fairly) assigned to the category that will be given a specific score or letter grade.

Dealing with Student Complaints and Dishonesty

Unfortunately, it is inevitable you will face students who will complain and students who will cheat. You will need to deal with them. Having some ideas on how to do so in advance may keep these situations from possibly getting out of hand when they arise.

Student complaints: You will prevent many complaints simply by establishing fair policies, explaining them clearly from the start, and applying them consistently. However, on occasion students will still have issues with the grades you give them, which can be a stressful and potentially acrimonious situation. If a student comes with a grade or other complaint, listen as sympathetically as possible without giving in to pressure or guilt. Ask the student to explain what would have justified a higher grade; most often the student will back down. However, occasionally you will make mistakes, and if warranted, you can offer to regrade the work. Still, you may not be able to make everyone happy; treat disgruntled students with continued respect and fairness. If you feel seriously intimidated by a student, do not hesitate to inform someone in a position of higher authority.

Student dishonesty: It is best to prevent cheating by dealing with the matter as a topic for discussion early in the course. In addition to including school and your personal policies on the matter in your syllabus, also consider addressing the issue more directly, though not necessarily the first day. (Remember, you want to set a positive tone from the start.)

> *It's what you learn after you know everything that counts.*
>
> —John Wooden

In most institutions, classroom teachers are not allowed to simply accuse a student of cheating and take punitive action. Just about every school will have a policy requiring cases of academic dishonesty be submitted to the dean of students or someone else in authority; if you do this, you will be on safe legal ground, even if the dean does not handle the situation in the way that you would. One advantage of submitting these problems to the dean is that repeat offenders will not go unnoticed. If the student confesses and you feel strongly that going to the dean would not be in anyone's best interest, you can always do things your own way, though you will be assuming some risk. In any case, you should amass all possible evidence and give students the opportunity to admit what they have done before confronting them with it.

Plagiarism should be given special attention. You should not assume that your students know and understand the conventions of academic credit; in some cases in high school or other classes, assignments may have permitted them only to copy and reproduce. Therefore, you may need to demonstrate the difference between paraphrasing an idea and honestly giving it credit. Help them to understand what constitutes "common knowledge" (as opposed to information that needs to be cited) in this subject, since for many introductory students the entire field is new. Also, be aware of online and traditional "paper mills" that sell prewritten assignments. If possible, design assignments that are specific to the class and the student and not easily met by an off-the-shelf paper. A good check against this problem is to ask students to bring in drafts, which will keep them on schedule as well as honest.

Assigning Marks

Different schools or departments may have their own system for indicating summative grades. Here is a typical way to designate the level of achievement of students:

A+, A	superior	I	incomplete
A−, B+, B	good	IP	in progress
B−, C+, C	fair	P	passed
C−, D+, D	poor	NP	not passed
D−, F	fail	DR	deferred report

Schools may also use a point system to translate letter grades into numerical equivalents. A common system would assign points as follows:

A+	4.0 grade points per unit	C	2.0 grade points per unit
A	4.0 grade points per unit	C−	1.7 grade points per unit
A−	3.7 grade points per unit	D+	1.3 grade points per unit
B+	3.3 grade points per unit	D	1.0 grade points per unit
B	3.0 grade points per unit	D−	0.7 grade points per unit
B−	2.7 grade points per unit	F	0.0 grade points per unit
C+	2.3 grade points per unit		

(Once again, make sure the kind of system you use corresponds to what you are expected to use by your department.)

Making the Grade—Assessment for Course and Teacher Evaluation

Chapter 9

Throughout Chapter 9 and in the first part of this chapter we have addressed the question of "How well are your students learning?" Now we address a different but equally important question: "How well are you teaching?"

There are a number of different sources of information regarding the quality of your teaching that offer feedback about areas that may need improvement. Student performance is one. If students are not learning or learning well this, of course, may reflect what your students are doing or not doing. At the same time, the quality of their learning may be a reflection of your own teaching behaviors as well. Indirect indicators of how *you* are doing can come from your student assessments (either summative or formative). More direct indicators can come from the use of course and instructor evaluations. There are a number of methods for generating this information. These can also be either formative or summative in nature. In some cases, your department may provide guidelines for evaluations and even give you actual evaluation forms to use. What we discuss here are designs for your own evaluations.

In what follows, we briefly overview the most important elements of any good course design and teaching practices. We then recommend procedures for gathering the information you will need to answer questions about the effectiveness of your instruction. To get you started, here are three general considerations that represent best practices in teacher and course evaluations.

Three Basic Considerations

A range of factors contributes to the effectiveness of your teaching, and well-designed evaluation instruments should be broad enough to address as many of these factors as possible. At the same time, your evaluation efforts should be narrowly focused in order to home in on specific concerns you may have. For example, they should address questions such as "How should I allocate class time for each topic?" "Can I introduce a particular topic in a more effective way?" "What parts of my course do my students find most valuable?" "How will I change my course the next time I teach it?"

The following are three fundamental considerations for designing reliable and valid evaluation procedures:

Use multiple sources of data: Just as your students benefit most from a variety of assessment procedures, you will also. Using a variety of sources of information and feedback will make your evaluation more reliable, valid, and just as importantly, fair. (It is possible that supervisors may use your evaluation to judge the quality of your work.) These sources include not only your students as the most obvious source of feedback, but yourself and colleagues as well.

Tailor your forms of evaluation to your specific courses: There are many ways to construct evaluation instruments, and many ideas for developing these can be found on the Internet. Although general suggestions and templates can be helpful, you will want to match the form with the specifics of your class(es) as much as possible. Using questions and criteria that are not appropriate to your subject matter, instructional design, and practices may create a distorted and inaccurate picture of you and your class.

Evaluate across courses and across time: Evaluate all your courses each semester rather than just the one course that you may be having a problem with or that you are doing particularly well in. This will enable you to make comparisons with yourself over time and among your courses that went well and those that may have been a challenge. Also, try to get most, if not all, students in your classes to evaluate you. Otherwise, any one student or a few students may have too much influence on the feedback you get.

> We distinguish the excellent man from the common man by saying that the former is the one who makes great demands upon himself, and the latter who makes no demands on himself.
>
> —José Ortega y Gasset

What Elements of Your Instruction Should You Evaluate?

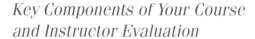

Unit 5

The goal of your course evaluation is to measure the gap between the *planned* instruction, the *taught* instruction, and the *learned* instruction to determine whether you have met your stated course objectives and how you can improve our instruction. To achieve this goal, we suggest that you organize your evaluation system around what we know are the specific and demonstrable characteristics of good teaching. (In the introduction to this unit, we summarized some of the qualities scholars have identified as fundamental to student success. We also return to this topic in Unit 5. The following table consolidates some of this information into four clusters for the purposes of course evaluations. (*Note:* These same areas are largely what you should cover in your initial course planning.)

Key Components of Your Course and Instructor Evaluation

Teacher Content Expertise

● Demonstration of your knowledge of your subject matter.

Course Design

● Clarity of purpose and organization of course elements.

● Establishment of high but realistic expectations.

● Skill in matching the instruction to students' learning needs and interests.

Presentation and Learning Activities

● Use of good communication skills.

● Design of learning environments that encourage time on task.

● Engagement of students so they take a deep approach to learning and actively utilize knowledge.

● Use of an appropriate array of methods.

● Encouragement of students to work together to learn.

● Provision of regular, helpful evaluations of learning.

Teacher–Student Relationship and Learning Climate

● Expression of enthusiasm and interest.

● Creation of respectful relationships.

● Acknowledgment of individual differences.

It is easier to perceive error than to find truth, for the former lies on the surface and is easily seen, while the latter lies in the depth, where few are willing to search for it.

—Johann von Goethe

(continues)

- Fair and impartial dealings with students.
- Openness to receiving feedback and adjusting courses appropriately.

Sources of Feedback—Documenting the Quality of Your Course and Teaching Practices

There are many possible sources of information you can use to document and improve your teaching. As we already have said, in many cases the same practices you use for formative student assessments can be used as a source of feedback on your course and teaching effectiveness. There are, however, additional and somewhat more direct sources of information that can provide valuable insight. These include student, peer, self-, and administrative evaluations. It is best if your evaluation approach is organized and charted over time, with these distinct sources brought together into a system. The following is a convenient evaluation matrix you can use:

Course and Instructor Evaluation Matrix

COURSE AND INSTRUCTIONAL ELEMENTS	STUDENTS	SELF	PEERS	ADMINISTRATORS
Instructor Content Knowledge				
Overall Course Design				
Presentation of Content and Learning Activities				
Teacher–Student Relationships and Learning Climate				
Professional Development				

> We judge ourselves by what we feel capable of doing, while others judge us by what we have done.
>
> —Henry Wadsworth Longfellow

Teachers can find evaluations of their courses and themselves rather intimidating, especially if the information gathered is to be interpreted and used by administrators. However, it need not be so. Unless there are departmental or school polices on mandatory formats and procedures for course and instructor evaluations, we suggest you begin as simply as possible. Whichever of the instruments described below (student surveys, self-evaluation checklists, etc.) you choose to use, focus on questions that cover the course and instructional elements over which you have direct control. There are many elements of teaching–learning transactions that you cannot control, such as those that arise from the personal background and life circumstances of each student or issues of program design and school management. Also keep in mind that because of the number and complexity of the factors involved in determining what is quality instruction, ultimately the validity of your measures and their meaning can be best judged only by you, not determined by the interpretations of others.

Student Evaluations

There are several ways to get and document student evaluations—students' feedback on your instruction.

Student Course Survey. It should come as no surprise to you that your students often do not "get" what you think you have "given." Student feedback is like going for a medical checkup. Everything may seem fine, but you need to get a reading on your "vital signs" to really know how well you are doing. Your students are obviously in an ideal position to report and comment on the quality of your teaching and their learning experience in your classes. The most customary and perhaps the simplest way to assess your instruction is via anonymous student surveys.

You can embed these short questionnaires in regular lessons at intervals (say one-third and two-thirds of the way through the course) and/or give them at the end of a term. Obviously, the sooner you get feedback, the sooner you can make needed adjustments. Student surveys should cover the core and most important features of your course from *their* perspective. Among other topics, they should include the following:

- Which instructional strategies helped students learn the most?
- Were you available enough for help?
- Did you provide useful comments on students' work that were encouraging and helped them make improvements?
- How much did the lessons and/or course challenge students?
- Did students feel comfortable asking questions?
- Did your teaching impact the level of interest in the course?

This type of assessment is for your own use. It is not necessary to record the data, do any statistical analysis, or officially report details.

> The most important knowledge teachers need to do good work is a knowledge of how students are experiencing learning and perceiving their teacher's actions.
>
> —Stephen Brookfield

Refer to Field Guide

However, the following are some simple things you can do to get the greatest value out of your course surveys:

- To get the most honest feedback, make these surveys anonymous and have someone other than you pass them out.
- Review the responses as soon as possible and write down your overall impression of the feedback. Right after class is best.
- Create a folder and use a notebook or file for storing and summarizing your written observations of the feedback.
- Think about how you might use the feedback to modify teaching strategies, and write down any specific ideas or plans with a short rationale.
- As you move forward with each lesson, be mindful of student responses and any changes you have decided to make with attention to how and when is best to introduce them.
- Consider talking to colleagues about the feedback, and reflect on any ideas they may suggest. Take a moment to add these thoughts to your other feedback summary.

Student Attitude Questionnaire. In addition to a course survey, you may want to develop and administer a student attitude questionnaire as a precourse and/or postcourse assessment. This type of survey focuses on student perceptions of their personal classroom experience. It includes general attitudes toward the course, the discipline, and their own learning and can help you identify elements in your course that best support student learning. For example, they ask questions about whether a student had a shift in interest in the course subject matter or chosen field of study because of having taken your class. They may also deal with how students feel about themselves as learners and whether they have confidence in their learning abilities. When given as a precourse and postcourse evaluation, these offer insights into possible shifts in student attitudes toward the subject that may have occurred as a result of your class. Attitudinal surveys may take many forms and address a range of issues; however, they typically consist of a series of statements with which students are asked to rate their agreement or disagreement. Ratings are placed on a scale of, say, 1 to 5, with 1 indicating little or no agreement and 5 very strong agreement.

Whatever forms of student evaluation you use to document how you are doing, do not use them alone. Student responses to surveys can be highly subjective. You will want to use additional sources of feedback, which can be consolidated into a more comprehensive statement of who and where you are as a teacher. For this purpose, we suggest creating a teaching portfolio.

It's not the strongest of species, who survive, nor the most intelligent, but the ones most responsive to change.

—Charles Darwin

Your Teaching Portfolio

The teaching portfolio, analogous to an art portfolio, has been proposed as one solution for some of the issues regarding the validity and reliability of more typical ways of evaluating instruction. Like a student portfolio, a teaching portfolio usually contains thoughtful and thorough narratives of your professional activities, supported by appendices of teaching materials. Portfolios are increasingly becoming a part of hiring and other personnel decisions at many schools and thus can be very useful not only for improving your teaching, but also for winning a teaching award or for applying for future positions.

There are several sources of materials you can include in a teaching portfolio. The items selected will depend on your particular teaching assignment, experiences and other professional activities.

Self-Generated Feedback. Self-analysis is far too often overlooked in the assessment of teaching and learning, yet it is central not only to the process of assessing teaching, but also to the process of improving it. Any feedback that provides new information has the potential to produce change, and self-reports should be an essential part of any teaching portfolio. You can provide your own perspective on virtually every aspect of instruction. These reports should be primarily descriptive as opposed to evaluative. They should focus on and document what you were trying to do, why, and how and the result. These descriptions will more easily reflect your professional development than those from other sources.

Self-reports should also be compared with data gathered from other sources. Data that you have collected over time might include the following:

- A statement of your philosophy of teaching and factors that have influenced that philosophy.

- A list of courses you have taught. This should include brief descriptions of course content, teaching responsibilities, student information, and a sample syllabus or lesson plan.

- Examples of course material you have prepared or published materials you may have modified to accommodate unanticipated student needs.

- A record of teaching insights and subsequent changes made to courses you regularly teach.

- A description of your professional-development activities and efforts to improve teaching. Included here can be your participation in seminars and workshops, your reading of teaching and other education journals, reviews of new teaching materials for possible application, and use of instructional-development services.

- Evidence of reputation as a subject-matter expert and skilled teacher, such as awards, invitations to speak, and articles you have written.

- Personal reflections on your growth and change as a teacher.

(*Note:* Much of this information can also be of value to your students. It can help you establish your credibility and authority as a teacher and should be considered in abbreviated form to be part of your course syllabi.)

Data from Others. Obviously, different people can and will provide different kinds of information about your teaching. We have already suggested the use of student surveys. However, students are not necessarily qualified to comment on all areas of your practice. For example, it is probably inappropriate to ask students about the breadth and completeness of your content knowledge since, from their point of view, such expertise should be a given. The more suitable judges of this information would be your colleagues. At the same time, colleagues are usually not good judges of whether you were regularly prepared for class, arrived on time, or were available for office hours. Clearly, getting the right kinds of input from right groups of individuals is what will give a portfolio its strength and depth.

Students: Besides customary student surveys and questionnaires, there are other ways of obtaining student feedback on your teaching that you can include in your portfolio, such as the following:

- Interviews with individual students after they have completed the course.

- Informal (and perhaps unsolicited) feedback, such as letters or notes from students.

- Examples of your comments on student papers, tests, and assignments.

- Precourse and postcourse examples of students' work, such as pretests and posttest, writing samples, along with laboratory, project, or fieldwork reports.

- Testimonials of the effect of the course on future studies, career choice, employment, or subsequent enjoyment of the subject.

Peers: Your colleagues within the department/school are best suited to make judgments about course content and objectives, your collegiality, and preparedness for subsequent courses. These judgments can be based on classroom observations, but they should also rely on other sources, including your course outlines, syllabi, texts and references, homework and assignments, graded exams, instructor comments on student work, etc. The feedback given should consider the following:

- Mastery of course content and clarity of organization.
- Ability to convey course content and objectives.
- Suitability and quality of specific teaching methods and assessment procedures for achieving course objectives.
- Commitment to teaching as evidenced by expressed concern for student learning.
- Intellectual challenges posed to and interactions with students.
- Ability to work with others on instructional issues.

All in all, when it comes to evaluating you and your courses, you are the final judge of whether you have succeeded as an instructor. We are confident you want this determination to be based on sound measures. Incorporating some, or better yet, all of the above suggestions into your evaluation system should make the process a rewarding one.

CHAPTER WRAP-UP

This chapter dealt with grading policies and procedures and course and teacher evaluations. These topics often come up for consideration, mostly at the end of a course and are, therefore, sometimes given short shrift. They should not be, and we trust we have given you reasons why they should not.

When it comes to how you go about assigning grades many subtle and complex factors come into play. Many instructors, especially inexperienced ones, fail to appreciate the significance of these factors. As a result, grading can become more of an onerous and burdensome task than it has to be. Moreover, unexpected but otherwise preventable problems with students arise because of perceptions of—or actual—unclear and even unfair policies and practices that result in student complaints and other issues.

Similarly, your course and teaching evaluation—just as your teaching itself—should be understood as a complex, multifaceted endeavor. This evaluation must be examined from different viewpoints. Any system you choose to use should obviously begin with data gathered from qualified, firsthand sources. But it also should include as many sources as possible in order to provide the most appropriate and accurate information on each of the many dimensions of your course and teaching. Doing so will eliminate obvious mismatches (e.g., students being asked to interpret your content expertise), reduce the possible use of methods that may be too complicated, inefficient, or potentially unfair, and finally enhance the reliability of your methods by reducing arbitrary and confusing elements. Clearly, different teaching conditions require some flexibility in selecting what combination of sources and what methods are most suited to particular disciplines or even courses. However, the general parameters described above offer a balanced framework for ensuring a flexible but consistent evaluation system.

If you are new to teaching, we trust that this brief overview of grading and evaluation policies and procedures will get you off on the right foot. If you are more experienced, we hope it has provided helpful insights on how to improve what you may already be doing.

SPRINGBOARDS FOR FURTHER LEARNING

Key Terms

course evaluation	instructor evaluation
grading	student evaluation
grading tips	student surveys

INTERNET ACTIVITY

Grading and course evaluation procedures are topics that have not attracted much attention from particular scholars or researchers of note. Using a key term search on the Internet should suffice in helping you access additional resources on these topics. Also, we suggest you use "college" and/or "postsecondary" as part of your search to narrow your results.

Unit 3
Learning without Limits: Proven and Powerful Strategies for Learning That Lasts

> *A man should keep his little brain attic stocked with all the furniture that he is likely to use, and the rest he can put away in the lumber room of his library, where he can get it if he wants it.*
>
> —Arthur Conan Doyle

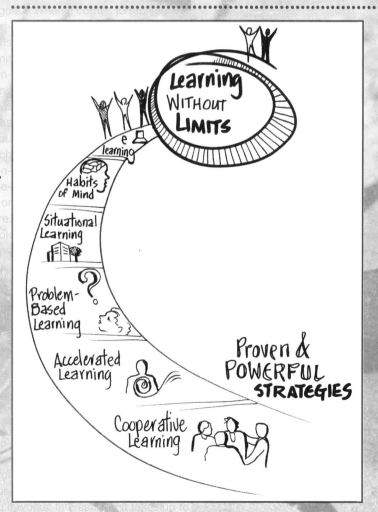

The following are the topics and some of the questions that will be addressed in this unit:

- *Cooperative/Collaborative Learning:* How can I use cooperative learning and still keep control of the class?

- *Accelerated Learning:* Just what does accelerated learning mean and how can I use it?

- *Inquiry/Problem-Based Learning:* Why is inquiry learning so valuable for deep learning?

- *Situational Learning:* What is it? and What is the best way to set it up?

- *Critical Thinking and Habits of Mind:* What are the most valuable skills I should teach to encourage critical thinking and habits of mind that promote better learning?

- *Teaching with Technology:* What different ways is technology being used today? and What are some of its benefits and limitations?

In Unit 3 you will find specific details on six methods that will increase student acquisition and retention of material. Each concept and practice takes careful planning and execution. We have selected what we have found to be the most valuable and viable tools for your toolbox. The chapters are easy to read, in a shorter format meant to excite you about finding more in-depth information on the methods to which you best relate. The basics for each of the following are included in this unit.

You have experienced these strategies in your learning experiences and perhaps used them in your instruction. Research on the brain and learning provides a strong foundation for using multiple strategies for engaging students in learning so that learning is embedded in long-term memory and secure deep understanding. And isn't that our goal?

When it comes to techniques, educators use what they know and have experienced. That is both good and bad. The good is that you know it works. The bad is that you limit your options to provide the most powerful learning for your many different students. In this unit we offer clear descriptions of each of the above techniques and illustrate the value of each as well. Descriptions are shared that will give you ideas on how you can adopt or adapt each technique. We refer you back to your most enjoyable, memorable teachers and learning experiences. It is probably true that they had one or more of these techniques in their repertoire.

Your most important task as you read this book and learn more about how you can become more effective is to experiment. What this means for you as an experienced instructor or a beginning teacher is that you can refine tools in your toolbox to use them "in the moment." It has often been the case that circumstances in a classroom dictate a change in the careful plans you have made. Because you have probably not done "scenario" plans for every contingency, it is necessary that you have a repertoire of skills that you can call on at a moment's notice. The only way to gain that repertoire is through experiment and practice.

As you read these chapters think how you can use each technique. Determine how you may have to adapt it for your course and your students. You may surprise yourself by trying something and finding it works. Interestingly, it takes up to 6 repetitions to remember something and up to 28 times practicing to form a new habit. (Ever wonder why diets are usually for 30 days?) Most people try something new once or twice and if it doesn't work they quit. Use these again and again. Share with your students that you would like to try something and need their help. Get their feedback on how to improve your instruction and on the technique. You will become more skilled with more input. You have to be persistent in the pursuit of excellence. You have to be a continuous learner.

Cooperative/Collaborative Learning: Remember a time in a course or learning environment when the instructor had you work with a small group to discuss, plan, or carry out an activity. This technique has been used since the beginning of time to engage learners. In Chapter 11 you will learn the specifics of setting up cooperative learning experiences. These situations can be very short in duration or set up as a cohort group over a period of time.

Accelerated Learning: There are teachers or learning experiences that stand out for most of us. These powerful learning experiences sometimes occur when the stars align and we have no influence in the experience. When instructors intentionally create powerful learning, they use multiple strategies and methods to do so. Perhaps you experienced that great science teacher in high school who posed questions, and you were responsible for solving a problem or discovering flaws in reactionary thinking. You may have worked in a group or perhaps individually to complete the task. The teacher used music to smooth the edges and had numerous posters around the room. Positive sayings were evident and the teacher spoke in ways that made you know you would be successful. You always felt relaxed when in that class. Accelerated learning as described later provides you with the tools to create those experiences regularly.

Inquiry/Problem-Based Learning: Although used in the sciences as a tool to do research, inquiry/problem-based learning is really about nurturing curiosity and asking questions. It goes against traditional education in that the instructor must not only be open to questions that are often difficult to respond to but also to nurturing students in their

questioning skills. When using this technique you must be ready to accept results that you may not like or be familiar with in your experience. There is a good deal of critical thinking that has to be nurtured as well as curiosity. Ultimately inquiry/problem-based learning is knowing how to gather data and make sense of it.

Situational Learning: We noted that one of the findings on learning is that learning needs to be situated. We used to believe that we could teach something in the classroom and students would be able to figure out how to apply that knowledge outside the classroom. It was a predominant practice, and unfortunately, it still is for many educators. To be more effective, learning should be situated to the real world. So the instructor who plans classroom activities and includes "bridge" and real-world situations will have better success in meeting the objectives of deep learning. By doing so you will be facilitating transfer of new information to more situations.

Critical Thinking and Habits of Mind: Critical thinking (or thinking critically) is an important skill for every successful person. Unfortunately, common sense, which is related to critical thinking, is not very common. As the guide on the side of your classroom, you need to plan for critical-thinking exercises and include higher-order thinking in your planning. Learning is messy, not stair-stepped, as we used to believe. There may be certain steps for a procedure to follow when implemented; however, learning the procedure may be less linear. Think about your experiences as a student. You were likely not as focused as the instructor may have believed. The same is true in your classes; yes, even in your most engaging moments you do not have everyone's attention. Thinking is not a linear process; it is much more chaotic.

Critical thinking also uses what is sometimes referred to as "habits of mind." We will offer more details about this concept and how to promote habits of mind in your instructional planning and design. Students should be able to question the content and your presentation of topics with clear thinking and no fear. So often it is the case that the instructor is the expert and should never be questioned; we know that this posture does not promote critical thinking. Strong habits of mind offer a classroom more valuable and robust discussions. In addition, these discussions provide healthy dialogue for deeper understanding and more profound learning.

Teaching with Technology: Technology is being used very successfully in the classroom for instruction and reinforcement. On-demand learning is being used more and more by colleges and universities around the world. Advances in software and hardware have made understanding technology a requirement for every student, even at the kindergarten level. When you are considering your courses you must consider how will you use technology and the resources that might be available.

306

In Chapter 16 we offer an overview that will help you make decisions about the use of technology in the classroom.

What It Means for You

This unit is a quick guide for you to understand some of what we believe are the most useful tools in planning for student learning. These are models, and entire books have been written on most of these—in some cases, multiple books. You may find that you are especially interested in a particular item. Go to the Internet and spend some time researching the topic to gather more information. As with every other chapter we have provided some key names and terms at the end of each chapter. This unit is not intended to include all the details; rather it will give you enough information to include some of the ideas in your design and practice and to "springboard" to more ideas. Spend time getting this short dose of information and then go deeper by finding the resources to learn more. You will find information in the companion Field Guide that offers more detail for implementing these methods.

Most instructors use their own method of teaching, the one that seems comfortable and most often works for them. It is usually a combination of more than one model, and it becomes their model. This will be true for you unless you consciously make a commitment to try different strategies. When you plan purposefully to use various methods your students will respect you and you will be among the top 20 percent of educators. You can move from good to great.

Refer to
Field Guide

CHAPTER 11

Cooperative/Collaborative Learning

Just imagine what we could achieve if we all knew what each one of us knows.

—John Browne

Do You Know:

- There are several cooperative learning models?
- How to use cooperative learning to help students gain individual mastery?
- The best ways to set up collaborative learning with adult learners?
- How to grade students when using cooperative learning methods?
- Ways to use cooperative learning with other methods of instruction?
- How to teach students to work in cooperative groups?

Introduction

Donald Trump's television show *The Apprentice* is based on a cooperative learning concept. If you have watched it, you have seen how it can become competitive and not very productive. Using that example will not benefit your students in mastering a subject. There are other models that are very helpful in the learning process and enhance the depth of learning significantly. Competition is more valuable in sports

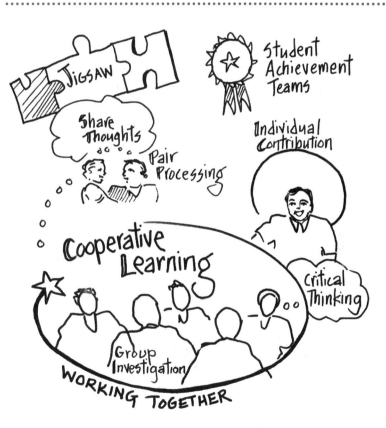

than in a classroom. We will use the term *cooperative learning,* as it seems more common in education circles. (The term *collaborative* can have the same meaning.)

Cooperative learning has been used successfully for many years at every level of education, and since the 1970s it has been studied and refined to its current level of sophistication. Roger and David Johnson of the University of Minnesota, Robert Slavin at John Hopkins, and Spencer Kagan of California have studied and researched results from using cooperative learning. They helped set the stage for much of the value currently understood from this instructional strategy. There are many iterations of cooperative learning, some more reliable than others. These variations offer you a multitude of options in providing students cooperative group activities. One of the reasons that cooperative learning works is that research in educational psychology notes that social interaction is a helpful tool for learning. Even as the research bears out the value, the truth is that people like working with other people.

The next section offers an overview of four models of cooperative learning for you to consider. As with the other chapters in this unit, the information presented is purposely just enough to get you started and is not more comprehensive. Our intent is for you to have a big picture with enough detail to try some of these models and then to pursue further study by pursuing more comprehensive sources.

The most important discoveries have been suggested to me by my failures.

—Sir Humphrey Davey

Two Keys to Making Learning Cooperative

All successful models of cooperative learning incorporate two key elements—interdependence and individual accountability.

Interdependence

Each student depending on every other student in the group and each student being individually judged on their contribution to the group as well as their own learning are the components that make the learning cooperative. There has to be a sense that it is "one for all and all for one," in order to build on the idea of cooperation. We learn from others by listening and doing real work together. Everyone works and everyone benefits in a true cooperative learning model. The idea that everyone must participate to be successful is paramount to successful use of cooperative learning. When every student recognizes that they have to participate, they live up to that expectation. Many instructors have allowed groups to be influenced by the one person who happens to do all the work or is the most assertive. That is not cooperative learning. There are variations that actually assign roles for students to fulfill, which will be described later in this chapter.

Accountability

The second key to cooperative learning is that students are graded for their individual contribution. Individuals, when held accountable, will perform whether in a group or alone, so individual accountability is just as important as group performance. One of the benefits of cooperative learning is that communication is important, and individual social skills become more attuned to group needs. Research tells us that when students talk about a topic with each other they will process information in a different manner, thereby creating multiple pathways in the brain for remembering and applying the information.

Four Types of Cooperative Learning

There are four basic versions of cooperative learning: group investigations, student achievement teams, pair processing, and jigsaw. From these basics there are many variations and styles that have been developed by Johnson and Johnson, Slavin, Kagan, and individual educators. Literally dozens of variations occur in classrooms around the world every day.

Group Investigations

Group investigations are students working to complete a project or process and use higher-order thinking skills. The instructor has only partially presented the content. Students are encouraged to research, analyze, synthesize, and evaluate content to complete the project. One of the variations of this version that you are familiar with is brainstorming. Even though it may not have a project associated with it, brainstorming involves higher-order thinking and students working together.

Group investigations are intended for projects that take more time to complete—a week a month or sometimes longer—using material that may have been partially presented in class. You might use this model for a project for which you expect students to do more extensive research and produce some public display or presentation. It is likely that you did this type of activity with a science project in elementary or middle school. This model involves a specific topic to pursue in depth. Each student takes a part of the topic—for example, history, use in society, or value to the legal system. Once assigned, students find sources to build a better product or presentation than they might be able to do on their own. Social skills and project management are important to the process that serves them in the real world too. By having them use these skills in class, you provide a lab for not only content learning but process learning as well.

> Cooperative learning is the instructional use of small groups through which students work together to maximize their own and each other's learning.
>
> —Johnson, Johnson, and Holubec

Student Achievement Teams

Student achievement teams are used to review and expand content that has been presented by the instructor. Students in heterogeneous groups work together to gain the greatest amount of knowledge available in the time frame offered on the given topic. The group has a task to complete—be it a presentation, a project, or completing a process. Students are held accountable for their own achievement, while in some cases working for group recognition as well. Teams study together and take tests individually. Scores are recorded for team and each individual.

After teacher input, students are divided into teams to study and work together. Teams are mixed with varying abilities, genders, and ethnicities. This method was developed at John Hopkins University, and research has shown that it is valuable in developing interracial appreciation and tolerance.

Students work together reviewing the material presented by the teacher and are graded on how they perform individually as well as how they fare in relation to other teams. It is a more competitive model than others described here. Competition is a motivator for many students, and this method provides a safety net for students who are not as capable as others. It is most valuable with subjects that are well defined and with questions that have one right answer. It can be used with many subjects as long as the area of study is specific, such as learning a set of principles, historical data, or math formulas.

Pair Processing

Pair processing is a valuable tool for short-term cooperative learning activities. It consists of a pair of students answering questions, recording thoughts, and sharing thoughts and responses. This may be an initial stage of moving students into longer-term cooperative activities. Pair processing can be used during lectures or skills practice to give students the opportunity to discuss their personal responses to content. More students can be involved in the process than during a teacher-led discussion. Of course, this is true of cooperative learning in general—students are more involved and have more opportunities to share their thoughts ideas, questions, and responses.

Pair processing is one of the most useful methods because it can be easily implemented in many situations. It is easy during a teacher presentation to have students discuss with a partner what they have just heard. It can be used for short periods of time to process information and also to prepare students to work together in long cooperative learning models. You can choose to do this spontaneously as you notice during class that students are fading or have quizzical looks. You also have a choice to move from pairs to small groups of four or six to

> We must act as if our institutions are ours to create, our learning is ours to define, our leadership we seek is ours to become.
>
> —Peter Block

expand the discussion. One benefit is to generate questions that may need to be answered before proceeding with the topic. Students can select partners or you can assign them. You may choose to have students use this method for sharing minute papers or reviewing papers. This could be a more long-term relationship that eventually can build into a larger group cooperative learning activity.

Jigsaw

Jigsaw is used with narrative material. This is a great method to promote peer-to-peer teaching and learning. Each student is given or chooses a particular section or chapter of material to review. Each group has a student doing the same sections. Students regroup with the peers assigned the same sections. They review and discuss the critical points. Students listen to each other as they review and study their like sections. They determine ways to engage others in presenting the material. After students have prepared their section or chapter they return to the original groups and each person shares their section with the rest of their group. Hence the puzzle pieces come together.

Jigsaw is a great way to get students, rather than you, to present lots of information from a text. You work as a facilitator for each group, helping them to develop their material to present, ensuring that they emphasize the critical points. This method can go on for several class sessions and over a number of text chapters. It is a helpful way for students to learn from an article or other ancillary information.

You might also use the jigsaw method to prepare students for tests. Assign each student to a group and assign a particular area of the exam to each group. Once they have prepared their material, it is presented to the whole group, and you act as facilitator. Your role is ensure that the information is accurate and actually includes what will be on the test.

> *Tell me and I'll forget. Show me, and I may not remember. Involve me and I'll understand.*
>
> —Native American saying

Planning for Cooperative Learning

Cooperative learning helps develop skills and characteristics that employers desire. Personal and academic skills that include listening, paraphrasing, explaining, writing, reading for understanding, and working with others, to name but a few, are discovered through cooperative learning. Students do not come by these skills naturally; you have to teach them explicitly and describe what they may be learning as a result and how it can be used in the real world (i.e., listening, paraphrasing, explaining, writing, reading for understanding, working with others). You will also need to structure the groups and group activities to make cooperative learning successful.

Teaching Students to Work Cooperatively

If you want to make it easy on yourself, remember that you have to teach students how to work in cooperative learning groups. You might believe that your students have the skills to be productive with other students—forget it. They don't, even as young adults or adults—mainly because they have not had enough experience working with others to accomplish a goal. It is unlikely that anyone has ever taught them the teamwork skills. Interestingly, many companies are pleased to have prospective employees who have had cooperative learning experiences. Because many organizations use a team approach to projects, they seek employees who have worked in cooperative learning groups in their schooling. You will be doing your students a service by teaching teamwork and using cooperative learning methods in your classes.

If you decide to use cooperative learning in your classes, and we hope you do, you need to carefully plan time to teach the basic skills of working in a group. An easy way to start is by assigning roles for each group member. Facilitator, recorder, reporter, materials manager, timekeeper, and checker are some of the roles you may consider. As you name each role, have your students determine what the responsibilities of that person would be. Once you have lists for each role, work with students to determine by consensus what might be the most important.

Provide time for skills practice in each role so that students know what a good job looks and sounds like. You can do skills practice in a large group and get student feedback to refine the necessary skills for each role. "Fishbowl" is a technique in which a group practices the skills while the rest of the students look on. Once they have worked in the fishbowl for 5 or 7 minutes ask them to make observations about the skills used. By offering students time to practice the specific skills of working in a group, when it comes time to actually do real work in a group they will be ready.

> *Ten geographers who think the world is flat will tend to reinforce each other's errors. . . . Only a sailor can set them straight.*
>
> —John Ralston Saul

Group Size

Cooperative groups seem to function best when small. Three or four students work very well in a group, whereas when you group seven or eight or even more the value decreases, not to mention the conflict increasing. The fewer the students, the more accountable each individual must be. Randomly placing students in groups has value for certain tasks, and heterogeneous and homogeneous grouping strategies work as well. When deciding you want to use cooperative learning, you have to consider the length of the working group (Is it short term, a few minutes, or days or weeks?) and the learning objective toward which you are moving.

Smaller groups require students to participate more, which is one of the great benefits of cooperative learning. They learn from each other and other groups too. Students are more likely to ask questions when working in small groups. As the facilitator, it is important to remember that they are working in groups, and hence you should answer a group's questions rather than responding to individual questions. Groups should process questions and ask for responses as a group. Then again, you do not have to answer questions if the group has resources to find the answers on their own—another benefit of cooperative group work.

Duration

Some groups can be together for an entire semester or quarter, while some will be together for only one class session or even just a portion of a class session. Minutes to months are your choices. You need to decide the model you want to use and its purpose. The longer students work together, the more they get to know each other and can work efficiently. On the flip side, if you have groups that are working well and others that are not, you need to be sure that every student is having a valuable learning experience. It is useful before forming groups over a longer period of time to plan for many short-term cooperative activities that will help set the stage for longer cooperative projects.

Forming Groups

There are different ways to form cooperative groups. Research would indicate that heterogeneous groups are more effective for both group and individual achievement. Giving students choices in forming their own groups can pose problems. Some students may be left out and others may end up with less-capable colleagues. You have to determine the best way to form groups.

You can predetermine long-term groups based on your observations and grading during the beginning stages of a class. This will ensure that each group has various abilities, genders, work ethics, and races represented. If you want to do a spur-of-the-moment activity you can have the students number off by fours or fives to form four or five groups. Paired shares can be with a person next to them or you can ask students to stand and find someone they have not talked with or worked with recently.

Classroom Management with Cooperative Learning

The main reason instructors do not use cooperative learning more is that they feel a loss of control. Too often that is the case, but it does not have to be that way. Just like teaching the skills of cooperative group work, you have to teach students classroom management. You would

> Our large schools are organized like a factory of the late 19th C: top down, command control management, a system designed to stifle creativity and independent judgment.
>
> —David T. Kearns

think this would be a greater challenge with younger students; however, as students get older instructors have lower tolerance for noise or "lack of control." This arises from the belief that as students are older they should "know" how to behave and work independently or in groups. Again, it's not true! You have to teach them or work with them to create an environment that works for everyone, including you.

One issue that must be considered is noise level. There may be other classes nearby, or it could be that you appreciate a quiet work environment. Students can be easily distracted by too much noise, and it seems to build so that everyone can hear everyone else. Work with students to determine some standards for group work. Set your expectations and agree on a signal to remind them to maintain quieter interactions. Noise does not indicate more productivity, but it also does not indicate less.

Instructions

Clear instructions will have a strong effect on the results you get with any activity or assignment. First you have to know what your expected outcomes are and how you expect the students to get there. Understand that there may be more than one way to arrive at the outcomes. When you know that, you can break the outcome down into steps that students have to complete to accomplish the goal. When you give instructions, have students repeat them or review them in groups before moving to the activity. Also, make sure they know what to do if they get stuck or do not understand something when it comes up later. (What do we do if we don't know what to do?)

Walk Around

The very best managers walk around regularly. They get the "pulse" of the workplace. The same is true of the best teachers. When you walk around during group work two things happen:

1. Students have easy access to ask for assistance and

2. students stay more focused on the task at hand.

Assistance may be answering questions, making process observations, or providing feedback on group interaction. When students are more focused on the task, it is less likely that the noise level will rise to unbearable.

> *Some persons talk because they think sound is more manageable than silence.*
>
> —Margaret Halsey

CHAPTER WRAP-UP

Cooperative learning groups are not just a method to have students teach each other or process content. Well-designed cooperative learning offers students personal insight, multiple ways to process information, practical skills for the real world, and a sense of accomplishment.

This method can be used in any content area, which makes it a very valuable tool. If you follow the suggestions presented here and do some more studying on your own, you will find this to be one of the most versatile methods you will use in your instruction.

Students interacting together and creating a sense of interdependence are positive influences on their learning. Accountability for learning and cooperating with others is important. They can take the skills used in cooperative learning activities and apply them in many real-world settings from family to work to volunteer activities. Cooperative learning is helpful as a learning tool and also for individuals to reflect with others on their thoughts, ideas, aspirations, and accomplishments.

SPRINGBOARDS FOR FURTHER LEARNING

Key Names

Roger and David Johnson   Robert Slavin
Spencer Kagan

Key Terms

cooperative learning   pair processing
group investigation   student achievement teams
jigsaw

CHAPTER 12
Accelerated Learning

It is written he who governs well, leads the blind; But that he who teaches gives them eyes.

—David McKay

Do You Know:

- Accelerated learning is as much a philosophy as a method?
- That learning can be accelerated?
- There are 10 key components of accelerated learning?
- Accelerated learning has a learning cycle with six parts?

A Little History

There is a tremendous amount of information on the history and background of accelerated learning. It has been called various names and described in several ways. During the past 40 years there have been thousands involved worldwide in these rapid learning ideas. Many people around the world acknowledge Georgi Lozanov, of Bulgaria, as the founder of the movement for Superlearning, which he called Suggestopedia. The concepts have actually been around for much longer. From Socratic dialogue to the inclusion of pictures and stained glass in cathedrals, we have been building to

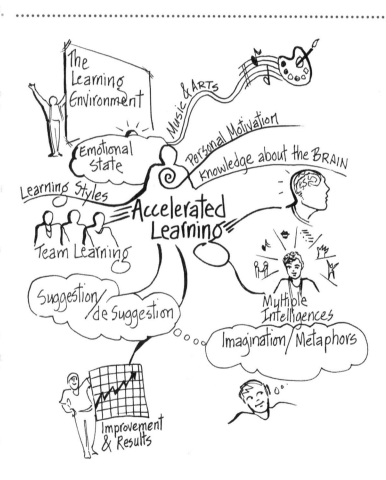

our current understandings about learning. Lozanov's contribution is significant in terms of determining and refining key elements of powerful learning.

Lozanov did his work in Bulgaria experimenting with teaching second languages using music, suggestion, relaxation, mental maps, concert readings, and activations. His method is very refined and requires considerable preparation. The results are astounding. In language courses using these methods it was discovered that a semester-long Spanish course using traditional methods could be taught in one-third the time using Suggestopedia.

There are many other contributors to the philosophy of accelerated learning (AL), and it is as much a philosophy as it is a method. You will find more names at the end of the chapter. AL is the primary focus of the International Alliance for Learning (IAL). You can visit their Web site at http://www.ialearn.org. At the end of the chapter you will find names of some of the leaders in the AL world.

Accelerated learning is a philosophy that offers engaging, memorable, and powerful opportunities for learning, with the learner as the focus of instruction creating their own meaning and value, from relevance of the content to their experience and world. Its basic premises are that everyone can learn and that learning in limitless. AL becomes especially powerful with relationships created between and among the content, the learners, and the instructor/facilitator. Accelerated learning is positive, joyful, fun, and painless. It uses components of several different methods/models of teaching and learning, including (but not limited to) cooperative learning, inquiry, experiential learning, problem-based learning, and others.

> *If we remain wedded to the way education is currently provided we cannot imagine other ways. We need some imagination, some fantasy, some new ways of thinking—some magic in fact.*
>
> —Hedley Beare

Learning Can Be Accelerated

Lozanov designed language courses that brought the same level of proficiency in a shorter period of time. Perhaps *accelerated* gives the wrong impression. In an AL setting students feel as though they are learning faster when the reality may be that they are experiencing learning that is more aligned with how we learn, and therefore it is more efficient. When all the 10 elements come together and the learning cycle is considered, it does work; learning seems to happen more quickly. Learning either happens or not, so the process may not be faster with AL, but AL is very different from traditional learning. AL is very aligned with the latest research in neuroscience as it relates to learning. Practitioners keep up with the latest research by reading and attending conferences. The research findings change and are added to regularly, so it is imperative that one keep up.

The 10 Elements of Accelerated Learning

Over a number of years the IAL developed and now subscribes to the following 10 elements as those that are critical to AL. It is helpful to know that these elements need not all be present and are in no specific order of importance. Each element includes a short description and some include examples for clarity.

Knowledge about the Human Brain

Knowing the latest scientific knowledge about the brain as it relates to learning is a key to being a better instructor using any method or model. Neuroscientists are at work every day discovering more about how the brain processes information, builds networks of synapses, and stores knowledge. AL facilitators use their understanding of implications for learning to enhance learning while being careful to not make assumptions that have no merit.

*All learning
has an
emotional base.*

—Plato

Emotional State

All learning is emotionally based. Yes, there is logic, but we are influenced by emotion more than by any other factor when in a learning situation. A positive mental attitude, especially about learning, helps create the emotional state for learning to occur. The environment is emotionally safe, so students are more relaxed. Instructors work purposefully at creating and maintaining this atmosphere.

The Learning Environment

Chapter 5

The learning environment is described in detail in Chapter 5. AL considers every aspect of the environment—the physical and the emotional. It feels fun, exciting, and inviting to learners as they enter and work there. The details are attended to with great consideration and care. The use of color, sound, art, furniture, peripherals, and light make all the difference because "everything speaks."

The Role of Music and the Arts

Music and the arts have been underused in the learning setting, yet research indicates that both have a significant influence on learning. Music provides rhythm and pacing to learning while affecting mood and energy. Music helps to create the relaxed alertness during which the brain is most receptive to learning. Like music, the arts contribute to our conscious and unconscious being. They offer models of language and visual input that cannot be represented in words alone. The arts and music engage learners naturally.

Personal Motivation

Motivation to learn and continue learning is internal and can be influenced by all of these elements. AL subscribes to the notion that students do things for their reasons, not the instructor's, which means that cooperation and opportunity must abound. Setting learning goals and discovering desires is important to the AL instructor.

Multiple Intelligences and Learning Styles

Knowing and understanding multiple intelligences and many learning style models is a critical part of AL. Respecting the differences in how people learn and designing lessons that take those differences into account is essential. Following the latest research on both these topics is important to the success of AL.

Imagination and Metaphors

Metaphors and analogies are valuable tools in the learning process. Offering them as representations of concepts is valuable and helpful in the learning process. Imagination is one of the earliest elements of learning for children, and AL aims to recreate childlike experiences; imagination does that. Visualization is important in imagination and enhances many areas of learning.

Suggestion and De-Suggestion

The idea that mental imagery influences behavior has long been adhered to in sports. It is also true in the classroom: what we believe and what is suggested can enhance or decrease our learning. In other words, if we think we can succeed, it is much more likely that we will, whereas if we think we cannot succeed, it is likely we will not. Through direct as well as subtle suggestion, teachers can influence performance and success. Like all these elements, each is connected to others. Personal motivation and emotional state are connected to suggestion. The idea of de-suggestion is removing what might be barriers to learning and achieving.

Team Learning and Cooperation

Designing activities that acknowledge the importance of the social aspects of learning is key. By structuring cooperative learning and team events for learners, AL instructors support the development of

> *I would rather have a mind opened by wonder than one closed by belief.*
>
> —Gerry Spence

interpersonal skills and learning from peers. AL is used with the notion that many techniques and models can be integrated to accelerate learning.

Improvement and Results

If there is no measurement or assessment, how do we know what is being learned? Looking carefully at results and adjusting instruction based on those results is crucial to greater student success. *Kaizen,* the Japanese word meaning continuous improvement in small steps, is what AL facilitators aim for. Regular and specific feedback contributes to students' success and helps them monitor their steps to improvement.

Six-Part Cycle

AL has a number of different proponents, and each has developed a particular cycle. The one that is most commonly agreed on is that supported by the IAL. Many of the current pioneers in AL are active in IAL and have contributed to an extensive study of AL. Every teaching model has some framework, and although AL is as much philosophy as model, the framework below moves AL to a model to implement. You will recognize some repetition of ideas from earlier chapters in the book.

Preparation of the Learner

Chapter 5

As discussed in Chapter 5, preparing the learner happens before the class begins. Some instructors offer prework or ongoing homework to help prepare students. The basic premise is to ensure that each student is ready to learn and has a desire to be present. Welcoming each student by name at the door as they arrive is one method of inviting them into learning. Students should be physically and emotionally ready to learn. You are in charge of providing the transition from the outside to the inside. The learning environment you set up with them will have influence over how prepared they are for learning.

Creating an Individual, Emotional Connection to the Learning

Have you ever been sent to a seminar or class? Someone in your organization thought it would be good for you. The content might not be particularly relevant to you, so the instructor is challenged. Your job as that instructor, even though your student will not be sent, is to bring some relevance to the content and enroll students in your class. They need to be provided an opportunity to find their own relevance and share that with others. That helps enroll everyone at a higher level.

Presentation of the Content or Process

You have many choices about how to present material or processes. In designing a course you will use many alternatives. We have described some of your options and have chapters that offer you models to use. It is imperative that you use a variety of techniques and get feedback form your students as to what works for them.

Practice

In AL, the majority of time students are interacting with the content in some fashion. Activations, games, skits, skills practice, and guided or interactive lectures all offer practice with the content. The more students can interact in multiple situations the better chance of earlier mastery of the content.

Performance

Practice leads to demonstrating skills and content knowledge in personal ways. Questions arise about the use of the skill or content in various unique situations. Performance on various formal and informal assessments provides the instructor with necessary feedback for grading and/or reviewing content.

Integration, Reflection, and Celebration

Action plans devised in class and carried out in the real world help to integrate skills and content knowledge for learners. Providing a means to reflect on their practice leads to improvement at using the newfound knowledge or skill. And the one thing we do not do enough of in traditional setting is celebrate learning. Celebrations can be over the small step of mastery or the implementation of a whole new set of strategies.

> We must act as if our institutions are ours to create, our learning is ours to define, our leadership we seek is ours to become.
>
> —Peter Block

CHAPTER WRAP-UP

Accelerated learning has the potential to improve learning in every setting. It is used in the settings of education and business training. Many schools, universities and businesses have used these techniques to improve their delivery of content. Accelerated learning offers people powerful learning experiences on a regular basis. Think back to that best class or teacher. Unfortunately, there were only a few, not nearly enough. Every class should be memorable for all the right reasons; one has positive experiences and learns more than expected. By improving instructional practices of every educator, education would be improved dramatically. Using AL, or any other model described in this book that you have not used before, will enrich you and your students.

SPRINGBOARDS FOR FURTHER LEARNING

Key Names

Bobbi DePorter
Gail Heidenhein
Eric Jensen
Charlotte LaHecka
Georgi Lozanov

Doug McPhee
Dave Meier
Sheila Ostrander
Colin Rose
Lynn Schroeder

Key Terms

accelerated learning
de-suggestion
International Alliance
   for Learning

suggestion
Superlearning
Suggestopedia

CHAPTER 13

Inquiry/Problem-Based Learning

The test and use of man's education is that he finds pleasure in the exercise of his mind.

—Jacques Barzun

Do You Know:

- We lose our creativity starting during kindergarten?
- Curiosity is one of our most valuable assets?
- How to teach students to ask good questions?
- The human brain loves to solve problems?
- Questions are an instructor's friend?

What Is Inquiry?

They say curiosity killed the cat, which is really not a good metaphor because curiosity is a characteristic that is very important to learning and understanding. When we do not know something we need to know, our brain seeks the needed information. *Inquiry is seeking information or knowledge.* Inquiry is driven by curiosity—and questions. We learn when we are curious and ask questions. The unfortunate thing is that students in school ask fewer questions and are less curious as they go through each grade. By the time they reach postsecondary education students not only do not ask many purposeful questions,

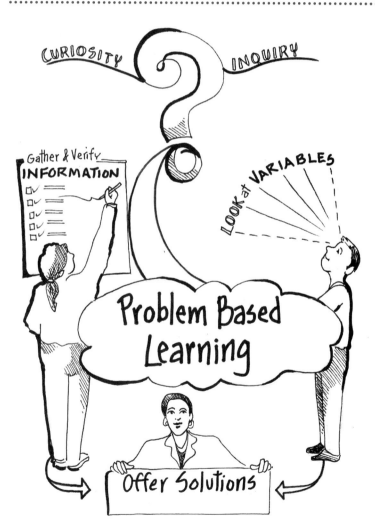

327

they have also lost that sense of curiosity they had on entering formal schooling. Cats are notoriously curious and our students should be as well. They will learn more by being so.

The Challenge of Using Inquiry

The loss of curiosity is challenging for educators who want students to be inquisitive. Our traditional education system consists more of one-right-answer questions than of dialogue. Educators are taught the way they were taught, wherein lies the problem. In the previous century information seemed finite. Hence, education and educators emphasized facts and information versus knowledge and understanding—one right answer. The accumulation and memorization of facts, formulas, and data was paramount to educational success in the 20th century. That is our experience. "It worked for me so it will work for my students." It was not really true then, and it certainly is not true now. The true success of education is when students come away from a class with as many questions as answers. The key is that they should be learning the tools for where to find and how to discover answers. They should also be learning the skill of asking good questions. They should know how to ask the questions that will get them to the information they seek.

Why Do You Know What You Know?

As an expert you have real-world experience with the content you are teaching. You know most everything about your subject. However, you actually know more than you think you know. You have built multiple contexts for subject-matter applications. You do things intuitively based on your prior experiences. You do not really have to think about it because you have "muscle" memory of how it works. You know what you know because of your many years of interacting with the subject that you are teaching. You discovered more and more about how the topic fits in the real world with each experience. You solved problems when things did not work as expected. You experienced failures that led to successes. All the while your brain was creating a vast network of neural connections about your experience. It created pathways that you have used unconsciously, and you have probably forgotten the specific experiences that made you an expert.

Your knowledge is difficult if not impossible to transfer to students through traditional teaching. Even when you use nontraditional methods they will not lead to complete mastery until students have more experiences with the subject and all its "connective tissue." That is why we have written this book. You have to provide as many varied opportunities as possible for your student to build context for their learning around your subject. By designing powerful experiences and using various methods to present and have students experience the content,

> *Do not go where the path may lead; go where there is no path and leave a trail.*
>
> —Ralph Waldo Emerson

you will provide them with valuable knowledge. That knowledge will be in the context of the application of the content in real-world situations. Using the inquiry model, you will improve the depth of learning for your students.

The person most associated with coining the term *inquiry learning* was J. Richard Suchman from the University of Illinois. He coined the term, but the method has been used from before the time of Socrates. Inquiry has probably been used in the science community more than in any other discipline. It is a natural process in science because there are questions that are pursued, as answers are not known.

If I knew what was going to happen in ten years I would do it now. I just follow my nose.

—Stephen Hawking

Suchman's Model

Suchman formalized inquiry by suggesting a model that included the following: you present a situation; students gather information, identify variables, hypothesize and test relationships, organize data, and propose improvements. In more detail, the model works well with any topic in any discipline. However, because it has been utilized mainly in science and mathematics, inquiry has not been as widely used as it might be. Looking more closely at each of the above items you will see how inquiry can be applied to any discipline or topic.

Prepare a Puzzling Situation or Event

When you prepare your inquiry-based lesson you will look closely at all the ideas about your topic. Determine what it is that students need to know to gain mastery, and design a puzzling scenario or situation that they will analyze. When presented, students can ask you questions about the situation or event; however, you can answer only yes or no.

As practice for inquiry you can use a story for which students can ask only "yes or no" questions. I've done this exercise successfully with many groups from youth to adult. Curiously, young people often think more vividly about the possible answers than adults do. One story I used is about a man lying on the floor of his jail cell dead. Besides the standard bed, small table and chair, sink, and toilet, there is a pool of water on the floor beside his body. What happened?

Students can only ask questions that offer a yes-or-no answer. As the facilitator you can only answer "Yes" or "No," and if you want, "It doesn't matter." In this particular story, the man used an icicle to kill himself. So questions that would lead to that conclusion might include: Is there a window in the room? Is the cell door open? (Doesn't matter.) Would it help to know about the weather? Is it cold outside?

(continues)

Is the window open? Students ask these questions and will ultimately get to the solution.

I often have to offer some prompt for questions, and this is part of the setup for using inquiry as a strategy in my classroom. As with any new learning experience it is most important for you to set up students for success. Early in my career I discovered that if I spent time teaching the skills I expected students to use during a new strategy like inquiry, it ultimately saved time. Students need to know how to ask effective questions before starting an inquiry lesson. You need to teach that.

Gather and Verify Information

Once you have presented a puzzling situation and students have asked questions to discover more from you, then they work in groups to gather more information and verify what they know. They determine as much as possible about the situation or event. As an example, it might be that you have described a legal case that has a curious twist or perhaps an archeological scenario that poses a puzzling question. You should have the basic information and not necessarily a conclusion. And if you are familiar with the situation or have experienced it yourself, you can proceed with confidence. The point is that students should be looking for possibilities as to why such an event occurred.

> *If you are looking for a big opportunity, find a big problem.*
>
> —Anonymous

Identify Variables and Hypothesize and Test Relationships

Once they have gathered as much information as they can students then look for the variables that make a difference. They look carefully at the causes and effects of relationships and data. Then they hypothesize. This higher-level thinking is critical to success.

Chapter 15

Organize and Present the Data

The next step is a critical one. If you have not taught students how to organize data, then do that first. Give them an example or model of what organized data look like. You might have a discussion before you begin the inquiry about this. After organizing the data they have collected, students can present it to the group for feedback. Other groups do the same and compare what they have hypothesized and concluded with each other. Once all the information is laid out for everyone, new insights are realized, and potential solutions are suggested, send the students back to their groups for the final phase.

It is not necessary to do presentations if you choose not to. It may be that you have not included time to do them. Or perhaps you have determined that you want the results from each group uninfluenced by other groups. It is really up to you. (Another of the thousands of decisions you still have to make as a masterful teacher.)

Propose Solutions or Improvements

The final phase is for the groups to determine improvements and/or solutions to the situation or event. Also, they should take time to analyze their methods of inquiry. By taking time to analyze and evaluate their work, they can better determine what to do the next time they are asked to work in groups with an inquiry exercise. A thought for you to consider is to have students do an inquiry session on inquiry. They can learn the model by studying it through the model.

Although Suchman provided one framework, there are others, and you can adjust his to make it work for your discipline and topic. If you have the basics and you are preparing your students for success by setting the standards for success you will be successful at implementing not only inquiry, but also all the methods in this unit.

Questioning Strategies for Inquiry-Based Learning

Before you use inquiry, as suggested earlier, you need to teach questioning skills. In the 1950s Benjamin Bloom created his taxonomy of questions and thinking at six levels, including knowledge, comprehension, application, analysis, synthesis, and evaluation. Dennie Palmer Wolf has also offered a valuable taxonomy for questions. He suggests that there are five major types of questions: inference questions, interpretation questions, transfer questions, questions about hypotheses, and reflective questions. Both of these resources are valuable in learning to pose better questions and teaching students to ask questions as well. Do not shy away from asking questions that promote thinking at higher levels. Do not allow yourself to be guilty of asking questions that require yes-or-no answers. Model strong questioning techniques and your students will work at that level as well. They may end up asking you difficult questions, and that is a good thing. It shows that they are thinking about the topic and want to know as much as they can.

Wolf's Questions

Inference Questions

Inference questions are those that ask the learner to conclude things from the evidence. Students go beyond the facts of the matter and

The first people had the questions, and they were free. The second people had answers, and they became enslaved.

—Wind Eagle

Chapters 8 and 9

draw conclusions based on all they see and hear about something. Why do students need to make inferences? Not everything is obvious in our world, much less in the subjects that are taught in schools and colleges. Inference questions are a test of knowledge and understanding of the topic. Drawing inferences is a critical skill that all students should have.

Example: What can you determine is true about [insert topic] but not known from what you have learned?

Interpretation Questions

Interpretation questions help us understand the consequences of information. This is valuable because it moves students from a surface understanding to a deep understanding of the topic or subject. Instead of an inch deep and a mile long, which many courses provide, your students will better understand if you include and they ask interpretation questions.

Example: How would this be different if . . . ?

Transfer Questions

We transfer by substituting another consequence and describing an application of knowledge in a different situation. In Bloom's model this is at the synthesis level. It presumes that the student has a deep understanding of the topic and can use the knowledge in a completely different situation from the one in which the information was learned.

Example: What if you applied the information in [describe situation]?

Hypotheses Questions

Questions about hypotheses are usually used only in the sciences—what a shame. Students can create a hypothesis in any discipline and then test to see if it is true through the same process that might be used in science. A hypothesis is a statement about what one believes might be true about something, a prediction. The questions around that hypothesis can be answered by experimentation.

Example: What facts did you consider when you wrote your hypothesis?

Reflective Questions

Reflective questions are discussed in Chapter 8, and here they are basically the same. Students are asked how they know they know. They are challenged to think about their thinking. This, of course, is what distinguishes us from other mammals. We can be reflective about our thinking and about the practice of teaching.

> *If you can change your mind, you can change the world.*
>
> —Joey Reimer

Unit 2 Chapter 8

Example: What are you assuming about [insert topic], and why is it an assumption and not a conclusion? How would I know you know you know?

A Bloom Refresher

To refresh your memory, here are the key words from each of Bloom's levels to use in creating questions that encourage quality thinking. These words also apply to Wolf's model and others that are used to improve thinking and learning.

- *Knowledge and Comprehension:* Identify, locate, listen, name, match, observe, and ask what, where, when, and who questions
- *Application:* List, teach, construct, paint, manipulate, report, interview, stimulate, and ask how questions
- *Analysis:* Classify, compare, dissect, separate, contrast, survey, categorize, and ask why questions
- *Synthesis:* Combine, hypothesize, predict, infer, write, create, invent, estimate, and ask what if questions
- *Evaluation:* Choose, decide, judge, evaluate, debate, discuss, recommend, and ask which and why questions

CHAPTER WRAP-UP

We teach what we need to learn and write what we need to know.

—Gloria Steinem

The human brain loves closure. Have you noticed that you feel cheated if you miss the end of a movie or TV show? You feel cheated because your brain did not reach a conclusion. You usually try to make up an ending based on the facts that you know. You may be right or wrong, but at least you have closure. This is useful to know when you are using the inquiry method to teach because it will help students work efficiently to finish the work. They want to solve the problem that you have posed.

Once again, you have many choices when it comes to designing your lessons and course. Inquiry is valuable and can be used in combination with the other models presented in this chapter. The challenge we ask you to meet is to use each method enough times so it becomes more natural. When you use inquiry you become a facilitator of learning, and you have to listen carefully to support the process. You will find that student questions at other times will challenge you and indicate that the students are really learning.

That "guide on the side" role of facilitator versus "sage on the stage" instructor shifts student thinking about their role in class. You sometimes will discover the obstacles to their learning at the same time they do. You are learning together. You do not have all the answers.

Your job becomes one of support and steering students to the resources they will need to accomplish their goals. With the stress on skill development, students learn at a deeper level and appreciate their learning more because they have a sense of personal and group achievement. The knowledge they gain is different than the information model that is more typical from lecture format. This is helps create the learner-centered classroom.

SPRINGBOARDS FOR FURTHER LEARNING

Key Names

Benjamin Bloom   Dennie Wolf
J. Richard Suchman

Key Terms

case-based learning   problem-based learning
inquiry-based learning

CHAPTER 14
Situational Learning

Anyone who stops learning is old, whether at twenty or eighty. Anyone who keeps learning stays young. The greatest thing in life is to keep your mind young.

—Henry Ford

Do You Know:

- You've experienced situational learning many times?
- There are many ways to provide situational learning?
- Businesses use several methods of situational learning?
- Successful athletes benefit from situational learning?

Introduction

Situational learning has been around since the beginning of time. Hunters and gatherers were situational learners. Nomads were situational learners. Adventurers and settlers learned situationally. Cultures across the globe have used situational learning formally and informally in families and societies to pass on values, attitudes, and cultural perspectives. You probably experienced the formal use of situational learning when you took a driver's training course in high school. Perhaps you were in a skills class in woodshop or sewing, where you learned by doing. Everyone at some point in schooling

Unit 1 Chapters 2 and 3

is exposed to situational learning. The trouble is, this does not occur often enough. If you want the best learning outcomes, you should be designing situations for real-world learning for your students on a regular basis.

By designing classes that include real-world situations, educators take advantage of one of the most powerful learning tools available. From a social learning perspective, schools too often provide abstract learning by removing content and learning activities from the settings in which they need to be applied. Students are asked to reason about and practice with rules and principles preformulated by others, expected to use and act on information (formulae, specialized terms) in a rote manner, and resolve well-defined problems that often fail to reflect the kind of challenges they will face outside the classroom. Thus, students end up with a surface and inflexible understanding that does not transfer well to new situations and real-life settings. Theories of situational learning suggest that deep understanding is naturally tied to authentic activities and contexts that reflect the conditions and character of the work of professionals in a particular field and learners' communication with peers and experienced practitioners about those contexts. Think about military pilots who train with flight simulators, which is required before they actually fly in an unfamiliar aircraft. They spend many hours and experience a variety of scenarios before moving to the real thing. When one of the troubling scenarios comes up during an actual flight they are prepared to deal with it because of their simulated experience. Your expert experience in the real world can help you develop situations that will improve learning for your students.

When I was 12, my brothers and I had a go-cart. It was vary fast, about 60 miles per hour, and we learned many of the skills for driving a larger vehicle from that go-cart. Both brothers were older, and the oldest, Alan, was already learning to drive. Alan didn't use the go-cart as much as Pete and I did. It was apparent when he continued his quest for a driver's license that his skills were lacking. Alan struggled and scared us all while he was learning to drive. He did get his license and is a good driver now. When Pete and I experienced driver's training and sought our licenses several years later, we breezed through the courses and easily passed the written and road tests. We have had a few frightening moments and could maneuver easily through them, calling on our go-cart experiences. Those were real-world moments. Our experience on the go-cart was the defining difference. I loved that go-cart!

Cognitive Apprenticeship

Contrast the traditional approach with the way most apprentices learn their craft, called "cognitive apprenticeship." They reason with unique models and cases, act on authentic situations, and resolve complex, ill-defined problems. This learning is typically based on discovery and exploration and practice, with knowledge and the "negotiation" of understanding through the relationship with practiced professional and possibly other learners. Treated and taught as novices, learners' knowledge evolves and grows and deepens because there are constantly new occasions of use and new situations that recast basic knowledge and understanding into deeper forms. Situational learning and cognitive apprenticeship hold the conviction that just about *all* learning happens most easily and effectively through such activities and experiences. In this approach, students collaborate with their instructors and one another in settings and relationships that seek to approximate "real-life" situations, together progressively moving toward a shared knowledge base and understanding. Instructors who advocate such an approach believe that this involves creating a "culture" of learning that resides in a naturalistic learning landscape and "community of practice" that is comprised of the knowledge, skills, values, and ways of thinking and behaving of those who occupy this place.

Obvious examples of situational learning can be found in the arts and most trades and crafts, which usually are taught through explicit and formal apprentice–master relationships. But if you are trying to think of a situational approach for your own courses taught in a didactic manner, think about how your field or trade may have been taught before there were formal educational institutions. Most likely, the knowledge and skills were taught by way of apprentice-like situations. Architects learned to design by working with master architects. Physicians learned to operate by watching and assisting other physicians. Capable practitioners mentored carpenters, masons, etc. Teachers even learned by observing and practicing in the presence of those more experienced.

Considering your own classes in this way need not to seem offbeat or unorthodox. The focus of much current cognitive research is understanding teaching and learning by studying how experts operate in their fields and then using this understanding as a guide for effective instruction. Proponents of *cognitive* apprenticeships believe we can then take the principles that underlie traditional apprenticeships and apply them to most courses of study to draw students into a "culture" of expert practice by teaching them how to think and behave like experts.

Where cognitive apprenticeship differs from traditional apprenticeship is in the scope of tasks and problems used. Generally, topics and skills for study are more selective, chosen to highlight and illustrate primarily the most critical concepts, techniques, or methods in order to "make visible" the knowledge and reasoning skills of those who work as

> Even today, many complex and important skills, such as those required for language use and social interaction, are learned informally through apprenticeship-like methods—that is, methods not involving didactic teaching, but observation, coaching, and successive approximation.
>
> —Allan Collins and John Seely Brown

Chapter 2

experts. At the same time, like a traditional apprenticeship, a cognitive approach gives students plenty of guidance and chances to observe, model, and practice in applying new knowledge in diverse settings that slowly increase the complexity of tasks so that component skills and models can be integrated and mastered. The instructional technique used to foster this process is known as "scaffolding."

Simulations

Flight simulators, first developed after World War II, have changed over the years. They were first just cockpits with hydraulics to move the simulator based on the pilot's actions, with no visual feedback. In the 1960s, visual capability became available and this was added for more realistic simulations of real-life situations. Computers of that era were mammoth and usually filled up an entire room. The development of computer technology with much smaller memory chips versus tape has helped provide even better simulations and more realistic situations. The move from video programs developed in the 1970s to computer-generated graphics in the 1980s and 1990s brought flight simulators to a level of performance that is very close to actually flying an aircraft.

Present thinking people kill the future.

—Ken Blanchard

The gaming industry has used simulations for years with great success and profit. From Atari to Xbox and PlayStation, young and old have enjoyed the simulations available to the gaming community. And there has been controversy over the violent nature of many of the computer/video games. Even so, these leading-edge products have contributed to raising the level of sophistication of computer simulations with the development of very high-end graphics.

There are real-world computer simulations that have been developed for many subject areas. These simulations are very sophisticated and have been successful at all levels of education. Computer-based simulations can be found for everything from archeological digs to business situations to mathematical conundrums. There are virtual reality computer programs, which seem to put you directly into the action, that offer instructors and students even more options.

You can find simulations for your subject area by doing a search on the Internet. It would be worth doing to look at samples to consider for your courses or at least to get ideas on how you might add elements to the design of your courses.

Internships

Talk about learning that is situated, internships offer the best, especially if there is a planned immersion program and ongoing training. When you are actually doing the real work in a real work setting you learn more. Many students who have taken an internship position have decided not to pursue the particular career. On the other hand, if you are already convinced and committed, an internship is a great way to learn the basics of a particular career. Internships are sometimes referred to as service learning. A basic component of the school-to-work movement is internships.

Internships are paid or volunteer positions. Both have value for students. Of course, paid internships are helpful to the budget and sometimes offer more responsibility. Interns learn the ropes of their chosen field by doing some of the menial work associated with the field. Like a beginning position, internships are a vehicle for organizations to get tasks done at lower or no cost. Also, companies offer internships to potential employees without the same level of obligation. Internships turn into actual job offers when the company needs to fill a position and the intern has proven that he or she has the competence and confidence to fill the position. Once a manager observes work habits and personality they can be assured of hiring a contributing employee. They can also determine that there is not a fit with a particular intern.

The medical field requires internships for doctors. Depending on the specialty, the internship could be several years or a shorter rotation in general medicine for general practitioners. Education requires internships in most states, where student teachers work in a classroom with an experienced teacher. In California, students do a rotation in elementary schools so that they have lower- and upper-grade experience. In many programs, students also have to spend time in schools with disadvantaged students. Obviously, the value is found significant in these areas and other professions as well.

If you are working teaching a subject for which you can provide internship opportunities for your students, they will learn more than if you do everything in class. In designing your course, you can include internships if you find employers who will work with you and your students. You have to make sure the employer has a formal way to provide the intern with the basic skills needed and that the students will be doing meaningful work related to the subject. This takes more than a phone call and agreement. You will have to visit the organization and meet with those who will be supervising the interns. In that meeting you will share what your expectations are for interns and hear what the employers need. By doing this you will find where the crossovers are and negotiate a stronger program.

Interns should do real work to contribute to the bottom line and should also be assigned some of the necessary tasks that help businesses run. They should not be doing filing or copying during their hours of internship. And it would not be expected that they work on sophisticated projects with senior managers. Proprietary information

> *From error to error one discovers the entire truth.*
>
> —Sigmund Freud

requires a nondisclosure release and should be addressed in your meeting with the company. Interns are better served when they have one contact to report to and work with. It is helpful for you to have only one contact as well. You might set up internships as extra credit for your class. The experience will be well worth the time students spend.

Case Studies

Case studies are actual cases from the real world used for discussion and learning. (They are also common for structuring and extending inquiry-based learning strategies.) The case puts forth all the particulars about a situation and students discuss a plan to respond to the case. This is done in groups just as it would be in the real world, so you would be using cooperative learning with this example. Actually, you can use cooperative learning with any of the classroom examples of situational learning.

Case studies offer students real situations that they may face in the future and have the benefit of not being real in the moment. There are solutions or response that were used in the case and those are usually shared after students have a chance to come up with how their group would respond. You can have students complete a number of case studies with a variety of challenges in a shorter period of time than a simulation or internship.

Case studies are great preparation for students before they complete a course of study. Students can use skills and knowledge to review, analyze, evaluate, and come to some conclusions regarding the application of their knowledge. They also learn to work together, as in other cooperative learning activities. Case studies can be presented as part of a lecture, on a handout, by an audio CD or tape, or by video. Each is viable to present the real-world situations in case studies.

Perhaps you have experienced a group activity for which the scenario is of survivors from a ship on a remote island or a disaster in space. There are many of these simulations that might be considered case studies. The skills used to process these case studies are more personal and general in nature than those associated with a specific workplace case study. They test communication skills and challenge values to clarify personal beliefs and actions. What would you do if . . . ? This type of activity offers students the opportunity to work together on a case or simulation that is less likely to happen in the real world and yet is a powerful learning experience.

Every reform was once private opinion.

—Ralph Waldo Emerson

On-the-Job Training—Apprenticeships

If you are a subject-matter expert, you have been in the job market for some time. Your career was spent learning your craft and you spent time on the job in training to get more proficient at it. Although you cannot offer your students much on-the-job training by giving them some experiences that are situated in the real world of the subject, you can increase the likelihood of their success. Apprentice programs in trade fields are very well designed and include benchmark expectations that if not met prevent apprentices from moving forward. The requirements are sometimes stiffer than college or university courses.

There are trade occupations that require as much training as a 4-year degree and ultimately can reward journeymen with very high income. These programs are not easy by any means and hold high expectations for those who choose to pursue journeyman status. Again, you cannot offer these particular internship-style programs, but the design should be just as robust for what you can offer. Details should be carefully considered and high expectations should be well established and publicized for any situational learning program you plan.

> *Scenarios do not predict the future, they highlight our perceptual limitations thus allowing us to spot issues, trends, and developments that we would be otherwise unaware.*
>
> —Joe Willmore

Scenario Planning

In business, companies often use scenario planning to prepare for possible future events. It is future-based, with present knowledge taken into account. One of the most memorable uses of this was Royal Dutch Shell's scenario planning around a potential oil shortage in the 1970s. Because they had actually played out the scenario, when the gas crisis hit they had a plan that they could implement. Other oil companies had to develop plans from the ground up, while Shell simply instituted their already-designed plan. They responded quickly and with agility and managed the crisis more effectively than their competitors. Scenario planning helps in determining potential weaknesses in infrastructures before it impacts present circumstances. Companies can correct flaws without suffering the possible consequences.

Scenario planning also has advantages in that an organization can find out how flexible it might be in a particular scenario. Can the right people respond quickly? Are resources readily available should scenario A or B occur? Where is the most appropriate place to store materials, or from which to deploy resources? If New Orleans and the federal government had done more scenario planning before Hurricane Katrina it might not have been so devastating. The Army Corps of Engineers actually knew that the dikes might collapse in a level 4 or 5 hurricane but did no planning as to what should occur when that happened. Had they done so, it would have promoted a more detailed evacuation plan for the Ninth Ward. The fact is, there was a plan in place at one point to use city

I never hit a shot even in practice without having a sharp in-focus picture of it in my head. It's like a color movie. First, I "see" the ball where I want it to finish, nice and white and sitting up high on the bright green grass. Then the scene quickly changes, and I "see" the ball going there: its path, trajectory, and shape, even its behavior on landing. Then there's a sort of fade-out, and the next scene shows me making the kind of swing that will turn the

busses to evacuate those who had no personal transportation; it was not used for Katrina.

Scenario planning is a little different from case studies in that the actual situation is not present. It is a brainstorming and creative process to prepare for future possibilities in business, to realize our perceptual limitations. Scenario planning is an important component of systems thinking. In systems thinking, one takes into account all the possible consequences of even the smallest change in a system. A system is anything that has more than one part or component. For example, if you were to offer your course as pass or fail, that would have implications for other courses and also the way you might determine the criteria for passing. It would also have an effect on students' perception of the value of the course and the amount of time they might spend studying for it. A further implication might be the value the course would be to the institution where you work. No decision is as simple as it may seem. Systems thinking is always looking at the big picture and how any change impacts the whole system or smaller systems within the system.

You can use scenario planning with your students in looking at the entire course you are teaching. By being offered options for projects, presentations, internships, and exams. students can develop scenarios that indicate the implications of each possible combination of course options. You can also custom tailor the course for each subsequent group of students. Once you have laid out the goals and your expectations, reaching them can be through many channels. If the students have a say-so in how that happens, they will be more likely to complete all the requirements and meet your expectations.

The other arena in which scenario planning is used extensively and has been for many years is the military. The smartest military leaders have always depended on alternative planning to give them the best advantage on the battlefield. In 340 BC Sun Tzu wrote the *Art of War,* which has stood the test of time and offered the earliest thoughts on strategic planning for the battlefield. It is considered one of the greatest books on warfare ever written and it offers the reader scenario planning as a strategy for winning battles and hence wars.

When companies and organizations take scenario planning to another level, they engage in strategic planning. Unfortunately, it is too often the case that a company has not looked at all of the implications of a strategy before implementing it. Such was the case for Coca-Cola when they removed their main product and replaced it with "New Coke." It was a major failure until the company decided to introduce "Classic Coke," which was the old familiar product and flew off the shelves once reintroduced.

Strategic planning has become very important to successful organizations. It works only if it is done with systems thinking in mind and constantly reviewed based on current circumstances. The same is true for your teaching. You can have the best plan and if you do not *previous images into reality. Only at the end of this short private Hollywood spectacular do I select a club and step up to the ball.*

—Jack Nicklaus

pay attention to the fact that you have numerous students who are non-English speakers and you do not adjust the plan, you will fail.

Mental Imagery

Although mental imagery is not specifically situational learning it can be a valuable learning tool and seems to fit here. Mental imagery is based on possible scenarios that create positive results. In order to have a positive mental image, the student must be able to visualize the specific experience. Athletes create a picture of their success at their particular event. Athletes also use imagery that includes the use of their athletic abilities to achieve the positive outcome. They "preconstruct" an end result that they desire.

Mental imagery exercises are perceptual, without the benefit of outside stimuli. You reconstruct what you have experienced and then adjust the image to create a different and usually more positive outcome. And imagery can be suggestive to help in changing behavior, say about healthier dieting. When we imagine ourselves thinner and eating healthy foods while avoiding junk food we practice mental imagery. All of us have used mental imagery at times. Using this tool you can create a positive outcome for your students by describing their success in your course. You can create vivid images and detailed positive activities that contribute to higher achievement of students in your classes.

The power of suggestion is strong, and it works. You read in Chapter 12, on Accelerated Learning, about Suggestopedia, which is based on the power of suggestion. Mental imagery is suggestion with purpose, because you are not only suggesting, you actually have a picture and feeling in mind and in your body as you go through a mental imagery exercise. Use of mental imagery is a valuable tool and you can increase productivity of your students if you suggest it.

CHAPTER WRAP-UP

As you see, there are many options for involving students in their own learning. Situational learning activities in the formats described should be considered as you plan and design your course and classes. The more students can apply their new and previous knowledge in real-world situations the better they will value their learning. They also are more active about seeking further and deeper information because they have more specific circumstances to apply their skills and knowledge. Students practicing their skills in a lab setting, your classroom, is less risky than sending them out in the world.

It will take a strong commitment on your part to use any of the methods described in this unit. You must first develop your instructional skills in setting up situational learning or any other method. Involve your students in that process, as suggested earlier. Ask them for feedback on the methods you use. Refine your practice by reflecting and refining future practice.

In using situational learning models your preparation is critical to success. You can find simulations and case studies online, or with your expert experience you can write you own case studies. The extra time you spend may well be worth it, as the case would be very real and firsthand, and therefore easier for you to respond to students about it. Simulations can be time-consuming and very detailed to develop and you will have to use one several times to make sure you have included all the pertinent details. You might do as well to search online for simulations that work for your purposes.

A key to success in using simulations is to have a planned outcome or goals for using this method. There are many reasons to use situational learning and deciding to start with a more general experience that draws on personal skills rather than knowledge gained in your class has merit. You support students' growing skills at working in groups and communicating clearly before they have to apply newfound knowledge that may not yet be well defined in the real world.

Whatever you decide, remember to try each method enough times to make sure you have learned the best ways to use it. Remember, you can use something once and it may not work, and the next time it will. Our desire is for you to develop a repertoire of instruction skills so you can make better decisions more often on your journey to becoming a masterful teacher.

> *Self-Confidence is the first requisite to great undertakings.*
>
> —Samuel Johnson

SPRINGBOARDS FOR FURTHER LEARNING

Key Names

Chris Argyris	Allen Collins
John Bransford	Jay Forrester
John Seely Brown	Peter Senge

Key Terms

active learning	on-the-job training
anchored instruction	scenario planning
case studies	school to work
cognitive apprenticeship	service learning
computer gaming	simulation
communities of practice	situational learning
internship	virtual reality
mental imagery	

are what what we live we live by, the by, the ways ways we go we go about about our our daily daily tasks. tasks. Chang Chang ing a ing a habit or habit or adding adding a habit a habit to our to our routine routine is a is a chal chal lenge lenge be be cause cause habits habits are so are so em em bedded bedded in our in our minds minds and and bodies, bodies. Have Have you you ever ever tried tried putting putting on your on your shoes shoes in a dif in a dif ferent ferent order? order? Or Or using a using a knife knife and and fork dif fork dif ferently ferently from from what what you are you are used used in? Habit is Habits an act an act re peated peated so so often often that it that it be be comes comes auto auto matic, matic, so so much much so that so that many many habits habits we do we do not not even even think think about about —we —we just do just do just do them.

CHAPTER 15

Critical Thinking and Developing Habits of Mind

Thought is the strongest thing we have. Work done by true and profound thought—that is a real force.

—Albert Schweitzer

Do You Know:

- How to cultivate habits of mind?
- Strong habits of mind will improve learning?
- Intelligent questions are important in the real world?
- Intelligence is "ability on demand" and can be improved?
- You should label habits of mind for your students?

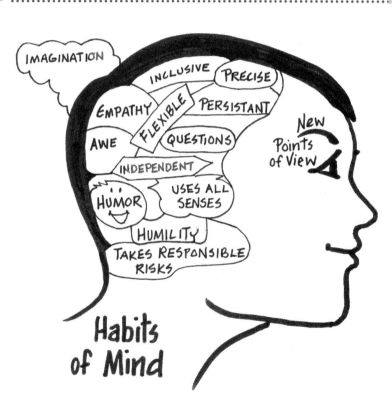

Introduction

Habits are what we live by, the ways we go about our daily tasks. Changing a habit or adding a habit to our routine is a challenge because habits are so embedded in our minds and bodies. Have you ever tried putting on your shoes in a different order? Or using a knife and fork differently from what you are used to? Habit is an act repeated so often that it becomes automatic, so much so that many habits we do not even think about—we just do them.

Habits of mind are no different. They are mental behaviors we engage

345

> *Improved learning is best achieved by improving teaching and learning relationships.*
>
> —Deborah Meier

without thinking consciously about them once we have learned them. They help us in our understanding of knowledge and can significantly improve our learning on any topic. These habits help us know what to do when we do not know what to do. When learned and practiced, each habit becomes a valuable tool, and when used together they are a full toolbox that we can open as needed. The more these tools are used the more proficient we become at applying them in different situations.

Habits of mind as predispositions to and capacity for critical thinking have been discussed for years in education, especially in the humanities, math, and science. The logical use of a set of skills to analyze, estimate, solve problems, convert, or question ideas and concepts has long been an aim of effective instruction in these areas. It is now clear that these skills can and should be used in every discipline. Indeed, in many discussions of educational reform, the topic of teaching critical thinking is at the top of the agenda, and for some it is the "holy grail" of true learning. All good reasoning should be guided by standards or habits of mind that include seeking clarity, accuracy, precision, relevance, depth, breadth, logic, and fairness in everything we encounter. In a world constantly bombarded by new discoveries and ever-increasing amounts of knowledge, the ability to think critically about this new information—and to reflect on what one has learned from it—takes on a new urgency. Knowing what to accept or reject and how to effectively and efficiently modify one's current knowledge base and thinking and to integrate new understanding into them has become a basic survival skill. Given the breadth and depth of the topic of critical thinking, we focus on an overview of the habits of mind that are a foundation for developing critical reasoning abilities.

Three Habits-of-Mind Models

Chapter 14

Educators have used their own means to teach habits of mind, sometimes working in concert with other teachers, and often on their own. Educational organizations have created and nurtured habits at every level of education. A cognitive apprenticeship is one model that educators are encouraged to use. Three other models used in many curriculum areas are described here, as they seem to have elements that are the easiest to integrate into any curriculum area.

Art Costa and Bena Kallick

Costa and Kallick offer a model that includes 16 specific "attributes of what humans do when they behave intelligently." Their series, published by the Association for Supervision and Curriculum Development (ASCD) is titled *Habits of Mind*. Each of four books is written with a different emphasis, including describing the 16 attributes, using them in classrooms, sustaining their use, and assessing them. They are straightforward and easy to understand. We offer a short description of each below. With this information you can begin to use these attributes to increase your students' involvement in higher-order thinking, not to mention to enhance your results for student learning. Costa and Kallick do not suggest that these are the only these 16 ways in which humans think intelligently. With this in mind, there are two other sections on these habits. This gives you a good sampling of things to experiment with and use over the long term. The 16 attributes for the Costa–Kallick model are discussed below.

1. *Persisting:* Not giving up easily is the key to this habit. By using a range of strategies you can ensure completion of problem solving. Have you ever faced a problem or challenge and been frustrated because you did not find an answer in a reasonable amount of time? By teaching students a systematic approach with multiple alternatives to problem solving they will learn to be more persistent.

2. *Thinking and communicating with clarity and precision:* Specificity is an important skill. Expressing our thinking out loud is crucial to others understanding what we have to say. You have probably been in a situation in which you asked yourself what someone really was saying. Because of vague or incomplete expressed thoughts, we are misunderstood. Encouraging precision and clarity in your classes will help students build a skill that will be valued well beyond your class.

3. *Managing impulsivity:* One problem that makes working with young people an ongoing challenge is that they act before thinking. Adults are just as likely to do the same thing. This is impulsive behavior. Making sure you give students time to think before expecting an answer will encourage them to think more deeply. Wait time is important for receiving better answers to questions. By learning to think and reflect more carefully, students will make fewer errors and consider more alternative solutions to problems.

4. *Gathering data through all senses:* The five senses are the channel through which all information reaches the brain. By presenting a problem and modeling all the sensual stimuli that it presents, you will help students understand that they too can observe more fully by using all their senses. We noted in Chapter 12 that using music can enhance learning; this is an example of sense having to do with learning and thinking. "Show Not Tell" is a writing mantra that emphasizes the value of using senses to learn at a deeper level. Our experiences have much to do with our learning; that is why we suggest the models of instruction included in this book.

> *Those who have most at stake in the old culture, or are most rigid in their beliefs, try to summon people back to the old ideas.*
>
> —Marilyn Ferguson

5. *Listening with understanding and empathy:* You probably know someone with whom you love to talk, because they listen to you without interrupting. Listening is a skill that is so important that we were given two ears and only one mouth. Yet there is not a secondary school system that requires a listening course for graduation. Are you a good listener? What do good listeners do that makes them stand out? They can repeat what they have heard, paraphrase in their own words for understanding, and ask questions that get to the concepts being described. Good listeners have the sensory acuity to know the nonverbal signals that help understand the words at the level of intent. You have to be careful not to let your thinking influence what someone else is saying. Do not think of what you have to say next! Walk in the other person's shoes. Teach your students this and they will be successful in life.

A former student wanted to talk about a Civil War veteran when we were studying the Grand Canyon. Of course, there was a connection for him, in that he had taken a trip to Grand Canyon and learned of a former Civil War soldier who was the first to explore many of the areas of the Grand Canyon. It wasn't random for him to bring that up, although it sounded random for the other students in class and me! His nonlinear thinking (at least in my mind) was actually a great example of how the brain works to seek familiarity with every new learning (connections to prior knowledge). It also is an important reminder that we need to listen to and understand our students.

> Carpenters bend wood; fletchers bend arrows; wise men fashion themselves.
>
> —Buddha

6. *Creating, imagining, and innovating:* We all have the capacity to do more than we think we can. By learning creativity techniques we realize what we are capable of accomplishing. Creative people are driven by problem solving and not by rewards that may be associated with a solution. By encouraging your students to take risks and fail you will nurture their ability to be more creative and feel more successful. Failure should lead to success. When teachers support innovative solutions and imagination, students will gain better habits of mind.

7. *Thinking flexibly:* Looking at a problem from more than one perspective is helpful in arriving at a solution. Flexibility is useful in thinking and living situations. Your job as an educator is to encourage unique approaches to problems and projects. If you are open to your students, you will model what you want them to practice. You should be able to shift your thinking when approached with a solution that you have not thought about.

Keeping the "big picture" in mind at all times helps to promote flexibility. If you are flexible in your thinking, you are okay with dissonance. You can sift through conflicting data to arrive at creative solutions to challenges faced.

8. *Responding with wonderment and awe:* The world is wonderful and amazing. There are so many opportunities to learn about everything around us, yet some people try not to learn anything new. This habit of looking at the world with awe brings appreciation to us. Because the brain is so diverse in its capabilities, we should look at every experience as an opportunity for learning. Curiosity is a key to this habit and to the survival of lifelong learning.

9. *Thinking about thinking (metacognition):* We have talked about metacognition and its importance to learning. Reflection is useful as a practice. We get in touch with our inner self and evaluate our progress on the task at hand. When reflecting on our thinking and becoming aware of strategies we use, we learn to broaden our thinking because usually we have a limited view. Acting before thinking is usually a result of a lack of metacognition. When we think about our thinking and the consequences of our thinking, we act differently. If you know what you know and can filter out what do not know, you will seek knowledge that will make a difference in performance.

10. *Taking responsible risks:* Have you ever taken an unreasonable risk? Perhaps not on purpose; it was only after you started down a path that you realized it was unreasonable. Taking risks helps us grow and learn. The balance is that we take risks that may have some physical challenges but are not life-threatening. Aversion to risk should be in the context of the situation. Taking a financial risk if you have money to lose is different from taking that same risk when you are scraping by every day. Teach your students to take risks in the classroom with questions that they are not confident to ask. Support failure in learning and its value to the learning process. Risk when repeated helps us create a set of values around it and determines how far to go with the next risk. The plan is that our students learn to take physical risks and also learn to take intellectual risks.

11. *Striving for accuracy:* Do you ever go back and look over your work before feeling it's complete? You probably do that because you want it to be complete and accurate. If you as a teacher expect accuracy, you have to explain it and also offer suggestions on how to scrutinize work for accuracy and precision. If your students are turning in incomplete or sloppy work, do not accept it, and be careful about penalizing them. If you have set the

We know at lot more now than the "last time around"—the 1960s and 1970s—about how to work for smart schools. . . . The smart school finds its foundation in a rich and evolving set of principles about human thinking and learning.

—David Perkins

standard and created the rubric for students to follow, only then do they have a picture of what accurate work looks like. Crafting good work is a skill and habit that is useful in every aspect of school and work life.

Accuracy Illustrated

If we accepted 99.9 percent accuracy as "good enough":

- The U.S. Post Office would misdirect 18,322 pieces of mail each hour
- 1,314 phone calls would be misrouted every 60 seconds
- The IRS would misplace 2 million tax forms this year
- 12 babies would go home with the wrong family each day
- 22,000 checks would be drawn from the wrong account every 60 minutes

Source unknown

12. *Finding humor:* Humor is healing, and it helps us understand the human condition. A valuable premise is that if you are not having fun, you not doing it right. Taking our place in the world and ourselves too seriously is not useful or healthy. In the scheme of things, a humorous frame about our lives helps us go through the journey more easily. Discovering the humor in a situation is helpful in the creative process. Learn to laugh at yourself and with your students and you will be remembered.

13. *Questioning and posing problems:* We have emphasized the use of good questions in several places in this book. Questions help students understand a topic and lead to deeper learning. Asking questions at higher levels in Bloom's taxonomy (analysis, evaluation, and synthesis) will encourage better thinking. Teaching students to ask questions is as important as you asking effective questions.

Chapters 7, 8, and 13

14. *Thinking interdependently:* We have emphasized the value of students working together. Research indicates that the social aspect of learning is critical to deeper understanding of any topic. Our thinking and reflection is directly related to our personal experience. By working in groups, students hear other perspectives and have to define positions they may hold. Their thinking may be challenged, and as a result they either change an opinion or realize that they do have good perspective.

15. *Applying past knowledge to new situations:* In Chapter 3, where we discuss memory, we note that using prior knowledge to cement learning is an important tool for long-term memory. We learn from experience—good or bad. Being reminded of a past experience in a new or different context will improve our thinking.

Your job is to remind students that they have had a similar experience and to guide their thinking to take advantage of that experience. Experiences do not happen in isolation, they are connected to everything else that happens to us. As teachers we have to facilitate our students in making the connections to prior knowledge.

16. *Remaining open to continuous learning:* Knowing what we do not know and wanting to learn more is an essential human attribute. Continuous learning is not just important, it is essential to being successful.

Ted Sizer and the Coalition of Essential Schools

At the Coalition of Essential Schools, a school reform organization, Ted Sizer suggests the following statements as habits of mind. They overlap some of the habits that Costa and Kallick propose above as well as Debbie Meier's below.

> *Smart people don't learn . . . because they have too much invested in proving what they know and avoiding being seen as not knowing.*
>
> —Chris Argyris

- *The habit of perspective:* Organizing an argument, read or heard or seen, into its various parts, and sorting out the major from the minor matters within it. Separating opinion from fact and appreciating the value of each.

- *The habit of analysis:* Pondering each of these arguments in a reflective way, using such logical, mathematical, and artistic tools as may be required to render evidence. Knowing the limits as well as the importance of such analysis.

- *The habit of imagination:* Being disposed to evolve your own view of a matter, searching for both new and old patterns that serve well your own and others' current and future purposes.

- *The habit of empathy:* Sensing other reasonable views of a common predicament, respecting all, and honoring the most persuasive among them.

- *The habit of communication:* Accepting the duty to explain the necessary in ways that are clear and respectful both to those hearing or seeing and to the ideas being communicated. Being a good listener.

- *The habit of commitment:* Recognizing the need to act when action is called for, stepping forward in response. Persisting, patiently, as the situation may require.

- *The habit of humility:* Knowing your right, debts, and limitations, and those of others. Knowing what you know and what you do not know. Being disposed to and able to gain the needed knowledge, and having the confidence to do so.

- *The habit of joy:* Sensing the wonder and proportion in worthy things and responding to these delights.

As you can see, Sizer's habits are straightforward and would be easy enough to use with your students and label them as habits of mind. The list is not as comprehensive as the Costa–Kallick model and may be easier to use. There are similar themes and results of using either will provide students with a robust experience in thinking.

Deborah Meier and the Central Park East Secondary School Model

Debbie Meier and her staff at Central Park East are part of the Coalition for Essential Schools; they decided they did not want a long list of habits to remember. In conjunction with the Coalition of Essential Schools they came up with a series of questions that help promote habits of mind. These are clear; hence, no further explanation is required.

- The question of evidence, or "How do we know what we know?"
- The question of viewpoint in all its multiplicity, or "Who is speaking?"
- The search for connection and patterns, or "What causes what?"
- Supposition, or "How might things have been different?"
- Why any of it matters, or "Who cares?"

Following the Meier model makes your job easier. The drawback is that you may not be serving the highest needs of your students. It may be effective to use the three models in conjunction with each other.

> Habit is a cable; we weave a thread of it each day, and at last we cannot break it.
>
> —Horace Mann

CHAPTER WRAP-UP

It really doesn't matter if you choose one model or combine elements from these and other models. The point of offering the information in this chapter is so you will purposely teach habits of mind. You will discover that when you spend time building the intellectual capacity of your students you will also help them to become more competent in the subject they are studying. When you are explicitly teaching a skill, it should be identified by a name.

Habits of mind are not a particular method; rather they can be used with any method or model of instruction. You can include questions during lectures that will promote these habits. You might choose to pose questions that encourage habits when you set students on a cooperative learning exercise. If you use accelerated learning, you have another opportunity to include habits of mind. These habits of mind should be taught and encouraged in every class and with every topic or subject.

SPRINGBOARDS FOR FURTHER LEARNING

Key Names

Art Costa

Bena Kallick

Debbie Meier

Ted Sizer

Key Terms

critical thinking skills

habits of mind

intellectual habits

mental habits

CHAPTER 16

Teaching with Technology: A Field of Dreams—If You Build It, Will They Learn?

Great, I say, because of the excellence of the things themselves, because of their newness, unheard of through the ages, and also because of the instrument with the benefit of which they make themselves manifest to our sight.

—Galileo's Siderius Nuncius

Do You Know:

- What kinds of instructional technologies are available today?
- What the different definitions of e-learning are?
- What benefits drive the adoption of e-learning by schools?
- What the strengths and limitations of e-learning are?
- What ways technology can be used to support face-to-face classroom learning?

Introduction

Over the past 30 years, increasingly diverse and powerful technological tools have been introduced into schools: Personal computers and personal digital organizers; CDs, DVDs, and on-demand video communications; hypertext, multimedia, and simulation software; local, wide-area, and wi-fi networks and the World Wide Web; e-mail, wireless voice mail, and instant

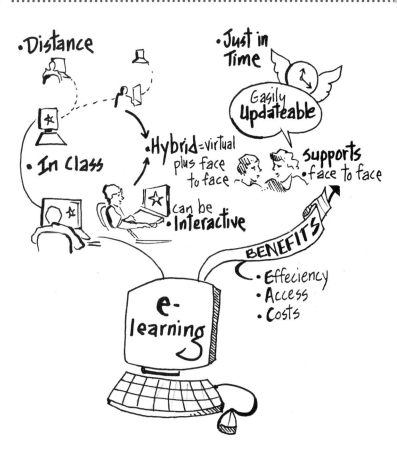

text messaging. Across the spectrum of postsecondary education, schools have been scrambling, and continue to try to keep pace with and take advantage of these innovations to better meet the interests and needs of their students, as well as to increase organizational productivity and efficiency and reduce costs. Classroom computers, networks, computer-mediated instruction, and user support systems are present in many schools, and the infrastructure and tools continue to be put into place. Indeed, the majority of postsecondary institutions offer some type of electronic-based instruction, or e-learning, today. A large majority of traditional 4-year residential schools offer online courses, and among 2-year public institutions just about all offer distance education today, with estimates that well over 100,000 distance education courses are offered.

These institutions include traditional "bricks and mortar" schools, and more recently, virtual, totally online universities. Both types are seeking to engage a generation of learners raised and absorbed in a rapid-paced, multimedia world of high-speed computing, communication, and entertainment technologies to meet student expectations of instantaneous access to both a real and a virtual universe of information and digital experiences. Schools are also embracing distant learning technologies to serve the increasing numbers of nontraditional students, whose harried and demanding lives make "education on a digital platter" a need. In this brave new world of technology, enthusiasts hail the ability of students to learn independently of time or place, arguing that e-learning will boost quality and expand access to postsecondary education. Some have gone so far as to prophesy the demise of traditional, residential campuses and the rise of a "new virtual age" in education and training.

Yet, despite investments of countless billions of dollars and the belief of many that technology is a solution for many of the challenges of education today and the face of its future, others are more cautionary. There are those who see some e-learning tools being adopted as "old wine in new bottles," sometimes used to achieve narrow learning objectives with limited application to the kind of education and training individuals need to become capable, lifelong learners in a knowledge economy. Furthermore, there are those who are concerned about schools, excited by the prospect of tapping into new student markets; with only dollar signs in their eyes, their attention is more on cost control than on learning outcomes. Therefore, despite the wave of e-learning technology sweeping across the teaching/learning landscape today, many are left uneasy, with many unanswered questions.

The purpose of this brief chapter is to touch upon both the enormous promise and limits of technology *in* the classroom, as well as look at technology *as* the classroom. It is hoped that this discussion can create a perspective for understanding new information and

> One of the enduring difficulties about technology and education is that a lot of people think about technology first and education later.
>
> —Martha Stone

communication technologies that can help you can use these technologies appropriately and for the greatest benefit.

Does IT Really Matter? The Main Issues Today

You may recall your first exposure to and journey along the road of innovations in IT, or information technology. Perhaps it began with word processors and DOS computers and the loud clatter of daisy-wheel printers. Then came along Windows-based systems and Macs, laser and color printers, scanners and increasingly sophisticated hardware devices and software programs. Of course, there was the World Wide Web, and now the development of high-speed networks and powerful search engines—all offering computing that is progressively less frustrating and more fun. We can only wonder what tomorrow might bring. Clearly, these and other innovations have transformed business and entertainment and communications. Possibly with every step, you may have believed that each new innovation would create a moment of critical mass that would also bring education across a threshold that would lead into a new world of teaching and learning.

So, where does the world of education really stand today, and what does the future have to offer? To a degree, the diffusion of e-learning technology into postsecondary classrooms and programs has progressed at a relatively slower and more uneven pace than it has in other fields. At the same time, as we have noted, e-learning is rapidly moving forward, and there is no disputing that teachers must master electronic teaching tools or likely will be mastered by them. What this all means, however, and whether we have entered a "promised land of learning" is a matter of debate. There are several issues at the heart of this matter.

A good teacher feels his way, looking for response.

—Paul Goodman

The Issue of Access

When it comes to the issue of access to postsecondary education, e-learning offers a definite plus. Technology—particularly the Internet and distant learning programs—has provided greater opportunities than ever before for students to participate in postsecondary education and career training. For the growing population of adult learners trying to balance the demands of work, family, and study, the availability and flexibility of e-learning have made pursuing and completing their education much easier. These benefits are proving to be valuable for traditional college-age students as well. Students, in general, now more often work as they study, and they have frequent scheduling conflicts because of other activities; e-learning provides them with options for fitting these other activities into their education. Ease of access through technology helps them keep their academic program on track as

A professor is one who talks in someone else's sleep.

—W.H. Auden

budget cuts in schools, especially public ones, have reduced the number of on-campus class sections and offerings. Moreover, education and training through the Internet is becoming big business worldwide, offering additional options for all types of learners. The clear trend is that online enrollments are predicted to increase, not only in terms of absolute numbers but growth rates as well.

Without question, e-learning has a growing presence in postsecondary education and training and is expanding access. Yet discussions about implementing and the educational value of e-learning continue to lack consensus.

I remember the first computer I bought in 1985. It was a no-name IBM-compatible with a 12-inch monochrome monitor, DOS operating system, 16-MHz CPU, 20-MB hard drive, and a 5½-inch floppy drive. I did get a modem a year or two later, but without the Internet all I could do was connect computer-to-computer with a more tech-savvy friend to get his help on occasion. Basically, I used it for word processing, printing out documents on a very slow and noisy letter-quality printer that was basically a typewriter hooked up to my PC. Today I have lightning-fast desktop system and a convenient laptop, wireless broadband Internet connections, and lots of sophisticated software programs. You might say "we have come a long way, baby" in the past 20 years.

Still, when it comes to the educational application of today's advanced technologies, I have witnessed little significant improvement in teaching and learning. Things may be easier and more convenient and productive in some regards. Yet, despite all the hoopla surrounding the latest and greatest and next innovations, many of the changes in education seem to be largely "skin deep." Some schools and faculty, in an effort to use the latest gadgets such as iPods in the classroom, are testing technology simply for the sake of technology, rather than using technology as a tool for learning. What I have observed is that the technology has often come first and the quality of learning is frequently an afterthought. Students often become the guinea pigs in "IT-enabled" classes as schools test whether the latest innovations actually help learning. When people focus too much on technology, they lose sight of the true purpose of technology, which is to facilitate learning in the classroom.

I believe, however, there is much promise with e-learning. The convenience and efficiencies provided by technology in the classroom are of clear value. Moreover, some institutions are now using advanced information and communication networks to create complex virtual learning environments that enrich learning and change the "heart" of education in dramatic ways. More than just virtual classrooms, these schools are using technologies to build and

sustain computer-supported communities. These are densely knit groups of learners that offer a "human face" to even remote relationships by providing personal support and sociability, as well as information and instrumental aid through an emphasis on collaborative learning approaches rather than on individual learning. I trust that these kinds of online learning communities represent the wave of the future as we move further along in the 21st century.

Beyond the Numbers—Two Concerns

Some educators look beyond the increasing numbers of students with greater access to postsecondary and have questions regarding how to use e-learning for other purposes.

What Is E-learning?

Part of the problem is the definition of *e-learning* itself. Is it online courses delivered at a distance? Is it the use of online tools to enrich, enhance, and extend content or learning? Is it totally online instruction, or are only portions of a course online? The terms surrounding e-learning can also be confusing. *Distance learning, distributed learning,* and *e-learning* are often used interchangeably to describe the delivery of postsecondary education programs and courses independently of fixed time and place (asynchronous), as well as those that are conducted at a fixed time (synchronous). On top of all this, students participating in such programs are a mixed bag. They can be residential, commuting, or at a distance, possibly even across the world.

In general, many educators assume *e-learning* to mean an entire course, with all the interactions between instructors and students conducted online. However, more recently the definition has been shifting from fully online courses to the use of technology in other settings. These are primarily:

1. to support face-to-face classroom instruction with students and teacher physically together for all teaching, and

2. to an offer instruction through *hybrid* courses that integrate intermittent face-to-face meetings and online components. (These are becoming more common as institutions struggle with increasing enrollments and inadequate classroom space, and are described at length below.)

Who *Really* Benefits Most?

Another issue with e-learning has to do with confusion about the expectations and needs of students themselves. As already stated, many of today's younger postsecondary students have grown up with technology; they expect technology not only to make their lives easier and more convenient but also to enhance and improve their learning experience. They want immediacy and automation as well. Just the idea of filling out a paper form, mailing it, and waiting for a response may be anathema to them. Yet, despite such expectations, we still need to be circumspect, for the common assumption that students want *more* technology may not be valid.

In theory, younger students should learn better through Internet courses because they have been surrounded by computers all their lives. Yet, some studies indicate that younger students are less satisfied with online learning than older students. Those who have to work a job and go to school at the same time so they can better schedule their learning opportunities prefer distance education—through Internet and video courses. But just the opposite is often true for those we might call members of the "Net Generation"; more technology does not necessarily mean more satisfaction. These students want interaction, not isolation. Rather than the demands of their daily lives, relationships are a driving force in their learning process. They desire the social experience and frequently need the structure that comes with being physically present in class with their peers and want to work face-to-face with their instructors. They also do not just want information pushed at them; they want engagement. Using an LCD projector and animated PowerPoint slides in a lecture, despite what many instructors would like to believe, is not necessarily using technology in an engaging manner.

Regardless of your views on and perceptions about the value of e-learning, it is here to stay. The train has left the station, and just about everyone needs to get on board. Although some may already be quite familiar with the many dimensions of e-learning, there are certainly others who may not yet be completely comfortable operating in e-learning environments. Wherever you personally position yourself, it is important to keep your focus on the learning and not just the technology. What follows are considerations for you to keep in mind to help you unleash student learning rather than possibly constrain it through the technology you may employ.

> *Acquire new knowledge whilst thinking over the old, and you may become a teacher of others.*
>
> —Confucius

The Different Faces of E-Learning

As alluded to in the issue regarding the different definitions of e-learning, computer-based instruction can take on different shapes and forms depending on student needs and institutional purposes and settings. The two dominant forms are virtual classrooms and hybrid classrooms.

The Virtual Classroom

A virtual classroom is a completely digital learning environment, with all course communications, interactions, and student work accessed and exchanged through networked computer and information systems. Everything occurs in a nonphysical, cyber environment. This is the environment of a distant learning course.

The Basic Features of a Virtual Classroom

The key technologies and features found in the virtual classroom can be grouped into three areas—communication/interaction, assessment, and support. Each of these has certain tools that enable success of education in the virtual classroom. Central among these areas are the communication or participation tools. These include the following:

- e-mail
- class announcements
- discussion boards
- file transfers and file management
- chat rooms
- virtual whiteboards
- journals or notes

All of these are the means of communication and transfer of information between students and the teacher. Some of these tools, such as the chat rooms and whiteboards, enable real-time (synchronous) communication, which is similar to face-to-face communication. Other tools, such as the discussion boards and e-mail, enable communication to occur at convenient times that suit student schedules and are not necessarily accessed at simultaneous or prearranged times (asynchronous). Schools commonly use any number of commercially available class management systems (CMS). Most prevalent are WebCT, Blackboard, and Prometheus. Each of which provides a convenient structure and tools for building and managing an online course. A free, open-source software program for creating online communities is MOODLE (from Moodle.org), which can be found easily on the Internet.

There are two basic kinds of virtual e-learning environments, independent, teacher-centered learning and collaborative, student-centered learning environments. Both styles contribute to the student's education, with collaborative learning often seen to be better suited to enhancing the quality of student learning.

The Independent Virtual Learning Environment

The independent virtual environment, which comprises the vast percentage of most e-learning, is conducted entirely online. It is teacher-centered learning, in which students learn in isolation without interaction with each other. All exchanges take place exclusively between the teacher and the student, whose learning is self-directed. The teacher

Two basic rules of life are: (1) Change is inevitable. (2) Everybody resists.

—W. Edwards Deming

provides information and feedback rather than facilitating learning activities. Students receive and respond to this information without collaboration and feedback from other students.

The structure of the content within an independent virtual classroom is relatively similar to a physical one. Both generally have content, lessons, assignments and homework, assessments, and some form of interaction between students and instructor. However, the means by which information and work is communicated or transferred from the teacher to student differs greatly. In a teacher-dominated virtual classroom, content that goes beyond what may be found in a course textbook is presented as online material, and it is rarely complemented by verbal discussions or explanations and little expectation for student-to-student interaction. (However, there may be informal discussion boards, chat rooms, and e-mail communications and supplemental online material that allow for but do not *require* student-to-student exchanges.)

Advantages of an Independent Virtual Classroom. In addition to the convenience of access, there are a number of additional advantages of an independent e-learning classroom over a traditional one for both students and teachers.

Personal and Hands-On Experience. Many concepts are difficult or impossible to represent or practice in a traditional classroom. For example, in a large number of disciplines, data analysis and interpretation is an essential but difficult concept to learn and practice by any means other than computer.

Archived Discussions and Other Materials. The technology allows convenient and instant access to information for reviewing and study. Having these materials available on demand not only promotes better learning opportunities but also accommodates the needs of students who may have missed an online activity.

The Development of Knowledge-Management Skills. The presence of technology in the classroom reflects the dramatic rise in the availability of readily accessible knowledge and communication tools online in the today's knowledge-centered workplace. Faculty can share their discipline-specific uses of technology with students that mimic some of their real-world applications.

Greater Flexibility and Adaptability. Electronic content can be updated more easily than printed material, saving time when preparing and adjusting material to suit lessons and individual student needs. These changes are instantly accessible to everyone enrolled, offering benefits to students, too.

> We teachers—perhaps all human beings—are in the grip of an astonishing delusion. We think that we can take a picture, a structure, a working model of something, constructed in our minds out of long experience and familiarity, and by turning that model into a string of words, transplant it whole into the mind of someone else.
>
> —John Holt

More Time to Respond to Student Communications. Teachers have a chance to construct the best possible response to students. This is often not possible in a traditional classroom, where answers are usually expected right away.

Collaborative Virtual Learning Environments

In contrast to an independent environment, in a collaborative e-learning course, technology is not just used as a platform to deliver instruction and manage the course (post syllabi, give and receive assignments, take attendance, request clarification and make comments via e-mail, etc.) Rather, learning emerges from an active and ongoing dialogue among both students and instructors to better understand and apply course material.

Collaborative e-learning systems go beyond posting materials on the Internet and the use of standard e-mail systems and informal discussion boards. They can include sophisticated conferencing/online collaboration systems designed to support classroom-like experiences, particularly group discussions and joint projects. They also may incorporate video and audio streaming of content, or video/audio conferencing for live and delayed interaction between students and teacher. Generally, these technologies are designed and used to support collaborative learning through structures that can transcribe discussions, stimulate and direct active participation, allocate assignment topics, and provide electronic assessment and feedback systems. Participation is generally asynchronous or "anytime/anywhere," with students able to connect at any time and from any location rather than having to be online at the same time, though the more ambitious programs occasionally bring students together in real time for live interactions. These enhanced systems may also organize and archive all student work and entries, marking and separating new from old content that has already been seen for greater efficiency.

It is important to appreciate, however, that as sophisticated as these technology tools are, they will only support group collaboration and facilitate the desired behaviors—they cannot produce them. For the group to adopt a structure of interaction that is collaborative in nature, an instructor must shape, model, and encourage the desired behaviors, and the students must be able and willing to participate regularly.

Advantages of the Collaborative Virtual Classroom. Well-designed online collaborative learning experiences offer all the benefits of an independent virtual classroom, along with additional ones. At their best, virtual classrooms become an immersive experience that fosters student interest, involvement, imagination, and interactivity. Some claim they can even be more engaging than a traditional classroom because of what is offered by new technologies.

The most incomprehensible thing about the world is that it is comprehensible.

—Albert Einstein

Expanded Knowledge Base. When properly designed and implemented, more information and knowledge can be shared and gained through the interaction and involvement with class members rather than just from print or electronic media or the teacher as sole authority.

Increased Opportunities for Active Learning. In a collaborative e-classroom, relatively passive learning approaches such as lecturing may still be valid. However, they are best used to introduce basic concepts that can be expanded on using technology-enhanced active-learning exercises. The one-on-one nature of computers and the highly interactive nature of many software programs enable a high level of individual engagement.

An Equal Chance to Be Heard. Often people's inhibitions are reduced in an environment in which text-based, online dialogue is used instead of face-to-face communication. Consequently, they are willing to get involved more by asking questions and participating in discussions.

Greater Classroom Diversity. As with any e-learning class, students from many geographical locations can enroll in collaborative virtual class-rooms. Because of the focus on student interaction, students have the advantage of working with others with diverse backgrounds and knowledge that can bring different ideas to their learning activities and projects.

The Development of Communication Skills. Although some students (particularly younger ones) may have a habit of relying on a very informal writing style with their e-mail and instant messaging, the reliance on regular course-related communications encourages the development of formal writing and social skills.

More Focus on Teaching Methods That Foster Understanding. Instructors can spend less time transferring information and knowledge and more time on helping students develop higher-order learning skills. They can also become facilitators of social learning as they guide students through collaborative assignments.

Disadvantages to Virtual E-Learning

As with any instructional approach, both independent and collaborative e-learning courses have their downside as well as their upside.

The Character of Class Communication. The most obvious limitation is the absence of verbal and visual tools typically found in the real class-room. Communication in the virtual classroom is, of course, completely text-based; body language, eye contact, and other verbal/visual cues are not present. This lack of face-to-face interaction is considered by many to be one of the most important elements of any learning experience. A good number of experts in the field of virtual classrooms and technology are concerned that the computer is replacing the "friendly face" of the teacher, and the absence of human qualities in the virtual classroom prevent students from experiencing some of the most important qualities of the best teachers—their passion for what they do, respect and concern for their students, an engaging manner, etc. This lack of a direct social experience also inhibits the building of trust among the students themselves.

Access. Proponents champion e-learning as a way to promote access to education. However, it also poses its own barriers. The technological requirements needed to enable full participation in the virtual classroom can become a disadvantage to some students. Such a classroom can be successful only if learners have personal access to and can use the communication tools used in the course. For example, if some students do not have a high bandwidth and adequate computer memory needed to efficiently access the Internet and download course material, they will be at a disadvantage. Also, the technological dependence of the virtual classroom can pose problems if there is an Internet connection failure or a similar technological problem that prevents students from completing a task. If there is no back-up plan in the case of a technological hindrance, students will miss out on the learning activity that was scheduled.

Problems only exist in the human mind.

—Anthony de Mello

Technology and Learning Skill Challenges. Generally, students must have adequate computing and communication skills. More importantly, since the majority of learning is text-based and self-directed, if students are used to being in a structured, scheduled environment they will be at a disadvantage and could likely get confused and fall behind. Moreover, because teachers are not as readily available in the virtual classroom as they are in the traditional classroom, students who usually need the ongoing support of the teacher may feel isolated. In addition, synchronous communication tools can also put some students at a disadvantage. They consist of real-time, text-based communication in which responses are often out of sequence because of varying typing abilities and differences in the Internet bandwidth among students. This can create confusion.

Suitability of Course Content and Instructional Activities. A difficult task that teachers face is the development of educational content that is interesting, relevant and important to students, and in an appropriate format. Instructors need to develop content to suit a class of students more diverse than they would expect to have in a traditional class (maybe from across the world) and whom they will never meet face to face.

They are also challenged to make the classroom inclusive and accommodative for the convenience of the students. It is tempting to simply transfer the syllabus of the traditional classroom to the virtual classroom. However, if this is done without modification to suit the unique character of the online environment, a valuable opportunity to improve educational content by taking advantage of the online format will be lost.

What follows is a description of a kind of e-learning format that many see as the answer to many of the challenges of completely virtual online instruction, the hybrid course.

The Best of Both Worlds?—Hybrid Classes

Although the term *e-learning* most commonly refers to learning spaces that exist completely independently of physical classrooms, e-learning tools also can work in conjunction with traditional classroom environments in what are known as "hybrid classes." The goal is to combine the best features of in-class teaching with the best features of online learning to promote active independent learning and reduce class seat time.

Hybrid courses are those in which a significant portion of the learning activities have been shifted from face-to-face instruction to online activities. Time traditionally spent in the classroom is reduced but not eliminated. In these settings the Internet is used to provide additional communication and material, but does not necessarily replace the learning that occurs in the physical classroom. At the same time, some activities conducted in the real classroom can be presented differently in virtual spaces, thus accommodating a wider range of student needs. Given these features, many traditional instructors who have little or no interest in teaching online courses are beginning to use information technology to enhance what they are already doing. In the process, classroom teaching is being expanded and redefined.

Different approaches to the hybrid model can be adopted based on personal instructional styles, course content, course sizes, and course goals. Some instructors may reduce class time by 25 percent to 50 percent, such as eliminating one class per week throughout the semester, meeting for several weeks and then not meeting for several weeks, or cutting nonproductive time from a longer evening course. Other mixes, of course, are also possible. Using computer-based technologies, instructors can use the hybrid model to redesign some lecture or lab content into new online learning activities, such as case studies, tutorials, self-testing exercises, simulations, and online group collaborations.

Advantages of Hybrid Courses

Hybrid courses offer a number of clear advantages over totally online courses, and there is evidence that a hybrid course model allows

Reality is the leading cause of stress among those in touch with it.

—Lily Tomlin

instructors to accomplish course learning objectives more successfully than traditional courses do.

Convenience Combined with Immediacy. Students and instructors experience greater convenience afforded by the online component without losing the valuable and much appreciated immediacy and social experience and interaction of face-to-face learning.

Flexibility. Instructors have more flexibility with and can add richness to their class activities. For example, teachers can use online options to expand access to course content for students. They are also able to better approximate a real-world setting through simulations and create more complex learning environments for students.

Efficiency. Instructional time can be used more efficiently. Face-to-face class time that in the past was needed to conduct classroom activities such as taking attendance, giving assignments, or providing directions can often be done online.

Quality of Learning. Students tend to learn more in the hybrid format than they do in traditional class sections or purely online environments. They have higher-quality work, better exam performance, and more meaningful discussions on course material.

Disadvantages of Hybrid Courses

About the only downside of a hybrid course is that for most instructors its development requires more time than developing a traditional one. This is primarily because of the effort needed to redesign the course and learning new techniques and technology skills. Still, the benefits can clearly outweigh these challenges.

Keys to Developing Hybrid Courses

The following instructional principles can help you tie together the face-to-face and online components of a hybrid course. In general, you will need to reexamine your course goals and objectives to design online learning activities that meet those goals and objectives. You will also need to figure out how to effectively integrate the online activities with the face-to-face meetings and prepare students to succeed in this unique learning environment.

Think Learning Rather Than Technology. As with any kind of course, consider what you want students to be able to do at the end of the term and what you must do each step along the way to get them there. When planning a major integration of digital communications technologies into a current course, however, your attention to learning objectives becomes even more important. You want to begin with attention to

One can resist the invasion of an army but one cannot resist the invasion of ideas.

—Victor Hugo

interactivity rather than the technology involved to avoid a counter-productive focus on the technology tools themselves. Simply putting materials on the Internet does not ensure that students will engage with and learn from them. You want to incorporate activities that require that students become involved in higher-order learning tasks and that get them to interact with each other.

Plan How You Will Use Classroom Time That Connects with the Online Work. Remember, a hybrid course brings together dissimilar elements of face-to-face and virtual instruction to perform common functions and achieve a shared result. Therefore, you will need to thoughtfully connect what happens in your classroom components with what goes online, as well as sequence assignments so that they go back and forth between one format and the other as seamlessly as possible to create a common learning space. You have to consider which in-classroom activities can be shifted to your online environment and how you will mix and match these activities. What information can be better transmitted online (such as your lectures), and what kind of teacher–student interactions should remain face to face (such as classroom discussions, question-and-answer sessions, and exams)? What would be the best mix of face-to-face meetings with online instruction (50–50? 25–75? Etc.)?

Decide on the Technological Tools You Will Want and Need to Use. With your learning goals in mind, ask yourself what technological tools will best serve these purposes. Will simple e-mail and the World Wide Web suffice? Or will a better choice be more comprehensive tools, such as course-management systems that facilitate the use of technology? The tools available have matured significantly. There are the course management tools mentioned already, such as Blackboard. Also, you can search archives of downloadable lessons and other material. For example, free major collections, such as Multimedia Education Resource for Learning and Online Teaching (MERLOT), the National Science Digital Library (NSDL), and the Co-operative Learning Object Exchange (CLOE), reduce the challenge of finding content. Other tools enable the editing of video and audio and the development of digital collections.

Be Prepared to Help Students Develop New Skills. As with any shift from a traditional classroom setting to something less familiar, your students may have to learn new skills to cope. For instance, they may find it challenging with the way course requirements are distributed over time, or have to learn how to cope with a possible new dependence on each other if you have created a collaborative learning environment. In addition, while many applications, such as e-mail, Web surfing, and

> It's a funny thing about life; if you refuse to accept anything but the best, you very often get it.
>
> —Somerset Maugham

word processing, may already be part of your students' lives, they may not have the full complement of skills needed to operate successfully online. They may need an orientation conducted in the physical class-room at the outset of the course to help them get up to speed on the technology and understand how to best manage their time.

These suggestions only offer a place to begin. As with any new approach to your teaching, there will be more things to learn and the need for practice. The rewards of pursuing a hybrid course, however, can be great for both you and your students.

CHAPTER WRAP-UP

In response to the question of "Does IT really matter?" we offer a definite "yes." You, of course, must ultimately answer this question for yourself. To help you do so, we conclude by breaking this rather broad question into a few more specific ones.

If you are going to achieve excellence in big things, you develop the habit in little matters. Excellence is not an exception, it is a prevailing attitude.

—Charles R. Swindoll

How do you personally expect to use e-learning? For some, this may mean teaching a fully online course. For others, it may mean the use of a course management system for a customary face-to-face course or a hybrid class. Or perhaps it means using computer and other technol-ogy in a traditional physical classroom settings to support instruction and learning.

What experience and expectations do students bring to your courses? You should not assume you understand your students' experience and expectations regarding e-learning, and you may need to ask them. Many students, not just younger ones, desire the personal character of traditional instruction and will resist the impersonal interface of some e-learning tools and environments.

Are you focused both on technology and on learning? Your students are much more likely to focus on "learning" than on "e-learning." Recall the qualities of those considered the best teachers. Personalization and interaction are important facets of successful learning environments. Students consistently say they want to interact with faculty who are ex-perts and who care about them, and they are frequently less concerned about the medium of the interaction. Therefore, can you personalize, customize, and increase interaction and improve learning *without* using technology? If so, you may want to forgo the high-tech stuff and focus on the overall quality of the learning environment.

It is our belief that the if you want to use technology, the inclu-sion of technology in hybrid courses offers the best use by bringing together the strengths of traditional face-to-face teaching with those of an online course. Ideally, when making your decisions about what tools to use and when to do so, we suggest using those that do the following:

1. augment teaching and learning to meet the needs of individual learners or groups of learners,

2. help students to develop information and knowledge inquiry, management, and display skills,

3. simulate real-world phenomena, including modeling physical, social, and conceptual relationships, and

4. call for student communication and collaboration, including the effective use of multimedia and online collaboration tools.

When properly designed and implemented, e-learning can prove to be a powerful way to reinvent the teaching that you already do. And e-learning will certainly have an increasingly important role in post-secondary education. However, just as students do not focus on the technology but on what they want to accomplish, we also need to do so. Hopefully the "e" of e-learning will slip into the background and the technology will take its proper place as an enabler rather than as the focus.

SPRINGBOARDS FOR FURTHER LEARNING

Key Names

Blackboard
Co-operative Learning
    Object Exchange
MERLOT

MOODLE
National Science Digital
    Library
WebCT

Key Terms

computer-mediated instruction
computer-based instruction
distance education
distant learning

e-learning
instructional technology
online learning
virtual classrooms

> *Respect your fellow human being, treat them fairly, disagree with them honestly, enjoy their friendship, explore your thoughts about one another candidly, work together for a common goal and help one another achieve it. No destructive lies. No ridiculous fears. No debilitating anger.*

—Bill Bradley

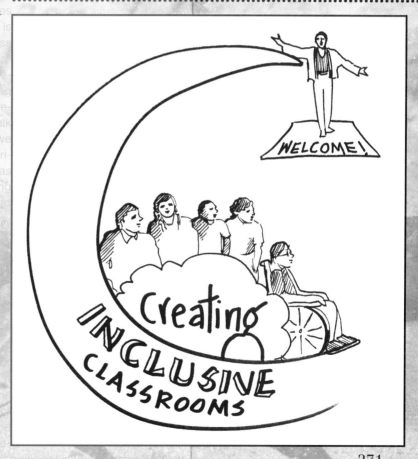

371

Introduction

American society is more diverse now than at any time in the past, and this diversity is reflected in postsecondary education today. Students bring with them rich and varied backgrounds and experiences that shape their interpersonal interactions inside and outside the classroom. To teach effectively in such an environment, you will want to understand the different backgrounds and experiences your students bring into your classroom and explore ways to foster an open, supportive environment for all. No matter what subject you teach, you may also need to examine some of your own unconscious assumptions with the goal of creating inclusive classrooms.

Inclusive classrooms are settings in which you and your students work together to create and sustain an environment in which all students feel safe and encouraged to express their ideas, views, and concerns. Such classrooms are places in which thoughtfulness, mutual respect, and the success of all are valued and promoted. In large part, this means teaching using many of the strategies we have already suggested throughout this text. Teachers who follow these strategies create strong personal relationships and continually build rapport. Instructors in inclusive classrooms use a variety of teaching methods in order to facilitate the academic achievement of each student. This means teaching content that can be appreciated from the multiple perspectives and varied experiences of your students. The content is presented in a manner that reduces students' feelings of being ignored or marginalized and, whenever possible, helps them understand that their experiences, values, and perspectives influence how they construct knowledge in any field or discipline.

An inclusive classroom is also one in which you attempt to be responsive to students on both an individual and a cultural level. This will largely depend on the kinds of relationships created between and among you and the students in the classroom. The nature of these interactions will be a function of many factors, including:

1. your assumptions and awareness of potential multicultural and gender issues in classroom situations;

2. your knowledge about the diverse backgrounds of your students;

3. how you plan class activities, as well as the ways students are grouped for learning; and

4. your decisions, comments, and behaviors during the process of teaching.

In addition, your effectiveness in creating an inclusive classroom will depend on your leadership and the example you set. Through your modeling and direction your students can become more aware of their assumptions, and be more informed, sensitive, and conscious about ethnic, racial, and gender issues. Unless students are informed about their own attitudes—and the possible ramifications of those attitudes in interactions with others who are different—their fears and reactions can generate tension in the classroom.

In this unit we explore the factors that you need to be aware of when working to create an inclusive learning environment, including issues and differences in language, culture, gender, age, and learning abilities. We also address ways of dealing with the inevitable problems and conflicts that will arise in your classrooms despite your best efforts to make them supportive of all students.

CHAPTER 17

Grace under Fire:
Dealing with Difficult Students
and Difficult Situations

*Difficulties are meant to rouse, not discourage.
The human spirit is to grow strong by conflict.*

—William Ellery Channing

Do You Know:

- What are some of the common problems you may encounter with students?

- What are some reasons for these problems?

- How you can prevent these problems?

- How you can best handle these problems once they arise?

- What skills you may need to manage these problems appropriately?

Introduction

Imagine, you have just finished what you experienced as a great class. Your students were engaged. They freely shared ideas in a lively discussion, made insightful comments and asked probing question. Feeling good as you pull together your class notes and materials, a student comes up to you to tell she was offended by some things several students said during the class and by the fact that you failed to realize anything inappropriate had even happened. You are caught off guard

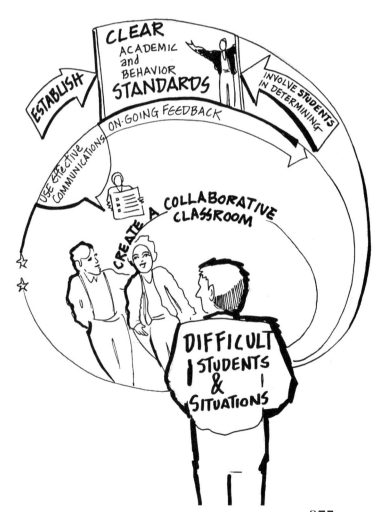

375

and at first have no idea what to say. How would you respond to this or another challenging situation?

A problem or conflict with a student or group of students or among students themselves in the classroom is a stressful experience that many teachers encounter at some point during their teaching careers. Indeed, if you teach long enough, it is almost inevitable that you will encounter difficult students and situations, and there is evidence that suggests that disruptive, uncivil, and unethical behaviors are becoming more common. This may range from insensitive jokes or offensive comments or plagiarism to outright harassment and cheating. When conflict occurs, you and your students may leave the classroom angry, distressed, uncomfortable, and perhaps feeling hurt. No two conflict situations or problems are exactly alike. Problems and conflict situations involve different individuals—individuals who possess distinct values and unique communication skills—and each may call for its own unique solution.

There are a number of reasons for problems and conflicts. Sometimes they may be age- or gender-related. For example, some research indicates that young male students are less concerned at times with ethical considerations and less aware of how their behavior may impact others. Or it may be personal beliefs, attitudes, or problems students bring into the classroom that negatively affect their learning, that of others, and/or a classroom environment. Lack of self-confidence, a learning disability, or family or financial concerns, for instance, may raise anxiety levels and create tension that can cause a student to act out. Also, as mentioned in the unit introduction, our schools are more diverse than at any time in our history, composed of students who lack awareness regarding the values and customs of others.

Further compounding this diversity is that students are often in competition for seats in overcrowded classrooms. In both public and private institutions, responses to budget cuts and taxpayer-driven accountability have, in some cases, resulted in downsizing faculty, the creation of larger classes, and greater competition for admission into courses required for degrees. Finally, according to some authors, the changing characteristics of college students have amplified conflict in postsecondary education. For example, students' need to obtain a degree to secure employment or advance their careers is stronger than ever. Increasingly, students also seem to expect to receive a desired grade, regardless of performance. This particular issue, in part, may be related to the notion of *student-as-consumer*. This is no longer a just a perspective within the for-profit segment of postsecondary education and is becoming increasingly influential in private and public nonprofit institutions as well. Within this model, education is a product to be sold, and students exchange money for knowledge. Some believe that among other things, this perspective lowers quality and effectively undermines social and civic values. Students who expect a passing

> Trust men and they will be true to you; treat them greatly and they will show themselves great.
>
> —Ralph Waldo Emerson

grade in exchange for their tuition can become oppositional and/or hostile when this exchange does not transpire.

Practical Strategies to Reduce or Eliminate Student-Related Problems

Chapters 4 and 5

Have you ever wondered why some teachers seem to have so little trouble with classroom management? Are they just born good instructors who command the attention and respect of their students? Although this may be true in part, it is hardly the whole story.

What many good teachers intuitively grasp or have learned from experience is that there are many good teaching practices that can be used to prevent conflicts and problems from occurring. Also, when they find themselves on the "front line" of a conflict or problem, they have learned ways of effectively handling them. Some of these strategies and skills were briefly introduced in Chapter 7 (e.g., regarding the facilitation of good discussions and group interactions). Elaborations on these and additional ideas are addressed here. These include some you can use individually, such as the use of effective communication skills, not being defensive, setting a good example, spelling out expectations, defining appropriate conduct, getting regular feedback, establishing a collaborative learning environment, reframing potential conflicts, and reengaging students. Effective approaches also include supportive school policies and processes, such as student grievance and faculty orientations.

Refer to Field Guide

Establish Clear Academic and Behavioral Expectations

Chapter 4

Establishing clear academic and behavioral expectations begins with your course syllabus. A good syllabus is more than a statement of educational objectives and activities. Consider it also as a contract between yourself and your students, as well as a contract among students themselves. As stated in Chapter 5, during the first class, rather than simply distributing your syllabus, carefully review the contents of the document to ensure that your students understand course objectives, expectations, classroom behavioral standards (which should be agreed-upon ground rules stated in a positive way), and evaluation criteria. A careful review with students can hopefully preempt misunderstandings (such as regarding assignment dates or procedures) or frustration that can result from ambiguous or poorly constructed syllabi. Also, be ready to continually evaluate syllabi to ensure that expectations are clear and concise. Student anxiety and resentment grows when there is a lack of clarity. A common concern among students is faculty who arbitrarily and independently change course objectives and expectations. When such behavior occurs, students can become confused and even angry regarding the direction of the course and newly established expectations. In short, students dislike professors who abandon initial learning agreements, alter assignments, and re-design courses in midstream without proper notice and explanation.

Also use your syllabus to communicate appropriate interpersonal boundaries and classroom behavior. Spell out unacceptable behavior, such as chitchatting and mindless talking during lectures. Also articulate student codes of courtesy. To set standards and the desired tone for a civil classroom, consider beginning with yourself. As mentioned in Chapter 5, establish your authority and credentials early on. This includes not only what you tell them about yourself, but how you project yourself—your professionalism and leadership. Ignoring important professional boundaries between yourself and students can quickly lead to a loss of student respect and possibly contribute to student confusion about their roles and place in the classroom. This, of course, does not mean you cannot be friendly and informal with your students; however, it does mean knowing what is appropriate in the context of your classroom. For example, in an effort to get your students to like you and create a relaxed environment, you may begin to fraternize with students or use frequent humor. Although sounding innocuous, you may unknowingly cross a boundary at the cost of your credibility and their respect.

Use Effective Communication Skills and Set an Example

You can remain respectful and manage student behavior through effective communication and interpersonal skills. This can include:

- Using polite language
- Demonstrating an inclusive attitude
- Teaching the language of disagreement
- Respectfully listening to students
- Using "I" statements
- Serving as role model for respect, common courtesies, and understanding

In general, work toward speaking *with* rather than *at* students. Students who sense you are genuinely trying to understand and honor their perspectives are probably less likely to feel disregarded or belittled in front of their peers. Conversely, students who feel insulted or need-lessly ridiculed may retaliate by inviting other students to complain about the course requirements or by constantly challenging you or the content. Clearly, communication may take a good deal of effort with some students, and do not underestimate the value in having other

> *The glue that holds all relationships together—including the relationship between the leader and the led—is trust, and trust is based on integrity.*
>
> —Brian Tracy

Refer to Field Guide

Chapter 5

students observe your concern and regard for a student who may be struggling to articulate an idea or response. Moreover, setting a tone of respect and patience can be invaluable when establishing an overall trusting rapport with students.

With regard to serving as a good example, it is not uncommon for even the most experienced teachers to fail to recognize that they may be the source of problems. You and your students are partners in generating and exacerbating conflicts. You can inadvertently provoke disruptive and even hostile student behavior by publicly criticizing, embarrassing, or invalidating students (e.g., remarking that a question is ridiculous). As we have emphasized already, it is very important to create a positive learning climate. You can do so in large part by acting warm, friendly, and motivational; maintaining a positive attitude toward students and demonstrating an interest in them will do much to establish conditions that can prevent many problems from arising in the first place. So if you want your students to treat each other respectfully, begin by doing so yourself and show your students the same courtesies you want from them.

Trust, but verify.

—Ronald Reagan

Create a Collaborative Learning Environment

We have presented throughout this text the value of designing classroom experiences that focus on collaborative learning. Doing so not only fosters better learning but also can reduce the competitive character of many classroom environments. Therefore, as we have encouraged you to consider already, try replacing a traditional transmission model of education with learning environments influenced by constructivist learning principles, which value prior experience and knowledge and welcome appropriate challenges, questioning, and debate from students. This will support both better learning and strong student connections. Establishing a cooperative learning environment involves several key ingredients such as effective social and team-building skills. When creating a cooperative learning environment, your role modeling can be a powerful tool. As alluded to earlier, the onus is placed on you to remain sensitive to the needs of your students and, more importantly, their behavior and responses toward their classmates.

Chapters 2 and 3

Personally, my main strategy for managing my classrooms is to devote a significant amount of time to creating a respectful and friendly classroom environment, starting with the first class meeting. When I began my teaching career I did this with a focus on better student learning, but soon saw how it prevented many potential problems

(continues)

and conflicts. I have over 25 years of teaching, yet I still experience conflicts and inappropriate student behavior. Early on, I learned that my initial response often determined whether the classroom conflict situation would escalate.

Ideally, your initial response should be to realize that conflict exists. This seems like a fairly obvious step to take; however, for many new teachers or those who may be teaching a course for the first time, admitting to yourself that classroom conflict exists can be a truly difficult step to take. Interpersonal conflict is not generally perceived as a pleasant or positive experience, and thus it is tempting to avoid it altogether. Avoiding or ignoring this conflict may be a way for one to "cope" with it. However, it is rarely productive in the long run, and I have learned that conflicts need to be addressed.

One approach I've learned to use involves a shift in my thinking about conflicts. I realized that a conflict in the classroom setting does not have to be viewed as a negative experience, but rather as an experience that my students and I can learn from. Productive conflict resolution demands that one engage in active discursive listening and dialogue, and I have explored specific conflict resolution models to assist with successful resolution.

One model that I have found valuable is Adam Curle's four-step "Framework for Moving to Peaceful Relations." Curle recommends that we:

1. educate ourselves about the conflict we are involved in (this requires that we also educate ourselves about specific power imbalances that exist in the conflict relationship),

2. confront the conflict situation through controlled communication,

3. negotiate the groundwork or rules that will help prevent future conflict, and

4. then work in support of a sustainable resolution and peace.

When steps 1 and 2 are practiced regularly so that conflict does not recur, we can move successfully to long-term harmonious interpersonal relations. Of course, not everyone perceives and addresses conflict in the classroom in a similar way. You will need to adopt distinct conflict practices based on your own personality, values, and teaching styles and on the specific factors—the student's personality, values, and class dynamics—that are involved. But one thing that I have consistently found is that seeking to resolve conflicts rather than ignoring or dismissing them creates positive interpersonal relations that powerfully reaffirm our commitment to our students, and in turn, our students' commitment to productive learning.

Chapter 9

> When people honor each other, there is a trust established that leads to synergy, interdependence, and deep respect. Both parties make decisions and choices based on what is right, what is best, what is valued most highly.
>
> —Blaine Lee

Build In Ongoing Feedback

This also is not a new idea. Feedback in the form of formative assessments and course evaluation not only improves student success and the quality of your instruction, but also gives your students a voice and a sense of control over their classroom experiences. When reviewing student feedback, look for patterns (both positive and negative) or blind spots that can be addressed to prevent or defuse hostile student-teacher or student–student interactions. Many problems arise not because they are ignored but simply because they go unrecognized. Exhibiting a willingness to evaluate your own work and being open to student observations helps you keep track of where your students are at, and contributes to an open, honest, and flexible learning environment. In addition to student evaluations, try consulting with peers or peer reviews to help you identify and confirm patterns, strengths, and needs.

Reframe and Defuse Conflicts

Clear classroom policies, ground rules, and strong expectations about classroom behavior can be helpful in averting problems or addressing conflict and tension that may emerge during classroom discussions. But what can you do when ground rules fail and conflict emerges between you and/or among students?

The purpose of reframing behavior is to sidestep unnecessary power struggles. In essence, reframing can assist faculty in viewing student behaviors in a different light. To reframe, you need to plan ahead and understand that such situations will arise despite your best efforts to create a respectful learning environment. For example, the perspective that a student challenge may be an attempt to seek clarification or get additional information is useful in helping to avoid personalizing ill-mannered student responses or reactions.

The reframing process allows you to *respond* productively rather than *reacting* harshly to students. This means avoiding personalizing student remarks and responding nondefensively and respectfully to a student's comment or behavior. Rather than reacting and entering into arguments with students, simply acknowledge concerns or empathize with their frustration. For example, if a student excessively criticizes the content and process of a course, there is obvious disappointment, which can be acknowledged. Further, behind a criticism is a willingness to speak out for the betterment of the course that can be noted.

When it comes to defusing a situation, consider some of the following:

- *Time Out.* It works for little kids, and it can work for you and your students. For example, if a friendly debate escalates into an angry exchange between one or two students, or between you and a student, signal a time out and break up the debate or end the argument. This action allows you to regain control of the class and for everyone to regain their composure.

- *Teachable Moment.* Sometimes awkward situations or misunderstandings can be used as teaching tools. If you or a student makes a comment that is misunderstood or inappropriate, apologize (if appropriate) and get the class engaged in a discussion of the issue. Strong emotions not only create problems, they also can provide a powerful impetus for students to become more involved in what is going on in your class.

- *Deflect the Issue.* Deflect the conflict and dialogue away from the individuals involved and get the whole class into a discussion on the topic. For example, you might say: "The comment stated is a reflection of the beliefs of many others. Are the assumptions underlying such a view valid? What do you think about this issue?"

- *Address the Concerns of All Involved.* When you do have a difficult situation, you should address the behaviors, views, issues, and concerns of both those directly involved in the incident as well as the student(s) who may have witness or been the object of a controversial or hurtful statement or action. One strategy is to state that if anyone needs to talk to you specifically about the incident, they can do so after class. If you have a good relationship with the affected students, you might initiate an out-of-class meeting to hear their concerns.

> *Respect Commands itself and can neither be given nor withheld when it is due.*
>
> —Eldridge Cleaver

A Simple Approach to Handling a Difficult Situation—Stop, Assess, Listen, Respond

- *Stop.* This is basically the old "count to 10" technique. Before you say or do anything, give yourself a few moments to step back and collect yourself emotionally so you can move forward in as calm a manner as possible.

- *Assess.* Here you reflect on what has happened to examine the circumstances and people involved. There may be clues to the context of what happened that can give you insight into how to handle the situation. These can include the trigger for the problem or crisis, the facial expressions, tone of voice, and bodily language of those involved, etc. It may be even the time of day (e.g., perhaps it is a night class and students are tired and overreact to a rather innocuous remark).

- *Listen.* Before speaking yourself, give others a chance to be heard. Your listening will, of course, give you more of the information you will need to figure out how to deal with what has happened. Just as importantly, listening to those who may be aggrieved or distressed and making them feel they have been heard in itself can defuse emotions and possibly be all that is needed to resolve a conflict.

- *Respond.* For many, this is the first step. It should be your last. After stopping, assessing, and listening you will be much more prepared to say something or take action that can lead to the best solution. And remember not to be defensive or judgmental, which for most of us are typical responses.

> What women want is what men want. They want respect.
>
> —Marilyn vos Savant

Repair Relationships with Students

Despite your best efforts, there is still the likelihood of strained relationships, and you will need to reengage students and resolve differences. The process provides you with opportunities to identify patterns or issues that would otherwise persist. Some of you may be reluctant to pursue this approach out of a concern regarding the loss of status. On the other hand, investing in the reengagement process shows that you are someone who is genuinely committed to student learning and personal growth, and that can increase student recognition and respect.

Although you are encouraged to establish mutually satisfying relationships with students, we advise you to meet with uncivil students to resolve issues in the company of other staff. In cases in which a male faculty member wants to reengage a female student, a female colleague should be invited to participate to reduce the possibility of allegations of faculty misconduct.

Remember, You Are Not Alone

Institutional Support

Each school administration should establish clear policies regarding student behavior and ethics. The information you include in your syllabus should include these policies. Discussing these policies openly may seem a distraction that uses time needed for instruction, but the issue goes much deeper than possible problems in your classroom. Your students' behavior in your classroom is a reflection of who they are and who they will be when they enter the workplace to practice their disciplines. Thus, ethical issues related to their intended professions can be an important element of their future success that students need to appreciate. This can prepare students to recognize conflicting circumstances they may encounter in their professional practice and to guard themselves against behaviors that may be self-defeating.

We also suggest a "back-to-the-basics approach" of conflict resolution during college/university or departmental gatherings. Although it sounds simplistic, it is important that faculty be reminded of the potential ramifications of uncivil student behavior, with possible workshops designed to avoid classroom conflict and introduce conflict-management skills to faculty and staff. Although some faculty may scoff at the notion of discussing the importance of promoting civil behavior in the classroom, the negative ramifications of such behavior cannot be ignored.

Our lives improve only when we take chances—and the first and most difficult risk we can take is to be honest with ourselves.

—Walter Anderson

Student Grievance Process

Unfortunately, it is not uncommon for students to report that their concerns are trivialized and easily dismissed. For this reason and to prevent student–faculty conflict from escalating, just about all schools and departments have student grievance processes in place. These policies and procedures provide a platform for student complaints and concerns to be taken seriously and appropriately investigated.

If fair and effective student grievance procedures are lacking (sometimes the procedures may be only symbolic and lack integrity), you and your students should request an institutional policy change. Training for faculty and students about the grievance procedure should be implemented. The institution must also make a determination about the privacy and right-to-know issues surrounding the grievance process.

CHAPTER WRAP-UP

There is no "magic formula" for working with distressed students. In some situations your normal ways of coping may not work. Consequently, you may feel unable to manage the situation, which can lead to feelings of panic, an inability to think, or a tendency to act impulsively or overemotionally and in ways you may regret later.

Afterward, it is not uncommon to think of different ways you could have coped with the situation. There can be a tendency to try to find out whose fault it was, or to assume that the situation occurred because things went wrong. Such blaming is not helpful, as fault is rarely the issue, and the factors leading up to such situations by their nature are often complex and difficult to handle. It is more useful, therefore, to consider in advance the possibility of such situations and be prepared to deal with them.

We encourage you to continually examine how your teaching styles, conduct, interpersonal communication, and overall learning climate can inadvertently contribute to unruly (and potentially dangerous) classroom environments. Be realistic in your expectations of student performance. Be aware of unreasonable demands in terms of course content, assignments, and examinations. In other words, rather than holding a narrow perspective wherein students are viewed as culprits, remain introspective regarding your personal attitudes and behaviors.

Still, there will likely be situations in which problems and conflicts will arise. Thus, you should consider how you can improve your conflict-resolution skills, be ready to seek out the advice of colleagues, and of course, get administrative support. Discontent among students can also swell when issues remain unresolved. Remaining isolated, feeling trapped, or allowing matters to intensify can result in elevated stress, job dissatisfaction, and even personal harm.

We also suggest that you remain vigilant to the changing landscape of the postsecondary classroom (e.g., greater diversity, larger student numbers in classes, the student-as-consumer perspective, the pressure to obtain degrees for employment). There should be open, in-class discussions of how competitiveness and personality-type factors impinge on individual personal and ethical behavior. Consider reaching beyond the traditional responsibilities of knowledge transfer and inspire students to reflect on the importance of behaving in ways that will lead to honorable and mutually respectful relationships. Encourage students to examine their own characteristics and appreciate alternative ways of behaving as an important step toward preparing them to be ethically responsible citizens and successful professionals.

SPRINGBOARDS FOR FURTHER LEARNING

Key Names

Conflict Research Consortium
Adam Curle

Key Terms

academic dishonesty	mediation
civility	student code of conduct
college classroom management	student ethics
college student behavior	student conflict resolution
conflict resolution	

CHAPTER 18

Diversity: Including All Learners

We all live with the objective of being happy; our lives are all different and yet the same.

—Anne Frank

Do You Know:

- The student population will become even more diverse in the future?

- Diversity is not just culture and gender?

- Multiple instructional methods better meet diverse student needs?

- We all have unconscious prejudices?

- Meeting diversity head on is healthy?

Introduction

Our world continues to change. Diversity has always been a part of all of us. Diversity is what makes our world a wonderful place. The unfortunate thing is that most of us did not grow up with much diversity. This makes it difficult to adjust to the diversity that shows up in our lives. We have our own personal cultural experiences, and as important as they are, we are missing the understanding of all the alternative perspectives that make diversity easier to live with and accept.

387

Now, as you begin teaching students from many diverse groups, you may wonder what to do to make it work. Perhaps you have spent years working in isolation from a diverse culture. Or maybe you worked with many people from different cultures. Either way you need to consciously attend to diversity issues in your classroom.

What Do We Mean by *Diversity*?

Diversity refers to race, culture, class, gender, age, sexual orientation, religion, language, and physical abilities.

- *Race* refers to populations distinguished by skin color, hair color, body shape, eyes, and other physical characteristics.
- *Culture* refers to ideas, art, customs, skills, etc. of a group of people passed on from generation to generation.
- *Class* often refers to status, power, or wealth.
- *Gender* refers to being male or female.
- *Age* refers to generational differences.
- *Sexual orientation* is being heterosexual, gay, lesbian, or bisexual.
- *Religion* refers to an organized belief in a divine or superhuman power and specifically how one practices that religious belief.
- *Language* refers to those in the United States who do not speak English as a first language.
- *Physical abilities* refer to any physically handicapping condition.

Now the question arises in your head, "How do I possibly deal with all these diversity issues?" Our simple answer is: One issue at a time. Every diversity issue will not show up at the same time in the same class. You still must be prepared for the eventuality that you will be faced with students from diverse backgrounds. Preparation is critical to your success in providing the most open classroom possible.

What About You?

Have you had experiences with discrimination? Were you the receiver or perpetrator? Do you hold prejudices that you are aware of and have dealt with? Have you grown from these experiences? If you have lived in a diverse community or worked in a setting that included people from many backgrounds you have formed opinions based on those experiences. Opinions are important, and too often we generalize about an entire group based on an isolated incident, even ones that do not directly involve us. Be careful not to fall into that trap. Learn about others by listening and asking questions. Everyone likes to talk about

> I grew up in a military family. My Dad was a Navy chaplain. We moved lots of times and I went to eight schools. When we were stationed on a military base, we attended school with everyone who was on the base. There wasn't a lot of diversity, but there was some. I vividly remember moving from the base at Guantánamo Bay, Cuba, to the one at Norfolk, Virginia. I was going into 5th grade. We lived in a new subdivision, and the second year there I attended the new school in our neighborhood. An eight-foot fence surrounded it. Just on the other side of that fence was a depressed black ("colored" in those days) community.
>
> I didn't have any black kids in my class; in fact, there were none in the school. I discovered prejudice secondhand because it wasn't about me but certainly it was about people I could see. We were in the midst of segregation. I had not experienced that, and was distressed that it was so. Over the years I have reflected on that experience a lot. And because of it I have done my best to accept others not by the color of their skin or the sound of their voice but for who they are on the inside. I don't claim to be free of prejudice, but I work on being accepting of others every time I meet someone different from me. It makes me sad today to think of how we have held people back in the United States because they didn't fit a certain mold. I work to change that every day.

themselves. Think about your life experiences and reflect on your openness factor.

As a teacher your job is to accept all those who come into your class. Students are graded on merit, nothing else. When you set your standards of performance you cannot have a double standard. Fair is fair. Let's look at each of the diversity issues more closely.

Race

This is probably the biggie for most people. Because we all belong to a race, we accept that ours is not only important but in most cases the best. Race is not so simple, though. Recent DNA samples gathered from around the globe are being studied to determine early migration patterns. What this project, sponsored by National Geographic, has concluded is that everyone comes from somewhere in Africa. It is estimated that migration started over 40,000 years ago, and the DNA traveled far and wide. By securing samples from over 100 countries, the project has mapped migration over the globe.

Since we all seem to come from the same gene pool originally you must be careful about race beliefs. Do not assume what you do not know. Race discussions used to happen more often in the 20th century than they do now. We have become less open about these discussions, probably because of globalization and terrorism. Your job is to assure each student that he or she is valued and respected in the same way as every other student. You also need to protect students from each other when you observe or hear prejudicial comments. That under-current (sometimes more obvious) can undermine your classroom and credibility. Set students up to live with a high standard of acceptance and most of them will.

Culture

Culture can be deceiving; one cannot determine by seeing someone what culture they grew up in. Again, do not assume anything by looks alone. People migrate around the world and grow up in cultures that may be quite different from what their race would indicate. Black tribes in Kenya have a completely different cultural upbringing than blacks in Jamaica. You may have many races in a class and few cultures. Culture is based on how we grew up, not necessarily where. Culture comes from our family and traditions they value. It has to do with art and stories, music and food, not location.

Learning about other cultures is exciting and helps us to appreciate and respect the differences. Travel is a great cultural experience, even if you take a road trip around the United States. We have many cultural differences from Maine to California and from Alaska to Florida. Of course, if you have traveled to other countries you have experienced those cultures as well. You will have multiple cultures in your classes; learn about them, as that will help you understand more about your students and the values they bring to class based on cultural upbringing.

> We have become not a melting pot but a beautiful mosaic. Different people, different beliefs, different yearnings, different hopes, different dreams.
>
> —Jimmy Carter

Class

Class is more evident these days in more primitive societies; however, we have vestiges of class in our everyday lives. Class is determined by a number of factors, including occupation, education, income, wealth, land ownership, social status, power, cultural refinement, and manners. Students who come from privileged backgrounds often feel entitled to more and better things, not the least of which sometimes includes grades in your class. Because of the large middle class in the United States, class has come to have less meaning here. Those who have more income or own large plots of land are lucky and have experienced an upbringing that might have included class-based experiences. Those who have less or come from underprivileged backgrounds have just as much to offer and are often hesitant to participate as readily because they feel "unworthy." As an instructor, your job is to be as inclusive as possible. It is important that you provide the same opportunities to every student, regardless of their background. One other consideration is that of overcompensation. Sometimes the underprivileged feel entitled because of the lack of opportunities in their lives. Walking this fine line is tricky and yet is important to the success of all your students.

Gender

You have heard of the "glass ceiling" and maybe even have experienced it. There are only a handful of women CEOs of Fortune 500 companies. And remember, women make up about 50 percent of the population. In your classes it will be important ensure that you are calling on both genders equally. Provide opportunities for both genders to participate at equal levels. If you are in a field in which one gender dominates classes and courses of study, you have to be especially careful to be inclusive.

As with race, there are subtle comments that show disrespect for one gender or the other. Call attention to this and offer corrective feedback so that these comments do not undermine. Be aware of your own remarks as well, and be open to student feedback. Defensiveness will not solve a perception, and perception is reality. Too often someone has little awareness of his or her lack of sensitivity. With tact you can provide a new perspective. Also be leery of making sexual comments or innuendos, as they can be offensive as well. This could be the basis for a sexual harassment charge.

Age

Age discrimination happens. You may be older and your students younger, and both ages are to be valued. Older students are showing up in colleges and universities around the country, in fact, around the globe. Retirees who want to start a new career or those who just want to take advantage of inexpensive classes are coming in droves.

The mix of young and old in a class can be a challenge if you do not anticipate it and have discussions in class about how to learn from each other. The alternative perspectives can make learning very exciting and engaging. People with lots of life experiences can learn from those who are using technology in ways never dreamed of. Young people can hear about traditions that are lost because of our fast-moving society. History comes alive when we talk to someone who was there. Take advantage of the age differences in your classes. Use all those resources to grow knowledge.

Sexual Orientation

In the past 20 years sexual orientation has become a regular topic of discussion. People have "come out" whom we never would have believed to be gay or lesbian. Our society has opened up to lively debates about gay marriage in particular and gay lifestyle in general. How does this affect your classroom? First, you have to acknowledge in your own mind that you will have gay and lesbian students. You may have bisexual and transsexual students as well.

With this in mind you have to be just as sensitive to these needs as to any other diverse group. How you respond to the outrageously dressed gay man will indicate to students how accepting you will be of their particular diversity issues. Numerous churches around the United States have become open and affirming, meaning that they openly accept into their congregations those who are gay, lesbian, or bisexual. It is a commitment to practice acceptance of those against whom other religions and many in society discriminate. Even those who do not disclose a different sexual orientation, who struggle with the discovery around their sexual orientation, are accepted. Because of your position of authority (teacher) it will be valuable for you to carefully consider how you will include these students in your classes.

Religion

Many cultures, many races, many religions—all perhaps different from yours. What do you do? Accept the differences and learn about them. You may be faced with holiday celebrations that are not recognized by your institution. What do you do? We suggest you allow an excused absence and provide a vehicle for students to keep up or to make up work.

Religious differences can also impact other diversity issues. Conservative Christians may speak out against gay men. This is a challenge for even the most accomplished instructors. As the saying goes, "Don't talk about religion or politics." You have to be careful here and still be accepting of all viewpoints. No one is right or wrong—they are all interesting. Of course, they will believe they are right, so be careful. Acknowledge the differences and note that you will not accept undue tribulation in your class.

Language

You will encounter students who do not speak English well. You may actually have several languages in one class. What do you do? Make sure that the students know the standards and understand course requirements. Determine how proficient they are with English. You should not adjust your standards unreasonably to accommodate these students' lack of English proficiency. And you have to be sensitive to their desire to learn and desire for success in your class. Refer them to any academic support services on campus and offer them a bit more attention than those who are proficient in English. Think of what you would need if you were attending a class being conducted in a language other than your first language. Acknowledge their challenges and discuss often what they need to be successful.

Physical Abilities

If we cannot end now our differences, at least we can help make the world safe for diversity.

—John F. Kennedy

This area includes those with wheelchairs or crutches. It also includes obese students and those with speech and hearing deficits. When you have a student with disabilities in your class, the law in the United States says you must make accommodation to serve that student's needs. However, you only need to accommodate the physical needs, not adjust your academic standards. Your institution should be prepared to make modifications if a student cannot move easily around the buildings or campus. The challenges come when other students do not respect those who are different because of a physical handicap. Many students who have physical challenges are open to discussing the particular challenges they face and will share their journey with others. The discomfort is more from those who are whole than those who are not. It is a wonderful thing to hear from a disabled person how she or he copes with everyday things. Experience would indicate that many have a wonderful sense of humor and can make others feel at ease. Take advantage of this if you can.

CHAPTER WRAP-UP

Acknowledging diversity is one key to successfully dealing with it. If you discuss the existence of oppression around the diversity in the world and your class you will be one step ahead of other instructors. You have to make your students comfortable talking about these issues because that is how we learn. The best people to learn from about diversity are those whom we know and can listen to. You can purposely create your learning groups to include diverse students— that is the way they will learn more about themselves and others.

The key to understanding others and their diverse backgrounds is to ask questions. It is like going to another country and taking part in the cultural activities there. Your experiences would be different if you ate only at American chain restaurants while traveling in other countries.

And, unfortunately, there are those who do just that, losing wonderful opportunities to experience a life different from their upbringing. Live life to the fullest by learning from your students how different they are from you and what they know that you do not as a result of the diversity in your classroom.

SPRINGBOARDS FOR FURTHER LEARNING

Key Names

There are literally hundreds of people who are associated with diversity issues. We have chosen not to include names here.

Key Terms

ADA   race
cultural diversity   religion
gender   sexual orientation
open and affirming

Unit 5
The Pursuit of Teaching Excellence: Personal and Organizational Learning and Development

Life is difficult. This is a great truth, one of the greatest truths. It is a great truth because once we truly see this truth, we transcend it. Once we truly know that life is difficult—once we truly understand and accept it—then life is no longer difficult. Because once it is accepted, the fact that life is difficult no longer matters.

—M. Scott Peck

"What lies behind us & what lies before us are small matters compared to what lies within us."

—Emerson

Matters of Institutional Accountability

In the introduction to this text, we briefly discussed some of the challenges faced by postsecondary schools today. One of the most significant is the need to better prepare students for the ever-accelerating economic and technological changes and the advanced skills required in today's workplace. There is also the challenge that arises from the growing expectations of the public, accreditation groups, and governmental agencies for improvements in the quality of instruction offered by schools, along with efforts to hold schools accountable for what they produce. These outside interests are seeking to develop evaluation methods to answer the basic question, "What is the quality of your finished 'product'?" These measures are intended to generate indicators of the outcomes of instruction, together with ways to meaningfully compare this information across institutions so prospective students can make better decisions about where to invest their time and money.

In addition to these external pressures, there are related internal management issues within schools, which are beginning to place direct demands on classroom teachers. These issues arise from the public concerns mentioned above regarding accountability, but they also arise from the enormous competition that exists among schools (both for-profit and not-for-profit postsecondary) for limited education dollars. As a result, administrators are increasingly holding classroom teachers accountable for student retention and graduation rates and, in some cases, even rates of job placement and other indicators of students' educational performance.

Teachers, especially those in postsecondary institutions, are perhaps the only professionals who habitually isolate themselves from peers and others behind closed (classroom) doors to practice their profession. Physicians, surgeons, lawyers, and nurses and just about all other skilled practitioners perform their work daily in front of their peers and in visible settings. They are also constantly subject to peer and/or administrative review and feedback and held accountable for what they do or do not do on a regular basis. Furthermore, with the exception of some career and vocational education programs, few postsecondary schools require teacher certification or formal teacher preparation as a condition of employment. In general, all that is needed to teach is evidence of knowledge of the subject matter, usually represented by a degree, or an adequate amount of related on-the-job experience. Given this state of affairs, one can appreciate the concerns of those who are left wondering what goes on behind the door of your classroom.

As a classroom teacher, you may know implicitly the value of what you do (especially if you are using assessments properly and regularly conduct course evaluations. But those outside your classroom who are now, perhaps for the first time, "looking in" do not know this, and it is becoming increasingly clear that these observers will not passively accept the work of teachers who cannot demonstrate that they produce a quality "product."

Matters of Personal Responsibility

The issues of both school and teacher performance today are most often framed in terms of matters of *accountability*. However, it is important to bring a moral dimension to these concerns—and the topic of teacher ability and learning as discussed in this unit—by approaching them also as matters of *personal responsibility*. Your teaching performance depends, of course, on your knowledge and skills. But teaching is not just a technical activity. It is a moral activity as well, and cannot be fully examined independently of the personal values and commitment you bring to your duties as an instructor, especially your sense of moral obligation and your commitment to personal excellence, together with the professional standards that define and establish the benchmarks for what you do.

Matters of Professional Standards

Aside from selected state requirements for the certification of vocational and technical educators working in public programs (e.g., adult education, occupational programs, and vocational–technical schools), there are rarely any explicit statements of professional standards for postsecondary educators. What standards do exist are rather informal, commonly established by individual schools as expectations and guidelines for their own faculty. There are also guidelines for professional standards from accreditation agencies. But these are presented as suggestions, not formal requirements. Consequently, for guidance in this area we need to look to efforts to establish standards for K–12 teachers, for which a general consensus is evident.

A prominent example is the National Board for Professional Teaching Standards (NBPTS). Founded in 1987, the NBPTS has been involved in creating a voluntary national certification system for experienced elementary and secondary teachers. The Board has adopted a policy statement entitled *What Teachers Should Know and Be Able to Do* (1990). The statement sets out the following five core propositions, which reflect what the Board values in teaching:

1. Teachers are committed to students and their learning.
2. Teachers know the subjects they teach and how to teach those subjects to students.

3. Teachers are responsible for managing and monitoring student learning.

4. Teachers think systematically about their practice and learn from experience.

5. Teachers are members of learning communities.

What is evident in these statements is that formal knowledge of subject matter—the primary and sometimes only criterion for the hiring of instructors in postsecondary education—is only one of several standards. In addition, these standards emphasize the critical importance of knowing how to practice the craft of teaching and learning from experience in a systematic manner and being part of a community of practitioners who support each other in their practice.

This unit focuses on these matters of systematic professional growth and the activities that promote it. It provides some select guidance for you to consider in developing a personal framework for learning and growing as an educator. We believe this pursuit of excellence is a matter of personal responsibility. First and foremost, it is what those who aspire to become good teachers are freely willing do. And it is also the right thing to do as an expression of your commitment to your profession and your students. Besides, if *you* do not hold yourself responsible, in this "age of accountability" someone else likely will.

ing to rather
teach." straight
It is a for
decep ward,
tively easily
simple under
phrase, stood
one proc
that ess.
sug Widely
gests a held
rather and
straight some
for what
ward, con
easily flicting
under "folk"
stood theo
proc ries
ess. abound
Widely about
held teach
and ing.
some "Just
what about
con anyone
flicting can
"folk" teach."
theo "If you
ries know
abound your
about sub
ject.
you
just can
about teach
anyone it."
"Good
can teach
teach ers are
If you born
know not
your made."
sub What
ject, you
you can need to
teach know
about
teach
ing can
ers are be
born learned
on the
What "Learn
you ing to
teach."
it is a
decep
tively
simple
phrase,
is that one
of the that
sug
gests a
rather
straight
It is a for
decep ward,
tively easily
simple under
phrase, stood
proc

CHAPTER 19

Teachers as Learners: Becoming a Reflective Practitioner

A teacher can never truly teach unless she is learning herself. A lamp can never light another flame unless it continues to burn its own flame.

—Rabindranath Tagore

Introduction

"Learning to teach." It is a deceptively simple phrase, one that suggests a rather straightforward, easily understood process. Widely held and somewhat conflicting "folk" theories abound about teaching. "Just about anyone can teach." "If you know your subject, you can teach it." "Good teachers are born not made." "What you need to know about teaching can be learned on the job."

Despite their prevalence in popular culture, however, there is little research support for these beliefs. Indeed, the phrase "learning to teach" covers many conceptual complexities that resist easy analysis. Just as we do not have a singular perspective on human learning, there is no single model available that can explain how individuals go about "learning to teach." Becoming an accomplished teacher—like all learning—is a complex social-psychological process that occurs over time and is influenced by many factors. Many very specific questions need to be asked and answered if

399

we hope to build a model of how people go about learning to teach. Among these are:

1. Who is doing the learning?

2. What needs to be learned?

3. How can learning best proceed? and

4. What will the context or setting of the learning be?

We cannot possibly do justice to such a complex process in this short unit. But we can outline some of the theoretical and practical issues that can give you some valuable insight into what "learning to teach" is all about.

Chapter 1

A Learning-to-Teach Chronology

It is hard to say when the process of learning to teach begins for any particular individual. From an early age, teaching by parents and teachers surrounds us all. As pointed out in Chapter 1, these early experiences have created and shaped each one's personal and mostly unconscious perspective on teaching, with the influence of our school experiences being especially strong. We all have spent many thousands of hours in elementary, secondary, and probably postsecondary classrooms watching and absorbing what teachers do, and in the process have developed our individual dispositions toward teaching, learning, and our professional field of study.

The informal and implicit character of this "apprenticeship" distinguishes learning to teach from other kinds of professional learning, and poses unique challenges for each of us who wants to develop as a teacher. The beliefs and attitudes rooted in these formative experiences can be quite resistant to modification. Indeed, a variety of research has documented that even explicit teacher education courses have a limited impact on a prospective teacher's preexisting orientations to teaching; new instructors commonly leave these programs with the same basic attitudes and orientation about teaching with which they entered.

Although little teacher preservice training is available, much less required, for postsecondary instructors, many K–12 teachers, in addition to having a bachelor's degree as evidence of their knowledge of subject matter, are almost universally required to enter into preservice programs designed to lay a foundation for their classroom practice. Although there is some evidence that certain kinds of innovative teacher preparation can affect the way teachers think about teaching and learning, as well as their students and subject matter, most of these programs have been shown to have little value when it comes to giving teachers a solid foundation for their early teaching experiences. New teachers consistently report that neither their prior subject-matter expertise nor their teaching preparation did much to prepare them for the realities of classroom instruction.

> *What lies behind us, and what lies before us are small matters compared to what lies within us.*
>
> —Ralph Waldo Emerson

This finding is also supported by educational investigations into a variety of teacher-training formats. This research has exposed a persistent and widely accepted myth in education today—that good teachers can be produced if we start with people who are smart and who have subject-matter degrees, and then give them basic pedagogical knowledge and classroom-management skills. For example, there have been studies in which prospective teachers were asked to explain and apply the knowledge of their college majors as a teacher would in a classroom, and they were no more able to do so than nonmajors. In general, it seems that neither academic success in a college major nor preservice teacher training guarantees that teachers have the *specific* kinds of knowledge and skills needed for effective teaching.

Although the reasons for this have yet to be determined conclusively, we suggest that the education-related coursework taken by teacher candidates in college, like many courses taught in our present school system, rarely requires a deep approach to learning. Most education professors are content to provide massive amounts of information that students memorize, while paying little attention to the meaning or significance of the material covered. Thus, once prospective teachers graduate, they often think about their subjects as little more than lengthy lists of facts, with limited or no consideration given to relationships among principles and concepts learned. The result is that they have no idea how to explain and represent these relationships in their teaching. It was never modeled, much less discussed and analyzed. Once in their own classrooms, they find themselves unable to engage students with important, substantive ideas and have few ideas on how to examine their own instructional practices in order to improve them. Thus, in order to survive in their classrooms, most new teachers fall back on and operate from the unconscious and somewhat inflexible pedagogical predispositions and belief systems that developed during their earlier schooling experiences. They simply teach the way they were taught.

To find yourself, think for yourself.

—Socrates

Stages in Professional Growth

Given the above state of affairs, just about everyone who enters the profession must inevitably learn to teach on the job. Indeed, it is said that new teachers essentially have two jobs during the early years of their practice—they have to teach *and* to learn to teach at the same time. There seem to be three stages teachers go through in learning to teach:

1. a formative stage of survival and discovery,
2. a stage of experimentation and consolidation, and
3. a stage of mastery and stabilization.

In the early years, new teachers begin to develop self-knowledge of their professional identity mostly through struggles and trial-and-error explorations of their students and subject matter. These years are extremely difficult for most teachers, and many leave teaching in the first 5 years. Over time, those who persist become more accomplished, developing as novices with a handful of consistent instructional routines and a growing understanding of both what students need and what to expect from them. Additional experience brings greater confidence and flexibility and a sense of independence that encourages greater experimentation and more risk taking. It is reported that after 5 to 7 years, most teachers enter into the third stage and feel they know how to teach (though the degree of mastery depends on how we define *mastery* and *expertise*). Of course, learning and change do not necessarily stop once teachers consolidate and establish a firm teaching style during this period. Still, it becomes more difficult to describe a common path for further professional development after this final step has been reached. Personal dispositions, varying opportunities to learn, and changes in the social and political landscape (think national standards and accountability) create incentives for continued learning. But whether learning is incremental or dramatic after this point seems to vary with individual teachers, the particulars of the school settings within which they work, and the larger sociopolitical context and trends that influence public perceptions and expectations.

If you don't know where you are going, any road will take you there.

—Alice in Wonderland

Beyond Subject-Matter Expertise— What Makes the Difference?

Even though you may have been hired primarily because you were acknowledged to be a subject-matter expert (SME), if being one does not necessarily qualify you to be an effective teacher, what can you do to become the best teacher you possibly can be?

An immediate and the likely response of many is, "Well, I'll attend an in-service or go to a seminar." This is a widely accepted approach to professional development. Indeed, it is the most common one. Unfortunately, it may not be the most fruitful. In-service education programs, workshops, and other training formats are almost invariably short-term, many no longer than a half-day and some just an hour or so long. The idea that such short-term workshops are an effective means for improving teaching practice is another widely held myth in teacher education. Just think, if a yearlong teacher preparation program rarely produces a teacher ready to teach successfully, why should we assume that a single, short-term or even extended series of workshops can make significant and lasting changes in teacher knowledge and practice?

Certainly, the expectation that customary professional development efforts should help teachers improve what they do is a reasonable one. And these efforts can accomplish a good deal when designed using insights into what teachers most need to learn and be able to do and when implemented using the best of what we know about good teaching and learning. This is especially so when we focus on and include a good mix of the primary content areas that comprise the core foundation for good teaching: building of instructor knowledge of subject matter, revisions to thinking about classroom roles, and learning how to manage substantially different teaching techniques to actively engage learners. Yet, even when *all* these elements are present, teacher change and growth can still be problematic and difficult. The learning that does occur is rarely solid enough to give teachers the confidence and skills they need to make consistent and sustainable improvements in what they do.

There seem to be several reasons for this lack of meaningful improvement. From what we know from how people learn best, what holds true for their students holds true for teachers themselves—teachers cannot just be told about new teaching ideas and techniques and be expected to understand and master them. They must also have significant and ongoing opportunities to observe others using them and deeply reflect on these techniques, plus they must experiment with and practice them in their own classrooms. *All* these experiential elements are needed to bring together a deeper understanding of the critical components of effective teaching—knowledge of the subject matter, of how diverse students are inclined to learn it, and of the best ways to help them do so. Teachers who receive assistance in only one of these aspects of teaching are frequently unable to significantly modify old approaches or develop new and more engaging teaching practices.

Ultimately both the content and processes of learning to teach must be brought together. Until now, programs have emphasized the "what" of teaching—knowledge of subject matter and teaching theory—rather than the actual "how" of teaching. For this reason, many, if not most, teacher-preparation courses, in-service education programs, and workshops have failed to significantly influence teacher thinking and improve their classroom practice. There is no single theory to describe how to best integrate content and process, but a clearer picture of what works is emerging, offering a number of important insights into how teachers learn best. We explore a few of these here.

The "How" of Learning to Teach

To understand how teachers learn to teach, we need to look at two areas of professional development:

1. the changes in teacher thinking—the cognitive processes that need to be modified (e.g., beliefs, perceptions, attitudes, orientations, understandings, and knowledge), and

2. the conditions that facilitate the needed learning—the particular opportunities or the contexts of learning (e.g., programs, settings, interventions, and social interactions).

Most research on how teachers learn has tended to focus on either one or the other but not on both of these dimensions. Thus, they fail to capture the essential character of effective teacher learning,

The great aim of education is not knowledge but action.

—Herbert Spencer

which is the ill-structured *interaction* between learners and the learning opportunity.

Fortunately, scholars and researchers are now beginning to define the nature of this interaction. They are doing so by investigating what the experience of participating in training is like for teachers—the sense teachers make of it and how they go about doing so. This research indicates that how teachers learn is no different from any other kind of student learning and that if we want to create an appropriate learning opportunity, we have to clarify the following:

1. what we want the learners (teachers) to learn,

2. what kind of thinking that will entail,

3. where learners (teachers) are in relation to the desired outcome, and

4. what kinds of resources and activities are needed to help learners (teachers) move in the desired direction.

In what follows, we briefly explore two of these dimensions to suggest how you individually as well as in partnership with other teachers can learn to teach more effectively. We focus on understanding what you want to learn and where you are in relation to this desired knowledge and skill. (In Chapter 20 we will look at the contexts of teacher learning and some of the activities that can help you learn what you most need.)

Becoming a Better Teacher— Changing Your Mind

We all have bad days in the classroom. This is true of the most experienced instructors and the freshest teaching recruit. Of course, there are differences in the kinds of things that can go wrong and the frequency with which they may do so. But this is not the point. The most notable distinction between masterful teachers and those who have yet to achieve mastery, even after years of experience, is not the challenges they face, but how they handle and learn from them.

So how does one develop more skillful ways of doing and being? There is no common trajectory, as we stated previously, for the personal and professional growth process of teachers. However, there does seem to be a common element as to how the best teachers go about learning and improving their practice that leads them to make lasting changes in their thinking and classroom behaviors. It is a predisposition to systematic and careful self-reflection and self-evaluation.

Conceptual Change and Learning to Teach

It is becoming clear that substantial changes in teaching practice are likely to occur only when teachers have or create ample opportunities

> *Reflection is what allows us to learn from our experiences: it is an assessment of where we have been and where we want to go next.*
>
> —Kenneth Wolf

Chapter 1

The unexamined life is a life not worth living.

—Socrates

to think deeply about what they believe about learning and teaching and observe and examine their behaviors in their classrooms on an ongoing basis. This means developing an awareness of what is happening *before* it happens, *while* it happens, and *after* it has happened.

This may sound like you are being asked to become a Zen master. However, it is not quite so complicated. As we have briefly discussed here and in greater detail in Chapter 1, this kind of reflective thinking begins with your understanding of your teaching philosophy. This philosophy plays a paradoxical role. Teachers as learners, like all learners, can only learn and change by drawing on their own beliefs and prior experiences to provide frameworks for understanding, interpreting, and assessing new and sometimes conflicting information. However, these same preexisting beliefs and experiences may also serve as barriers to change. They become problematic when they are not examined and when they limit the range of ideas and actions we are willing to consider as growth opportunities and possible solutions to teaching challenges and problems. Moreover, even when we understand and examine these beliefs and attitudes, as we have stated, they can still be quite resistant to change. This is true for both prospective teachers and experienced ones as well. A field of inquiry known as conceptual change theory offers a possible explanation for this and the conditions under which people are more likely to change their minds.

Briefly, conceptual change theory suggests that several conditions seem necessary to induce a conceptual shift that leads to changed behavior. First, you need to recognize discrepancies between your own views and those underlying the potential solution(s) to a specific pedagogical problem or, on a broader philosophical level, the gap between your overall philosophy and an entirely new vision of teaching and learning. Second, you need an opportunity to consider why new practices and their associated values and beliefs are better than your present or conventional approaches. Third, vivid examples of these practices need to be presented, preferably under realistic conditions, and ideally where you can experience and practice with them firsthand. Furthermore, you may also need regular support and guidance to effectively incorporate these ideas and sustain these practices in your teaching on an ongoing basis (as explained in the next chapter).

Fundamental to this process of teacher learning through conceptual change is self-observation and reflection.

The Role of Self-Reflection

Educational philosopher and theorist John Dewey recognized that it is the reflection on our experiences that leads to learning, not merely the experience itself. We learn only from those experiences that we ponder, explore, review, and question. Today, researchers are looking at the developmental aspects of critical reflection in teaching to reveal more fully how it is reflection, not experience alone, that provides the greatest opportunities for professional understanding and growth.

The Nature and Process of Reflection

Reflection is an evolving concept and has many definitions in the context of teacher thinking. Dewey saw it as a proactive, continuous examination of the origins and impacts of beliefs, attitudes, and practices. The work of Donald Schon is also closely linked to teacher reflective practice. Schon construed reflection as an approach to decision making and problem solving. The concept also includes constructivist notions of individuals actively examining their past and current knowledge and experiences to generate new ideas and behaviors. In addition, a humanist element is evident in the importance of personal growth and understanding what restricts that growth.

Reflection as an element of professional growth begins with a state of doubt, a challenge or perplexity. It may be in regard to a specific problem that needs a specific solution. It may also be something that calls into question your professional identity. This would be a challenge to your fundamental teaching philosophy that leads to an inquiry into broad issues of pedagogy and curriculum, the underlying assumptions and consequences of your actions for both yourself and your students. This uncertainty is followed by research into ideas, techniques, and materials that will resolve this doubt and settle the perplexity.

Reflection, however, is more than just thinking hard about what you do. Becoming a critically reflective practitioner requires active engagement or mindful involvement in an experience. This includes the following:

- Giving careful attention to your experiences and how meaning is made and justified through these experiences.
- Analyzing and prioritizing issues, using tacit and resource-based knowledge, and developing a feasible plan of action.
- Understanding the influence of context and how that shapes your behavior.
- Looking beyond the technical aspects of an experience (methods and techniques) to the personal and moral dimensions of teaching implicitly embedded in this experience to examine values and questions of whether or not you are being the teacher you want to be.

When fully appreciated for its power as a tool for professional growth, this reflection is not about a single event in time, but occurs over time as you begin to construct meaning for yourself.

Our deepest fear is not that we are inadequate. Our deepest fear is that we are powerful beyond measure. It is our light, not our darkness, that frightens us. We ask ourselves, who am I to be brilliant, gorgeous, talented and fabulous? Actually, who are you not to be?

—Marianne Williamson

Sometimes for me, a transformation in teaching has come in a dramatic moment, other times in a subtle but growing awareness, and still on other occasions as the accumulation of many small events. But whatever the case has been, it always has led to a change and an improvement in my teaching only through a thoughtful reflection on the experience. The initial impetus may have been the emotional impact of the experience, but the commitment to pursue the meaning and lesson of the experience has always emerged out of a willingness to sit with and contemplate the event and then decide to gather whatever resources I needed to learn something new.

I recall one particular incident early in my teaching career. I had assigned a chapter from a text, instructing the students to read and study a selected passage. During the next class, when I opened a discussion on it with several questions as prompts, not a single student was ready to participate. At first I assumed it was because no one had done the assignment. But rather than operate from this assumption, I decided to question my students and discovered this was not the case for most. The majority of the class had followed my instruction to "read and study" the material. What became apparent was that what to "read and study" meant for the students was quite different from what it meant to me and what I expected them to do. I realized I could not take anything for granted when communicating with my students. I could not assume that things that were "obvious" to me were as readily apparent to them. From that day on, I began to explore ways to understand my students' thinking, beliefs, attitudes, and concepts about the subject matter and what teaching and learning meant to them. Ever since and over a period of time (meaningful learning does take time), not only have I gained a deeper respect for my students, but I have also gained their respect and become a much more effective instructor.

Levels of Reflection

Essentially, reflective learning is learning by doing. But this is not an innate talent possessed by all those in the teaching profession, nor one uniformly learned. It is a learned habit of mind. In order to understand and become skilled in the process of reflective learning, it is helpful to distinguish between two kinds or levels of reflective activities, technical and philosophical reflection, together with differences between reflection-*in*-action versus reflection-*for*-action. These levels are somewhat developmental, and not every person will progress through them until they reach the stage of critical reflection at the deeper philosophical level.

> *We must become the change we want to see in the world.*
>
> —Mahatma Gandhi

The Technical Level

Technical reflections are concerned with refining teaching strategies. Many, if not most, teachers reflect only at this level. It involves examining your teaching behaviors after an incident or event, such as a problematic situation or a class. The focus of the reflection is on the effective application of knowledge and skills in the classroom and is primarily focused on the techniques. This type of reflection is the one most accessible to most teachers, especially novices.

Although this level of reflection can bring some value and change, it tends to operate at a somewhat surface level. Unless you look at the connections between what you are doing (technique) and the deeper reasons for these actions (philosophy) it can be difficult to adopt new methods and ways of doing things that will endure or have a significant impact on your students' learning. Generally, a focus on practice alone will not permit you to move far from your basic predispositions and inclinations—no matter how many new ideas you are exposed to.

Philosophical Level

The philosophical level is where you reflect on the roots and character of your teaching perspective. It is the *why* and not just the *what* of your thinking and actions. We have explored this topic in Chapter 1 and return to it in the companion Field Guide. An examination at this level can be triggered by and occur as a spontaneous recognition of a pivotal moment. There are two kinds of reflective activity at the philosophical level: reflection-*in*-action and reflection-*for*-action.

Reflection-in-Action: In reflection-*in*-action, there are two possible concerns. Your concern may be with what you are doing in the classroom *while* you are doing it. It also may arise *after* the fact, when you take the time to step back and think back on an incident and the reasons why something happened or why you did what you did. Reflective practitioners working at this level focus on the contextual dimensions of their practice. They concentrate on the sometimes complex relationship between a problem or challenging situation and their own beliefs, attitudes and values, and actions. At this level, reflection is contemplative of and is expressive of commitment to meaningful change as a guide to future actions rooted in new ways of thinking, not just new techniques.

Reflection-for-Action: Reflection-*in*-action is spontaneous reflection in the midst of the action itself, arising as a response to an incident or problem in the course of a particular class session. Reflection-*for*-action, on the other hand, is structured rather than spontaneous, and it is proactive rather than reactive. It is gaining knowledge by planning, reflecting on action before and after an event in order to explore an issue that has been predetermined and to arrive at possible alternative approaches.

Chapter 1

Refer to Field Guide

Ultimately, man should not ask what the meaning of his life is, but rather must recognize that it is he who is asked. In a word, each man is questioned by life; and he can only answer to life by answering for his own life; to life he can only respond by being responsible.

—Viktor Frankl

Despite their difference in temporal focus, the practical differences between reflection-in-action and reflection-for-action may not all be that significant. Both forms ultimately call for retrospective analysis of action to understand the relative successes and failures of previous events, with some sort of analysis before taking the next step. Also, all reflection, even as it remains connected to the past, by its nature is focused on the future and the development of new ways of thinking and practicing. Whatever its expression or scope, reflection ideally becomes a cumulative body of knowledge that can then be used to help teachers integrate introspection into their teaching to improve practice.

The Process of Reflection

Whether you are prompted to reflect "on-the-fly" or to pursue it in a proactive and preplanned manner, the process of skilled teacher reflection includes similar phases and tasks.

Basic Steps of Teacher Reflection

The process of reflection can be described in terms of the following steps or tasks:

1. *Identification:* the concern or problem to be solved or question to be answered. *What happened?*

2. *Description:* the relevant details that identify the critical element of the event. *The Who? What? How? When? and Where? of the issue or situation.*

3. *Analysis:* the possible causes of the issue. *Why did it happen?*

4. *Evaluation:* the significance of the event in terms of its impact on you and your students, and its relationship to lesson or course goals, personal philosophy, etc. *What does it mean?*

5. *Actions:* actions that can lead to improvements in your practice. *What should I do?*

When going through these steps, consider these key elements of teaching and learning transactions to guide your investigation and actions. They apply whether your reflection is planned proactively or as a response after the fact. (*Note:* They are also suitable for the design of your course evaluation instruments.)

Chapter 5

Teaching Philosophy: Are your beliefs and values and attitudes about teaching and learning conducive to producing the most significant learning outcomes possible, as evidenced by current theory and research?

Content Knowledge: Do or did you possess and/or demonstrate a thorough knowledge of the subject matter that meaningfully organizes content and helps your learners grasp its deeper significance?

Preparation: Do or did you make the appropriate preparation, using the necessary pedagogical practices to support instruction?

Instructional Delivery: Do or did you present instruction in a manner aligned with student learning goals that resulted in active student involvement, a deep approach to learning, appropriate teacher–student interaction, and meaningful lesson plans resulting in high levels of student achievement?

Classroom Setting and Management: Do or did you demonstrate classroom-management skills supportive of diverse student learning needs that create an environment conducive to student learning?

Student Assessment: Do or did you implement assessment techniques based on appropriate learning standards that not only measure student learning (summative) but also help guide and motivate it (formative)?

The snow goose need not bathe to make itself white. Neither need you do anything but be your self.

—Lao Tse

Personalizing the Process

The separation of teaching into convenient phases or steps as described here does not necessarily represent the realities of teaching and learning. A linear chain of events or series of questions cannot do justice to describing the complexity of the teaching/learning process. What actually happens during teaching and learning occurs within a fuzzy "field" or a "space" within which a complex of intersecting and nonintersecting relationships occurs, arising at many levels and in many different moments.

What's more, the activities and elements of teaching described as separate aspects persistently overlap. They feed into and out of one another and generate other experiences and activities not even mentioned here. Moreover, at any moment, any of the players—you and/or your students—engaged in the teaching/learning transactions going on in your classroom may be simultaneously doing any number of things. For these reasons, at times it proves difficult to contemplate content, preparation, presentation, etc. as discrete aspects of teaching—or as distinct and separate focuses for reflection and revision. For these reasons, most reflective teachers end up devising their own ways of representing the full complexity of their teaching with the guidelines outlined above as only one way among many of representing this complexity.

With this in mind, we suggest the following, particularly when taking a proactive, reflection-*for*-action approach. This is a simple protocol for creating a relatively easy cycle of action–reflection–action, etc.

- Try to figure out your own way of representing the complexity of your teaching practices and student learning activities.
- Break the "big picture" of your instruction down into areas of activity that you can easily identify and describe.
- Devise a cycle of reflection—action, evaluation, reflection, revision, and new action—in a single area that most interests you.
- Sustain the action–evaluation–reflection–revision–action cycle until you have achieved and can maintain the quality you want in that area.
- Then do the same in the next area of personal interest.
- Make a practice of recording what you do in each area of activity, and of putting the records in a teaching portfolio.

The ability to perceive or think differently is more important than the knowledge gained.

—David Bohm

The Collaborative Nature of Reflection

Reflection as a method of inquiry into teaching can be collaborative as well as individual. Indeed, the opportunity to share with colleagues and friends is extremely helpful in becoming a more reflective practitioner and can lead to the most significant and sustainable transformations.

Collaboration includes requesting feedback on a particular question or issue, or it can also take the form of discussion with colleagues who assist you in identifying appropriate actions to help you clarify your beliefs and dispositions. Feedback, comments, and discussion about your reflections might come from a mentor, supervisor/coordinator, and/or your peers in the program. For example, questions from a friend can help clarify an issue for you, just as a probe or comment from a supervisor can help you look deeper into the situation. Also, your peers can help each other in learning how to reflect alone, in pairs, and in small groups. You can show each other how to keep reflective journals, record classroom episodes, and put together portfolios about teaching and learning in your classrooms.

Learning collaboratively is a complex process. It requires learners to understand themselves, their motives, and their thoughts and beliefs, as well as the motives, thoughts, and beliefs of others. In its most powerful expression it also requires merging of individual interests into a collective aspiration and ways of behaving that create a bond of trust, belonging, and purposefulness among group members. People involved in collaborative learning can address these complexities more easily

Chapter 20

when they take time to build relationships, plan methods for learning together, and adopt processes that support generative thinking and reflection. Ways of doing this are discussed in Chapter 20.

CHAPTER WRAP-UP

Teachers who have or who develop the right disposition for reflection—open-mindedness, a sense of personal responsibility, and professional commitment—study and question their own beliefs and practices in order to learn. They take time to ponder the "ordinary moments" in their classrooms, sharpen their understandings and insights, and, as a result, make better decisions that improve teaching and learning.

Reflective practice begins quite simply, with an awareness of a need to change. It involves stories that describe classroom episodes that are problematic and proceeds with questions about what happened and why, the meaning of the episode, and how the experience can inform their teaching in the future. And when practiced skillfully and with commitment, it becomes a continuous cycle of self-observation and self-evaluation.

As you pursue self-reflection, keep these points in mind:

1. The learning of different aspects of teaching is more or less suited for different settings and different kinds of learning opportunities.

2. The dispositions and beliefs, knowledge, and understanding you bring to any learning opportunity will affect what you learn from it and set the foundation for subsequent learning.

3. How you personally prefer to learn will affect what you learn.

Reflective practice is not without its challenges. It requires a commitment to self-development and the time to achieve it. Developing new habits of mind will come only through experience, experimentation, and practice. It may also prove to be emotionally challenging when you find yourself confronted with uncertainties about your teaching philosophy or possible competence.

Still, the benefits are clear. Reflection as a method of professional development is very flexible. It springs from your needs and the particulars of your own unique teaching situation and can address what concerns you most. It is also very practical. Opportunities to explore and reflect on ideas, techniques, and approaches are built into the process, and links between theory and its applications are easily evident. It brings a high degree of professionalism, responsibility, and intellectual rigor into your teaching. It improves your ability to plan and implement instruction in more fruitful ways, as well as improving your ability to

I've always wanted to be somebody, but I should have been more specific.

—Unknown

react and respond as you are teaching to whatever may come up. Finally, it is sustainable. Reflective practice creates a cyclical process of observation, reflection, and implementation that becomes a regular part of good teaching.

SPRINGBOARD FOR FURTHER LEARNING

Key Names

Stephen Brookfield
John Dewey
Donald Schon
The National Center on Teacher Effectiveness
National Center for Research on Teacher Learning (NCRTL)
Teacher Education and Learning to Teach Study (TELT)

Key Terms

reflective practitioner
reflective teacher
teacher self-reflection
teacher education
teacher preparation

teacher learning
teacher preservice
teacher professional development
teacher reflection

CHAPTER 20

Schools That Learn: Enhancing Teacher Learning

It must be considered that there is nothing more difficult to carry out nor more doubtful of success nor more dangerous to handle than to initiate a new order of things; for the reformer has enemies in all those who profit by the old order, and only lukewarm defenders in all those who would profit by the new order; this lukewarmness arising partly from the incredulity of mankind who does not truly believe in anything new until they actually have experience of it.

—Machiavelli

Introduction

Reflective practice is the hallmark of teachers who are deeply committed to improving their teaching. But are reflective teachers necessarily better teachers? Is reflection enough to make a difference in student learning? As with other questions we have asked in this text, there is no simple yes-or-no answer. Many factors determine its value, especially what teachers learn from analyzing classroom episodes and how effectively and consistently they apply what they have learned to improve their daily practice.

At the end of Chapter 19, we pointed out that teachers examining and evaluating their actions and then devising new approaches oversimplifies complex reality. Teacher reflection, as

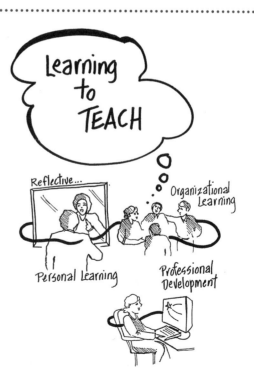

Learning to TEACH

Reflective...

Organizational Learning

Personal Learning

Professional Development

415

powerful as it is as a tool for teacher learning, does not automatically lead to improved practice. Teacher reflection, however, does offer an excellent chance of improving teaching and learning when it becomes part of a teacher's basic repertoire of skills, *and* is encouraged and supported by others (colleagues, program directors, staff developers, and administrators), as well as linked to other opportunities to learn.

The Big Picture

In the introductions to this unit and to this text, we spoke of the importance of professional development for educators. Interest in professional growth has been longstanding in K–12 education and is becoming an ever-increasing concern in postsecondary education. These concerns arise from those outside and those within education. Legislators, policy makers, funding agencies, the general public, and school program directors and administrators all want to know whether teacher training can really make a difference in student learning.

Through efforts to address this issue, professional developers and educational scholars have come to understand that teacher learning *must include organizational development to support individual development.* Different forms of professional growth processes are being proposed and implemented to include not only teachers but also others, with attention on the improved performance of *entire* school organizations and staff. There is interest in what is known about various organizational characteristics and structures and how all persons and programs interact to impact student learning, retention, and other indicators of institutional effectiveness.

Research on Professional Development—A Mixed Bag

The research base on professional development in education is quite extensive. Those who look to this research for guidance on how to best promote professional growth, however, quickly find themselves faced with seemingly paradoxical and at times apparently incompatible findings. The following are some examples:

- Some research suggests that professional-development efforts must be practitioner-specific and focus principally on day-to-day activities at the classroom level, while other work indicates that an emphasis on organizational approaches are more productive.

- There are experts who stress that professional development is best conceived and carried out by individual teachers and on-site school personnel. Others believe that teachers and school-based individuals generally lack the capacity to design and implement worthwhile improvements on their own. They argue that the most

> *We know a lot more about what can be done to improve higher learning. Solid research on how learning occurs, how it can be best facilitated, and how organizations that foster it should be structured has burgeoned over the last few years.*
>
> —Peter Ewell

successful programs are those developed by those from outside an institution.

- Some propose that the most effective professional development is best approached in a gradual and incremental fashion, without expecting too much at one time. Others insist that the broader the scope and vision of a professional-development program, the more likely the program will generate the enthusiasm of teachers and be implemented successfully.

These and other contradictions can easily leave those promoting and designing professional growth opportunities confused. The issues seem clear, but positive efforts can seem elusive.

When I first began doing professional-development workshops, I was quite excited about all the things I had learned through over a decade of reading and study of emerging concepts in educational and cognitive psychology, and the neurosciences and their implications for teaching. Changing my own practice took a good deal of time and consistent attention and effort. Yet over time I felt I had made significant improvements and wanted to share my knowledge and experience with my peers. So, with grand visions of classrooms taught by well-informed and equally enthusiastic teachers working with highly engaged students, I decided to design and conduct seminars. Well, as you might already expect, I was not only possibly a bit overzealous, but also somewhat naive.

This naiveté did not last long, however. Within a few short years I experienced just how difficult it is to introduce change into the practice of other teachers. I witnessed that even among the most dedicated and committed educators, occasional workshops and intermittent in-services were rarely enough to create sustainable improvements in their classroom practices. I realized, moreover, that good ideas and brief practice sessions were not enough if new insights and understandings were to be effectively translated into meaningful gains in teacher effectiveness and student learning. Even with the best designed and delivered training, more was needed if personal change and professional growth was to move forward at other than a glacial and highly uneven pace. With additional experience and research, it became clear that the "more" needed included collaborative teacher learning supported by school leaders and administrators. In my experience, such efforts, unfortunately, have not been and are not common. At the same time, when these efforts are put forth, I have seen how they do contribute to creating the

(continues)

essential conditions needed to produce the results I originally envisioned when I began conducting workshops. This is not only my own experience, but is supported by the well-respected thinking and research of others. My current hope is that ideas so briefly introduced in this chapter will provide the initial impetus for teachers, program directors, and staff developers to look more deeply into the theme of creating *sustainable* change through an organizational commitment to teacher learning.

The Right Stuff

Research shows that successful teacher training—like all good instruction—incorporates and balances three elements. As articulated by the National Staff Development Council these are content, process, and context.

Content

Content is what is to be learned. A problem with some teacher-training programs is that topics are not always selected in a systematic and predetermined manner. The value of a particular topic is often left to the judgment of a staff developer or to each individual teacher's interest. Also, much of the content offered is frequently a prescription of general practices described in broad and perhaps vague terms. Teaching of algebra, for example, calls for quite a different knowledge base and set of instructional practices than the teaching of a course in business-management theory. Generic content and approaches may not offer adequate guidance to practically minded teachers who want to know *precisely* what to teach in their own courses and how to do it. Moreover, teachers might possess a repertoire of teaching tools and techniques but still not know the appropriate times to use them. Staff-development activities should bring all these elements together. Unfortunately, they rarely do.

The Right Stuff. Effective professional training should focus on the deepening *discipline-specific* subject-matter knowledge and effective teaching approaches that individual teachers need. Content should highlight the conceptual framework for a discipline that reveals the deeper relationships between core principles, problems, and questions around which each field of study is organized. It should show instructors how to communicate these key ideas to their learners and help students grasp these ideas on a deep level.

Process

The processes of effective professional development should incorporate everything we know about powerful teaching and learning, as has

Organizational learning is learning that occurs as a result of an infrastructure and support that expands learning beyond the individual level. Its three core activities include research, practice, and capacity building.

—Peter Senge

been presented throughout this text. However, many staff-development events do little more than present information with minimal or no attention to ways to facilitate deep and lasting learner understanding. Lectures and PowerPoint presentations are too often substituted for interactive learning. And where there is interaction, it is often conducted at a superficial level because of time constraints. Also, there is very rarely any means of evaluation or follow-through in place. Where there is some sort of evaluation, it often is not much more than participant self-report surveys with questions about what was of interest, what was learned, and the degree of participant satisfaction.

The Right Stuff. Effective professional development should be learner-centered, engaging, and focused on understanding and should have plenty of opportunities for interaction and meaningful practice. There should be a balance between covering content and "uncovering" learning. Information should be embedded in settings and contexts that reflect the real-life challenges teachers face and will face. There should also be some sort of assessment and evaluation procedures that provide feedback on the success of learning.

Context

Most professional development at all levels of education, including the postsecondary level (where it does exist), consists almost entirely of occasional on-site in-services or requirements for instructors' participation in off-site workshops. What is neglected in nearly all these efforts is the powerful impact of *context*. The uniqueness of the individual setting— the teachers, the program, the students, and the school—is always a critical factor in education. What works in one situation for one teacher may not work in another situation for another teacher. Although some general principles may apply throughout, most will need to be adapted, at least in part, to the unique characteristics of the instructional setting and those involved. There is a good deal of research that indicates that teacher learning efforts that assume uniformity across teachers and contexts repeatedly fail to achieve significant outcomes. The complexity of the teaching and learning process and the diversity of contexts in which this process is embedded makes it difficult, if not impossible, to come up with universal, all-purpose approaches.

The Right Stuff. Some contexts and occasions require professional development that focuses on teacher-specific activities, while others may call for a more systemic or organizational approach. In some situations teacher-initiated efforts work best, while in others a more top-down approach may be needed. And while some contexts demand that professional development take a gradual approach to change, others may demand immediate alterations at all levels of the organization. Efforts that effectively facilitate teacher learning focus, therefore, on finding

> A bridge, like professional development, is a critical link between where one is and where one wants to be. A bridge that works in one place almost never works in another. Each bridge requires careful design that considers its purpose, who will use it, the conditions at its anchor points . . . and the resources required to construct it.
>
> —Susan Loucks-Horsley

the right mix of professional development processes and methods that work best in each specific setting and time. This means linking teacher learning to their immediate or greatest needs at particular moments in particular classroom settings and program configurations. To make these connections, teachers and schools must work collaboratively and systematically to create ongoing learning opportunities that are shaped and integrated in ways that best suit organizational and individual contexts. Recognizing the importance of contextual differences also means considering the dynamics of systemic change and acknowledging that organizations must develop along with the individuals within them.

Pathways to Successful Teacher Learning

Though it is not possible to make precise statements about the elements of effective professional development without regard to the context of the learning, there are certain principles that do appear to be critical to the teacher learning process. These are based on thinking about teacher development, as well as about how people and organizations change. These guidelines provide a simple framework for developing an optimal mix of professional-development processes that can help resolve the paradoxical and conflicting research findings mentioned previously. There is no guarantee that following these principles will always bring success. Still, evidence indicates that neglecting the issues described in these guidelines will likely limit success and result in programs and activities that fail to bring about significant or enduring change.

Principle 1: Make It an Individual and an Organizational Endeavor

Professional growth often begins as an individual endeavor through personal initiative. A teacher faces a problem or challenge and wants to know how to deal with it. However, when seen as *only* as an individual process, professional development can become overly arduous. Also, teachers, like professionals in many fields, are reluctant to adopt new practices or procedures unless they feel sure they can make them work; for this, they need encouragement and support. Furthermore, to focus exclusively on individuals in professional-development efforts, while neglecting factors such as organizational politics and culture, severely limits the likelihood of success. A nonsupportive environment can constrict any change effort, no matter how much individuals are encouraged to persist. The key is to find the right chemistry of individual *and* organizational practices that will contribute to success in a particular context. Change happens when it is *both* bottom-up *and* top-down.

> *The issue is having professional development that is sustained, content-rich, and curriculum-embedded instead of what we call the sort of "drive-by-workshop" or "spray and pray" approach. . . .*
>
> —Linda Darling-Hammond

In other words, individuals have to have the desire to learn and grow and school leaders need to offer the means to do so.

Principle 2: Don't Make It Too Big or Too Small

There also needs to be a good balance between the ultimate goals of a professional-development effort and how the change process is managed. Few people feel comfortable with radical changes. Trying to take on too much at any one time is an easy way to undermine just about any effort. At the same time, however, the vision of change needs to be compelling enough to ignite interest; otherwise, few will bother to make a sustained effort to achieve it. Thus, efforts need to be broad enough in scope to challenge teachers and motivate them to take risks *and* at the same time be conducted in an incremental manner. A good maxim to follow is "think big, but start small." Have a powerful vision of what is possible and the benefits to be gained, plus have a practical, strategic plan with short-term goals that can bring small successes along the way.

> *People don't resist Change; they resist being Changed.*
>
> —Peter Senge

Principle 3: Make It a Process, Not an Event

This may be the most common misunderstanding about teacher learning—believing that professional development can be seen and conducted as an event, rather than as a continuous process. Finding meaning in something new or learning to be proficient at something new is difficult. Change that holds great promise for increasing individual ability or enhancing an organization's effectiveness is likely to be slow and will certainly call for sustained work. It is imperative, therefore, that improvement be seen as an ongoing endeavor. It must become a natural part of each practitioner's repository of professional skills and built into their normal practices, as well as the organization itself. For this to happen, continued support and encouragement are essential.

This process approach will also help integrate and give greater credibility to innovations. More so than just about any other profession, education seems full of "reforms du jour." These commonly bring as many problems as solutions. New practices, policies, and programs are often introduced without any effort to show how they relate to the ones that came before or to those that may come afterward. Furthermore, there is seldom any mention of how different innovations contribute to a growing professional knowledge base. The result is often fragmented, uncoordinated, and ephemeral attempts at change. This pattern of constant yet unrelated, short-term innovations not only confuses improvement, it often creates cynicism. Many teachers come to view new ideas as isolated and temporary fads that will be replaced by yet other ideas. If professional-development efforts are to succeed, they must include explanations of how these innovations are to be incorporated into regular classroom practice. This can happen only when they are presented as part of a coherent framework for change. It is only when several strategies are carefully and systematically integrated that substantial improvements become possible. Coordinating and combining ideas in this way can release great energy in the improvement process. No longer lost, not seeing the forest for the trees, participants begin to see the forest *and* the trees.

Principle 4: Make It Worthwhile

Participants need to see results. What works will be reinforced and likely repeated. Evidence of success, therefore, is critical, and there must be specific procedures to provide this feedback. This information can be provided in a variety of ways, again depending on the circumstances. The most immediate and obvious feedback can come from students themselves by monitoring student learning on a regular basis using formative assessments and other classroom assessment tools. (These take many forms, as explained in Chapter 9.) Teacher reflective practices also play a central role here. If external feedback procedures are involved, such as those called for by supervisors or program directors, it is best they focus on outcomes meaningful to everyone involved and suited to teacher and program needs and constraints, such as the time that may be involved. Otherwise, they may interfere with desired changes rather than support them. The key is to find the optimal balance for each program or school's context, with an understanding of the interpersonal dynamics of the individuals involved and the culture of the organization in which they work.

Principle 5: Make It a Group Effort

Enduring and significant change is rarely easy. Fitting new practices and techniques to unique on-the-job conditions can be an uneven process, and it will require extra time and effort, especially at the beginning. Few persons can successfully move from a professional-development experience directly into implementation. In fact, few will even take the risks associated with the uncertainty of implementation unless there is an appreciation of the difficulties that are a natural part of the process and support is provided. Moreover, difficulties can be compounded if teachers perceive that they have no say in the change process or feel isolated in their improvement efforts. Teamwork can make a huge difference.

This teamwork should be based on collegial interaction, mutual respect, and the expectation that all involved are constantly seeking and evaluating potentially better practices. People working together make it easier to build the capacities needed to deal with the

Chapter 9

Faculty know there's a problem indeed with learning . . . and they know it will take more than a new mantra to turn that around.

—Ted Marchese

> *Not I, but the City teaches.*
>
> —Socrates

challenges, uncertainties, and doubts that will arise when teachers attempt to implement new ideas. Working in teams also allows tasks and responsibilities to be shared. This reduces the workload of individual team members and enhances the quality of the work produced. In addition, working in teams helps focus attention on the shared purposes and improvement goals.

Group work can consist of simply offering opportunities for practitioners to interact and share ideas with each other, such as during informal meetings. However, we suggest that this support take the form of coaching, especially peer coaching (see next section). This can provide individual teachers with the guidance each may need in adapting the new practices to their unique contexts, help them to analyze the effects of their efforts, and urge them to persist in the face of what will likely be minor setbacks.

Peer Coaching

Research into best practices suggests that there is a powerful synergy when several different training components (listed below) are used in combination.

- The presentation of a theory or description of skill or strategy
- The modeling or demonstration of skills or methods of teaching
- The practice of these skills in simulated and classroom settings
- The offering of structured and open-ended feedback on performance
- The support of peer coaching on application (hands-on, in-classroom assistance with the transfer of skills and strategies to the classroom).

> *A tradition of vigorous criticism and reflection is essential to successful organizations. Neither uncritical loves nor unloving critics make for organizational renewal.*
>
> —John Gardener

It is the last element, peer coaching, that is often missing in the mix of these components. Yet there is evidence that it has a central, indeed essential, role in enabling teachers to extend their repertoire of teaching skills, consolidate new practices, and transfer them successfully among different classroom settings. Peer coaching allows learning to be learner-driven and makes the entire process more positive and empowering through support, companionship, and specific feedback over an extended period.

What Is Peer Coaching?

Although there are several types of peer coaching, in its broadest sense it is a process in which two or more professional colleagues work together for a specific, generally predetermined purpose in order to improve and/or validate teaching. The purpose can vary. It may be to reflect on current practices or to expand, refine, and build new skills to integrate teacher learning with everyday practice. In some forms, it is evaluative and public, while other forms are confidential and conducted without evaluation to encourage more open communication and risk taking in the learning process. In the latter format, peer coaches do not "teach" teachers but teach *with* them in a highly personal manner. This assistance is about more than technical concerns. Coaches help teachers to envision and create new possibilities and to engage in regular, reflective discussions about instruction. The aim becomes about trying to connect to the "heart and soul" of teaching and not just to improve technique.

The Benefits of Peer Coaching

There are a number of clear benefits to peer coaching, as discussed below.

Reduces Isolation and Creates a More Cohesive School Culture

Teachers often experience isolation from their peers. Coaching reduces isolation by providing the professional dialogue that increases the connections among faculty. Peer coaching also has the potential for improving school climate, and, ultimately, enhancing school effectiveness when a model appropriate to school goals is applied.

Coordinates and Combines Individual Resources and Talent

Peer coaching helps teachers form the types of relationships they need in order to pool knowledge, skills, and resources. They learn new knowledge and skills and how to apply this knowledge in their classrooms from peers who are more experienced. When teachers work with other teachers, it is possible that they will suggest instructional techniques or interventions not familiar to those others. Such collaboration is especially important in enabling teachers from a variety of disciplines to become familiar with and value the contributions of the others.

Overcomes Limits of Short-Term Efforts

Peer coaching is also a positive solution to some of the problems of traditional in-services and other short-term efforts used to educate teachers. Instead of one-time workshops with no follow-up, peer coaching provides the ongoing assessment of a specific skill or strategy that enables teachers to continue their training in the classroom.

As we mentioned earlier, even when teachers are receptive to using a new technique and have good intentions for implementation, rarely do they effectively transfer a new skill into their practice simply as a result of learning a theory. Nor are they able to apply a new skill even when a demonstration or an opportunity for practice is provided within the context of the training. Successful application occurs consistently

> *All human beings, by nature, desire to know.*
>
> —Aristotle

only with all these components coming together with practice and support in the context of their regular teaching activities.

Peer coaching can create the opportunity for this grounding of new concepts and behaviors in the reality of everyday classroom experiences. This follow-up and continued professional dialogue are particularly valuable among teachers whose educational training and philosophy may vary widely. In coaching conferences, peers can discuss specific individual and school needs as well as give and receive feedback about the specific skill being observed from a perspective each alone may not have considered.

Approaches to Peer Coaching

There are a number of possible strategies for peer coaching. It may involve in-class training by a supportive peer who helps a teacher apply new ideas and skills and/or it may be conducted outside of class in a workshop or less formal setting.

Technical Coaching

Coaching can be of a technical nature for the purpose of facilitating the transfer of in-service training to classroom practice. It can begin with two or more teachers jointly planning instructional segments in which new knowledge and skills will be applied. The teachers review and discuss the data together. Actions that might improve the use of the skills and knowledge are explored. New applications are planned, observed, and analyzed. Another strategy assigns a teacher who is more skilled than other teachers to conduct model lessons to illustrate the use of new skills and knowledge. The other teachers, in turn, use the model on similar lessons to practice the new instructional processes in their own classrooms. Model lessons and the analysis of what occurred both take into account the classroom context and the particular needs of each teacher.

Collegial Coaching

This model shares the goal of refining teaching practices with technical coaching but also emphasizes and promotes a climate of cooperation and culture of dialogue for discussing professional views and activities. It also seeks to encourage teachers to be more self-analytical and self-reflective about what they do in the classroom. The long-range goal of collegial coaching is a self-perpetuating cycle of improvement in teaching. For example, a teacher who is to be observed may want to learn more about how to improve in a particular area. This desire becomes the focus of the coaching sessions. The coach gathers classroom data on the teacher's instructional practices and analyzes and interprets teaching/learning strategies while encouraging applications to future

Collegiality in higher education is a pattern of behavior characterized by an emphasis on teaching and learning, frequent interaction, tolerance of differences, generational and workload equity, peer evaluation and consensus decision-making.

—W. Massey, A. Wilger, C. Colbeck

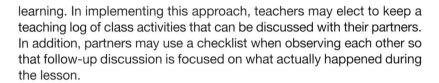

A gem is not polished without rubbing, nor a person perfected without trials.

—Chinese proverb

Chapter 19

learning. In implementing this approach, teachers may elect to keep a teaching log of class activities that can be discussed with their partners. In addition, partners may use a checklist when observing each other so that follow-up discussion is focused on what actually happened during the lesson.

Cognitive Coaching

This model focuses on helping teachers define and reshape their thinking and problem-solving skills rather than on directly developing new teaching practices. The goal is to help teachers better learn how to learn so that they can learn on their own more successfully and continuously engage in new learning. It is based on the assumptions that thoughts and perceptions produce behavior and that to learn something new requires engagement and shifts in thinking. In some ways, cognitive coaching can be seen as a form of collaborative self-reflection, with the coaches helping their colleagues become more aware and understand their thinking. A large part of the role of the coach is based on trust and rapport with the person being coached. The person being coached, not the coach, evaluates what is good or poor, appropriate or inappropriate, effective or ineffective about their work.

Challenge Coaching

This is the application of coaching techniques to the resolution of specific problems or situations that may arise spontaneously. Like reflection-in-action, it is unplanned and may come at any time. Pairs or teams work together to resolve the problem. Though the initial impetus for challenge coaching is unplanned, it often results in a formal plan proposed by participants for the resolution of a given problem.

Team Coaching

This is a variation on peer coaching and team teaching. Mentors or resource teachers, instead of observing classroom teachers, teach right alongside them. These resource teachers have expertise in the methods being used by the teachers they are coaching. The coach and teacher plan, teach, and evaluate the lesson as partners. These teachers coach their peers intensively in their classroom settings to assist them in applying effective methods for students. The success of team teaching supports the notion that people other than regular classroom teachers can be coaches. However, the coach should always be someone who is a peer; otherwise, teachers may perceive the coaching as evaluation rather than collaboration.

These separate approaches to coaching can be put into three general categories based on the strategies used.

1. Technical coaching and team coaching each focus on incorporating new instructional techniques into teachers' routines.

2. Collegial coaching and cognitive coaching seek to improve existing teacher practices by assisting teachers to reflect on their teaching, refining techniques, developing collegiality, and increasing professional dialogue.

3. Challenge coaching concentrates on identifying and treating a specific problem and can be used in a larger context than the classroom, such as at a school or departmental level.

The positive impact of peer coaching on student and teacher learning is well documented. Yet peer coaching programs are not common. Peer coaching, as any comprehensive staff development program, must have the involvement and commitment of teachers and administrative leadership and the buy-in of other members of a school community if it is to be successful. This kind of shared and systematic effort may call for a shift from the customary concept of schools as organizations *for learning* to a new vision of schools as organizations *that learn*.

A New Vision of Schools: From Teaching Institutions to Learning Communities

The idea of a school as a learning community or learning organization captures the character of what we have been discussing about the teacher as learner and the organizational policies and culture that support it.

There are various definitions of what constitutes a learning organization; however, commonly it is seen as an institution that has the culture, values, and capacities that support the sharing and building of knowledge and resources in order to achieve a common purpose. The concept of learning organizations is not new. For the past several decades, a good deal of business-management theory and literature have given attention to the culture of the workplace and how businesses can operate as learning organizations that can yield higher quality, productivity, and profits. However, the notion of schools as learning communities is relatively new.

What Is a Learning Community?

A school as a learning community is not a school whose mission is teaching. Rather, it is a school whose underlying culture is one of learning. A community of learners is a community whose most important condition for "membership" is that one be a learner—whether a student, teacher, staff member, or administrator. A learning community is an organization that exists to promote the learning of all who are part of it and to create the conditions under which profound and sustainable levels of learning can flourish. The irony is that schools have to work to

> *The ability to learn faster than your Competitors may be the only Sustainable Competitive advantage.*
>
> —Arie P. de Gues

become learning communities. Most are not, including just about all postsecondary institutions.

How Do You Create a Learning Community?

It seems clear that transforming a school into a learning community can be done only with leadership and active nurturing of the entire staff's development as a community. To begin, leaders must provide a strategic vision of change that aligns the *why, what,* and *how* of change; encourage and sustain schools as reflective communities; and provide the necessary resources. Traditional notions of in-service training or the dissemination of best practices need to be replaced by opportunities for knowledge sharing based on real situations. The conventional belief that teachers teach, students learn, and administrators manage needs to be completely altered, with the understanding that all have something to contribute. Administrators and teachers must be learners who together question, investigate, and seek solutions for school improvement. These new roles and relationships call for shared leadership, collective creativity and practice, common vision and values, and supportive policies and conditions. Among the critical elements of such an endeavor are the following:

> You do not lead by hitting people over the head— that's assault, not leadership.
>
> —Dwight D. Eisenhower

Leaders who work to:
- encourage open dialogue about change and the change process
- connect smaller endeavors to a larger effort or grander vision
- balance innovation with its impact on individuals

Teachers with regular opportunities to:
- share what they know
- discuss what they want to learn
- connect new concepts and strategies to their own unique contexts

Systems that allow:
- access to successful models of (new) practice
- time for teachers to work and learn collaboratively
- strategies for team planning, sharing, learning, and evaluating initiatives

Personal capacities for
- trust and respect
- skillful communication
- critical inquiry and ongoing change

When these skills and capacities are in place, teacher learning becomes embedded into the day-to-day activities and operations of a school. Teacher development no longer stands apart from organizational development. Learning becomes intimately interconnected to and part of a school's entire organizational culture, processes, and purposes, driving a continuous cycle of improvement and growth.

CHAPTER WRAP-UP

The ideal in professional development is becoming increasingly clear. That ideal sees practitioners in education respected for their professional knowledge and teaching skills. It sees educators at all levels constantly in search of new and better ways to address the diverse learning needs of their students, exploring knowledge about the nature of learning and how it might be implemented in different and changing contexts. It sees schools as learning communities where teachers, students, and staff are continually engaged in inquiry and stimulating discourse with time for reflection and plenty of opportunities to integrate theory into their everyday practice.

Do or do not. There is no try.

—Yoda, Jedi Master
(*Star Wars*)

Some may consider this view as an overly optimistic perspective on the processes and potential of professional development in education. However, the vision is not far-fetched. Nor is it revolutionary. Although the process of professional growth and change can be complex, we do understand how to facilitate that process through pragmatic adaptations to specific contexts so that ongoing improvements in professional practice are ensured. To summarize, program designs should have the following characteristics:

Teacher Involvement	Teachers should be involved in all aspects of planning and implementation of the staff development, which should be driven by and grounded in personal inquiry, reflection, and experimentation.
Individualized Focus	Efforts must take into account teachers' experiences, levels of expertise, disciplines, teaching assignments, and professional goals, as well as the resources available to them.
Thoroughness	Programs involve a good mix of (1) the background or theory for innovations, (2) demonstrations with interactive activities, (3) opportunities for practice, and (4) feedback to teachers about their efforts.

(continues)

| **Sustainability** | Development activities regularly engage teachers in practical tasks, create opportunities to observe, assess, and reflect on their new practices, and are connected to other aspects of school development and change. |
| **Coaching** | Efforts are collaborative and involve the sharing of knowledge, with expert or peer coaching provided to support teachers as they try new ideas in their classrooms that can assure "transfer of training" for everyone. |

The essential conditions of everything you do must be choice, love, passion.

—Nadia Boulanger

The ideas presented suggest that greater success in professional development rests not so much on the discovery of new knowledge, but in a capacity—individually and collectively—to use the knowledge we have wisely. This is true regardless of whether professional development is viewed as an integral part of a career cycle, as a structured effort to keep yourself abreast of advances in your field, or as a self-directed journey to find meaning and appreciation in your work.

These ideas also illustrate that, in the final analysis, successful professional growth requires teachers who are willing and able to rethink their own practice and possibly teach and act in ways they have never contemplated before. This means being able to both unlearn previous beliefs and practices and learn new skills. Indeed, teachers who desire to grow professionally need to demonstrate the personal and intellectual virtues they hopefully seek to cultivate in their students—curiosity, open-mindedness, the ability to question conventional wisdom, and a love of learning.

SPRINGBOARD FOR FURTHER LEARNING

Key Names

Art Costa
Linda Darling-Hammond
Michael Fullan
Robert Garmston
Thomas Guskey

Bruce Joyce
National Staff Development Council
Peter Senge
Beverly Showers
Margaret Wheatly

Key Terms

effective staff development
educational leadership
learning organizations
models of teacher
    professional development

organizational change
organizational learning
peer coaching
professional learning communities

CONCLUSION:
Thinking about the Future
of Postsecondary Education:
Where Are We Headed?

The most surprising future is one which contains no surprises.

—Hermann Kahn

Don't try to innovate for the future. Innovate for the present.

—Peter Drucker

Shoot for the moon. Even if you miss it you will land among the stars.

—Les Brown

Where We Are Now

On two occasions in the past half-century, American higher education engaged in a comprehensive examination of its purposes and effectiveness. The first investigation was the Carnegie Commission on Higher Education in the late 1960s and 1970s. The commission posed a set of key questions: "What broad purposes does higher education fulfill in society? Who benefits from it? Who shall pay for it?" Several recommendations emerged from the work to answer these questions. These became the foundation for increased public investment in access to postsecondary educational opportunities, with the rationale that higher education serves not only the individual student but also society as a whole by providing a more educated citizenry and a more productive workforce.

431

In the 1980s came another examination of education, *A Nation at Risk,* which reignited the national debate about education and its social, political, and economic consequences. The primary focus was on the declining quality of learning in the nation's primary and secondary schools. However, it also helped establish a framework for a similar look at higher education. Among the findings that emerged were the need for higher expectations, greater student involvement in learning, and better assessments of students' learning outcomes.

At the turn of this new century, once again policy makers, scholars, and educational leaders are looking at higher education's purposes and the best means for achieving them. In the decades since the recommendations of the previous investigations, major societal and economic changes have occurred. These have impacted every major American institution, including our colleges, universities and entire system of postsecondary learning, and have led to the need for a new assessment of where higher education stands now and where it is headed. New kinds of questions are being asked. These are arising from the success of efforts to increase access to postsecondary education and a rapidly expanding knowledge base, combined with sometimes dramatic changes in demographics, technology, and the nature of work. Schools and the public agencies that support and monitor their efforts have discovered that the recommendations of prior reform seem ill suited to address these new issues. Current reform efforts are too often ad hoc and understate the challenges and potential risks while overstating the possible benefits of suggestions for change and improvement. Even as they try to keep pace with the shifting educational landscape and look ahead to the future, postsecondary institutions find themselves trying to navigate uncharted territory.

> *Don't judge each day by the harvest you reap, but by the seeds you plant.*
>
> —Robert Louis Stevenson

Where We Are Headed

Throughout history people have tried to develop methods for predicting the future. By reading palms and tea leaves or gazing at the stars, soothsayers have sought to know what changes time will bring. Today, those who strive to anticipate the future are called futurists, and include scientists, sociologists, and operations researchers using modern objective quantitative and qualitative methods to forecast the future. The future, of course, cannot be known with absolute certainty, and futurists recognize that many different futures are possible, depending on current events, long-term trends, and the decisions people constantly make in the present. An important aspect of methods of futures studies, therefore, becomes the assessment of the probabilities of alternative futures. Considerations of possible futures are generally designed to help people better understand these possibilities in order to make better decisions today to manage future uncertainty.

The purposes of futures studies are often divided into three divisions, imagining the possible, assessing the probable, and deciding on the preferable. Most methods of futures studies focus on just one or two of these goals. For instance, analyzing a present trend will give some information about the possible and the probable if the trend continues or we understand what may cause the trend to change. Yet, the investigation of a trend tells us relatively little about what we like to have happen. On the other hand, visioning techniques may tell us something about the possible and, as we brainstorm a range of alternatives, the preferred future. However, it may tell us relatively little about the probabilities of preferred futures without the help of other techniques. There almost always will be the need for multiple methods if on is to work through the full range of futures studies.

Futures research methods are both descriptive and prescriptive. Descriptive methods attempt to explain what the future might be. Prescriptive methods try to help people clarify their values and preferences so that they can develop visions of a desirable future to be able to take the best steps to create the preferred future. Although the methods remain somewhat amorphous, a consensus on the best methods is developing. In general, a method's value is seen to lie in pulling together the judgments of many people, generating questions and ideas to produce different judgments, and demonstrating consistencies and inconsistencies among and within competing views of the future. One method used by all futurists is trend analysis, which involves the use of a variety of techniques based on historical data, including identifying emerging trends or nascent changes in the world around us.

> *What we see depends mainly on what we look for.*
>
> —John Lubbock

Trend Analysis

Most things tracked by trends are events whose magnitude and direction are so well established that there is little that decision makers can do with them other than hope to use their power effectively. In general, these are the relatively dominant social, demographic, technological and economic forces operating within a particular industry, society or even the world. Still, trends do not continue forever, and today often shift with increasing frequency or even come to unexpected ends. Either they die forever or become dormant to rise again in a new form at a later time, with the cycle of growth and decay occurring again. Also, trends rarely, if ever, occur alone. They always interact with other already-established conditions, trends, and events in varying and unpredictable ways. This interaction leads to new trends or emerging issues.

Emerging issues are trends that are identified *before* they become trends. First they are obscure and weak and need to be evaluated in terms of their potential for growth and whether this growth should be encouraged, discouraged, or ignored. Emerging issue analysis requires an additional technique called "scanning," which is basically a way of looking for the very beginning of emerging issues. It involves looking for ideas that are obscure and even outside the mainstream and assessing its potential value and growth. In recent decades, large businesses and governmental agencies have become increasingly concerned with and adept at tracking trends and identifying emerging issues, much more so than education. However, education policy makers and scholars have also recently begun to participate in the processes of future forecasting.

Forecasting Alternative Futures—Creating Scenarios

Change is the essence of emerging and developing futures and forecasting attempts to predict possible outcomes of change. Since the precise outcome of a trend or an emerging issue cannot be predicted, the best that can be done often is to forecast alternative futures of trends or emerging issues based on different theoretical and factual assumptions about the structure, environment, and interaction among different trends and emerging issues. This is where scenario creation comes into play.

One who asks a question is a fool for five minutes; One who does not ask a question remains a fool forever.

—Chinese Proverb

As described earlier, the creation of alternative futures through scenarios consists of describing and characterizing the future expression of emerging issues and the range of possible futures they can create. Futurists will combine probable and possible future assumptions—including social, cultural, and economic trends and potential decisions, especially political interventions—to generate predictions and alternative descriptions for the future of entire societies, as well as the individual industries and organizations—including the educational institutions—that operate within them. Forecasts of alternative futures offer options for the strategic design and development of plans to bring about the chosen future. They provide a framework for what possible futures to investigate, analyze, and assess in terms of their possible impacts, consequences, and outcomes before choosing a plan to accommodate this future. This is what the National Education Association (NEA) did in 2001, when it developed two alternative scenarios for the future of higher education.

Two Scenarios: Alternative Futures for Postsecondary Education

Scenarios are, in part, streams of trends and emerging issues moving together in varying ways according to different theories of social change, as well as facts surrounding these changes. Events and continuities from the past and present will be combined with trends, emerging issues, and potential decisions, and, according to different theories of how the world works, frame and forecast several alternative futures or scenarios. The NEA applied this method to take a look at possible futures for higher education and came up with two scenarios—a market-driven one and a quality-driven one.

Market-Driven Scenario

In the market-driven scenario, higher education is no longer primarily the government's responsibility or for the public good. It is a system that permits individual consumers to get the kind of education they want for their own private purposes. In this scenario, increasing public-sector fiscal constraints are seen to lead to growing cutbacks in public support for postsecondary education. Public 2- and 4-year schools are forced to reduce costs. This largely involves a massive commitment to electronic instruction and the packaging of services in order to compete for targeted segments of the growing market for postsecondary education.

This market-driven scenario produced five distinctly different types of institutions of postsecondary learning:

- MacUniversity—a cheap franchise of community colleges
- Educational Maintenance Org—higher education owned or guided by the needs of major corporations,
- Outsourced U—where all student services, such as libraries, food, sports, dormitories, and teaching itself, are provided by outside contractors with oversight by a handful of full-time administrators,
- Warehouse U—schools established to deal with rising unemployment and the decline in the need for mental as well as manual labor, as a way to keep youth and the unemployable out of the job market and in schools to study as long as possible
- Wired U—schools that feature media-based delivery by star faculty performers, specializing in delivering teaching with high entertainment and production values

Quality-Driven Scenario

According to the quality-driven vision, higher education is a public good and an important investment in societal well-being. In NEA's quality-driven scenario there is a new national political consensus, which forms around the critical connection between higher education and future economic performance. Congress enacts legislation to underwrite 2 years of postsecondary schooling for every American, and further

We cannot hold a torch to light another's path without brightening our own.

—Ben Sweetland

funds an electronic infrastructure to ensure universal low-cost access to distance learning. States then create a seamless articulation between their secondary and postsecondary systems. The legislation initially promotes an explosive growth in postsecondary enrollment, overwhelming existing school faculties and facilities, degrading the quality of the traditional postsecondary learning experience, and giving rise to new types of high-quality/high-tech low-cost public postsecondary institutions.

These institutions are part of a system of two year and then four-year community-based colleges. They maintain a residential character, but with a shifting student population. This is because students leave school intermittently to complete off-campus, community service that can extend their access to free public education by two years. Also, consortia of universities eventually link into a global system of education at the graduate level. Although campuses remain, most classes are conducted as seminars held by video-conferencing. Upper-level students are assigned faculty mentors and in-turn serve as mentors to lower-level students. As workers find their jobs changing, they increasingly turn to distance learning to update their skills; with students given is a faculty tutor whose responsibility is to seek out new materials to challenge the adult learners.

This is not the only formulation of alternative futures of higher education. For example, there is a new taxonomy of higher education offered by the National Center for Postsecondary Improvement that offers the following description of what is and what is to come: (1) brand name, selective, high-status schools that cater to mostly full-time students from traditional age groups and have a commitment to traditional academic values, (2) mass provider institutions, such as large public universities, with obligations to educate as best they can the citizens of their states, trying to be all things to all people, (3) and convenience institutions that are on the cutting edge of both the new technologies and new markets for education and operate a user-friendly businesses to serve job-minded students for whom liberal-arts degrees have little appeal.

> We have a hunger of the mind which asks for knowledge of all around us, and the more we gain, the more is our desire; the more we see, the more we are capable of seeing.
>
> —Maria Mitchell

So, What Does This Mean *to* and *for* You?

A particular feature of the above alternative future scenarios is that they are substantially different from one another—in terms of theories of social stability and change, what the major trends and emerging issues are, and how they should be monitored. Yet, at the same time, they all reflect the continuation of current trends and emerging issues. So what does this all mean?

Postsecondary education as it exists today, though facing fiscal and competitive pressures, and despite some notable progress since the 1960s and 1970s, remains largely unchanged. In the minds of many, this has rendered the enterprise of higher learning less than it should be and could be in today's world. Many of the items heading the agenda for change in the 1960s and 1970s remain today. Critics regularly question the learning exhibited by school graduates. These students may be able to faithfully reproduce facts and demonstrate routine procedures, but they often fail to demonstrate a deep understanding and an ability to transfer what they learned in school to complex and changing environments and unfamiliar problems. Moreover, achievement gaps in higher education persist between students of lower and higher socioeconomic status, and across ethnic and racial groups. Despite repeated calls to recast the preparation of future faculty and skills of those currently teaching, reforms and improvements of classroom practices proceed as at a glacial pace. Colleges and universities are making slow progress in building a faculty that reflects and is prepared to teach the increasingly diverse student population.

So have we reached the end of the line? Of course, not. Is there nothing new under the sun for higher education? Of course, not. There is always *you*.

Each of you who has read and reflected on the ideas presented in this text has made a commitment to continue your learning as a professional educator. And hopefully by the time you have reached this conclusion to the book, you have also begun to incorporate some of these ideas into your thinking and teaching. Whether you are a full-time or part-time instructor, this commitment sets you apart from many other teachers in postsecondary education. Indeed, you may not think of yourself as one, but you are a leader in many ways for having chosen to learn and, we trust, go beyond traditional educational philosophies and practices. Educational practice of teacher-leaders contrasts sharply with traditional pedagogy, based on theories of teaching as simply transmission of knowledge.

Whether as learners or teachers, most of us have spent a great deal of our lives in classrooms. Yet, despite all this experience in education, just about every postsecondary educator enters the teaching profession and begins to practice their craft knowing very little about teaching or learning. They end up doing what they do for the same reasons their students do not always strive for excellence. They prefer familiar routines. Thus, many teachers feel that the customary "stand and deliver" methods of teaching work well, or at least well enough that they need not bother trying to change.

However, you have made the decision to change, to grow and to learn what you can to improve what you do or will do in your classroom. Perhaps, you even have the long-term vision of your teaching practice you once held when you began your studies in your chosen field—to learn and become a teaching expert just as you became a

Good better best, never let it rest, until your good is better, and your better best.

—Traditional expression

Nothing worth doing is completed in our lifetime. Therefore, we are saved by hope.

Nothing true or beautiful or good makes complete sense in any immediate context of history. Therefore, we are saved by faith.

Nothing we do, however virtuous, can be accomplished alone. Therefore, we are saved by love. . . .

—Reinhold Niebuhr

subject-matter expert. This may seem a daunting enterprise. But it need not be. You can progress steadily and incrementally by following a simple formula, as discussed below.

- *Begin now*. You do not want your students to procrastinate when doing their class assignments. You should not either. If you are not sure where to start, just pick something that interests you. Just starting in itself can become the seed of a new habit of mind that can lay the foundation for significant improvements in your practice over time.

- *Think big but start small*. This advice works for any kind of change process, whether it be organizational or personal. It makes change compelling and at the same time manageable and achievable. You will want to see results quickly to judge the effectiveness and value of what you are doing. So build into your improvement process a lot of small steps that can lead to bigger, more meaningful change and take time to evaluate your success at each stage.

- *Include your students*. Do not just talk *to* them, but talk *with* them about what you are doing. Your students do not want to be guinea pigs in some experiment. Include them as partners in the change process and help them grow and learn with you. They will not always understand or necessarily appreciate at first what you are trying to do if it is outside what they are used to. This is simple human nature. Students will mostly expect the familiar and may seek out what appears to be the easiest path. Raise their own expectations of themselves and create a vision with and for them of what learning and teaching can really be.

- *Make it safe to err*. There is a common misconception about learning. Most repeat the old saying, "practice makes perfect," without thinking about whether it is true. Practice rarely, if ever, makes perfect. It does make for progress. So do not be too hard on yourself. Give yourself permission to make mistakes. Your students need this accommodation in their learning, and so do you.

- *If at first you don't succeed . . .* You know this one, *try, try again*. Twenty-eight times to form a new habit and repeat at least six times to embed new knowledge.

We wish you the best on your journey to becoming a masterful educator whose craft is informed by *both* the science of learning *and* the art of teaching.

The following is an annotated list of some of the educational and learning researchers, thinkers, scholars, and writers whose work has been a source of and influence on many of the ideas in this book as well as many our lifelong teaching practices. We also identify professional organizations of which you should be aware. We encourage you to take a closer look at these for your own information and inspiration.

We have grouped these materials into three categories that focus on the overarching themes of this text: the science of learning, the art of teaching, and professional and organizational development. Though we have placed each resource into a separate category, many of these books and resources touch on topics that range across themes. For example, there are books that discuss specific classroom practices (The Art of Teaching) but also preface these with explanations of the theory and research behind them (The Science of Learning).

Appendix: A Selection of Recommended Resources and Readings

The Science of Learning

The following resources focus on theory and research into our understanding of the brain–mind connection and provide a wide-ranging overview of thinking into how people learn and learn best.

- Wolfe, M. (2001). *Brain matters: Translating research into classroom practice.* Alexandria, VA: Association for Supervision and Curriculum Development.

Wolfe acknowledges that neuroscience and cognitive research applications to classroom are not always clear. With that premise, she sorts through the most relevant and important findings to provide an easy-to-understand and valuable resource for what we do know. It emphasizes (along with the resource that follows) the importance of educators becoming more familiar with how the brain works, so they can understand for themselves the applications of research in the classroom.

- Sylwester, R. *A celebration of neurons.* (1995). Alexandria, VA: Association for Supervision and Curriculum Development.

This text also focuses on brain research that has important implications for teaching and learning. Rather than just survey this information, Sylwester provides valuable insights into the significance of these ideas. Notable among them are his explanation of the concept of downshifting and how stress and perceived threats affect brain function and learning. Though Sylwester has revised some of his thinking over the years on this subject and others, this book offers a great place to begin to understand how the brain works as a learning tool.

- Goleman, D. (1996). *Emotional intelligence: Why it can matter more than IQ.* London: Bloomsbury.

Goleman's work is not without its critics. However, we still recommend it. It raises important issues and questions about the role of emotion in contributing to personal success in life, including academic achievement. It can start you thinking about the place of affect in the classroom and why creating a supportive learning environment plays such an important role in student learning outcomes. For a different, more complete and scientific understanding of how emotion affects the mind and personality, we recommend *The Molecules of Emotion* by Candice Pert and *The Emotional Brain: The Mysterious Underpinnings of Emotional Life,* Joseph Ledoux.

- Kolb, D. A. *Experience as the source of learning and development.* Englewood Cliffs, NJ: Prentice Hall, 1984.

David Kolb has made important contributions to both learning styles theory and how learning from direct experience provides an important foundation for classroom instruction. His thinking relates also to problem-based and inquiry-based learning instructional methods.

- Costa, A. L., & Kallick, B. (Eds.). *Habits of mind: A developmental series.* Alexandria, VA: Association for Supervision and Curriculum Development, 2000.

This is a series of books on how to help students develop the mind-set and intellectual skills they need to succeed not only academically but also in the workplace and in everyday endeavors as they encounter problems, dilemmas, and enigmas, the resolutions of which are not immediately apparent. Included in the series are *Discovering and Exploring Habits of Mind, Activating and Engaging Habits of Mind, Integrating and Sustaining Habits of Mind, Assessing and Reporting on Habits of Mind,* and *A Resource Book for Teaching Thinking.*

- Bransford, J. D., Brown, A. L., & Cocking, R. R. (Eds.). *How people learn: Brain, mind, experience, and school.* Washington, DC: National Academy Press, 1999.

This book summarizes important developments in the science of learning in a manner accessible to a nonspecialist audience. It examines topics such as differences between novices and experts, conditions that improve students' abilities to apply knowledge to new circumstances and problems, the design of learning environments, and teacher learning. It provides a thorough grounding in contemporary theory and research, and highlights important implications for teaching, with specific applications to a variety of disciplines.

- Caine, R. N., & Caine, G. (1991). *Making connections: Teaching and the human brain.* Alexandria, VA: Association for Supervision and Curriculum Development.

This is the first of three books on brain function and the process of learning or what is often referred to as brain-based learning. With attention to the activities and the types of environments that promote learning, the authors propose twelve principles for teachers to following in order to take advantage of natural brain processes to design enriching and appropriate learning experiences for learners. They explain the importance of teachers beginning by investigating their own thinking and beliefs about teaching and learning.

Multiple intelligences: The Theory in Practice

- Gardner, H. (1993). *Multiple intelligences: The theory in practice.* New York: Basic Books.

Howard Gardner's theory of multiple intelligences has informed many discussions about what the proper goals of learning and teaching should be and the need to accommodate all types of learning and expressions of learning. His earlier work introduced the concept of multiple intelligences. If you are familiar with the concepts but not their application to classroom practice, here is a good place to begin.

- Curry, L. (1983). *An organization of learning style theory and constructs.* ERIC Document no. 235.

Lynn Curry's thinking is referenced in Chapter 2. She has published a number of articles in professional journals that provide a valuable framework for sorting through the many different kinds of descriptions and inventories of learning styles that are available.

- Perkins, D. (1995). *Outsmarting IQ: The Emerging science of learnable intelligence.* New York: Free Press.

This book is an excellent overview of the history of indicators and measures of intelligence and why we need a new perspective on what it means to be smart by a renowned researcher in the fields of education and learning. Perkins distinguishes among three kinds of intelligence: "neural intelligence," based on the brain's raw processing power; "experiential intelligence," based on acquired knowledge; and "reflective intelligence," in which individuals learn new memory and problem-solving strategies and monitor themselves to see how the strategies are working.

- Bruer, J. T. (1993). *Schools for thought.* Cambridge, MA: MIT Press.

John Bruer holds that we must apply what we have learned from cognitive research and studies of problem solving by novices and experts to improve teaching and learning in schools. He discusses a theory of learning as a developmental psychology of performance changes. Bruer looks at specific educational practices in mathematics, science, and reading and writing, and provides numerous examples.

- Brooks, J. G., & Brooks, M. G. (1993). *In search of understanding: The case for constructivist classrooms.* Alexandria, VA: Association for Supervision and Curriculum Development.

This book provides a rationale for the development of classrooms based on constructivist learning. The authors describe five guiding principles for teaching derived from constructivism, with research support for and classroom examples of each principle. The book has a good balance of conceptual insight and practical applications.

- Jensen, E. (1998). *Teaching with the brain in mind.* Alexandria, VA: Association for Supervision and Curriculum Development.

Jensen is a noted author of several books on brain-based learning. After some criticism for failing to make appropriate connections between research and classroom practice, in this work Jensen not only offers a simple explanation of research on learning and the brain but also presents a model for interpreting the research and assessing the degree of confidence to be placed in its classroom applications.

The Art of Teaching

The following are resources that focus primarily on applications of research and thinking into best practices that have been demonstrated to improve curricular and course design and everyday classroom practice.

● Angelo, T. A., & Cross, K. P. (1993). *Classroom assessment techniques: A handbook for college teachers* (2nd ed.). San Francisco: Jossey-Bass.

This well-organized, user-friendly volume suggests "hands-on" strategies that teachers can use to collect feedback from students in order to assess student learning and learning readiness, to assess the effects of their teaching, and to make appropriate adjustments. Each strategy is illustrated with examples from a range of disciplines, along with brief case studies of how faculty from across the disciplines have used these techniques.

● Marzano, R., Pickering, D., & Pollack, J. (2001). *Classroom instruction that works: Research-based strategies for increasing student achievement,* Alexandria, VA: Association for Supervision and Curriculum Development.

The authors review decades of research findings to summarize the results into nine broad teaching strategies that have positive and powerful effects on student learning. Among these are rather common and deceptively simply strategies such setting objectives and providing feedback, summarizing and note taking, and reinforcing effort and providing recognition. However, there are others not so familiar, such as identifying similarities and differences and the use of nonlinguistic representations. This book is an invaluable resource for more complete descriptions of these nine strategies, many of which we could only touch on in this book. Each chapter presents extended classroom examples of teachers and students in action; models of successful instruction; and many "frames," rubrics, organizers, and charts to help teachers plan and implement the strategies.

● Marzano, R. J. (1992). *A different kind of learning: Teaching with dimensions of learning.* Alexandria, VA: Association for Supervision and Curriculum Development.

This book presents a practical model, "Dimensions of Learning," that teachers can use to improve the quality of teaching and learning in their classroom. It is based on educational research into how children learn, emphasizing learning a process of constructing meaning. The dimensions are loose metaphors for how the mind works during learning. Teachers plan for instruction, design curriculum, and assess student performance using instructional strategies within each dimension.

● Johnson, D. W., & Johnson, R. T. (1991). *Learning together and alone.* Englewood Cliffs, NJ: Prentice Hall.

Johnson and Johnson have done pioneering work in the area of cooperative learning. This book explores essential components of cooperative learning. These include positive interdependence, face-to-face interaction, individual accountability and responsibility, interpersonal and small-group skills, and group processing.

- Margulies, N. (1991). *Mapping inner space: Learning and teaching mind mapping.* Tucson: Zephyr.

Mind mapping, a form of thinking organizer developed by Tony Buzan, is a creative take on the development and use of visual thinking tools that can be used for multiple purposes. The book offers strategies for mind mapping to enhance thinking skills, encourage cooperative learning, and make learning more fun and more memorable. (You may want to take a look at the original source for mind mapping, Tony Buzan and Barry Buzan, *The mind map book: How to use radiant thinking to maximize your brain's untapped potential*.)

- McPhee, D. (1996). *Limitless learning: making powerful learning an everyday event.* Tucson: Zephyr.

This book offers a six-part framework for K–12 educators to follow in creating the kinds of classrooms that engage learners and enhance learning. Filled with practical tips and strategies, it has been a strong influence for many educators.

- Wilen, W. W. (Ed.). (1987). *Questions, questioning techniques, and effective teaching.* Washington, DC: National Education Association.

Questioning techniques are probably the most commonly used active learning instructional strategy in higher education. This book is a collection of nine papers that offer a review of relevant research on questioning techniques. Moreover, it examines the characteristics, purposes, and values of different kinds of questions and offers lots of specific techniques for using questions effectively.

- Grasha, A. (1996). *Teaching with style: A practical guide to enhancing learning by understanding teaching and learning styles,* Pittsburgh: Alliance.

This is one of our resources that falls into more than one of our categories. Part professional-development text and part guide to practical classroom techniques for improving your teaching, Grasha's book is an excellent resource for both new and experienced educators. It studies how awareness of one's own personality and teaching styles can lead to changing and improving teaching and learning practices. It is comprehensive, easy to use, and full of practical ideas on teaching and explanations of how to do it. It also does a good job of linking concrete assignments or exercises to the theories that support them.

- Wiggins, G., & McTighe, J. (1998). *Understanding by design.* Alexandria, VA: Association for Supervision and Curriculum Development.

The authors explore ideas for deep learning and understanding and teaching designs to promote them, together with common educational practices that interfere with this understanding. They introduce the notion of a backward design process when planning a course or unit of study. This begins with the purpose of the task or the desired results and then proceeds to a determination of what knowledge and skills are needed to provide evidence of achievement. The authors offer six indicators of student understanding to use in the design process, and put the process into an easy-to-understand framework with templates and extensive examples.

- Hyerle, D. (1996). *Visual tools for constructing knowledge*. Alexandria, VA: Association for Supervision and Curriculum Development.

This book is based on the premise that knowledge is more than information. Knowledge is information that is interconnected and interdependent. To help students see and make these connections they need the proper thinking tools. Visual representations of knowledge such as webs, organizers, and thinking-process maps, all of which can be used across disciplines, provide a means to make these connections and also to assess learning. They are explained with examples.

Professional and Organizational Growth

The following are just a few titles that discuss powerful paths to professional growth and the institutional processes and culture that best support it.

- Brookfield, S. D. (1995). *Becoming a critically reflective teacher*. San Francisco: Jossey-Bass.

According to Brookfield, "Critically reflective teaching happens when we identify and scrutinize the assumptions that undergird how we work." He suggests four "lenses" for getting at and investigating these underlying (and often problematic) assumptions, including teacher autobiography, the perspective of students, the perspective of colleagues, and the theoretical literature on pedagogy.

- Palmer, P. (1998). *The courage to teach: Exploring the inner landscape of a teacher's life*. San Francisco: Jossey-Bass.

Aimed at the activity of "teaching from within," this book seeks to help teachers understand one's teaching persona and to show how a teacher can develop the authority and skill to teach, in the midst of the complex forces of both the classroom and one's own life. Palmer promotes the need for "communities" of learning, but not without important qualifications. He recognizes that authentic, open relationships within organizations must be balanced by leadership that can maintain necessary boundaries and uphold the standards that define "community at its best."

- Senge, P. M. (1990). *The fifth discipline: The art and practice of the learning.* New York: Doubleday.

In *The Fifth Discipline,* Senge lays out plans for cultivating a "learning organization," one that constitutes an alternative to traditional hierarchical organizations. As discussed in Unit 5, significant improvements in schools can no longer be expected to result simply from staff-development programs designed to train individual teachers to perform in effective ways. The success of students also depends on a school's ability to improve itself as an organization. The book details five "disciplines" that serve as guides for creating learning organizations. It has been an influential and popular work among business professionals. As educational leaders begin to look to business for new information about management, the book can have an impact on the way educational administrators view school leadership.

- Covey, S. R. (1990). *Principle-centered leadership.* New York: Simon & Schuster.

Stephen Covey offers a vision of a humanistic process for developing the kind of leaders who can guide individuals and organizations amid tremendous change. The book introduces a paradigm founded on the belief that there are certain principles—trustworthiness, trust, empowerment, and alignment—that should guide personal and interpersonal relationships and form the foundation of effective leadership.

- Caine, R. N., & Caine, G. (1997). *Unleashing the power of perceptual change: The potential of brain-based teaching.* Alexandria, VA: Association for Supervision and Curriculum Development.

The authors introduce the idea that all teachers design their lessons based on their perceptual orientation. They describe three perceptual orientations that teachers take. It is through a process of transitioning from an external focus and reliance on outer authority to greater self-awareness and reliance that teachers are able to rethink their attitudes toward student learning and, in the end, design a learning environment that offers students the most meaningful and powerful opportunities for learning.

Selected Professional Organizations

In addition, to the above text resources, we also recommend you look into several professional organizations that provide both free and members-only information and resources for postsecondary education. These cover topics regarding trends and innovations in classroom teaching practices and paths for professional development, plus valuable updates and commentary on broader issues, such as social, legislative, and economic issues that impact career and higher education.

AACC—American Association of Community Colleges

The AACC represents about 95 percent of all accredited U.S. 2-year community, junior, and technical colleges in the United States—the largest and fastest-growing sector of U.S. higher education. AACC supports and promotes its member colleges through policy initiatives, innovative programs, research and information, and strategic outreach. Though focused on leadership and institutional development, it offers resources and important perspectives for classroom instructors on the shifting landscape of two-college education. A separate but related organization you may want to take a look at is the League for Innovation in Community Colleges.

ASCD—Association for Supervision and Curriculum Development

The members of this organization span the entire profession of educators from superintendents to classroom teachers. Though its primary focus is on education at the K–12 level, its resources and publications are, in our opinion, an invaluable source of ideas on all aspects of effective teaching and learning—such as professional development, educational leadership, and capacity building. It offers broad, multiple perspectives—across all education professions—on key policies and professional practices. Many of the books we have included in our list here have been published by the ASCD.

CCA—Career College Association

The CCA represents the specific interests of over 1,400 private, for-profit career-specific education and training schools. Its primary mission is to advocate for these institutions with attention to matters of critical postsecondary education issues involving legislation and the larger higher-education community. However, as a teacher it provides you important updates on legislative and regulatory issues that can and do directly impact your career as an educator.

IAL—The International Alliance for Learning

The IAL is one of a dozen worldwide organizations that have members who wish to learn more about accelerated learning and Suggestopedia.

They offer membership and regular teleconferences with experts. Their annual meeting is held in January.

NEA—The National Education Association

As the largest teachers' union in the United States, the NEA not only represents the interests of K–12 educators but also of adult and postsecondary educators. It has an entire subsection focused on higher education and offers great articles through its journal, *Thought and Action,* as well as free resources available online. Their work on future scenarios for the future of higher education, which we referred to in the conclusion of this book, is just a small example of what you can find.

Index

Note: Page numbers for topics in the Field Guide appear after the page numbers for the Core Book, and are preceded by FG.

A

449